Prophecies from the Book of Taliesin

Prophecies
from the
Book of Taliesin

edited and translated by

Marged Haycock

CMCS, Aberystwyth

CMCS Publications,
Department of Welsh,
Aberystwyth University,
Aberystwyth, Ceredigion
SY23 2AX, Wales, GB

© CMCS 2013

All rights reserved. No part of this publication may be reproduced, stored in a retrieval system or transmitted in any form or by any means, without the prior permission of CMCS

ISBN 978-0-9557182-7-4

The Leverhulme Trust

This research was supported by the AHRC
and by the Leverhulme Trust

Argraffwyd yng Nghymru gan Wasg Dinefwr
Printed in Wales by Dinefwr Press

Contents

Preface	vii
Abbreviations	viii
General Introduction	1
Bibliographical abbreviations and short titles	19

Texts, translations and commentaries

1	Daronwy	25
2	Glaswawt Taliessin	42
3	Kychwedyl a'm dodyw o Galchuynyd	61
4	Dygogan awen	83
5	Kein gyfedwch	98
6	Rydyrchafwy Duw ar plwyff Brython	109
7	Gwawt Lud y mawr	123
8	Yn wir dymbi Romani kar	151
9	Ymarwar Llud bychan	176
10	Darogan Kadwal[adyr]	186

Index of forms discussed in the textual notes	191
Conspectus of the Book of Taliesin	198

Preface

It is a pleasure to thank the kind friends and colleagues who have helped me in many different ways over the years: R. Geraint Gruffudd, Elissa Henken, Ceridwen Lloyd-Morgan, Morfydd E. Owen, Oliver Padel, Jenny Rowland, and the late J.E. Caerwyn Williams. I have been privileged to work for many years with a team of exceptionally dedicated scholars and teachers in the Department of Welsh in the Old College, Aberystwyth University, and I would like to record my thanks to these long-suffering colleagues. Former students, Andrew Hawke, Ann Parry Owen and Graham Isaac very kindly made available text concordances, and Jenny Day helped with questions about weapons and warfare. Support from the Arts and Humanities Research Council and the Leverhulme Trust is acknowledged with gratitude. In June 2011, the Center for Medieval and Renaissance Studies at the University of California, Los Angeles, gave me the chance to air some ideas about prophecy, and I thank them warmly, especially Joseph Falaky Nagy and Martha Nagy, kindest and most generous of hosts. The Centre for Advanced Studies at the Norwegian Academy of Science and Letters, Oslo, was a wonderful haven during the very last stages of the work, and I would like to acknowledge the generous scholarly advice and companionship of the warrior band, Jan Erik Rekdal, Ian Beuermann, Ralph O'Connor, Morgan Davies, Charles Doherty, Stefka Eriksen, Jon Gunnar Jørgensen, Clémence O'Connor, Melissa and Susannah Davies, and Sigrun Sigurðardottir. Especial and heartfelt thanks to Marit Finnemyr Strøm and Maria Sætre. At home, Patrick, Gwen and Gwilym Sims-Williams were encouraging and helpful at every turn. Diolch i bawb am bob cymwynas.

Abbreviations

<	deriving from	ModIr	Modern Irish
>	developing to	ModW	Modern Welsh
abs.	absolute	ms	manuscript
adj.	adjective	MW	Middle Welsh
BL	British Library	n.	note
Bret.	Breton	neg.	negative
cf.	compare	NLW	National Library of Wales
Corn.	Cornish	OBr	Old Breton
def. art.	definite article	OE	Old English
E.	English	OF	Old French
em.	emendation	OIr	Old Irish
et al.	*et alii*	ON	Old Norse
etc.	et cetera	OW	Old Welsh
f.	folio	p.	page
fem.	feminine	pl.	plural
Fr.	French	plup.	pluperfect
fut.	future	prep.	preposition
gl.	gloss(ing)	pres.	present
imperf.	imperfect	pret.	preterite
impers.	impersonal	pron.	pronoun
impv.	imperative	rel.	relative
indic.	indicative	s.n.	sub nomine
Ir.	Irish	s.v.	sub verbo
L.	Latin	sg.	singular
lit.	literal(ly)	subjunct.	subjunctive
masc.	masculine	trans.	translated
MBr	Middle Breton	vb	verb
ME	Middle English	VL	Vulgar Latin
MIr	Middle Irish	W.	Welsh

General Introduction

The manuscript
The Book of Taliesin (ms Peniarth 2),[1] kept in the National Library of Wales in Aberystwyth, is a small, plain, incomplete[2] manuscript with poem titles mostly in red, and with alternating red and teal-blue capitals marking the start of many of its sixty-one poems. It was written, and for the most part rubricated, by a single, 'excellent' hand using a disciplined textura script which Daniel Huws dates to the first half of the fourteenth century.[3] The letters are hearteningly easy to read and the pages can be viewed in high resolution on the Library's Digital Mirror, www.nlw.org.uk. This scribe with a clear hand, who wrote four other surviving manuscripts,[4] is likely to have been working in an institutional scriptorium in mid- or south-east Wales, possibly at the Cistercian house of Cwm-hir in Maelienydd. Certainly, by the end of the sixteenth century, the Book of Taliesin was in Radnorshire, just a few miles west of Offa's Dyke, in the possession of Hugh Myles, son of the historian John Myles of Harpton (Tre'rdelyn). And it may have been in the family before then: a reference by the fifteenth-century poet, Lewys Glyn Cothi, suggests it belonged to the Myles's cultured forebear, Dafydd ap Rhys ap Meurig of Old Radnor (Pen-craig). We can track the manuscript's path from then on through John Lewis, Llynwene (a relative of the Myles family), thence to the Hengwrt library, where it was examined by Edward Lhuyd in 1696, and on to Peniarth before it was bought by Sir John Williams, eminent physician and noted collector and connoisseur whose munificence provided the foundation collection for the National Library of Wales in 1909, thus ensuring that institution's fortunate siting in Pura Wallia.

---

[1] The title *Llyvyr Taliessin* first appears in the catalogue of ancient manuscripts published by Edward Lluyd in his *Archaeologia Britannica* (1707), but it may have been given by its seventeenth-century owner, the historian and textual scholar, Robert Vaughan of Hengwrt near Dolgellau.

[2] It lacks the first leaf of the first and fourth of its five quires; there may be a whole quire or quires missing between quires 3 and 4, at the beginning, and at the end (as the unmatched catch-word of the last quire indicates). This affects one of the poems included in this present collection, §10 Darogan Katwal[adyr]. On the possibility that a group of prophecies also found in the Red Book of Hergest preceded quire 1, see below, 5-6.

[3] MWM 79. The handwriting may be compared with the slightly more innovative script used by Gwilym Was Da, known to be holding a burgage in Dinefwr in 1302/3. He copied three law texts of the Blegywryd family (Peniarth 36A, Peniarth 36B, and Cambridge, Trinity College MS O.7.1). The script of the Bodorgan manuscript is also similar. Peniarth 9, written by Ieuan Ysgolhaig in 1336, appears to be somewhat later than the Taliesin group. Further details in 'Llyfr Taliesin', *NLWJ* 25 (1988), 357-86.

[4] NLW 3036 (Mostyn 117), a Welsh translation of Geoffrey of Monmouth's *Historia Regum Britanniae* belonging to the Brut Dingestow family of texts; Peniarth 6 part iv, containing part of *Geraint fab Erbin*; and BL Harley 4353 and Cotton Cleopatra A.xiv, law texts of the Cyfnerth group generally associated with mid- or south-east Wales.

General Introduction

The edition

In a companion volume, I reviewed the study of the contents of the manuscript from medieval times down to the collotype facsimile published by J. Gwenogvryn Evans in 1910 and the heroic age of hengerdd scholarship begun by John Morris-Jones and continued by his disciples, most notably by Ifor Williams in his editions, *Canu Llywarch Hen*, *Canu Aneirin*, *Armes Prydein* and *Canu Taliesin*, and by John Lloyd-Jones in his dictionary of early poetry, *Geirfa Barddoniaeth Gynnar Gymraeg*.[5] The Conspectus at the end of the present volume lists its sixty-one poems in their manuscript order:[6] eight are religious or Scriptural, with another three containing Christian doctrine and learning associated with the repertoire of the legendary Taliesin figure.[7] In a further twenty-three, his is likely to have been the imagined poetic 'voice'.[8] The 'core' of the Book of Taliesin, as edited by Ifor Williams in one volume in 1962, and assigned by him to the second half of the sixth century, consists of eight praise poems to and about Urien Rheged, an elegy for his son, Owain, two to another North British ruler, Gwallawg, and a praise poem to Cynan Garwyn of Powys.[9] Newer studies of Edmyg Dinbych and Echrys Ynys, also edited by Ifor Williams, have adhered to his dating of those poems, respectively 875-900 and 1000-50.[10]

The present collection is concerned with only nine of the ten poems in the Book of Taliesin that may loosely be termed prophecies (on which term see below). The tenth, *not* included here, is Armes Prydain 'The Prophecy of Britain', a focused and well-preserved poem of 199 lines, edited by Ifor Williams, and later published by Rachel Bromwich in an augmented English version with translation.[11] It is a well-known text, neatly sectioned, decisive, its vision of the past informed by, or shared with, the *Historia Brittonum* (829 or 830): the homeland is the whole island of Britain from sea to sea, and a savage ethnic clearance is imagined, so that the Saxons hucksters and stewards will be but a blip in history — a 'swarm that will be gone'. It ends by folding this all into the Christian end-time: the Welsh will be triumphant right up until Judgment

---

[5] *Legendary Poems from the Book of Taliesin* (Aberystwyth, 2007) [henceforth LPBT], 2-6.
[6] As well as the poems, there is a corrupt Latin sequence that describes the Day of Judgment, discussed and translated CC 248-9, 256-7, and see LPBT 5.
[7] All eleven are edited and translated in CC; the last three are edited and translated in LPBT nos. 13, 25 and 26.
[8] All edited in LPBT.
[9] Ifor Williams, PT.
[10] BWP 155-80; R. Geraint Gruffydd in *'Edmyg Dinbych': Cerdd Lys Gynnar o Lys Gynnar o Ddyfed* (Aberystwyth, 2002); and idem, 'A Welsh "Dark Age" Court Poem', in FS Mac Cana 39-48, not ruling out even a ninth- or tenth-century date for Echrys Ynys (p. 43).
[11] *Armes Prydein o Lyfr Taliesin* (Caerdydd, 1955); English edition and translation by Rachel Bromwich, *Armes Prydein: The Prophecy of Britain* (Dublin, 1972). There are also translations by G.R. Isaac, 'Armes Prydain Fawr and St David', in *St David of Wales: Cult, Church and Nation*, edited by J. Wyn Evans and J.M. Wooding (Woodbridge, 2007), 161-81, at pp. 171-81; and by John K. Bollard, in *The Battle of Brunanburh: A Casebook*, edited by Michael Livingston (Exeter, 2011), 29-37.

Day, and God will not fail them. It is a text surprisingly well-loved in many quarters.[12]

Williams contextualised Armes Prydain as a Deheubarth production, *c.* 930 (before the Battle of Brunanburh in 937), directed against the Saxons in general, but specifically against Æthelstan of Wessex and those of the Welsh who were coming to an accommodation with him. Although a later-tenth-century date has been suggested,[13] the most recent discussion, by T.M. Charles-Edwards, favours *c.* 939-42. More significant from the point of view of the present study is his argument that the poem is of Gwynedd provenance, but clearly aimed at the southerners at a juncture when Gwynedd, but not Dyfed nor Glywysing, were allied with the Norse leader, Olaf Guthfrithsson. (He explains the inclusion of the Bretons as allies as reflecting 'the established conventions of the genre' — taking the deliverer *Kynan* to be Cynan Meriadog — rather than 'contemporary reality'.)[14] It was the allegiance of the southerners to the English overlord, Æthelstan (and then his successor, Edmund), that Armes Prydain was intended to challenge, with the aim of persuading them to join the rainbow coalition of opposition to Wessex — Gwynedd, the Hiberno-Norse of Dublin, the Gaels of Alba, and the *Cludwys* (whom Charles-Edwards regards as Cumbrians by the tenth century).[15]

Another edition of Armes Prydain would be otiose here, but the poem is an important comparandum in the present textual study. The remaining item edited here is a mixed text, §3 Kychwedyl a'm dodyw o Galchuynyd, long regarded as problematic, but interpreted here as a form of propaganda using figures from the North British past. Owain fab Urien and Mabon fab Idno are not ciphers for deliverers, like Cynan and Cadwaladr in Armes Prydain and elsewhere, but rather glorious shadows whose names and feats seem to be lending lustre and weight to the struggles of their distant descendants in another North, another time.

This edition follows the same principles as before. The ten poems are given in the original manuscript orthography, but with all the help of silent

---

[12] See Bobi Jones, 'Ein cerdd genedlaethol gyntaf', *Barddas*, 190 (1993), 12-19, and also R.M. Jones, *Ysbryd y Cwlwm: Delwedd y Genedl yn ein Llenyddiaeth* (Caerdydd, 1998). But Thomas Parry did not admit Armes Prydain to his *Oxford Book of Welsh Verse* (1962), not because the anthology was intended (in the words of C.H. Roberts, Secretary to the Delegates at the Press) 'to do missionary work among the English', but simply because Parry had an eye to the quality of the material. He countered Rachel Bromwich's criticism by saying that he included other prophetic poems — the Afallennau and the Oianau from the Black Book of Carmarthen — 'because I liked them. Armes Prydain is historically most fascinating, and it is vigorous propaganda, but it has never struck me as being particularly fine poetry': quoted by Derec Llwyd Morgan, *Y Brenhinbren: Bywyd a Gwaith Thomas Parry 1904-1985* (Llandysul, 2013), 242 and 244.
[13] David N. Dumville, 'Brittany and "Armes Prydein Vawr"', *ÉC* 20 (1983), 145-59; and cf. the uncertainty expressed by Colmán Etchingham, 'Viking-Age Gwynedd and Ireland: Political Relations', in IWMA, 149-67, at pp. 164-6.
[14] WaB 520, and see p. 10 below on the contested identity of *Kynan*.
[15] WaB 532-5.

editorial capitalisation, punctuation, and word-division, and *w* is used rather than *6*. Italics indicate emendations to the text, explained in the commentaries. Lines are not emended *metri causa*, except where rhyme is a sure guide, but some account has been taken of syllabic as well as rhythmic norms when faced with corrupt portions of text.[16] The translations are meant primarily as a fog-lamp through what Keith Thomas called 'the cloudy language' of prophecy, or as a rough causeway across what Tatlock rightly recognised as 'quivering ground'.[17] The commentaries weigh up competing interpretations. They also set the linguistic features and poetic diction within the matrix of poetry composed up to the date of the copying of the manuscript in the first part of the fourteenth century,[18] that is the poetry known as hengerdd, and the work of the court poets (*c.* 1100 to *c.* 1283)[19] and their early-fourteenth-century successors. The prophetic stream, in poems from the Black Book of Carmarthen and the Red Book of Hergest especially, is an important touchstone, as is Geoffrey of Monmouth's *Historia Regum Britanniae* in some cases. But in general, the Welsh treatments of Galfridian material, and the billowing genre of prophetic poetry from the fourteenth century down to Thomas Pugh's *British and Outlandish Prophesies* (1658) is beyond the scope of the volume. Important textual work in this field has been done by Manon Bonner Williams (on the Welsh items in the Red Book and the multilingual Peniarth 50),[20] and by Gruffudd Fôn Gruffudd as part of a major project at Bangor University on the later prophecies attributed to Taliesin.[21]

---

[16] Metrical patterns have been outlined in LPBT 37-9.
[17] Keith Thomas, *Religion and the Decline of Magic* (Harmondsworth, 2003), 467; J.S.P. Tatlock, *The Legendary History of Britain* (Berkeley, 1950), 405.
[18] Definitions and comments from Lloyd-Jones's *Geirfa Barddoniaeth Gynnar Gymraeg* are given in English.
[19] Usually referred to here as the CBT corpus to avoid confusion with other kinds of 'court poetry': CBT = *Cyfres Beirdd y Tywysogion*, 7 vols, general editor R. Geraint Gruffydd.
[20] Manon Bonner Jenkins, 'Aspects of the Welsh Prophetic Verse Tradition in the Middle Ages', unpublished PhD thesis, University of Cambridge, 1990.
[21] General studies on the Welsh material include Margaret Enid Griffiths, *Early Vaticination in Wales with English Parallels* [published posthumously and] edited by T. Gwynn Jones (Cardiff, 1937); R. Wallis Evans, 'Prophetic Poetry', in *A Guide to Welsh Literature*, volume II, edited by A.O.H. Jarman and Gwilym R. Hughes (Swansea, 1979), 278-97; G. Aled Williams, 'The bardic road to Bosworth: a Welsh view of Henry Tudor', *THSC*, 1986, pp. 7-31; Elissa Henken, *National Redeemer: Owain Glyndwr in Welsh Tradition* (Cardiff, 1996), pp. 1-44; Jerry Hunter, *Soffistri'r Saeson: Hanesyddiaeth a Hunaniaeth yn Oes y Tuduriaid* (Cardiff, 2000), especially pp. 78-142; Dafydd Johnston, 'Proffwydoliaeth a Phropaganda', in *Llên yr Uchelwyr: Hanes Beirniadol Llenyddiaeth Gymraeg 1300-1525* (Caerdydd, 2005), 346-74, especially pp. 346-64; and Elizabeth Schoales, 'Welsh prophetic poetry in the Age of the Princes', *Proceedings of the Harvard Celtic Colloquium*, 24/25 (2004/2005), 127-39. Rupert Taylor, *Political Prophecy in England* (New York, 1911) and Lesley A. Coote, *Prophecy and Public Affairs in Later Medieval England* (Woodbridge, 2000) are useful ways into the vast field of medieval prophecy, the latter documenting work by Southern, Reeves and many later scholars, while Peredur I. Lynch, *Proffwydoliaeth a'r Syniad o Genedl* (Bangor, 2007), which is informed by more recent studies, is indispensable.

General Introduction

Contexts
Since the introductions and commentaries address the specifics of the individual poems, the discussion here will be limited to a few broader concerns: the ordering of the prophetic poems in the manuscript; prophecy as one of the special arts of the Taliesin figure; the main features of prophetic discourse; and a summary of how the orthographic and linguistic evidence is not inconsistent for the most part with the composition of these poems between the tenth and the thirteenth centuries. In some cases this broad dating can be refined, for example in conjunction with considerations such as the mention of Norman invaders.

The Book of Taliesin scribe, engaged in multiple text production, is likely to have been the copier rather than the compiler of the manuscript, but he may have assembled blocks of material already put together by others. There is certainly a rationale to the ordering of some parts, including the siting of the two great *Armes* poems: the secular prophecy, Armes Prydain, next to Armes Dydd Brawd, the long 'Prophecy about the Day of Judgment'.[22] Poems about mead and beer, respectively Kanu y Med and Kanu y Cwrwf, are paired together, in the same way as Kanu y Byt Mawr and Kanu y Byt Bychan. The manuscript's elegies are in a discrete section, as are the *Kadeir* poems, and the Urien Rheged group already mentioned.[23] Seven of our prophecies are close together in the last surviving quire of the manuscript, but only §§5-6 and §§7-9 run on in continuous blocks. The incomplete state of §10 Darogan Katwaladyr indicates that a further quire contained at least some of the same material. On the other hand, §1 Daronwy and §2 Glaswawt Taliessin are far removed in the first half of the manuscript, separated by one of the Gwallawg poems, while the mixed text, §3 Kychwedyl a'm dodyw o Galchuynyd, stands between the riddling poem about the wind (Kanu y Gwynt) and one of the drinks poems, Kanu y Med.

The companion volume discussed and edited the very first surviving poem of the Book of Taliesin, which is acephalous. Happily, the whole poem, beginning Prif Gyuarch Geluyd, is extant in the Red Book of Hergest (*c.* 1400), and it was suggested that the whole block of seven prophecies attributed to *Taliessin* which starts at column 1049 of the Red Book was at the end of the first missing quire of the Book of Taliesin.[24] The seven poems in question are Anrec Vryen (which recycles portions of material also found in the Book of Taliesin);[25]

---

[22] The latter edited in CC poem 20, and see also commentary by Pierre-Yves Lambert, 'Visions of the Other World and Afterlife in Welsh and Breton Tradition', in *Apocalyptic and Eschatological Heritage: The Middle East and Celtic Realms*, edited by Martin McNamara (Dublin, 2003), 98-120.
[23] See the Conspectus at the end of this volume, and further details in LPBT 5-7.
[24] LPBT 51-3.
[25] Most obviously the 'tag' found at the end of several of the Urien Rheged poems: *Minneu Dalyessin/ o ia6n llyn* (recte *llin*) *geirionnyd./ Ny dalywyf yn hen/ ym dygyn aghen/ ony mol6yf-i Vryen* (R1050.4-6). Also to be noted are *Vryen o Reget haelef* (recte *haelaf*) *yssyd/ ac a uyd ac a vu yr Adaf* (R1050.1, echoing PT III.1 and 21-2); *y lewenyd* (R1049.9, cf. PT III.5); and the use of the verb *gogyfarch* (R1049.7-8), and perhaps *eur ac aryant* (R1049.10).

Mal rot yn troi; Moch daw byt; Llynghes Von; Crist Iessu; Mor yw gwael gwelet; and Prif Gyuarch Geluyd itself. The significance of this connection between the Book of Taliesin and the Red Book of Hergest has been examined elsewhere,[26] but for our purposes now, what is important is the likelihood that our manuscript was even more weighted towards prophetic material than the extant prophecies — which, taken with Armes Prydain, represent about a fifth of the manuscript — might suggest.

Another consideration is that several of the legendary Taliesin poems, those overtly spoken by his distinctive know-all 'voice', contain prophecy cheek by jowl with displays of his other professed specialities, such as cosmology, natural science, Scripture and book-learning, mingled in with boastful accounts of his associations with characters of history and legend across the aeons, and assertions that he is an intimate of the *awen*, 'poetic inspiration', its founts and its ways. Three poems of this mixed Taliesin type contain significant elements of prophecy: they are the poems nos 1, 8 and 9 in the *Legendary Poems*: Prif Gyuarch Geluyd; Golychaf-i Gulwyd; and Kadeir Teyrnon. In addition, at the end of no. 5 Kat Godeu, after calling on druids and wise men to prophesy to Arthur (lines 238-9 *Derwydon, doethur,/ darogenwch y Arthur*), Taliesin reminds the audience for the second time of the key events of Christian chronology — the Flood, the Crucifixion and the Day of Judgment — before boasting in the final lines, 'I am splendid and I am enlivened by the prophecy of Virgil'.[27] The poet Virgil became renowned as a magician and sage in the Middle Ages, and was credited with having foretold the birth of Christ. The point here is that Taliesin too had done the same thing, as the Norman writer Wace and other sources testify — that he was, in effect, the Welsh Virgil.[28] This mantic facet of the legendary Taliesin sits easily with his other gifts, and is acknowledged in terms such as *syw*, *sywyd*, *sywedydd* and *derwyd* that blur the boundary between poetic inspiration and a heightened perception of the significance of things and events — revelation or prophecy in the widest sense — of past, present and future, not merely the gift of foreknowledge. How this works in practice may be illustrated by part of one of these mixed Talesin poems, Golychaf-i Gulwyd. After recounting his exploits alongside great men of native history and legend, he moves into prophecy to 'warn' of sea-borne raiders around Bardsey Island — a post-eventum reference to the Vikings in all probability:[29]

---

[26] LPBT 51-3.
[27] LPBT 5.248-9.
[28] In another poem, Angar Kyfundawt, Gwiawn — likely to be an alias of the Taliesin figure — speaks of the coming of 'a profound one' who could bring the dead to life, possibly an allusion to Taliesin's prophesying of Christ: LPBT 4.15-18. For an inventory of sources outside the Book of Taliesin which credit Taliesin with prophetic and visionary powers, see LPBT 12-21. For Welsh interest in the figure of the Sibyl, like Virgil, a pagan witness to Christ's first Advent, see Haycock, '*Sy' abl fodd, Sibli fain*: Sibyl in Medieval Wales', in *Heroic Poets and Poetic Heroes in Celtic Tradition*, edited by Joseph Falaky Nagy and Ellen Jones, *CSANA Yearbook 3-4* (Dublin, 2005), 115-30.
[29] LPBT 8.15-22.

General Introduction

> Ystyryem yn llwyr   kyn clwyr cyffes
> *Let us be mindful, before the confession cell,*
> dyfot yn diheu   agheu nessnes.
> *that death is certainly coming nearer and nearer.*
> Ac am tired Enlli   dybi dylles:
> *And misfortune will come around the lands of Bardsey:*
> dyrehawr llogawr   ar glawr aches,
> *ships will be deployed on the sea-flood,*
> a galwn ar y Gwr   a'n digones:
> *and let us call on Him who made us:*
> a'n nothwy rac gwyth   llwyth agh*y*mes.
> *may he protect us from the anger of the swarming host.*
> Pan alwer Ynys Von   tiryon väes,
> *When Anglesey is called a fair plain*
> gwyn eu byt wy gwleid*yad*on   Saesson ar tres.
> *blessed are the ravaging English hosts.*

Compare the assured movement from deep legendary time to the future and back again:[30]

> Bum yg Kat Godeu   gan Lleu a Gwydyon:
> *I was in the Battle of the Trees with Lleu and Gwydion:*
> wy a rithwys gwyd E*u*uyd   ac Elestron.
> *Eufydd and Elestron fashioned trees.*
> Bum y gan Vran   yn Iwerdon:
> *I was with Brân in Ireland:*
> gweleis pan ladwyt   ⋄mordwyt[31] tyllon;
> *I witnessed the slaying of mighty-thighed warriors;*
> kigleu gyfarfot a*n*gerdolyon
> *I heard the clash of the fierce men*
> a Gwydyl diefyl   diferogyon.
> *with the Irish devils, a wily lot.*
> O Pen*ryn* Penwaed   hyt Luch Reon:
> *From the promontory of Penwith as far as Loch Ryan:*
> Kymry yn vn vryt   gwrhyt *uo*ryon.
> *the Cymry with a common purpose, men of great valour.*
> Gw*a*ret dy Gymry   yg kymelri —
> *A salvation for the Cymry in [their] struggle —*
> teir kenedyl gwythlawn   o iawn teithi:
> *three ferocious peoples possessing true qualities:*
> Gwydyl a Brython   a Romani
> *The Irishmen and the Britons and the Romani*
> a wnahon dyhed   a dyuysci.[32]
> *will make war and turbulence.*
> Ac am teruyn Prydein —   kein y threfi —
> *And around the limit(s) of Britain — fair its dwellings —*

---

[30] LPBT 8.29-51.
[31] The ⋄ symbol indicates editorial deletion, and italic letters denote emendations.
[32] Exactly the same two lines (also rhyming with *teithi*) are found in the Black Book of Carmarthen, in the Oianau prophecy associated with Myrddin: LlDC 17.193-4.

keint rac teÿrned   uch medlestri.
I sang before rulers over vessels of mead.
Yg keinyon deon im   a'e dyrodi,
Noblemen would give me the first libation,
handwyf pensywet   ket ryferthi.
[for] I am a chief sage with an abundance of gifts.
Ys kyweir vyg kadeir   yg Kaer Sidi:
Harmonious is my song in Caer Siddi;
nys plawd heint a heneint   a uo yndi,
sickness and old age do not afflict those who are there,
ys gwyr Manawyt   a Phryderi.
as Manawyd a Phryderi know.
Teir oryan y am tan   a gan recdi,
Three instruments/organs around a fire play in front of it
ac am y banneu   ffrydyeu gweilgi;
and around its turrets are the wellsprings of the sea;
a'r ffynhawn ffrwythlawn   yssyd oduchti —
and [as for] the fruitful fountain which is above it —
ys whegach no'r gwin gwyn   y llyn yndi.
its drink is sweeter than the white wine.

In Prif Gyuarch Geluyd, the prophetic element is mixed up more promiscuously with questions:[33]

Eigyl, Gallwydel,
The Angles [and] the mixed-blood Irish
gwnaont eu ryuel.
shall make war.
Pan daw nos a dyd?
Where do the day and the night come from?
pan uyd llwyd eryr?
why is an eagle grey?
pan yw tywyll nos?
why is the night dark?
pan yw gwyrd llinos?
why is a greenfinch green?

or with moral condemnation of the Welsh and a foretaste of their roasting in Hell, before offering some limited hope of victory:[34]

Ymkaffwynt yn dirdan —
They will come together in the great conflagration —
Kymry yg griduan;
the Cymry in a state of lamentation;
prouator eneit
soul[s] will be put to the test
rac llwyth eissyffleit.
in the face of the damned host.

---

[33] LPBT 1.10-15.
[34] LPBT 1.52-72.

General Introduction

Kymry prif diryeit —
The Cymry [will be] the worst of the wretches —
rann rygoll bwyeit.
a group having utterly lost [God's] blessing.
Gwaed hir ucheneit,
[There will be] a wail of protracted groaning,
a*r*wyar honneit.
[and] manifest bloodshed.
Dydoent gwarthuor,
There will come — a sea of shame —
gwydueirch dy ar uor,
ships on the ocean,
Eingyl yghygor.
[and] Angles attacking.
Gwelattor arwydon
There will be seen portents
gwynyeith ar Saesson,
of vengeance on the Saxons,
***claudus* yn syon.**
faltering our murmurs.
O rwyuannusson
From among the leaders
bydhawt penn seiron!
there shall emerge a master strategist!
Rac Ffich*ti* lewon
Against the fierce sea-rovers
***marini* Brython.**
[will be ranged] the sea-borne Britons.
Ry daroganon,
They shall prophesy
a medi heon
and reap the scattered [soldiers]
am Hafren auon.
around the River Severn.

He combines profligate boasts — 'I don't praise menials', 'I'm a sage in contest' — with dire warnings of an end time when chaos will rule, when

Posbeird◇ bronrein a dyfi,
Haughty convoluted poets shall come,
a deuhont uch medlestri,
lording it over the mead vessels,
a ganhont gam vardoni,
composing false verse,
a geissont gyfarws nys deubi,
trying to secure a reward that they won't get,
heb gyfreith, heb reith, heb rodi.
without justice, without rights, without power to transact.
A gwedy hynny digoui
And after that, there'll come
brithuyt a byt dyuysci;
cataclysm and worldwide turmoil;

> **nac eruyn-ti hedwch, ny'th vi!**
> *don't ask for peace because you won't get it!*

These extracts illustrate the prophetic discourse present in the mixed poems, and show how political prophecy can feed off religious apocalypse, a feature common to many European traditions. We can turn now to the more sustained, arguably purer, form of prophecy in the present collection, where the Taliesin 'voice' is less strident, the discourse less personal. But poem §2, *Glaswawt Taliessin*, indicates by its title that this poem, at least, was attributed to him, and since prophecy was clearly part of his repertoire as an inspired as well as a knowledgeable creature, it may well be that some of the other poems, too, were tacitly attached to his name — just as the block of prophecies in the Red Book of Hergest which may have been in the initial missing quire of our manuscript is headed with the name *Taliessin*.[35] They may have been recited by their author or authors, using the distanced 'voice' of the prophetic poet, or else by declaimers. In some cases, as at the beginning of Armes Prydain, there might be an airy reference to the all-knowing *awen* 'inspiration'[36] or to a *deruyd* or *deruydon* 'prophet(s)',[37] or to *sywedydyon* 'sages'.[38] Frequent elements can be summarised as follows for convenience, but since comparanda are exhaustively noted in the individual poems' commentaries, they are not detailed here.

Deliverers are Cynan (§1 and §6) and Cadwaladr (§8 and §10), sometimes, as in Armes Prydain, as a pair (§2 and §7). Cynan has been equated, following Geoffrey of Monmouth, with Cynan son of Eudaf (Geoffrey's *Conanus Meriadocus*, founder of Brittany),[39] but the name is too common to be certain. Wade-Evans favoured Cynan Garwyn, the late-sixth-century ruler in Powys praised in the Book of Taliesin.[40] His late date would tend to rule out Cynan son of Rhodri (also known as Cynan Dindaethwy), d. 816, last of the Maelgyning kings, great-great-grandfather of Hywel Dda, and father of *Etthil* (or *Ethellt*), perceived as the legitimising link between the first and second Gwynedd dynasties since she was the mother of Merfyn Frych (or his wife in some

---

[35] R1049.7. Leaving aside the mass of later prophecy attributed to him: see above, p. 4, and n. 21. In our present collection, we have only one example (in §8.43) of the phrase *Gogwn* 'I know', a trademark of the Taliesin persona. Some very uncertain lines in §7.35 appear to refer to the *kerdawr*, the poet who perceives the significance of the cloud's torrent of rain as it moves over the high ground, a possible allusion to his occult abilities.

[36] AP lines 1 and 107. If Armes Prydain is a Gwynedd production, as argued by Charles-Edwards (see above, p. 3), then the second awdl's attribution of the wisdom to Myrddin may have been a sop to the men of the South whom the northern poet wished to sway, in the same way as the commendation 'to God and Dewi' — unless St David and his 'blessed banner' were already thought to be a rallying point for all the Welsh.

[37] A word limited in hengerdd to the Book of Taliesin: see on §7 lines 32 and 106.

[38] §7.104.

[39] See TYP³ 320-21.

[40] PT I; see WCD 163.

sources).⁴¹ Cadwaladr, associated with Anglesey in §8.34, is thought to be the mid-seventh-century son of the famous Cadwallon ap Cadfan, the ruler of Gwynedd who had been slain by the Angles at the battle of *Hefenfelth* in 634.⁴² Cadwallon himself is also remembered in one poem (§6), as having returned triumphant across the Irish sea to re-establish himself in power. This might have struck a chord or have been a rallying call down the centuries for supporters of banished or self-exiled Gwynedd claimants. Another Gwynedd deliverer, Hiriell, obscure to us but well-known to the twelfth- and thirteenth-century poets, shares the stage with Cadwaladr in poem §8.⁴³ References to Lludd are made in §4.6 (with Caswallon), in §9.11, and in the title of §7 Gwawt Lud y mawr. His brother, Llefelys, is paired with him in §9.11 *kyn ymarwar Llud a Llefelis*, a line similar to the title of the prose tale, *Cyfranc Llud a Lleuelys*. Disappointingly little is to be gathered about them as deliverers or otherwise in our texts. The *Gwr o Gud* 'The Man from Hiding' and the *Llyminawc* 'Leaper', two ciphers found elsewhere, appear in §4. Animal ciphers — not always easily differentiated from run of the mill animal metaphors — include §5.21 *Linx* (possibly for Henry III, crowned 1216); §8.44 *Arth o Deheubarth* 'the Bear of Deheubarth'; §8.18 *Arth a Llew* 'Bear and Lion'; §8.24 *Dreic o parth deheu* 'the Dragon from the southern region'; §6.23 *y Gath Vreith* 'the Speckled Cat'; and §7.49 *y Uuch Vreith* 'the Brindled Cow'.⁴⁴

The parlous state from which deliverance is sought is delineated conventionally in many prophetic traditions.⁴⁵ It usually portrays a striking inversion of the normal social order, the chaos referred to by the Welsh as the *brithuyt* 'mottled world' or the *byt dyuysgi* 'world in confusion'. It is seen very clearly in the Black Book of Carmarthen (and related Peniarth 3) prophecies, and those of the Red Book of Hergest. The signs of the times include inappropriate wealth distribution and lack of hospitality: 'empty-handed the poet, resplendent the priest',⁴⁶ poets not getting their deserts,⁴⁷ and servants eager to have the upper hand.⁴⁸ Father will be pitted against son.⁴⁹ Men and women will forfeit their proper characteristics, 'wives without modesty, men without manliness',⁵⁰

---

⁴¹ On the succession, see WaB 473. WaB 476-7 notes that Cynan is called *rex Britonum* in the Annals of Ulster (WaB 351), referring probably to his supremacy in Gwynedd as this title was not one which the Irish chronicles used for minor kings.

⁴² Cadwaladr died of the plague in 682 according to the Annales Cambriae, but in that of 664 according to HB ch. 64: see TYP³ 298-9 and WaB 355-6.

⁴³ The Gwynedd figures Beli Hir (if not Beli Mawr) and Iago, not here deliverers as such, are named in §2 and §4. Rhun (probably son of Maelgwn Gwynedd) effects a clean sweep of the South in poem §1, even engrossing its legendary dominions beneath the sea.

⁴⁴ The problematic list of animals in §1 Daronwy is discussed in the note to §1.39.

⁴⁵ See Graham R. Isaac, 'The end of the world in Welsh and Irish: a common disaster', *SC* 28 (1994), 173-4.

⁴⁶ R585.1-2 *gwaclla6 bard hard effeiryat*.

⁴⁷ LlDC 17.189 *Kertorion allan heb ran teithi*.

⁴⁸ Pen3 Afallennau 123.45 *gueissyoneu fraeth bit aruaethus*.

⁴⁹ LlDC 17.41 *ymlat mab a thad*.

⁵⁰ LlDC 17.211 *Gwraget heb gvilet, gwir heb gurhid*.

or husbands will be grossly overstretched, with 'twelve wives to each man'.[51] Incest reflects the confusion and godlessness which prevails, with sinful monks,[52] foreign bishops,[53] and no respect for churches and relics.[54] Similar things are found in our collection including: improperly loquacious women (§1.24); incest (§2.24 and perhaps §10.14); nobles reduced to churls (§1.25); servants ruling the roost (§4.13; §10.11); the erosion of generosity (§4.12); the devastation of consecrated places (§7.54); and inconsistency of various sorts (§7.69 and 95). Nature's very course is blighted as the sun loses its warmth (§7.31) and fails to shine in the summer (§7.108), leading to famine and distress (§7.67), while the arable land will be seething (§7.53). Even the cuckoos are fated (§7.68), just as a Red Book prophecy has the birds dying in May.[55] A riderless horse with its reins loose indicates loss and defeat (§4.10); horse- and cattle-raiding (or animal husbandry) are in abeyance (§7.64-5). No wonder, then, that there is a longing for the days of *med a marchogaeth* 'mead and horsemanship' (§1.26-7).

Following the lead of Gildas and then the *Historia Brittonum* — and naturally enough in view of the depredations of Vikings and Normans as well as the earlier Angles, Saxons and Irish — political prophecy is focused on Britain's island identity, and its successive waves of invaders and settlers,[56] comparable with Ireland's legendary history. In a few passages the Britons appear to be regarded as the heirs of Rome in some way.[57] This is not surprising in view of the admiring way in which Gildas (*De Excidio Britanniae*, ch. 25), had spoken of the British leader Ambrosius Aurelianus's membership of the *Romana gens*. Moreover Romanitas was closely identified with Christianity.[58] Hence when one of the prophecies refers to *Kessarogyon* 'people of Caesar' (§8.42) it is not clear whether it means the Romans or the Britons, nor whether it is hostile or favourable to them.

Not surprisingly, as in other prophecies such as Llynghes Von in the Red Book, we find approaching fleets, ships cresting the waves (§2.11-12; §7.16; §8.11 and 16-17; §8.68) and the oar dipping into the brine (§2.3). The undesirables are banished to the ocean, as in Armes Prydain (§8.33 and 8.55-6), while Cadwallon returns triumphantly across the Irish sea (§6.17). The listing of successive fleets, ethnic groups (*Kymry, Eigyl, Gynt, Gwydyl, Gwydyl Ffichti, Prydyn, Seis,* and an exoticised people from *gwlat Gafis*), sons and rulers, is a

---

[51] R1049.42 *deudeng wraged ac nyt ryued am vn g6r vyd.*
[52] LlDC 17.81-2 *Ac escib lluch lladron diffeith llannev/ A myneich a obrin beich o bechodev.*
[53] LlDC 17.186 *Escyp agkyueith diffeith difid.*
[54] R584 *by6 mall a g6all ar lannev/ torredaw6d geir a chreireu*; cf. AP line 139 *Neu vreint an seint pyr y saghyssant.*
[55] R584.35-6 *Mei mar6 cogeu rac ann6yt.*
[56] The word *gormes* 'oppression' is used only once in our collection, and not for a foreign invader. *Arymes* is used once only, in §2.12 *arymes kyn Brawt*: see note.
[57] See on §1.33 *o amtir Rufein*; 7.102 *Brython o vonhed Rufein*; 8.1 *Dymbi Romani kar.*
[58] See further references §1.33n, and discussion in WaB 226, 239 and 241; see also Alheydis Plassmann, 'Gildas and the negative image of the Cymry', *CMCS* 41 (2001), 1-15.

General Introduction

feature here.⁵⁹ Numbering by threes, fives and sevens is found (§2.12; §4.5; §8.29; §5.11-21; §7.16), as well as lists of battles, days of the week, river- and fortress-names and so on. Bloodshed and violence are routine, with some extreme motifs such as 'playing ball with the heads of the Saxons' (§6.22) bringing to mind the split heads and heaving corpses in the more savage lines of Armes Prydain. Normandy is named in §5.16, and there is a succession of (unnamed) Norman kings in the same poem, perhaps running down to Henry III (if he is the *Linx* in §5.21).

As indicated already in referring to the mixed Taliesin prophecies and the manuscript's pair of great *armesau*, there is seepage between the treatment of earthly time and the enfolding Christian schema of end-time and the eternal. The Day of Judgment was the greatest remaining event in the divine plan with an outcome already known and heeded, although its timing was known only to God, and expressly *not* to be calculated by mortals. Thus, the arrival of three fleets in the flood in §2.12 is an *arymes kyn Brawt*, an intimation of something momentous prefiguring the Judgment Day itself. In §7.99, ultimate victory will be proclaimed — actually read out⁶⁰ — a while before the Day of Judgment and the Britons will be resurrected (*datwyrein*), just as in the great Judgment poem the dead will arise from their graves to meet their God,⁶¹ with John the Evangelist and John the Baptist in attendance reading out from books.⁶² In our secular prophecy, as in the religious poem, enemies, the evil race of Cain, will be consigned to the swamps of Hell (§7.113-17).

To think about the future was to think of the patterning of the past as well. The past could be projected onto the screen of the future as though it was still to happen. That is the point of the Fool's comment in *King Lear*: 'This prophecy Merlin shall make, for I live before his time'. The prophecies, then, can be a species of history, harnessed to contemporary needs. Thus poem §6, 'foretelling' the Gwynedd forces acting in concert with Powys in a southern campaign which names the rivers Tywi and Teifi and the *llys* 'court' in Lonyon — modern-day Llonion near Pembroke Dock — may preserve a memory of some joint action which was being remembered for propaganda purposes. Poem §2 anticipates that 'there will be, on the River Conwy, (more suffering) that will wreak vengeance', a likely ex eventu reference to the 'Wednesday battle' on the Conwy which avenged the killing of Rhodri Mawr by the English in 878. Other such references can suggest a post quem dating, but the poems that contain them were not necessarily composed soon after the event, as Ifor Williams tended to assume,

---

⁵⁹ Not confined to prophecy, however.

⁶⁰ There is a possibility that the *llyfrawr* 'librarius' was regarded as redundant in the eyes of the Armes Prydain poet, not because he was an occult specialist akin to the poet himself (as suggested by Thomas Jones, see AP line 193n), but because the Armes was already committed to writing and being read out to audiences (a not-for-profit activity unlike that normally undertaken by the *agawr brydyd* 'the grasping bard').

⁶¹ CC 20.81 *Drychafant o vedeu*.

⁶² CC 20.155-8 *A chenwch, deu Ieuan,/ Ragof, y deu gynran,/ A deu lyfyr yn ach llaw/ Yn eu darlleaw*.

General Introduction

since the memory of such events would undoubtedly have held a live charge for centuries.

We may turn next to a summary of the language, leaving the details for the commentaries. Orthography is regular for the most part, with §5.17 *whechet* illustrating the southern or mid-Walian dialect of the scribe or his exemplar.[63] Poem 6, unusually, is attested in another version, in Peniarth 111. This derived from a medieval exemplar which used *d* for [-d], a feature often associated with the Black Book of Carmarthen-type of orthography (*c*. 1225-50), but which is used elsewhere, for example by the Alpha hand of the Hendregadredd manuscript (*c*. 1300).

The overall picture is that most of the language cannot be said conclusively to pre-date the language of the twelfth- and early-thirteenth-century court poets. Thus, starting with verbal forms, we generally see 1sg. present in *-af*, not the forms in *-if* which were still in use but in decline in the twelfth century, except for §10.8 *bydif*, although see on §8.85 for a possible emendation to *yolif*. The 3sg. present subjunctive in *-wy*[64] is used for a set of verbs in poem §1 Daronwy (§1.7 *amnodwy*; §1.11 *gwypwy*; §1.13 *tyfwy*; §1.14 *kymrwy*; §1.17 *gwledychwy*; §1.52 *dychyfrwy*), with a few elsewhere: §6.1 *Rydyrchafwy*; §6.14 *nothwy*; §8.24 *dydyrchafwy*; §8.30 *traghwy*. But the innovative *-(h)o* forms (which are on the increase in the twelfth century, and which will overtake *-wy* in the first half of the thirteenth century)[65] are attested too: as well as *bo* throughout (§1.5; §3.12; §5.27; §6.11), we see §1.28 and 32 *Dedeuho/Dydeuho*; §1.45 *karo*; §1.47 *caho*; §3.7 *llafaro*; §6.23 *trabludyo*; §7.50 *gwnaho*.

3sg. absolute endings *-it/-yt* are rare — uncertain pluperf. §1.47 *kewssit*; §8.14 *llywit* — but in any case, such forms are still used sporadically by thirteenth-century court poets.[66]

Our collection has plenty of scope for (marked future) endings in *-(h)awt*:[67] §2.8 *gwnahawt*; §2.19 *tardawt*; §2.21 *briwhawt*; §2.27 *tyfhawt*; §4.12 *kollawt*;

---

[63] See details, LPBT 7. Usually *t* for [-d]; *f* for [-v]; *f* and *u* for [-v-]; *v* and *u* for [v-]; *d* for [-ð] and [-ð-], and *t* as well as *d* for [-d-]. There is a tendency to avoid yod in plural and adjectival endings (e.g. *meibon*, *keinhawc*). The letter *i* is generally used for initial yod and in instances where yod *is* shown in the second element e.g. *Taliessin*. Lenition of initial p, t (and d) is not generally realized; heavy [-nn] is normally written with a single *n*; similarly heavy [-rr].

[64] See the full discussion by Simon Rodway, 'Two developments in medieval literary Welsh and their implications for dating texts', in HI 67-74, pp. 71-4; Rodway, Dating 81-3.

[65] See Rodway's discussion with graph at HI 73. The *-o* ending is the only form found in the saga englynion (five examples). It is found consistently in the Llyfr Llandaf *Braint Teilo* prose text (early twelfth century).

[66] See Simon Rodway, 'Absolute forms in the poetry of the Gogynfeirdd: functionally obsolete archaisms or working system?', *Journal of Celtic Linguistics* 7 (1998 [2002]), 63-84; Rodway, Dating ch. 4.

[67] For views on the origin of the ending, see Rodway, 'Absolute forms', 64; and Dating 62 and 90. Since Welsh present and future are coterminous for most verbs, these endings are distinctively future. Differing future forms of the substantive vb (*bi*, *adfi*, *dybi*, *dymbi*, *byd*, *bydhawt*, etc.) lend variety. Interestingly, the Welsh word *dyfodol* 'future' is not attested until 1595 (English *future* dates from the 1380s), nor *arddyfodiog* (adj.). The Red Book of Hergest

General Introduction

§7.36 *wylhawt*; §7.52 *berwhawt*; §7.109 *bythawt*; §8.27 *tyruawt*; §8.30 *traghawt*; §8.64 *bydhawt*; §8.63 *fflemychawt*; §8.82 *gwledychawt*. These are also found in the court poet corpus, with examples continuing into the thirteenth century (e.g. CBT VII 30.7 *llifa6d*).[68]

3pl. in *-(h)awnt* is limited to §8.55 *nuchawnt* (uncertain); §8.38 *pebyllyawnt*; §8.61 *bydawnt*; §8.62 *medhawnt*; possibly §2.14 if *gwnahawt* were emended to *gwnahawnt* (see note); cf. Armes Prydain [AP] line 7 *gwasgarawt* emended by Ifor Williams to *gwasgarawnt*; and AP line 8 *gwnahawnt*.[69] The forms in poem §8 are likely to be imitating AP.

Impersonal forms in *-(h)awr* are found: §7.54 *yssadawr* (uncertain); §7.80 *dygedawr*; §7.99 *darlleawr*; §8.50 *dydeuhawr*; §8.54 *galwhawr*. These may be compared with several *-(h)awr* forms seen in the twelfth century, especially in the work of Cynddelw, occasionally persisting into the thirteenth (e.g. CBT VI 8.38 *rygarha6r*; 15.41 *meflawr*).[70] Impersonal forms in *-ator, -etor, -ettawr, -odawr* are found in §7.53 *berwhodawr*; §7.55 *canhator*; §7.68 *tyghettor*; §9.12 *dysgogettawr*. Both *-itor* and *-ator* forms are found in the CBT corpus.[71]

A 3sg. pret. in *-t* occurs in §7.1 *gogant* (also in Prydydd y Moch, see note). There are no examples of the innovative 3sg. pret. *-awð* which spread across the board in the literary language by the late thirteenth century.[72] However, the ending *-w(y)s* which it tended to replace is not very frequent either: only §3.16 *efrefwys*, §3.21 and 62 *disgynnwys*, and §6.18 *atrefnwys*. Comparable *trefnwys* is still found in the twelfth century (Gwynfardd Brycheiniog, CBT II 26.228), while *disgynn6s* is normal in thirteenth-century prose mss (Pen. 16iii, 35^r; and Pen. 14, pp. 73 and 83), so the lack of *-awð* in our poems does not signify a pre-twelfth-century date.

Some features are sometimes referred to as 'early':[73] 3sg. imperfect in *-i*,[74] as in §2.34 *dygorelwi*; *rwy* as in §8.20 *Ryw keissynt*, and see on §1.14; the prepositions *dy* 'to, for', as in §8.11 and §8.57. But these are all to be found in the CBT corpus as well.[75] On the other hand, non-contracted *mäes*, not seen in CBT, seems likely in §7.90. Instances of generic consonantal or 'Irish' rhyme are not necessarily diagnostic for early dating in verse outside the court poetry corpus, as has long been acknowledged,[76] but they are noted in the commentaries.

---

bardic grammar uses the term *ffutur* to indicate 'that which may come ahead' (*yr hwnn a del rac llaw*), giving the subjunctive *karwyf* as an example: see GPC s.vv.

[68] See full listing in Rodway, 'Absolute forms'; and Dating 181-93.
[69] Rodway, Dating 62, finds no such endings in CBT and 13c prose manuscripts.
[70] See now Rodway, Dating 60-61.
[71] See §7.55n and Rodway, Dating 102-5.
[72] See Simon Rodway, 'A datable development in medieval literary Welsh', *CMCS* 36 (1998), 71-94; Dating ch. 7.
[73] In GMW xix-xx and elsewhere.
[74] Treated by Rodway, 'Two developments', HI 69-71; Dating 65-6.
[75] D. Simon Evans, 'Iaith y Llys a Beirdd y Tywysogion', FS Gruffydd 60-74; *dy* occurs in CBT II 26.287 (Gwynfardd Brycheiniog, end of the 1170s): see on §5.107.
[76] See comments, LPBT 39, n. 129.

The material presented in this section suggests that there is no pressing reason to date the poems of this collection *before* the work of the twelfth- and early-thirteenth-century court poets. On the other hand, we have no solid information about the language of eleventh-century poetry, and we are obliged to depend rather heavily on the dating of Armes Prydain to *c.* 939-42 as a tenth-century benchmark. Since the language of this poem is not radically different from that of our poems, we have little choice but to assign them to a broad tenth- to thirteenth-century period. It has been too convenient to assign our poems to the chronologically ill-defined rag-bag of so-called 'late hengerdd' or 'Y Bwlch' poetry and, by a lazy extension and wishful thinking, to what is sometimes defined as the 'pre-Geoffrey of Monmouth tradition'. On the grounds of content rather than language, some, such as §5, are patently late, and this might be true for others.

In dating anonymous prophetic material, there is perhaps need for especial caution, bearing in mind the recycling of phrases, lines and sentiments, and the possibility that the prophetic poems used waning forms to lend a distinctive archaic air (such as futures in *-awt*; impersonal *-awr* and *-itor* endings). Already giving a special feel to the discourse are the future forms, such as *bi, adui, dymbi, dyfi, rydybyd*. Of very particular significance as hallmarks are verbal forms with extra *dy-* prefixed, such as §1.18 *dedeuant*; §2.34 *dygorelwi*; §3.8 *dygyrchet*; §4.1 *dygogan*; §4.1 *dygobryssyn*; §4.5 *dyrchafyssyn*; §4.8 *dyderuyd*; §4.24 *dydaw*; §5.15 *dymgöi*; §7.32 *dysgogan*; §7.57 *dedeuant*; *dydybyd*; §8.50 *dydeuhawr*; §8.17 *dymdygyrch*; §8.50 *dyderbi*; §8.79 *dydyccawt*; §8.24 *dydyrchafwy*; §9.3 *dygorescynnan*; §9.12 *dysgogettawr*; §9.21 *dydyrchefis*. This is to be compared with eleven verbs used in this way in Armes Prydain.[77]

This volume, like its companion, is part of a larger attempt to map out a grammar of poetic diction, to understanding how the early poets to *c.* 1300 composed and were trained to manipulate their materials.[78] Assembling comparanda has already indicated some unexpected findings, most significantly that some of the putative hengerdd or old poetry, traditionally assigned to the pre-1100 period, overlaps with, or is in a complicated relationship with the compositions of the twelfth- and thirteenth-century court poets. In particular, eleven of the poems in the companion volume were seen to bear the distinct footprint of one particular court poet, Llywarch ap Llywelyn, also known as Prydydd y Moch, a bold and exceptionally inventive practitioner active in the royal courts of Gwynedd between *c.* 1174/5 and *c.* 1220.[79] A slighter case was made for a further five in that collection. As a young man, Prydydd y Moch served Owain Gwynedd's sons, Dafydd and Rhodri, as well as their cousins, Gruffudd and Maredudd ap Cynan, and was a canny survivor during the unsettled thirty years between the death of Owain Gwynedd in 1170 and 1199

---

[77] AP 78-9.
[78] See LPBT 25-7.
[79] Summarised in LPBT 27-36. See comments by G. Aled Williams, *CMCS* 59 (2010), 87; Thomas Owen Clancy, in *Beyond the Gododdin*, edited by Alex Woolf (St Andrews, 2012), 167 n. 4; and Charles-Edwards, WaB 653.

General Introduction

when Llywelyn ab Iorwerth (known to us as Llywelyn Fawr 'the Great') became ruler over the whole of Gwynedd.[80] Many of his finest poems were sung in his prime to Llywelyn, during a period of great cultural activity, when Llywelyn made huge gains at the expense of the Normans, recapturing the castle of Degannwy in 1213 and going on to bring much of Wales under his influence, including central and south-east Wales and Deheubarth.

In view of the likelihood that Prydydd y Moch was the author or adaptor of legendary Taliesin material (or both),[81] the same scrutiny has been accorded in the commentaries to these prophecies, too, to see whether they show any of the same symptoms.[82] Some of these could certainly be discounted as coming from a common stock (e.g. §3.1), or serving the needs of the genre (e.g. the use of *Prydein* and *Brython*) or as instances (e.g. §5.18 *heu*) where the sense of the rarely used verbal noun could hardly be expressed in any other way.

---

[80] LPBT 31-6.
[81] For possible contexts, see discussion LPBT 33-6.
[82] §1.15 *ar lan Gwyllyonwy*, cf. CBT V 22.28 *Dyfyrdonwy* (a nonce form thought to be based on Dyfrdwy).
§2.11 *droch drymluawc*, cf. predilection for unusual adj. formations in *-awc*. See note.
§3.1 *Kychwedyl a'm dothyw*, cf. CBT V 2.7 *Kychwetyl a'm dothy6*: three instances of *dodyw* as well.
§3.11 *Goleith dy yscarant amgant dy vro*, cf. pl. form used four times by Prydydd y Moch (but also by Cynddelw, twice); *amgant* is also a word favoured by Prydydd y Moch.
§3.15 *o Gludwys vro*, cf. the only other attestation of name + *vro*, in CBT V 28.3 *Carno 6ro*.
§3.35 *rac pedrydan dande*, cf. Prydydd y Moch's favouring of adj. formations in *-de*.
§4.7 *diwed plo coll Iago*, only other example of this rare word is by Prydydd y Moch, CBT V 23.137-9, who also rhymes it with *Iago*.
§5.1 *Kein gyfedwch*, use of this form rather than *cyfedach*. Cf. *-wch* form in CBT V 1.58 and 77 (but also used by Cynddelw). §5 is possibly about his patron Llywelyn ab Iorwerth's castle at Dolbadarn.
§5.2 *ryyscrifyat*. Use of preverbial *ry* with impersonal past as in CBT V 338 (*rygreat, ryerchit, ryanet*).
§5.18 *o heu hyt vedi*. Vb noun used uniquely here, and in CBT V 8.13 and 8.14.
§6.5 If *kyfleudon* be emended to *cyflawdon* as suggested by G, then note it is only used elsewhere by Prydydd y Moch, CBT V 4.23 and 25.17.
§6.14 *nothwy*, only paralleled in other BT examples and CBT V 23.3.
§6.17 *Pan dyfu Gatwallawn*; Cadwallon was a paragon in his praise of Llywelyn Fawr, CBT V 23.88-92, and in CBT V 23.136-8.
§6.22 *Gware pelre a phen Saesson*, cf. unique use of *pelre* in CBT by Prydydd y Moch, CBT V 14.6 *Dossa6c, hytola6c, ha6t y belre* (used, like *olwyn*, of horse's hooves).
§7.1 *Kathyl goreu gogant*, with the rare *-t* preterite of the compound vb *goganu*, as used uniquely in the court poetry corpus by Prydydd y Moch, CBT V 5.61.
§7.8 *ryodres rychwant*. *Ryodres* is used once in CA, but the CBT comparanda are entirely restricted to Prydydd y Moch, with three examples, see notes.
§7.25 *ar weryt* ? If *a'r weryt*, cf. CBT V 6.24 *Ef ry6r ryweryd digreid* for sole instance of *ry* with *gweryt*.
§8.58 *vrthenedic Prydein*, cf. 37 examples of *Prydein* in Prydydd y Moch (cf. 20 by Cynddelw).
§10 *Marchawc mwth misterin*. Although in CA line 3 and PT VII.9 and VIII.32, *mwth* is used in CBT only by Prydydd y Moch, all with *meirch* (twice *mwth*, and once pl. *mythyon*).

Nevertheless, it is surely tantalising that the rare word *plo*, in §4.7 *diwed plo coll Iago*, is matched only by Prydydd y Moch, CBT V 23.137-9, who also rhymes it with *Iago*.

Despite the southern or mid-Walian affiliations of the Book of Taliesin, the content of the texts, where we can judge, is overwhelmingly to do with North Wales. This includes the prophecies in this volume as well as most of the legendary Taliesin poems in the companion volume, and we can only speculate about their assembling in a northern exemplar or exemplars. Twelfth-century commentators, notably Gerald of Wales, tell us that prophecies were in oral circulation and in written texts. In St Davids a woman shouted an old Welsh prophecy in King Henry II's face as he returned from Ireland. The king requested translations of prophecies and Gerald 'sought the assistance of persons better acquainted with Welsh poetry' than himself to do the job. Gerald claimed to have found the raw materials 'long sought-for and desired' on Palm Sunday 1188 in a *libellus*, a little booklet, in Nefyn on the Llŷn Peninsula, 'in a most remote region of Gwynedd'. If that *libellus* really existed, did it contain the sort of prophecies we have in this collection? Was its discourse of violence, the 'playing ball with the heads of the English', simply too toxic? Perhaps it is no wonder that Gerald backtracked, saying 'the time was not ripe', that the truth, 'though most useful and desirable, should be concealed for a while rather than bursting forth into the light, over-hastily and dangerously causing offence to greater powers'.[83] Such material may have been viewed very differently in the courts of Gwynedd, and have been collected up, augmented and adapted. As to the date of our items, we remember that the Black Book of Carmarthen, the most senior partner of the Ancient Books firm (*c*. 1225-50), was not averse to including twelfth-century court poetry of local southern interest, nor indeed patently recent prophecies such as the Afallennau or the Oianau.[84] This is just as likely to have been true of a Gwynedd compiler, who, in the true spirit of Taliesin — 'I'm old, I'm young' — created a varied miscellany of verse spanning many centuries, admitting the new as well as the old.

---

[83] See Ad Putter, 'Gerald of Wales and the Prophet Merlin', *Anglo-Norman Studies* 31 (2008 [2009]), 90-103; Karen Jankulak, *Geoffrey of Monmouth* (Cardiff, 2010), pp. 82-3.

[84] See §6.24.

Bibliographical abbreviations and short titles

AC	*Annales Cambriae*, edited by John Williams ab Ithel (London, 1860)
AH	*Astudiaethau ar yr Hengerdd*, edited by Rachel Bromwich and R. Brinley Jones (Caerdydd/Cardiff, 1978)
AP	*Armes Prydein from the Book of Taliesin*, edited by Ifor Williams, English version by Rachel Bromwich, Medieval and Modern Welsh Series volume VI (Dublin, 1972)
AW	*The Arthur of the Welsh*, edited by Rachel Bromwich, A.O.H. Jarman and Brynley F. Roberts (Cardiff, 1991)
B	*Bulletin of the Board of Celtic Studies*
Bardos	*Bardos: Penodau ar y Traddodiad Barddol Cymreig a Cheltaidd, cyflwynedig i J.E. Caerwyn Williams*, edited by R. Geraint Gruffydd (Caerdydd, 1982)
BD	*Brut Dingestow*, edited by Henry Lewis (Caerdydd, 1942)
BGod	*Beyond the Gododdin*, edited by Alex Woolf (St Andrews, 2013)
Bleg	*Llyfr Blegywryd*, edited by Stephen J. Williams and J. Enoch Powell, second edition (Caerdydd, 1961)
BMax	*Breudwyt Maxen Wledic*, edited by Brynley F. Roberts, Medieval and Modern Welsh Series volume XI (Dublin, 2005)
BR	*Breudwyt Ronabwy*, edited by Melville Richards (Caerdydd, 1948)
BT	*The Book of Taliesin: Facsimile and Text*, edited by J. Gwenogvryn Evans (Llanbedrog, 1910)
BWP	Ifor Williams, *The Beginnings of Welsh Poetry*, edited by Rachel Bromwich (Cardiff, 1972, second edition 1980)
ByT (Pen. 20)	*Brut y Tywysogyon, Peniarth MS. 20*, edited by Thomas Jones (Caerdydd, 1941)
ByT (RBH)	*Brut y Tywysogyon, Red Book of Hergest Version*, edited and translated by Thomas Jones (Cardiff, 1955)
CA	*Canu Aneirin*, edited by Ifor Williams (Caerdydd, 1938)
CBT	*Cyfres Beirdd y Tywysogion*, 7 vols, general editor R. Geraint Gruffydd (Caerdydd, 1991-6)
CC	*Blodeugerdd Barddas o Ganu Crefyddol Cynnar*, edited by Marged Haycock (Abertawe, 1994)
CHAge	*The Celtic Heroic Age: Literary Sources for Ancient Celtic Europe and Early Ireland and Wales*, edited by John T. Koch in collaboration with John Carey, second edition (Malden, MA, 1995)
ChwT	Ifor Williams, *Chwedl Taliesin*, O'Donnell Lecture 1955-6 (Caerdydd, 1957)
CIB	Patrick Sims-Williams, *The Celtic Inscriptions of Britain: Phonology and Chronology c. 400-1200*, Publications of the Philological Society, 37 (Oxford, 2003)
CLlaLl	*Cyfranc Lludd a Llefelys*, edited by Brynley F. Roberts, Mediaeval and Modern Welsh Series volume VII (Dublin, 1975)

Bibliographical Abbreviations

CLlH	*Canu Llywarch Hen*, edited by Ifor Williams, second edition (Caerdydd, 1953)
CMCS	*Cambridge/Cambrian Medieval Celtic Studies*
CO	*Culhwch and Olwen: An Edition and Study of the Oldest Arthurian Tale*, edited by Rachel Bromwich and D. Simon Evans (Cardiff, 1992)
CPNS	W.J. Watson, *The History of the Celtic Place-Names of Scotland* (Edinburgh, 1926; reprinted Dublin, 1986)
Day, Arfau	Jenny Day, 'Arfau yn yr Hengerdd a Cherddi Beirdd y Tywysogion', 2 vols (PhD thesis, Aberystwyth University, 2010)
DB	*Delw y Byd*, edited by Henry Lewis and P. Diverres (Caerdydd, 1928)
Diarhebion	*Diarhebion Llyfr Coch Hergest*, edited by Richard Glyn Roberts (Aberystwyth, 2013)
DP	*The Description of Penbrokshire by George Owen of Henllys, Lord of Kemes*, edited by H. Owen, 4 parts, Cymmrodorion Record Series, 1 (London, 1892–1936)
DPNW	Hywel Wyn Owen and Richard Morgan, *Dictionary of the Place-Names of Wales* (Cardiff, 2007)
Dydd dyfydd	Ifor Williams, 'Dalen o femrwn', *B* 4 (1927-9), 41-8: poem I, pp. 45-7
EANC	R.J. Thomas, *Enwau Afonydd a Nentydd Cymru*, I (Caerdydd, 1938)
ÉC	*Études celtiques*
Echrys Ynys	BT 68.5-69.8, edited and translated by Ifor Williams, 'Two poems from the Book of Taliesin: II An early Anglesey poem', in BWP 172-80; also translated and discussed by R. Geraint Gruffydd, 'A Welsh "Dark Age" Court Poem', in FS Mac Cana 39-48
Edmyg Dinbych	BT 42.16-44.16, edited and translated by Ifor Williams, 'Two poems from the Book of Taliesin: I The Praise of Tenby', in BWP 155-72
EEW	T.H. Parry-Williams, *The English Element in Welsh*, Cymmrodorion Record Series, 10 (London, 1923)
ELl	Ifor Williams, *Enwau Lleoedd* (Lerpwl, reprinted 1969)
ELlSG	J. Lloyd-Jones, *Enwau Lleoedd Sir Gaernarfon* (Caerdydd, 1928)
EPN	Eilert Ekwall, *The Concise Oxford Dictionary of English Place-Names*, fourth edition (Oxford, 1960)
ERN	Eilert Ekwall, *English River-Names* (Oxford, 1928)
EWGP	*Early Welsh Gnomic Poems*, edited by Kenneth Jackson, second edition (Cardiff, 1961)
EWGT	*Early Welsh Genealogical Tracts*, edited by P.C. Bartrum, (Cardiff, 1966)
EWSP	Jenny Rowland, *Early Welsh Saga Poetry: A Study and Edition of the Englynion* (Cambridge, 1990)
EyB	Thomas Jones, 'The Black Book of Carmarthen "Stanzas of the Graves"', *Proceedings of the British Academy* 53 (1967), 97-137
FAB	*The Four Ancient Books of Wales*, edited by W.F. Skene, 2 vols (Edinburgh, 1868)
FS Gruffydd	*Beirdd a Thywysogion: Barddoniaeth Llys yng Nghymru,*

Bibliographical Abbreviations

	Iwerddon a'r Alban, cyflwynedig i R. Geraint Gruffydd, edited by Morfydd E. Owen and Brynley F. Roberts (Caerdydd and Aberystwyth, 1996)
FS Mac Cana	*Ildánach, Ildírech: A Festschrift for Proinsias Mac Cana*, edited by John Carey, John T. Koch and Pierre-Yves Lambert (Andover and Aberystwyth, 1999)
G	J. Lloyd-Jones, *Geirfa Barddoniaeth Gynnar Gymraeg* (Caerdydd, 1931-63)
GBDd	*Gwaith Bleddyn Ddu*, edited by R. Iestyn Daniel (Aberystwyth, 1994)
GC	*Gwaith Casnodyn*, edited by R. Iestyn Daniel (Aberystwyth, 1999)
GDC	*Gwaith Dafydd y Coed a Beirdd Eraill o Lyfr Coch Hergest*, edited by R. Iestyn Daniel (Aberystwyth, 2002)
GDG	*Gwaith Dafydd ap Gwilym*, edited by Thomas Parry, second edition (Caerdydd, 1963)
GDGor	*Gwaith Dafydd Gorlech*, edited by Erwain H. Rheinallt (Aberystwyth, 1997)
GEO	*Gwaith Einion Offeiriad a Dafydd Ddu o Hiraddug*, edited by R. Geraint Gruffydd and Rhiannon Ifans (Aberystwyth, 1997)
GGDT	*Gwaith Gruffudd ap Dafydd ap Tudur, Gwilym Ddu o Arfon, Trahaearn Brydydd Mawr ac Iorwerth Beli*, edited by N.G. Costigan (Bosco), R. Iestyn Daniel and Dafydd Johnston (Aberystwyth, 1995)
GGG	*Gwaith Guto'r Glyn*, edited by Ifor Williams and J. Llywelyn Williams (Caerdydd, 1961)
GGM	*Gwaith Gruffudd ap Maredudd*, edited by Barry J. Lewis and Ann Parry Owen, 3 vols (Aberystwyth, 2003-7)
GGGryg	*Gwaith Gruffudd Gryg*, edited by Barry J. Lewis and Eurig Salisbury (Aberystwyth, 2010)
GGrG	*Gwaith Gronw Gyriog, Iorwerth ab y Cyriog ac Eraill*, edited by Rhiannon Ifans, Ann Parry Owen, W. Dyfed Rowlands and Erwain H. Rheinallt (Aberystwyth, 1997)
GIG	*Gwaith Iolo Goch*, edited by D.R. Johnston (Caerdydd, 1988)
GLGC	*Gwaith Lewys Glyn Cothi*, edited by Dafydd Johnston (Caerdydd, 1995)
GLlBH	*Gwaith Llywelyn Brydydd Hoddnant, Dafydd ap Gwilym, Hillyn ac Eraill*, edited by Ann Parry Owen and Dylan Foster Evans (Aberystwyth, 1996)
GLlG	*Gwaith Llywelyn Goch ap Meurig Hen*, edited by Dafydd Johnston (Aberystwyth, 1998)
GLM	*Gwaith Lewys Môn*, edited by Eurys I. Rowlands (Caerdydd, 1975)
GMW	D. Simon Evans, *A Grammar of Middle Welsh* (Dublin, reprinted 1970)
GodA	*The Gododdin of Aneirin: Text and Context from Dark Age North Britain*, edited by John T. Koch (Cardiff, 1998)
Gosymdaith	R1055-6, edited by Nicolas Jacobs, 'Gossymdeith Llefoet Wynebclawr', in *Early Welsh Gnomic and Nature Poetry* (London, 2012), 21-5 and 61-7

Bibliographical Abbreviations

GP	*Gramadegau'r Penceirddiaid*, edited by G.J. Williams and E.J. Jones (Caerdydd, 1934)
GPB	*Gwaith Prydydd Breuan, Rhys ap Dafydd ab Einion, Hywel Ystorm, a Cherddi Dychan Eraill o Lyfr Coch Hergest*, edited by Huw Meirion Edwards (Aberystwyth, 2000)
GPC	*Geiriadur Prifysgol Cymru* (Caerdydd, 1950-2002)
GPC^2	*Geiriadur Prifysgol Cymru*, second edition (Caerdydd, 2003-)
Gruffydd, *Cerdd Lys Gynnar*	R. Geraint Gruffydd, *'Edmyg Dinbych': Cerdd Lys Gynnar o Ddyfed*, Darlith Goffa J.E Caerwyn a Gwen Williams (Aberystwyth, 2002)
GSCy	*Gwaith Dafydd Bach ap Madog Wladaidd 'Sypyn Cyfeiliog' a Llywelyn ab y Moel*, edited by R. Iestyn Daniel (Aberystwyth, 1998)
GSRh	*Gwaith Sefnyn, Rhisierdyn, Gruffudd Fychan ap Gruffudd ab Ednyfed a Llywelyn Bentwrch*, edited by Nerys Ann Jones and Erwain Haf Rheinallt (Aberystwyth, 1995)
HB	*Historia Brittonum*, in *Nennius, British History, and the Welsh Annals*, edited and translated by John Morris (Chichester, 1980)
H-cd	*Yr Hengerdd: Mynegeiriau Cyflawn*, edited by G.R. Isaac, CD (Aberystwyth, 2001)
HE	*Bede's Ecclesiastical History of the English People*, edited by Bertram Colgrave and R.A.B. Mynors (Oxford, 1969)
HGK	*Historia Gruffud vab Kenan*, edited by D. Simon Evans (Caerdydd, 1977)
HI	*Yr Hen Iaith: Studies in Early Welsh*, edited by Paul Russell (Aberystwyth, 2003)
HKB	Geoffrey of Monmouth, *The History of the Kings of Britain*, edited by Michael D. Reeve, translated by Neil Wright (Woodbridge, 2007)
HW	J.E. Lloyd, *A History of Wales*, 2 vols, continuous pagination (London, 1939)
IIMWL	Patrick Sims-Williams, *Irish Influence on Medieval Welsh Literature* (Oxford, 2011)
IGE^2	*Cywyddau Iolo Goch ac Eraill*, edited by Henry Lewis, Thomas Roberts and Ifor Williams, second edition (Caerdydd, reprinted 1972)
Ior.	*Llyfr Iorwerth*, edited by A.Rh. Wiliam (Caerdydd, 1960)
IWMA	*Ireland and Wales in the Middle Ages*, edited by Karen Jankulak and Jonathan M. Wooding (Dublin, 2007)
Juv	Juvencus manuscript (Cambridge University Library, MS Ff.4.42)
JuvTC	Helen McKee, *The Cambridge Juvencus Manuscript glossed in Latin, Old Welsh, and Old Irish: Text and Commentary* (Aberystwyth, 2000)
Lexique	*Lexique étymologique de l'irlandais ancien*, edited by J. Vendryes et al. (Dublin and Paris, 1959-)
LHEB	Kenneth H. Jackson, *Language and History in Early Britain* (Edinburgh, 1953)
LL	[Liber Landavensis] *The Text of the Book of Llan Dâv*, edited by J. Gwenogvryn Evans and John Rhys (Oxford, 1893)

Bibliographical Abbreviations

LPBT	*Legendary Poems from the Book of Taliesin*, edited by Marged Haycock (Aberystwyth, 2007)
LlDC	*Llyfr Du Caerfyrddin*, edited by A.O.H. Jarman (Caerdydd, 1982)
LlDW	*Llyvyr Du or Weun: Facsimile of the Chirk Codex of the Welsh Laws*, edited by J. Gwenogvryn Evans (Llanbedrog, 1899)
Marwnad Cynddylan	Marwnad Cynddylan, edited and translated by Jenny Rowland, in EWSP 174-89.
Moliant Cadwallon	Moliant Cadwallon, edited and translated by R. Geraint Gruffydd, 'Canu Cadwallon ap Cadfan', in AH 25-42, pp. 29-30
MWM	Daniel Huws, *Medieval Welsh Manuscripts* (Cardiff and Aberystwyth, 2000)
NLWJ	*National Library of Wales Journal*
Owen, TrArbennig	Morfydd E. Owen, 'Y Trioedd Arbennig', *B* 24 (1970-2), 434-50
Peirian Faban	'Peiryan Vaban' [from Peniarth 50], edited by A.O.H. Jarman, *B* 14 (1950-2), 104-8. References by line number
Pen.	A manuscript in the Peniarth collection, National Library of Wales, Aberystwyth
Pen3Afallennau	Ifor Williams, 'Y Cyfoesi a'r Afallennau yn Peniarth 3', *B* 4 (1927-9), 112-29. References by page and line
Pen3Cyfoesi	as above
Pen3Oianau	as above
PKM	*Pedeir Keinc y Mabinogi*, edited by Ifor Williams, second edition (Caerdydd, 1951)
PNP	B.G. Charles, *The Place-Names of Pembrokeshire*, 2 vols (Aberystwyth, 1992)
PNRB	A.L.F. Rivet and Colin Smith, *The Place-Names of Roman Britain* (London, 1979)
PT	*The Poems of Taliesin*, edited by Ifor Williams, translated and revised by J.E. Caerwyn Williams, Mediaeval and Modern Welsh Series volume III (Dublin, 1968)
R	*The Poetry in the Red Book of Hergest*, edited by J. Gwenogvryn Evans (Llanbedrog, 1911)
RBB	*The Text of the Bruts from the Red Book of Hergest*, edited by John Rhys and J. Gwenogvryn Evans (Oxford, 1890)
SBCHP	Peter Schrijver, *Studies in British Celtic Historical Phonology* (Amsterdam, 1995)
SC	*Studia Celtica*
Sims-Williams, Prepositions	Patrick Sims-Williams, 'Variation in Middle Welsh conjugated prepositions: chronology, register, and dialect', *Transactions of the Philological Society* 111 (2013), 1-50
Tal	John Morris-Jones, 'Taliesin', *Y Cymmrodor* 28 (1918)
TC	T.J. Morgan, *Y Treigladau a'u Cystrawen* (Caerdydd, 1952)
THSC	*Transactions of the Honourable Society of Cymmrodorion*
TT	*The Triumph Tree: Scotland's Earliest Poetry, 550-1350*, edited by Thomas Owen Clancy (Edinburgh, 1998)
Tymhorau	'An early Welsh seasonal poem', edited by Graham C.G. Thomas, *B* 34 (1987), 61-5
TYP³	*Trioedd Ynys Prydein*, edited by Rachel Bromwich, third edition

Bibliographical Abbreviations

	(Cardiff, 2006)
VGFC	*Vita Griffini Filii Conani: The Medieval Latin Life of Gruffudd ap Cynan*, edited by Paul Russell (Cardiff, 2005)
VM	*Life of Merlin: Geoffrey of Monmouth, Vita Merlini*, edited by Basil Clarke (Cardiff, 1973)
VVB	J. Loth, *Vocabulaire Vieux-Breton* (Paris, 1884)
WaB	T. M. Charles-Edwards, *Wales and the Britons, 350-1064* (Oxford, 2013)
WCD	Peter C. Bartrum, *A Welsh Classical Dictionary* (Aberystwyth, 1993)
WHR	*Welsh History Review*
WKC	*The Welsh King and his Court*, edited by T.M. Charles-Edwards, Morfydd E. Owen and Paul Russell (Cardiff, 2000)
WML	*Welsh Medieval Law*, edited by A.W. Wade-Evans (Oxford, 1909)
YB	*Ysgrifau Beirniadol*
YT	*Ystoria Taliesin*, edited by Patrick K. Ford (Cardiff, 1992)

1 Daronwy

The metrically mixed text may indicate that two poems, or portions of poems have been joined: lines 1-39 use the short Class 1, while the remainder, lines 40-53, uses a longer line, usually eight syllables, which has a consistent end cadence after the single caesura.[1] The problems of interpreting the drift of the text led Margaret Enid Griffiths to characterise it as 'a very curious and obscure poem',[2] and it is not suprising that it has received little attention. Lines 1-17 rhyming in -*wy* use several of the words used by the court poets when they are singing on this particular rhyme (see notes). The poem opens with what appears to be a reference to the biblical Flood, and again in line 8, to *balch Nefwy*, here interpreted as Noah's Ark, as discussed in the textual notes. The salvation effected by God at the time of the Flood leads into a rhetorical question about another sustaining or protecting agency — whether there is to be had a *pren* ('wood' or 'tree', a word used figuratively also for 'warrior') greater than *Daronwy*. Such questions, sometimes riddling or ambiguous, are a signature of the Taliesin persona, as are assertions of knowledge.[3] The name, *Daronwy*, gives the poem its title, and the context suggests that it may have been understood at one level as the *dar* 'oak tree' of Goronwy/Gronwy, especially since 'the men of Goronwy' are unequivocally present and praised in line 10. Another tree 'growing in the forest' is the magic staff (*hutlath*) of Mathonwy (line 12), an item which is well-known from the Fourth Branch of the Mabinogi. In that story, Math fab Mathonwy's *hutlath* effects the memorable punishment of the brothers, Gwydion and Gilfaethwy, for raping Goewin: it strikes them, turns them into a succession of male and female animals, and subsequently restores them to their own shape and form. Then the staff is used to prove whether their sister, Aranrhod, is a virgin and fit to replace Goewin as Math's footholder: she fails the test spectacularly, dropping two creatures behind her: Dylan, who heads for the sea, and Lleu who is incubated and reared by Gwydion. In our poem, this famous *hutlath*, now perhaps planted and growing as a tree, appears to be bearing fruit or benefits, and may perhaps be compared with Aaron's rod (sometimes equated with that of Moses)[4] which put forth buds, blossoms and ripe almonds (Numbers 17:8). In Christian tradition, this miraculously flowering staff of Scripture was connected typologically with the Incarnation of Christ, and its wood with both the Tree of Life and Christ's Cross.

---

[1] On metrics see LPBT 37-9.
[2] EVW 118.
[3] On questions, see LPBT 8, 11, 49. See on line 11 *odit a'e gwypwy* 'it is a rare man who knows it'. Whether Taliesin is the imagined speaker here in unclear as with other poems of this collection: see General Introduction, 6-10.
[4] Moses's staff (*Llath Voyssen*) is the subject of a poem in the Book of Taliesin: see edition and translation, CC 80-91. In that poem, God is praised for providing protection to the Israelite hosts against the ferocity of the waves (*tonyar* and *ryferthwy*), probably referring to the crossing of the Red Sea in Exodus 14.

1 Daronwy

The mention of Mathonwy, presumably Math fab Mathonwy or his father, might lead one to wonder whether Goronwy in line 10, and perhaps the person whose name might be associated with a protecting or efficacious oak tree (if *dar (O)ronwy*), is the same as Gronw Befr, the lord of Penllyn betrayed by Blodeuwedd in the same story. This is very uncertain, however, since there are others of that name, such as the Goronwy connected with the Taliesin persona in the poem Kat Godeu: 'now no-one visits me except Goronwy from the Water-meadows of Edrywy',[5] and various historical figures, such as those of the family of Ednyfed Fychan, as discussed in the notes.

The identity of Daronwy is further complicated by the incidental information at the end of the White Book of Rhydderch and Red Book of Hergest versions of Triad 26 *Tri G6rueichiat Ynys Brydein*, 'The Three Powerful Swineherds of the Island of Britain'. This notes that *Cath Balug*, 'Palug's Cat', was reared on the island of Anglesey by the sons of Palug, 'to their detriment' (*yr dr6c vdunt*), and that it was one of the Three Chief Oppressions (*gormes*) of Anglesey that had been reared on the island, together with Daronwy and Edwin of Northumbria (here called *brenhin Lloegyr* 'king of England').[6] Unfortunately, whether this Daronwy was a man or a monster, a beast or even a poison tree is not indicated. Gwilym Tew's cywydd '(Y) gŵr mawr hir a grym yr haf' which mentions *[Vn] o vaibion daro[nw]y/ [y] min y tan y maent wy/ brenin ywch noc wybrenwynt/ [b]rawd ynvam ac adam gynt* offers no help.[7]

A second complication is the township and stream, Dronwy, formerly Daronwy,[8] in the parish of Llanfachraith in north-west Anglesey, a few miles inland from Holyhead Bay. The stream Dronwy flows into the River Alaw, with Pont Dronwy and Pen-y-bont Dronwy as well as Dronwy, the substantial seventeenth-century house built by the Bulkeley family, which is still standing. The area is just north of Aber Alaw in the commote of Talybolion, famous as the place where Branwen died of a broken heart and was buried after returning with the seven survivors from the debâcle in Ireland.[9] Alaw'r Beirdd, as it was known in 1352, evidently took its name from poets who held land nearby: we know that Dafydd Benfras, *fl.* 1220-58, had held land in Cornwy, Talybolion, and that his kinsman, Gruffudd ap Maredudd ap Dafydd held land in Dronwy in 1352

---

[5] LPBT 5.228-9, and n.

[6] TYP³ 51-8.

[7] *Llanstephan MS. 6*, edited by E. Stanton Roberts (Cardiff, 1916), 193 (cf. NLW Llanstephan 134, p. 212). BL Stowe 959, 46ʳ has *vaibion da ronwy* ('sons of good Gronwy'?) and NLW 13063, 79ʳ, has *Dâr onwy*.

[8] Early forms include *Doronewey* (1291/2), *Davronwy* (1352), with later instances of *Dyronwy*, *Deronwy*, then *Dronwy* from the early 17c., per Bangor University, Melville Richards Archive, s.nn. *Dronwy, Daronwy*.

[9] PKM 45. In the Extent of Anglesey of 1352, Alaw'r Beirdd was 'held of St Beuno', indicating a connection with Clynnog Fawr explored further by Patrick Sims-Williams, 'Clas Beuno and the Four Branches of the Mabinogi', in *150 Jahre "Mabinogion": Deutsch-walische Kulturbeziehungen*, edited by Bernhard Maier and Stefan Zimmer (Tübingen, 2001), pp. 111-27, at pp. 122-3.

together with other heirs of Gwely Dafydd ap Gwas Sanffraid.[10] R.J. Thomas suggested that the stream- and township name Dronwy perhaps derived from a personal name Daronwy.[11] This would be either from the element *dar* found in *cynddaredd* 'anger',[12] or from *dâr* 'oak tree(s)', either as *Daron* (with *-on* forming an oak theonym)[13] comparable with *Ieithon*, *Aeron*, etc., or else an extended form in *-wy*, comparing the formation of personal names such as *Mathonwy* or *Euronwy* (rather than river-names in *-wy*, such as *Dyfrdwy*, or regional names such as *Ardudwy*, *Colunwy*, not entirely ruled out by Thomas). *Dar* is a common element in river-names, e.g. Daron in Llŷn, and Dâr, tributary of the Cynon. Alternatively, as suggested above, Dronwy may take its name from *Dâr Oronwy* (*dâr* leniting a following proper noun), comparing the formation of Darowen (*Dareweyne* 1254) five miles east of Machynlleth, and English names such as Hodsock ('Hod's Oak', EPN 244).

Since there no other Anglesey references in the poem, we might question whether there is necessarily any link between our poem and Daronwy, the second Great Anglesey Oppression of the triad (not a good thing, presumably), and/or the place in the north-west of the island. *Dâr*, as already noted, can be used as a figure for a mighty warrior and indeed it is a term for God himself in a fourteenth-century englyn by Gruffudd ap Maredudd ap Dafydd which also (coincidentally, perhaps) mentions *balch Noe* 'Noah's ark'. Is it possible, then, that an extended form has been created for rhyming purposes by analogy with Math > Mathonwy? If that were the case, *py pren a vo mwy/ noget Daronwy* would take its place in a pious introduction in praise of God's protective power, in readiness, perhaps, for the next section about the talismanic *hutlath Vathonwy* whose fruits will be secured by the secular deliverer Cynan when he comes to power. *Daronwy* was perhaps interpreted as a personal name and because it came early in the poem, and appeared to share its first element with the noun *darogan*,[14] was deemed suitable for abstracting as a title for a poem with a strong prophetic element. That still leaves unexplained the identity of the Great Oppression in the triad — unless that, too, had arisen through some misunderstanding of a poetic text such as ours combined with a knowedge of the Anglesey place-name. Yet more speculation is hardly in order, so we must set aside the dramatic events of the popular revolt of 1294 when Roger de Pulesdon the 'unpopular and extortionate sheriff of Anglesey' was hanged by the Anglesey rebels, Goronwy the sergeant of Twrcelyn and Trahaearn ap Bleddyn of Talybolion. Both were executed and their lands, including lands in Dronwy, were escheated to the crown: in the spring of the following year, Edward I spent

---

[10] See details in CBT VI 363-8; GGMD I, 1-8; A.D. Carr, *Medieval Anglesey* (Llangefni, 1982), 222-3.
[11] R.J. Thomas, 'Enwau Afonydd â'r olddodiad *-wy*', *B* 7 (1933-5), 133.
[12] G 297 suggests *dar* 'fierce' as a possibility.
[13] Discussed by Ifor Williams, ELl 46.
[14] Really the first element of *darogan* is *dar-* 'before'.

several weeks in Llan-faes on the island, ordering the establishment of Beaumaris castle.[15]

The following section of our poem, lines 18-27, foretells the coming of four sovereignties or dominions (*pennaeth* can also mean 'ruler') from over the sea, and a fifth 'no feebler', set on conquering Britain. Using a discourse much like that of other prophecies, especially those in the Black Book of Carmarthen, the poet describes a world in turmoil — women talkative or forward, free men bond — and expresses a longing for the certainties of the heroic code of mead and manly horsemanship. Then two 'unyielding ones', a widow and a slender wife, will come 'with iron wing, berating men', followed by champions from 'the region of Rome' who will be the subject of song. The five dominions or rulers of lines 21-2 are paralleled by lines 38-40 in which the innate properties of four different animals — dog, horse, pig, bullock — are noted, with a fifth a *llwdyn gwyn/ a wnaeth Iessu*, a blessed young animal or youth created by Jesus.

After warning that the Cymry will not be popular if they go to ground in a cowardly fashion, the poet's heart rises as he thinks of how past success may bode well for the future: 'he who has had good luck will not have bad'. This resurgence appears to be linked to the figure of Rhun (perhaps the son of Maelgwn Gwynedd). It is the fury (literally 'steam') of his battling which will spread out over a vast area. Here the names of fortified places (*din* and *caer*) mix real locations (the Old North *Dineidyn* 'Edinburgh', and possibly *Kaer Rian* in Pembrokeshire) with the invented and legendary (*Dineidwc* and *Caer Rywc*), all intended to indicate Gwynedd supremacy. The last name, *Caer Rywc*, if it is to be identified with one of the names in the drowned south-western kingdom of Teithi Hen, echoes the Flood or inundation material treated at the beginning of the poem, before the poem closes with the certain hope that 'our Lord God shall defend us'.

---

[15] Carr, *Medieval Anglesey*, 56-7; G. Rex Smith, 'The Penmachno letter patent and the Welsh uprising of 1294-95', *CMCS* 58 (2009), 49-68.

1 Daronwy
Book of Taliesin 28.22-29.20

Dvw differth Nefwy
God protected Noah
rac llanw llet ofrwy,
from the Flood, a radiant extent,
kyntaf *a tannwy*[1]
the swiftest thing to spread out,
a treis dros vordwy.
attacking beyond the (bounds of the) surging sea.

5   **Py pren a vo mwy**
What tree could be greater
noget Daronwy?
than Daronwy?
Ne*ut*[2] wy amnodwy[3]
He (i.e. God) will cherish those
amgylch Balch Nefwy.
around Noah's Ark.

Yssit rin yssyd uwy —
There is a secret which is greater —
10   **gwawr gwyr Goronwy;**
the radiance of Goronwy's men;
odit a'e gwypwy.
it is a rare man who knows it.
Hutlath Vathonwy,
Mathonwy's magic wand,
ygkoet pan tyfwy,
when it grows in the wood,
ffrwytheu *rwy*[4] kymrwy
promotes fruits/successes
15   **ar lan Gwyllyonwy.**
on the bank of the Gwyllionwy.
Kynan a'e kaffwy
Cynan will secure them
pryt pan wledychwy.
when he shall rule.

---

[1] ms *atarrwy*
[2] ms *nyt*
[3] ms *am nodwy*
[4] ms *nwy*

Dedeuant etwaeth
They shall come again
tros trei a thros traeth:
over ebb and over shore:
20   **pedeir prif pennaeth,**
four chief dominions,
a'r pymhet nyt gwaeth:
and the fifth, no feebler:
gwyr gwrd ehelaeth
strong, numerous men
ar Prydein aruaeth.
(with their) intent on Britain.
Gwraged a ui ffraeth,
Women shall be forward,
25   **eillon a ui kaeth;**
free tenants shall be bond;
ryferthwy hiraeth
a high-tide of longing
med a marchogaeth.
(for) mead and horsemanship.

Dedeuho dwy rein:
There shall come two unyielding ones:
gwedw a gwryawc vein
a widow and a slender married woman
30   **hëyrn eu hadein**
with iron wing
ar wyr yn goryein.
berating men.
Dydeuho kynrein
There shall come champions
o amtir Rufein.
from the region of Rome.
Eu kerd a gygein,
The poem about them shall be fitting,
35   **eu gwawt a yscein.**
the song about them shall spring forth.
Anyan[5] derw a drein
Like oak-trees and thorns

---

[5] ms *anan*

1 Daronwy

ar gerd yt gygein.
in song shall it be fitting.

Ki y tynnu, march y rynnu,[6]
A dog to sniff, a stallion to blow,
eidon y wan, hwch y tyruu.
a bullock to gore, a pig to root.

40 **Pymhet llwdyn gwyn a wnaeth Iessu**
The fifth a blessed youth/young animal whom Jesus made
o wysc[7] **Adaf y ᛞ**[8] **ymträu.**
of Adam's line . . . .
Gwyduilet[9] **coet kein eu syllu**
The wild animals of the wood, fair to behold them,
hyt yt uuant a hyt yt uu.
as long as they were, and as long as he was.
Pan wnel Kymry kamualhäu
When the Cymry cowardly go to ground

45 **keir aralluro pwy karo nu?**
near a foreign region, who will love them now?

Llemeis-i lam o lam eglwc —
I leapt a leap as a result of evident fate —
kewssit da nyr gaho drwc.
he who had good fortune will not have bad.
Megedorth Run yssef a wc[10]
The (battle-)steam of Rhun, that is what will threaten
rwg Kaer Rian a Chaer Rywc,
between Caer Rhian and Caer Rhywg,

50 **rwg Dineidyn a Dineidwc.**
between Dineidyn and Dineidwg.
Eglur dremynt a wyl golwc:
The gaze sees a clear (end in) view:
rac rynawd[11] **tan dychyfrwy mwc,**
before the onrush of fire, smoke shall rise,
an Rën Duw a'n ryamwc.
(and) our Lord God shall defend us.

---

[6] ms *rynyaw*
[7] ms *wisc*
[8] ms *ymra* with strike through and deleting points
[9] ms *gwyduet*
[10] ms *ao '6c* with deleting point beneath *o*
[11] ms *rynawt*

1 Daronwy

title **Daronwy** See poem introduction.

1 **differth** Subject-fronted sentence order, with rel. pron. not required before *di-*, GMW 61, and cf. also LPBT 13.12-13 *Mawr Duw digones/ heul haf a'e rywres*; Tymhorau line 9 *mawr Dduw ddymkawn*.

This 3sg. pret. form of vb *diffryt* 'defend', as in PT XI.5 (of Gwallawg) *Ef differth aduwyn llan lleenawc*, is also attested in prose texts (six examples), with three of *diffyrth*. *Diffyrth* is more usual in poetry, e.g. in CC 22.12 *Duu a'n diffirth*; CBT I 27.48 *Dyfyrth chwech oes byd rac pyd poeneu*, and in the triple collocation matching our text in CBT IV 16.184-5 *Kann g6ara6t g6erinualch Nef6y./ Kann diffyrth Trinda6t tri mack6y—o dan* 'since He saved Noah's arkload, since the Trinity saved the three youths from the fire'. *Duw* + forms of the vb *diffryt* are collocated in CC 25.6a-b *Y Duv y harchaw. . . . can dichaun vy niffrid*; Pen3Afallennau 123.73-4 *pan vo Duw dewin ym difrit i rac trin*; Peirian Faban line 2 *A ddifero di Duw rac Gwyddyl gynt*. With noun *diffret*, EWSP 417.9 *Duw diffret*.

1 **Nefwy** Cf. line 8 below, and note on §6.18 *yd atrefnwys nefwy yn Ard Nefon*. *Nefwy* 'court, citadel' with Ifor Williams, *B* 7 (1933-5), 30, who compared VVB 194 *nom* 'templa' supposedly from the same root as *nef, nyfed*, and OIr *nemed*, and possibly the first element of *neuadd*. But GPC notes no such common noun, and on *nom* see P.-Y. Lambert, *B* 30 (1982-83), 21-2, and *CMCS* 12 (1986), 112. Possibly 'Heaven' (as in LPBT 1.7), although Ifor Williams thinks that unlikely in our example. However, *llanw* 'flood, tide' in line 2 below and the past tense favour a form of the Biblical *Noa/Noe*, as does the similar collocation in CBT IV 16.185 noted above. CBT I 1.22 *o plant Nevuy* testifies to the use of Biblical *Noah* as a personal name in Wales: see further J. Vendryes, 'Gallois Noe, Neuwy, Nouguy', *Bulletin de la Société de Linguistique de Paris*, 43 (1947), 32-7.

2 **rac llanw llet ofrwy** *Gofrwy* LPBT 7.42 and 67 but not otherwise attested in hengerdd. The same collocation in CBT II 9.7-8 *I edryt uy lleduryd-y, a'e llet ourwy,/ Y edry[d] llywy lli6 tonn dylann* 'to tell of my sorrow, and her great radiance,/ to the dwelling of the fair one with the hue of the sea wave' (Hywel ab Owain Gwynedd to a girl, following *Hywel ab Owain Gwynedd: Bardd-dywysog*, edited by Nerys Ann Jones (Caerdydd, 2009), 204-5). *Llet ofrwy*, lit. 'radiance of breadth/expanse', is more naturally understood as describing the Flood rather than God. *Llanw* 'flood, flow', opposed to *trei* 'ebb', is not the usual word for the Flood, which is *dilyw* (< L. *diluvium*).

3 **Kyntaf a tannwy (ms atarrwy)** A form of vb *adara* 'to catch birds', or *adalwy* 'call back' (Noah's dove?) seems difficult to square with line 4. G's restoration of 3sg. subjunct. of vb *tannu* 'extend, spread' (GPC notes also 'disperse, put to flight') would suit a sea-flood. An alternative emendation might be *a cannwy*: see CBT IV 16.192 and note p. 296 on *kannwy* < *cannu* 'to maintain, keep, hold, possess', or < *cannu* 'to make white or radiant', and the suggestion that it might be a 3sg. form of *canuot* 'to perceive'. More difficult to explain would be scribal corruption of *tramwy* ('passage, course' or 3sg. of denominative vb); *tramwy* is collocated with *mor* (e.g. Peirian Faban line 5 *o dramwy mor llydan*), with *llanw* CBT VI 18.26 *En y trei tramwy llan6 rwy rwyd ha6l*, and with *mordwy* (CBT VI 19.18). Similarly it would be difficult to account for *trangwy* (vb *trengi* 'die'), found collocated with *gofrwy* CBT IV 16.165, in the passage cited in the note above on line 1; or *taflwy* (vb *taflu* 'surge, pound').

1 Daronwy

Kyntaf 'first, swiftest' may be subject (as in the translation) or object, 'the first which he may put to flight will attack'. If adverbial 'firstly', the antecedent of the vb would not need to be formally expressed (see GMW 72-3). Very uncertain.

4 **a treis dros vordwy** Lack of spirantisation appears to rule out the noun *treis* while unrealised lenition of *t-* is common enough in this manuscript. So *a* is understood as rel. pron. and 3sg. of vb *treisyaw* although *treis* is invariably a noun. Was *a* perhaps written under the influence of the beginning of *atarrwy*? *Treis + tros* is a common collocation: restore *mawrdreis* perhaps, as in CBT III 21.151.

5 **py pren** If Daronwy is a personal name, *pren* is perhaps a figure for a warrior, as in EWSP 429 *Vn prenn yg gwydvit*, and elsewhere: see LPBT 171-2. But it may be a figure for God himself: see on line 8 below.

6 **Daronwy** See poem introduction. Could this be a name for God, whom Gruffudd ap Maredudd addresses as *Dâr nef a daear* (GGM II 4.41) following an englyn on Noah's Ark: see on line 8 below.

7 **Neut (ms Nyt) wy amnodwy (ms am nodwy)** Uncertain. As it stands, 'it is not they who defend me', cf. CBT V 23.2 *A'm notwy rac auar*; §6.14 *ny nothwy dinassoed*, but it is unclear whether the subject *wy* would be trees such as Daronwy, or 'Goronwy's men' in line 10. Here, tentatively, the 3sg. subjunct. of vb *amnodi* is understood, as in CBT I 26.49 *Am 6un a 6udyt y hamnodi*; and CBT V 2.23 *tud amnoti*. *Wy* is object, and since *nyt* and *neut* are sometimes confused, the latter is restored.

8 **amgylch Balch Nefwy** G *balch* 'boat, ship' (< L. *barca*, cf. *madalch* ~ *madarch*, *arch* ~ *alch*), especially for Noah's Ark: J. E. Caerwyn Williams 'Balchnoe', *Y Traethodydd*, 134 (1979), 139–41; GGM II 4.40 *falch Noe deg i dir*; GSRH 12.122 *Gŵr o hil ddoeth balch noeth Noe*, etc. Curiously G lists our occurrence under the adj. *balch* 'proud'. On the possible pl. *balch(e)eu*, see on §8.17. On Nefwy, see above on line 1.

9 **Yssit rin yssyd uwy** *Yssit* is almost invariably in line-initial position in poetry; cf. LPBT 5.240 *Yssit yssyd gynt*.

10 **Goronwy** A character named Goronwy 'from Dolau Edrywy' is mentioned in the poem Kat Godeu (LPBT 5.229-30); Gronw(y) (Bebr) is a lord of Penllyn in *Math fab Mathonwy*. As noted in LPBT 235, the name Goronwy was popular especially in the north from the 11-12c onwards, e.g. Goronwy ab Owain ab Edwin whose sister Angharad ferch Owain was married to Gruffudd ap Cynan. He was the father of Cristin, who became the second wife of Owain Gwynedd, marrying within the prohibited limits of consanguinity. That line was associated with Tegeingl. The name Goronwy was favoured by the family of Ednyfed Fychan (d. 1246), seneschal of Gwynedd serving Llywelyn ab Iorwerth and then his son, Dafydd. Ednyfed's son Goronwy (d. 1268), whose mother was Gwenllian daughter of Lord Rhys ap Gruffudd, was highly regarded as a diplomat and counsellor. He was seneschal to Llywelyn ap Gruffudd, and in 1263 he led the Gwynedd army against the king's forces in Gwent. He dealt (from a distance) with the papal legate Ottobuono. His death notice in BTyw in 1268 indictates his eminence, as do two elegies, one by Bleddyn Fardd (CBT VII poem 45), and a four-englyn fragment by Y Prydydd Bychan (CBT VII poem 21); a further englyn is discussed in CBT VII, p. 533 n. From his father he held extensive lands in Anglesey, Arllechwedd and Ceredigion. His own grandson and

1 Daronwy

great-grandson were also called Goronwy. His son was the first to bear the name 'Tudor' (known as Tudur Hen in the genealogies). Another Goronwy, rhingyll of Twrcelyn, was active in the Madog rebellion of 1295 (see poem introduction).

11 **Odit a'e gwypwy** The 'singular knower' topos, cf. LPBT 9.45 *Nys gwyr ny vo taer*, and further examples LPBT 305. *Odit*, LPBT 4.51, and cf. §3.7 *Odit o Gymry a'e llafaro*. The movement of these lines is generally in couplets, and it is difficult to know whether this line belongs with lines 9-10 allowing for a regular couplet sequence from lines 12-17 (as in the translation) or whether it belongs with line 12. If the latter, *odit* is subject with *a'e* containing a proleptic infixed pron. referring to the *hutlath*; or if object, 'it is a rare thing that he knows' with rel. pron. in the form *ae* or else *a* + infixed pron. (see GMW 63).

12 **Hutlath Vathonwy** Unique example of *Mathonwy* in early poetry. The mention of the *hutlath* which Math wields in his story (PKM 77) suggests that Mathonwy is one and the same as the magician Math (on such doublets, see TYP^3 439) or else is his father. Math's *hutlath* is used as a chastity test and as a means of transforming characters into and out of animal form; it is not explicitly used to create microcosmic Blodeuwedd (pace TYP^3 440). A similar transformational property belongs to the *hutlath* wielded by Llwyd fab Cil Coed at the end of *Manawydan uab Llyr* (PKM 65). The Taliesin figure claims he was created by Math, and that he has been with him: LPBT 5.163; 1.80. Math's *hut* ('magic power') is the first of the *Teir Hut Ynys Prydein* in Triad 28 (and see TYP^3 438-40).

13 **ygkoet pan tyfwy** *Pan* is understood as 'when', although 'that' is possible.

14 **ffrwytheu rwy (ms nwy) kymrwy** *Ffrwytheu* 'fruits' in the literal or the figurative meaning. If negative *nwy* is retained, the sense might be that Mathonwy's staff, planted to grow in the wood, would function as a talisman to ward off any successes or gains (?by the enemy) on the bank of the Gwyllionwy. Slight emendation to *rwy* gives a marginally better sense with lines 16-17. On its use, restricted in hengerdd to the Book of Taliesin, with instances by Cynddelw and Prydydd y Moch, see on LPBT 5.50 *y Ren rwy digonsei*; 8.13 *vy ren rwy digones*; 9.60 *keluyd rwy katwo*; and 10.10 *detwyd Douyd rwy goreu*. *Kymrwy*, 3sg. *kymrwyaw*, G 'to strengthen, enliven, make powerful'; see PT 124; CBT IV 6.170 *Pan gymrwy ryuel ryhoffir*. Another possibility would be *rwy* 'plenitude, abundance' and the adj. *kymrwy* 'strong': 'a flourishing abundance of fruits . . . may Cynan secure'.

15 **ar lan Gwyllyonwy** A river, lake or stretch of coastal water would seem likely here. A formation from *gwyllt* 'wild', *gwyllyon*, the latter perhaps a personal name according to R.J. Thomas, 'Enwau afonydd â'r olddodiad -*wy*', B 8 (1935-7), 27-43, p. 33. But it is possible that it is based on pl. *gwyllyon* 'the wild ones', i.e. waves of the sea. Prydydd y Moch's curious formation, CBT V 22.28 *Dyfrdonwy*, is thought to be based on *Dyfrdwy* (R. Dee) and perhaps, according to W.J. Gruffudd, to contain *Donwy* (see CBT V 208 for details), but it is equally likely to be a metrically-driven nonce form, as is possible here.

16 **Kynan** See General Introduction, 10-11 on the deliverers, Cynan and Cadwaladr.

17 **pryt pan wledychwy** Cf. CA line 1196 *prit pan aeth*; CBT II 5.15 *Pryt pan eler*; CC 20.87 *Pryt pan dyffo*. LlDC 15.6 (Bedwenni) *Ac Edwin iMon ban gluedichuy* (recte *guledichuy*); 15.20 *Arbenygaul Mon a'e guledychuy*; LlDC 17.145 (Oianau) *ban vo pendewic Dyued a'e guledichuy*. Contrast CBT VII 25.80

1 Daronwy

gwledycho. The shift from *-wy/-oe* to *-o* in 3sg. pres. subjunct. forms has been discussed by Simon Rodway who showed that *-o* forms increase dramatically in the work of the early Gogynfeirdd. In the Book of Taliesin, he counted 24 instances of *-wy*, and 24 of *-o*: 'Two developments in medieval literary Welsh and their implications for dating texts', in HI 67-74, pp. 71-4 — and see now Rodway, Dating, ch. 3.

18 **Dedeuant etwaeth** On *etwaeth*, still being used in the 13c, see LPBT 355. The vb *dydyfot* is used below, lines 28 and 32 *dedeuho/dydeuho*; and cf. §7.57 *dedeuant* and CBT VI 10.53 *dedeuant*.

19 **tros draeth** Cf. collocated *traeth* and *pennaeth* 'sovereignty' in LPBT 18.2 *py ledas y pennaeth dros traeth Mundi*; CBT IV 16.59-60 *uch na6traeth—yssyd/ Ny symut y bennaeth*.

20 **pedeir prif pennaeth** The four régimes or dominions may relate to the four 'peoples' or 'nations' (*pedeirieith*) mentioned by Cynddelw (CBT III 7.26, 13.6) and Llygad Gŵr (CBT VII 24.116), although Loth's suggestion that these were the speakers of the languages Welsh, Irish, English and French was countered by J.E. Caerwyn Williams who favoured either the four parts of Wales, or of Britain: see CBT III 90. However, CBT IV 2.52 *O bedeiryeith d6fyn* 'from the four languages of the world' hints at a looser concept whereby wholeness was signified by quarternities, as noted CBT IV 29. In the present example, it is more likely that successive invaders are being called to mind: perhaps the Romans, Irish, English, and Scandinavians, with the Normans forming the fifth incursion. A similar but more detailed scheme, including Irish-Picts (or sea-raiders) and Normans is found in §5.11-22 *Pymp pennaeth dimbi — / o Wydyl Ffichti*, etc., and cf. also LlDC 17.32-5 (Oianau) *Ojan a parchellan oet reid gweti/ rac offin pimp penaeth o Nortmandi,/ a'r pimhed in myned dros mor heli/ y oreskin Iwerton tirion trewi*. Bede's list of the five languages of Britain (English, British, Irish, Pictish and Latin, HE I.i) was adapted by Geoffrey of Monmouth (HKB ch. 5 'five peoples'), leaving out Latin to include the Normans.

21 **a'r pymhet nyt gwaeth** The fifth dominion was no less strong or able (lit. worse) than the others.

22 **gwyr gwrd ehelaeth** *Gwrd* is very frequently collocated with *gwr* and *gwyr* and their compounds, e.g. CA line 47 *gwr gwrd eg gwyawr*; line 1003 *gwyr gorsaf gwryaf gwrd yg calet*; LlDC 18.34 *bet gur gurt yg kyniscin*; 18.164 *Bet gur gurth y var*; 34.4; CBT III 8.31 *A llawer gwr gwrdd yn ing*; IV 8.41; V 21.9; VII 44.25 and 50.21 *g6r g6rt*, etc. *Ehalaeth* is rhymed with *ffraeth*, as here, in §4.3 (= AP line 3).

23 **ar Prydein aruaeth** *Ar* 'on', sometimes 'towards'. The common pool of rhymes *traeth/aruaeth/ehelaeth/ffraeth/hiraeth* are found frequently: in the Gododdin; EWGP 24.24; EWSP 405.6; AP line 3 *A phennaeth ehelaeth a ffraeth vnbyn*, etc.

24 **Gwraged a ui ffraeth** Whether *ffraeth* means 'loquacious' or 'forward, eager', we see here the 'upside-down topos' discussed in the General Introduction, 11-12. The fut. forms, *bi* and *adui* (as well as *dybi*, *dyfi*, *dymbi*) mark prophetic discourse: §7.103 *A'm bi barnodyd o aghygres dieu*; CC 20.161 *Ac awch bi wynnyeith*; LlDC 17.126 (Oianau) *An bi ni inaeth guared guyd[i gu]aeth*; R577-83 (Cyfoesi) *passim*; etc.

25 **eillon a ui kaeth** *Eillon* is used of tenants, evidently men with a measure of freedom, not necessarily serfs or churls (see G on the debasement of the term; LPBT 1.89). Cf. the collocation of Edmyg Dinbych line 24 *noc eillon Deutraeth gwell kaeth Dyfet*, on which see Gruffydd, *Cerdd Lys Gynnar* 16.

26-7 **ryferthwy hiraeth/ med a marchogaeth** *Ryferthwy*, here and in CBT III 16.81 in the figurative, rather than literal meaning as in §8.16 *myr ryuerthwy*. *Hiraeth* rhymed with *marchogaeth* CBT I 15.24; IV16.48, a word somewhat uncommon in early poetry (LPBT 3.50, near *medfaeth* [recte]; Gosymdaith line 86). For collocation of *med* with *march* and its derivatives, as in CBT III 29.9-10 *meithuaeth—met/ A meuet marchogaeth*, see FS Gruffydd 54. The lines point up the nostalgia in the age of turmoil.

28 **dwy rein** *Rein* usually adj. 'stiff', as used of corpses, with *goryein* as here, by Cynddelw CBT IV 1.40-1 *Ual Gweith Uadon ua6r wrya6r oryein;/ Gweleis gadeu geirw a rut ueirw rein*. The compound *bronrein* implies a haughtiness of bearing, as in LPBT 1.94, and accompanies *balch* in EWGP 26.2 *gna6t bronrein balch*. EVW 119 proposes an unnecessary emendation to *riein* 'maiden'.

29 **gwedw a gwryawc vein** Who might the widow and the slender married woman be? Could the *gwedw* refer to the Empress Matilda (c. 1102-67) who was widowed in 1125 before her arrival in England? She remarried in 1128; after 1135, she contested the succession to the throne assumed by her cousin Stephen de Blois. Her name (which was also the name of Stephen's wife Matilda of Boulogne who directed some fighting) means 'battle might'. Or could this be an earlier person — Æthelflæd, the Lady of Mercians (who attacked Llan-gors in 917); Gwenllian daughter of Gruffudd ap Cynan; or Eleanor of Aquitaine who accompanied her husband on the Second Crusade 1145?

It may be that the poet draws in part on Revelation 9:8-10. Locusts are described like horses prepared for battle: 'And they had hair as the hair of women, and their teeth were as the teeth of lions. And they had breastplates, as it were breastplates of iron; and the sound of their wings was as the sound of chariots of many horses running to battle . . . and their power was to hurt men five months'. The adj. *gwryawc*, common in the Laws, is not otherwise found in early poetry.

30 **hëyrn eu hadein** *adein* can mean 'arm' in some instances as well as the more common 'wing'.

31 **ar wyr yn goryein** Unusual vb *goryein* 'to shout, cry, bawl' (< *gawr* 'shout'), otherwise only used by Cynddelw (see on 28 above), also in collocation with *rein*, and in GPB 7.33 (emended).

33 **o amtir Rufein** *Amdir* 'surrounding region' is not common in early poetry: LlDC 17.156 (Oianau) *Ban diffon brodorion o amtiret Mon*; CBT III 3.87 *Berth y mae Meiuot a'i hamdir*. See General Introduction, 12, on the Roman topos in prophecy; cf. §7.103 *Brython o vonhed Rufein*; §8.1 *Yn wir dymbi Romani kar*; §9.13 *rac pennaeth o Rufein kein y echrys*; R1050.14 *ac allwed Rufein gan r6yueu/ ac Allmyn heb allel kyrcheu*.

34 **Eu kerd a gygein** *Gwawt* in line 35 suggests *kerd* 'song' rather than 'craft'. It is used with the vb *kyngenni* 'to be contained; to suit, be appropriate' by Cynddelw CBT IV 6.120 *Cred a ched a chert rychygein—y'th bleid* 'Loyalty and gifts and song are appropriate for you' (to Hywel ab Owain Gwynedd). In both lines, it is understood that the *kerd* and the *gwawt* are sung about the champions, not by

1 Daronwy

them (*Gwawt Lud y mawr* is the 'great song *about* Lludd', *Canu Owain Gwynedd* is addressed *to* Owain, etc.).

35 **eu gwawt a yscein** The vb is commonly used with *clot* 'fame', as well as in the context of scattering arms, gifts, etc.: see LPBT 232.

36 **Anan derw a drein** G s.v. *auan* 'raspberry' suggests emending -*n*- to -*u*-. While this suits the botanical context with *derw* and *drein*, the force of the line is obscure to me. Other possibilities might include *anyan* 'nature' (since yod is not always realised orthographically in our manuscript, see LPBT 2 and 7), or *anaw* 'wealth, abundance; fruit, profit'. If the former, the song is perhaps imagined as shooting forth as do the leaves of the oak or the thorn blossom; if the latter, the song has the abundance of the oak and thorn trees. The blossoming thorn introduces part of Myrddin's prophecy in the Oianau, LlDC 17.146 *Ojan a parchellan neu blodeu drein/ gorlas kein minit eluit neud k[e]in*; and good coming from evil (the Virgin Mary contrasted with Eve's progeny) is conveyed in CC 33.41-2 *Y doeth o epil ennwir Eua,/ Mal y daw ar y drein, blodeu rosa*. If Adam is identified in line 41 below, beliefs about the Tree of Life may conceivably be relevant.

37 **ar gerd yt gygein** Unexpected repetition of vb form. Perhaps emend to reflexive vb *ymgygein*.

38 **Ki y tynnu, march y rynnu (ms rynyaw)** A change of metre to an unusual line, usually eight syllables with a central caesura (4+4). It would be possible to analyse lines 38 and 39 as containing four short lines rhyming (with emendation) in -*u*, but the Class 1 line is not typically four syllables, with the notable exception of PT IV. See LPBT 37-9 on metrics.

Lines 38 and 39 contain ambiguous *y*, either 3sg. personal pron. 'his', or else — as in the translation — the prep. *y* 'to, for' (with unrealised lenition) which is less strained. In either case, the point is to identify the distinctive characteristics of the four animals. Here, the dog draws breath in order to get the scent while the stallion blows out. The same vbs are used in a list of the human senses and functions in LPBT 25.12-13 *vn yw a rynnyaf,/ a deu a tynnaf*, and the two are found together in a description of a horse exhaling and inhaling to good comic effect in *Breuddwyd Ronabwy*: BR 4.15-17 *Ac eu hymlit a oruc y marchawc. A phan rynnei y march y anadyl y wrthaw y pellaei y gwyr y wrthaw. A phan y tynnei attaw y nesseynt wynteu attaw hyt ym bron y march*. See further *B* 3 (1926-8), 54-5; CA 242; G s.v. *grynnyaw*; and BR 39. Unlike *grynnyaw* (also in LPBT 2.40), the *grynnu* form of the vb noun, needed here for the rhyme, is not attested in poetry; it is however used in a Cyfnerth law text, WML 96.17-18.

39 **eidon y wan hwch y tyruu** Either 'trample' or 'pierce' would suit the context; the vb noun *gwan* is more common than *gwanu* in verse, but cf. LPBT 22.5a *gwanu Dylan*. Since the gender of *hwch* can be masc. and fem. in medieval texts, the ambiguous *y* mentioned above is still unresolved.

The function of these animals is not at all clear. Do the five (including line 40) parallel the five dominions of lines 20-21? The use of animal symbolism to represent kingdoms is found in Scripture, Augustine, Jerome, etc., and in medieval texts such as Merlin's prophecies in Geoffrey of Monmouth's *Historia Regum Britanniae*: the red and white dragon are the Cymry and the Saxons (HKB ch. 112), the boar of Cornwall 'will trample the foreigners' necks beneath his feet' to be followed by six successors. The German worm (*uermis*) and a wolf from the sea, a lynx which will 'pierce through everything', a 'warlike boar', a goat, and 'the boar of trade', 'the ass of wickedness', a 'stag with ten branches', a hedgehog, a heron which hatches a fox, a wolf and a bear are all mentioned. A mountain ox will summon the wolf and 'gore them like a horned bull'. Yet our list seems more concerned with noting the main characteristic of each animal (its *teithi*, as the Laws have it) before elaborating on the fifth.

40   **pymhet llwdyn gwyn a wnaeth Iessu**   *Pymhet* 'fifth' here rather than 'one of five'. *Gwyn* 'white' or 'blessed'. Since *llwdyn* generally denotes a young animal, and is figuratively used for a youth, it may have a similar meaning to *mab*, *maban*, referring to a promised deliverer. GPC s.v. *llwdn* notes such a usage from the 15c by Dafydd Offeiriad, *Er hyn y mae or hynedd/ llwdn glan llydan i gledd*. But it may be simply for humankind, created, according to Genesis 1, after the beasts of the earth, the fowl of the air and the creatures of the waters. *Iessu* is sometimes used of the Trinity.

41   **o wisc Adaf y ymträu**   G favours the personal name *Adaf* 'Adam' rather than *adaf* 'hand, wing; protection'. *Gwisc* is not impossible since there are various traditions about Adam's clothing, his covering of fig leaves, tunic of skin, shining raiment, etc. (see on §7.116). But if this represents ModW *wysg* 'track, path' rather than *gwisg*, then *o wysc Adaf* could mean 'in the manner of Adam', 'from Adam's line', i.e. a man (cf. §7.83 *o echen Adaf henyn*): see GPC s.v. *wysg*, where only late instances of *o wysg* (as well as common *yn wysg*) are cited. See further, J.E. Caerwyn Williams, '*Wysg* (river-name), *wysg*, *hwysgynt*, *rhwysg*', *Celtica*, 21 (1990), 670-8, pp. 676-7.

The scribe evidently had a problem with the end of the line: he wrote *yymra* then added deleting points under the last four letters and struck them through for good measure, then wrote *ymtrau*. Although it would give good sense ('to fight'), there is no evidence for a back formation *ymdrä-u* from *ymdrawr* 'fighter' (< vb *ymdaro*), and a rhyme is required in *-u*. The common locution *tra uu* for the last part seems unlikely given that the *a hyt yt uu* in line 43 would duplicate the rhyme.

42   **Gwyduilet (ms gwyduet) coet kein eu syllu**   Accepting G's emendation to *gwyduilet* 'wild animals', see GPC s.v. *gwyddfil*. For this use of *syllu*, cf. CBT II 5.14-15 *Ma6r uthret g6elet g6eilgi,/ Pryt pan eler y'6 syllu*.

44   **kamualhäu**   G 100 and 430 regards this vb as *cam* + **gwalhäu*, 'to become bold, presumptious', comparing *dywalhau*. A connection with *gwal* 'lair', and *gwalhau* 'to make a lair, hide' (see GPC s.v.) seems also possible, as in translation.

45   **keir aralluro**   *Keir* may be pl. of *car* 'sledge, vehicle' (CBT IV 14.11 is another possible poetry example), but G favours the well-attested variant of prep. *ker/ger*, and also considers *kein* 'fair'. On *aralluro* (and *arallwlat*) see on §3.5 *arallvro*.

45   **pwy karo nu**   *Nu* 'now', see LPBT 5.228; no other examples in rhyme position. *Pwy* contains obj. infixed pron., probably pl. (referring to the *Kymry*, or else the *gwyduilet* of line 42).

46   **Llemeis-i lam o lam eglwc**   The *i* spelling here (as in LPBT 4.37 and 197, 9.64) suggests the personal pron. rather than the prep. (invariably written *y* although the pron. is sometimes realised as *y* in this manuscript). Figura etymologica. The second *llam* is perhaps figurative, 'lot, fate', see EWSP 559. *Eglwc* 'visible, apparent', cf. LPBT 11.50 *aneglwc* 'invisible' (of the Wind) rhyming with *drwc*; CC 9.18 *drem aneglwc*; LlDC 18.63 *Madauc Mur Egluc*.

1 Daronwy

47 **kewssit da nyr gaho drwc** The line has a gnomic feel, 'once lucky always lucky', cf. CC 31.4 (Englynion y Clywaid) *'Kafas da ny chaffo drwc'*. Prefixing the antecedent *a* would yield a regular syllabic pattern, but is not grammatically essential.

48 **Megedorth Run** Cf. *mygedorth* in CA lines 307 and 317 (of horse); EWSP 459 and TYP³ 115 (battle descriptions); see TYP³ 121, and GPC s.v. *mygedorth* for other uses.

Rhun appears as a geographical designation in LlDC 16.27 *Awallen peren a tyf tra Run*. Rhun is also a reasonably common personal name: (1) Rhun son of Maelgwn Gwynedd, associated with an attack on the men of the North; (2) Rhun son of Urien Rheged (Rhun Rhyfeddfawr of the triads, TYP³ 503-4), on whom see Andrew Breeze, 'Northumbria and the family of Rhun', *Northern History*, 50, no. 2 (2013), 170-9; (3) Rhun son of Alun Dyfed and (4) Rhun fab Pyd both named in Englynion y Beddau (LlDC 18.74 and 18.30), the latter, probably a mistake for *Panna* 'Penda', in the same englyn as Cynon *in Reon Rid* (see Patrick Sims-Williams, *Religion and Literature in Western England, 600-800* (Cambridge, 1990), 28 n. 57). Also in Englynion y Beddau is (5) Rhun father of Meigen (LlDC 18.53 and 56), on whom see below on line 49.

Rhun son of Maelgwn was the most famous of these. Morfydd E. Owen (WKC 238-9) suggests that the name of Rhun, first born son of Owain Gwynedd, and the Gwynedd genealogies and other texts reflect 12c and early 13c interest in Maelgwn and in this son, Rhun, who also figures in the Triads, *Breuddwyd Ronabwy*, and Hanes Taliesin. Breiniau Gwŷr Arfon, in the Black Book of Chirk, relates how Rhun and the men of Gwynedd went to the North in pursuit of those northern leaders who had come down to Arfon to avenge the killing of Elidir Mwynfawr (Clydno Eidyn, Nudd, Mordaf and Rhydderch Hael). Supremacy was adjudged to the men of Arfon to cross *glann Gweryt* in the North (River Forth), and Taliesin 'sang' an englyn about their prowess there: *Kygleu urth wres eu llawneu/ Gan Run ynrudher bydyneu;/ Gwyr Aruon rudhyon yn rydieu*. Fourteen privileges (*breintiau*, whose loss gave rise to complaints, *gravamina*) were thus granted by Rhun to the men of Arfon. The mention of Rhun in the Cyfoesi prophecy (following Maelgwn) may reflect the precedence motif in the above story, but equally the second line may be a heroic commonplace about fighting in the van of the army: R577.40-2 *Run y en6 rugyl y fossa6t/ yg kynnor bydin br6ydra6t;/ g6ae Brydein o'r diwarna6t*.

48 **yssef a 'wc** The scribe wrote *ao* then added a deleting point under the *o*. There is a suspension mark ' immediately before *6c*. G 675 understands this as *66c*, the 3sg. of a vb with root *gwc* (cognate with OIr *-fich*) meaning 'to threaten, attack, fall upon, fight'. This gives a reasonable meaning here, and monosyllabic *(g)wc* would suit the cadence. *Amwc*, 3sg. pres. of *amwyn* 'to defend, guard', is unlikely, being used in the final line, and because it would give an atypical pentasyllabic cadence.

49 **rwg Kaer Rian a Chaer Rywc** Pertinent here perhaps is the place-name Llanrhian (Pembs.) and *Kader Rhian* (attested 1669), thought to contain the man's name *Rhian* (late 12c *Lanrian*) < *rhi* + diminutive *-an*: PNP I, 235. This is some five miles north-east of St Davids, near the port of Porth-gain, and therefore reasonably suitable for a length-and-breadth topos although that is usually phrased as *o . . . hyt*, as, for example, in AP line 173 *o Dyuet hyt Danet wy*

1 Daronwy

bieiuyd. Caer Hafod is just to the north-east (near Bickney tumulus), and Caerau and Castell Coch promontory fort are nearby, on the coast to the south-west of Abereiddi. There is a 9-10c cross-carved stone, known as Mesur y Dorth surviving just south-east of Llanrhian: see Nancy Edwards, *A Corpus of Early Medieval Inscribed Stones and Stone Sculpture in Wales*, vol. II, *South-West Wales* (Cardiff, 2007), 348-9. It is one of a dense cluster of stones in Dewisland (Pebeidiog), and may have been a marker on the pilgrim route to St Davids (ibid. 60).

There is no compelling reason to emend with FAB II, 401 to *Reon*, either the Old North *Reon* (at or near Stranraer on Loch Ryan, discussed LPBT 300-1) or a *Reon* in Wales (with *rhyd* or *caer* 'fort'), despite mentions in prophecies and in Englynion y Beddau: LlDC 16.84 (Afallennau) *yny del Kadwaladir oe kinadyl Rid Reon* 'until Cadwaladr comes to confront him at Rheon Ford'; LlDC 17.171 (Oianau) *a groar adar kir Kaer Reon*; LlDC 18.32 (Englynion y Beddau) *bet Kinon in Reon Rid*. An early-14c poem by Gwilym Ddu refers to the area of 'Arfon south of Rheon Ford' (GGDT 7.58), suggesting a Gwynedd location for Rhyd Rheon. The ms reading *Kaer Rian* is retained in our text.

49 **a Chaer Rywc** There are no other obvious examples. Skene, FAB II, 401 (noted by CPNS 368), identified the name with Crawick Water, a tributary of the River Nith, and the hamlet Crawick near Sanquhar ('old fort') in Dumfries and Galloway, perhaps because he identified *Kaer Rian* as Loch Reon (see above). However, Thomas Jones makes a plausible connection with the *Kaerrihoc* of which Teithi Hen mab Guinnan was the king. This occurs in the Inundation triad preserved in Latin in Exeter Cathedral ms 3514, printed in 'Triawd Lladin ar y Gorlifiadau', *B* 12 (1946-8), 79-83: *Regnum Thewthy Hen mab Guinnan, brenin Kaerrihoc*. This region was known as *Heneys Teithy Hen* and located between St Davids and Ireland. The king was the only survivor from the flood, escaping on his horse. Jones believes *-oc* may be a mistake for *-wc*, and cf. variation of these endings, as in *Cadwg ~ Cadog*, etc. It is interesting that this inundated region is mentioned in St Dyfrig's *Vita* and that of Euddogwy in the Book of Llandaf, associated in each case with an 'extent topos'. Dyfrig's see extends from Mochros (now Bellymoor, Herefordshire) *usque ad insulam Teithi* (LL 69 and 133), well beyond St Davids. As Jones remarks, the Llandaf propagandists had hit on a claim hard to disprove! The name would contain the territorial suffix seen in Seisyllwg, Morgannwg, etc. Presumably the first element would be *ri* 'king' (matching the element in *Kaer Rian*), or else *ry*.

Probing the Pembrokeshire locations, what connection might there be with Rhun? It is curious that the third region in the above Inundation triad is *Mays Maichghen* which Thomas Jones identified as (if not *Mechain*) 'the plain of Meigen', noting that a Meigen ap Rhun in Englynion y Beddau is buried in an *amgant* 'region', an *inis* 'island' covered by the sea (LlDC 18.51-3 and 54-6). He ventured that the englynion might preserve a memory of such an inundation story, noting how Seithennin who is connected with the Maes Gwyddnau inundation is drawn into the Beddau englynion. If Jones is correct, then that Rhun could be a candidate here. But if the Gwynedd Rhun, then perhaps we have northern propaganda, not unlike the impetus which moved the Dyfrig and Euddogwy supporters.

1 Daronwy

50 **rwg Dineidyn a Dineidwc** The first name is Edinburgh; the second is not attested elsewhere and looks like a nonce formation for the rhyme and alliteration. Dineiddwg is the name of a fine early-twentieth-century house in Milngavie near Glasgow built and fitted out *c*. 1904 by Honeyman, Keppie and Charles Rennie Mackintosh for the manufacturer William J. Beattie. It is likely to have been extracted from W.F. Skene's *Four Ancient Books*, published in 1868 (FAB I, 270, 'between Dineiddyn and Dineiddwg') since Beattie is known to have had antiquarian interests.

51 **Eglur dremynt a wyl golwc** *Golwc* collocated with vb *gwelet*, as in LPBT 11.52 (in rhyme block with *aneglwc*, *drwc*); CBT III 4.102; 5.102; VII 27.11-12; 42.46. *Dremynt* with *gwelet* LPBT 17.15-16; CBT III 3.161-2.

52 **rac rynawt tan** *Rynawt* with single -*n*- and -*t* is curious. The occurrences in CA line 446 *rac rynnaud Eithinin* and LPBT 9.57, 18.56 *rynnawd* suggest emendation here to *rynnawd* [ð] 'rush, attack', as does R1062 *Diga6n y6 g6are rynna6d*, where the other meaning 'a while, space of time' is more likely: see Diarhebion 14. The scribe may have been copying from an exemplar with final -*t* = [ð] (and with single -*n*-), as in LlDC 3.31 *rynaut*.

52 **dychyfrwy mwc** Cf. AP line 38 *dychyfroy etgyllaeth pennaeth lletfer* 'oppressive rule will give rise to sorrow', and see note AP 33-4 for *dychyfroy* as older orthography for *dychyffrwy*, and for its relationship with *cyffrwy*, and with vbs *cyffro(i)* and *dychyffro(i)*, the latter seen in CBT III 16.188 *Dychyfry fossa6d fwyrgna6d fer;/ Dychynne flamdreis y dan flamdei Lloegyr*. Ifor Williams paraphrased our example as 'where there is a great fire there will be an abundance of smoke, or more exactly "puffs" of it'. This is followed by GPC s.v. *dychyffrwy* 'to spring up, disperse, scatter'.

53 **an Rën Duw** Disyllabic *reen* uniquely collocated in poetry with *Duw* in CBT V 18.1 *Duw Ren dy-m-ryt kymwynas*; with *Dëws* CBT I 2.1. *An* at the beginning of the line is understood here as 'and our' (*a* + *yn*) but may be simply *an* 'our'.

53 **a'n ryamwc** 3sg. pres. ind. of *amwyn* 'defend', cf. CBT IV 16.175; V 27.18. The syntax (with no infixing of the pronoun after *ry*) may be compared with Echrys Ynys line 25 *na chyrbwyllwyf a'm rywnel da*; CBT I 17.7 *Hir aeth a'm rywnaeth rewin*; 28.32 *Parth a'r G6r arwr a'n rywara6d*; III 17.6 *A'm rybuch o'i wenllaw*.

2 Glaswawt Taliessin

The attribution of prophetic verse to Taliesin — and to the figure of Myrddin — is a medieval commonplace, and the explicit attribution in the title confirms that the speaking voice in the present poem was imagined to be that of the inspired legendary Taliesin claiming foresight of political and social upheaval, and of foreign incursions, stout defenders and fierce battles that were possibly quite far in the past by the time the poem was composed, post-eventum discourse being a staple of the medieval Welsh prophetic tradition.[1] The *glaswawt* of the poem title (possibly abstracted from line 34) is a compound of *glas* 'blue, green, grey, pale; fresh, verdant' and *gwawt* which, despite its etymological connections with words for inspiration and prophecy (cf. Ir. *fáth* and L. *vates*), is a very common generalised term for a poem or poetry, especially praise-poetry; note, however, that another Book of Taliesin prophecy (poem §7 in this collection) is entitled *Gwawt Lud y mawr* ('The Great Song concerning Lludd'). *Gwawt* is very frequently compounded, as in *gwenwawt*, *bardwawt*, *gwawtryd*, etc. GPC's interpretation of *glaswawt* as 'vigorous song' is possible, as is 'verdant'.

The poem is assigned a 'worth' of 24 points (*XXIIII a tal*), a value accorded to other poems in the manuscript including Kadeir Taliessin 'Taliesin's Metre' (or 'Song' or 'Chair') the title of which has been written by the main scribe at the bottom of page 31 in the manuscript. Higher values are given by the scribe to the almost adjacent series of three poems which follow: Kadeir Teyrnon (*CCC.*), Kadeir Kerrituen (*CCC.*), and Kanu y Gwynt (*CCC. a tal*).[2] Twenty-four 'points' are found again a little further on in the manuscript, in the rubric to the pair, Kanu y Med and Kanu y Cwrwf, while a unique value is assigned to the Scriptural poem on the Plagues of Egypt (*X.C.*).[3] These values, which are confined to the section between pages 30 and 44 in the Book of Taliesin, are matched only by those mentioned in the rubric in the Book of Aneirin (CA 55), found immediately after Gwarchan Cynfelyn. No other prophecies are given such values. The Gododdin rubric copied in the mid-thirteenth century implies that these 'worths' were, or were imagined to have been, operational in poetic contests where the recital of older verse as well as the composition of new items may have been adjudicated.[4]

Glaswawt Taliessin is concerned with Gwynedd — its greatest rivers, the Menai and Conwy are named in lines 7 and 8, along with its highest fastness of Snowdonia (*Eryri*, line 16) in the north-west. The mention of an 'iron man from the lineage of Anarawd' suggested to Ifor Williams that the poem 'in its present form' is to be dated later than 916 when Anarawd son of Rhodri Mawr of Gwynedd, styled *rex Brittonum* in the annals, died, or possibly when he was

---

[1] See General Introduction, 13-14.
[2] Nos 9, 10 and 11 in LPBT.
[3] Edited CC 72-9.
[4] Discussed LPBT 257-8.

2 Glaswawt Taliessin

already an old man.[5] But despite his tentative suggestion[6] that the poem *might* belong to the 916-46 generation, this is far from certain, especially since poets continued to make references to Anarawd and his lineage as paragons of martial prowess well into the twelfth century (see on line 26 below). Similarly, while mentions of Conwy and Eryri (lines 8 and 16) may well allude to the events around 881 when ealdorman Æthelred of Mercia was conclusively defeated by the men of Gwynedd (see note on line 8), they do not necessarily demonstrate that the poem was composed soon afterwards. For instance, the Cyfoesi prophecy, cast as a dialogue between Myrddin and his sister Gwenddydd, no earlier than the twelfth century in its present form,[7] recalls Anarawd's action in the 'Wednesday battle' on the Conway: *Ar lann Kon6y, kym6y du6 Merchyr;/ etmycka6r y deuawt:/ arbennic anian Anara6t.*[8] In the present poem, Cynan and Cadwaladr, the pair of deliverers well-known from Armes Prydain and elsewhere, are poised to attack and raze the dwellings of the Saxon and the foreign invaders (*Gynt*). The stylistic evidence of Glaswawt Taliessin does not rule out a dating later than the tenth century: indeed, some of the poem's prophetic topoi, such as the advent of the three fleets and the proliferation of incest, are seen in twelfth- and thirteenth-century material.[9] Nor is the lexicon conclusive, since much of the diction and some collocations (such as *durawt/Anarawt*, or *ysgwyt/yscawn* as in the Gododdin) are found in later verse. In short, the 916-46 dating suggested as a possibility by Ifor Williams, and confidently followed by others including Andrew Breeze, 'The Battle of Brunanburh and Welsh tradition', *Neophilologus* 83 (1999), 479-83, at p. 480, and Clare Downham, *Viking Kings of Britain and Ireland: The Dynasty of Ívarr to A.D. 1014* (Edinburgh, 2007), 214, remains uncertain.

The poem has been viewed as a early source for a potential reference to the battle of Brunanburh in 937. The notes below lay out in detail the competing interpretations of the crucial *kattybrudawt* in line 28 by which the Brunanburh reference stands or falls. The drift of a number of lines is summarised by Margaret Enid Griffiths (EVW 120-21), who notes the absence of any reference to the Normans. The text has been partially translated by Ifor Williams, ChwT 22-3 (lines 7-12, 17, 25-8), and my translation below is substantially the same as that which I published and annotated in *The Battle of Brunanburh: A Casebook*, edited by Michael D. Livingston (Exeter, 2010), 46-9, 177-82.

The disparate line lengths are united by the use of a single *-awt* rhyme throughout, or Irish rhyme as in lines 11-12, 28-9 and 30-31. The monorhyme is probably intended to echo the ending of the name *Anarawt* just as the rhyme *-ein* throughout *Marwnat Owein* (PT X) echoes the ending of *Owein*. The short Class

---

[5] ChwT 23.
[6] Reiterated in PT xxvi.
[7] This is not to say that it may not have been based on earlier (not necessarily poetic) materials, including a regnal list. Cf. O. J. Padel, 'Geoffrey of Monmouth and the Merlin Legend', *CMCS* 51 (2006), 37-65, at pp. 48-9; WaB 337-9.
[8] R579.4-6.
[9] See General Introduction, 11-12.

2 Glaswawt Taliessin

1 line takes over at line 23 leading to an increased urgency as the poem moves towards its close; the earlier part uses a more expansive tripartite line with two caesuras, four main accents, and a regular four-syllabic end cadence. Variety is provided by the use of the *toddaid byr*, as in lines 5-6, 13-14 (with short line 14), and an irregular *traeanog*-type patterning in lines 14-16 and lines 20-22.[10]

---

[10] On metrics see LPBT 37-9.

2 Glaswawt Taliessin xxiiii a tal
Book of Taliesin 30.24-31.20

Kennadeu a'm dodynt   mor ynt anuonawc!
Messengers have come to me, how splendid they are!
Dygawn   ym lletcynt   meint vyg keudawt.
The whole (preoccupation) of my mind causes me grief:
Gnawt rwyf   yn heli   — Beli wirawt;
frequent, an oar in the brine — Beli's drink;
gnawt yscwyt   yscawn   ar gefyn yscawt;
frequent, a light shield in the depth of night;
5   **gnawt gwyth ac adwyth   o yspydawt — gaer,**
frequent, ferocity and destruction (emanating) from a fortress of feasting,
   a naw cant maer marwhawt.
   and nine hundred stewards shall perish.
Atvyd Mei   ar Venei,   crei gyflogawt,
In May, on the Menai, there will be a place of carnage,
atvyd mwy   ar Gonwy, ◊[1] gwynyeith gwnahawt.
on the (River) Conwy there will be more (suffering) that will wreak vengeance.
Adoer lleith[2]   dyrreith —   anaw barawt —
Chilling the death which came about — ready reward —
10   **o hëyrn   erchwyrn   edyrn dyrnawt.**
from savage iron (weapons), an immense blow.
Tri dillyn   diachor,   droch drymluawc,
Three trim invincible ones, heavily-laden in the water with hosts,
teir llyghes   yn aches   arymes kyn Brawt,
three fleets in the flood, a tribulation before Judgment,
teir[3] diwedyd kat   am tri phriawt — gwlat:
three battles at dusk for/around three rightful land-rulers:
   gwnahawt bat betrawt —
   death will necessitate a grave —
15   **tri o pop tri, tri phechawt —**
   all three, three transgressions —
   ac Eryri vre varnhawt.
   and will try the high ground of Eryri.

---

[1] ms *creith*
[2] ms *lloeith* with deleting point beneath *o*
[3] ms *tri*

Llu o Seis, eil o Ynt,   trydyd dygnawt:
A host of Saxons, the second of Foreigners, the third a cruel one:
yg Kymry   yd erhy   gwraged gweddawt.
in Wales there will remain the widowhood of wives.
Rac baran   Kynan   tan tardawt.
Before Cynan's tumult, fire will spread.

20   **Katwaladyr a'e cwyn;**
Cadwaladr will scourge them;
briwhawt bre a brwyn,
he will trample hill and rushes,
gwellt a tho tei, ty tandawt.
thatch and the roofs of houses, a house conflagration.
Atvyd ryfedawt:
A strange thing shall come to pass:
gwr gan verch y vrawt.
a man (consorting) with his brother's daughter.

25   **Dyfynhyn durawt**
They (the Cymry) shall summon a man of steel
o lin Anarawt:
from the line of Anarawd:
ohonaw y tyfhawt
from him shall stem
coch *kattybrunawc*:[4]
a ruddy one of the battle for the settlement in Brun's region
nyt arbet na nawt
who will spare neither kin

30   **na chefynderw na brawt.**
nor cousin nor brother.
Wrth lef corn kadwr
At the call of the warrior's horn
naw cant yn afyrdwl,
nine hundred (shall be) sad.
O bedrydant dygnawt
Because of the powerful, harsh man
dygorelwi lesni   o Laswawt —
whom the verdancy of the 'Glaswawd' declaimed —

35   **ef ret**[5] **wrth a gawd y geudawt.**
he will swoop on those who inflame his mind.

---

[4] ms *kattybrudawt*
[5] ms *efret*

2 Glaswawt Taliessin

title **Glaswawt Taliessin xxiiii a tal** 'Taliesin's Verdant Song: worth 24 [points]': see poem introduction on the attribution and the poem-worth.

1 **Kennadeu a'm dodynt** The announcement of the arrival of tidings, often bad, for relayal by the speaker is found in a variety of verse, including court poetry and prophecy. The use of *kennat* 'message, messenger' (see below for examples) is, however, far less common than *chwedyl* and its compound *kychwedyl* 'account, news'. The latter is used to open §3.1 *Kychwedyl a'm dodyw o Galchuynyd*; and internally at the beginning of a new awdl, §3.39 *Kychwedyl a'm dodyw o leutired Deheu.* Cf. further Moliant Cadwallon line 16 *Kychwedyl a'm dodyw o Wynedd glawr* (AH 29); CBT IV 7.18 *Maurgof ar gychwetyl gychwynn*; CBT V 2.7 *Kychwetyl a'm dothy6 am dwythualch ri*; CBT VI 8.24 *Yr pan doeth kychwedyl am l6yth Kichwein.* Similarly, *chwedyl* often imparts bad tidings: see on §3.1. The less common *kennat*, pl. *kennadeu* 'message; messenger': CA line 848 *cennadeu amoded*; R579.9-10 (Cyfoesi) *kennadeu ansel* (see GPC s.v. *hansel* 'gift, payment'); R579.27-8 (Cyfoesi) *kennat g6astat* (of Serfen Wyn); EWGP 32.28 *diwyt gennat*; CC 31.60 *diwyt gennat*; CBT I 29.16 *Kennadeu agheu yn gyuarwyt,/ Kyn bod ym oerglat, boed ym Arglwyt*; elsewhere CBT IV 9.178 *kynnatyl kennadeu.* *Kennat* is used of a horse messenger six times in CBT II 15 (Owain Cyfeiliog), and also in CBT II 16.53. Of St Cadfan as heavenly emissary, CBT II 1.109. The use of the adj. *anuonawc* 'noble' (see below) suggests 'messengers', possibly horse-messengers or mounted envoys; since they are 'sent' there may be intentional word-play on the homophone vb *anfon* 'to send'.

1 **a'm dodynt** Forms in -*ð*- in sg. are used in CA line 1118 *Neu'm dodyw angkyvwng o angkyuarch*; B 26 (1974-6), 407 *Can dodyw pen Edwin lys Aberffraw* (Cadwallon fragment); LPBT 4.34 *neur dodyw*; by Cynddelw, Meilyr Brydydd, Dafydd Benfras, Hywel Foel, and Prydydd y Moch (3 out of 9 including one referring to prophecy, CBT V 11.45-8 *Kynan, darogan derwyton,—dyda6;/ Ef dodyw o Urython,/ Ana6 kwyna6 kertoryon,/ Un oet wel, ut mwynbell Mon*; Prydydd y Moch also uses the compound form, CBT V 2.65 *Dydoty6 y dyt, Dauyt dyuynfri*). Cf. CBT V 2.7 *Kychwetyl a'm dothy6*; CBT III 26.67 *Neu'm dothyv*; VII 49.10 *Etgyllaeth a'm dothyw*.

This precise pl. form is used by Meilyr alone of court poets: CBT I 5.5-7. *Ni dotynt tros uor etwaeth,/ Pobyl anhyuaeth Nanhyuer,/ G6ytyl, dieuyl duon.* Pl. vb form with pl. subject, as very common in poetry: LPBT 5.42; EWSP 449.7a *Yn Abercuawc cogeu a ganant*; EWSP 444.105 and 106 *Pedwarpwnn broder a'm buant*; CBT III 15.9 *Dynyadon oesga6t as g6tant—o'y varw*; CBT III 28.36 *Eryth-gwynant cant kerta6r*; CBT III 5.15 *Trybelid wylein a wylynt—arnaf*, etc.

1 **mor ynt anuonawc** See on LPBT 25.24 *mor ynt amrygyr*; this syntax continues in poetry at least to the end of the 13c. Instances of common 3pl. *ynt* are noted in LPBT 5.193n. See CA 157 on *anuonawc*, used for a noble warrior, CA line 318 *Issac anuonawc*; of a noble hall, CA line 388 *neuad mor anvonawc*; of warrior fame, CA line 250 *e glot oed anvonavc*; and of innate nobility, CA line 254 *anuonawc eissylud.* Of horses in CBT III 14.32 *Meirch anuona6c myna6c ma6r*. But some word-play is possible since messengers/messages are 'sent' (the vb *anfon* 'to send' is used of horses in CBT V 14.36 *Diamheu anuon granmwynyon gre*; other instances are CBT V 4.37 *yn olud anuon*; CBT II 14.2 *Galon yn anuon anuut dyghet*). *Anfon* is less common than *danfon* in court poetry (e.g. CBT V 5.63). Irish rhyme with *keudawt*.

2 Glaswawt Taliessin

2   **dygawn** G classes this with 3sg. *digoni* 'to make, cause' (generally *digawn*, cf. LPBT 2.4 *digawn gofal*; 6.78 *Digawn lawryded*; PT XI.34 *gwyr a digawn*; CC 31.11c *Digawn Crist trist yn llawen*). Compare Hendregadredd's spelling *dygawn* for adj., CBT VI 15.17 *Mor dygawn y mae digymroded—wedy*; and LlDW 129.21.

2   **ym lletcynt** *Ym* 'to me'. CA 248 'sadness, pain, grief': CA line 690 *neus* (em.) *gwn lleith lletkynt*; EWSP 441.87 *tew lletkynt*; LlDC 16.26 (Afallennau) *gwydi ev llettkint*; R581.9 (Cyfoesi) *G6endyd, gwaranda6 letkynt*; Peirian Faban line 1 *peit ti a'th letkynt*; CBT IV 5.81 *Essillyt Merwyt, maur a letkynt—yw/ Nad ynt vyw vegis gynt*; and seven other court poetry examples (as well as compound *diletkynt*).

2   **meint vyg keudawt** *Meint* understood as subject of vb, 'the full amount/whole of my mind, i.e. all that preoccupies me'. But if *meint* 'how much, how great!' (cf. CBT II 6.20 *meint y reufed*), it could be a separate statement, 'It causes me grief; how great is my mind'. Common *keudawt* (< L. *cavitat-*) 'mind, heart, breast', etc.

3   **Gnawt rwyf yn heli** Runs of nominal statements beginning with *gnawt* 'usual [is]' are found in gnomic verse (e.g. the Gnodiau series, EWGP 26-7) and in another prophecy, Peirian Faban lines 57-61. Compare the *dechymyd* series in AP lines 35-9. *Gnawt* (and *gnawt vot* and *gnawt y*) are extremely common in the CBT corpus (84 occurrences of the unlenited form alone), in many instances in runs (e.g. CBT I 13.11-18; CBT I 17.1-6; CBT IV 6.254-68; CBT VI 23.9-22; CBT VI 24.59-81, etc.). Lines 3-5 are understood as describing current woes which cause the distress alluded to in line 2 rather than referring to the future when such tribulations will become commonplace.

Rwyf is most often used in poetry for 'leader' (sometimes of God), especially by court poets: cf. CBT I 5.11 *rwyf myr*; CBT IV 10.37 *Wyf kerta6r y'm r6yf r6ysc morgymla6t—gwyrt*. *Rwyf* 'oar', as here, in R1051.5-6 (Llynges Fôn) *tr6st r6yueu trosti* (which also mentions Môn, and Conway).

3   **Beli wirawt** The *gwirawt* 'alcoholic drink' (used in conjunction with mead, bragget, and wine) of Beli appears to be a kenning for the sea, 'Beli's drink', Beli being either the legendary ancestor figure Beli Mawr ap Mynogan (see TYP[3] 288-9) or else Beli son of Rhun, grandson of Maelgwn Gwynedd. 12c and 13c court poets freqently refer to Gwynedd rulers as being of Beli's lineage, and to the region as 'Beli's land'. CA 181-2 notes Anwyl's unconvincing suggestion that in CA line 449, *ysgwyt vriw rac biw Beli bloedvawr*, 'Beli [Mawr]'s kine' might be a poetic figure for the sea waves; but since *biw* 'cattle' echoes the *alauoed* 'herds' of line 447, it is preferable to understand it literally, and to understand *Beli bloedvawr* 'a vociferous Beli' as a description of Cadfannan, the subject of the awdl, or else as a reference to a historical figure such as Beli son of Nwython.

The court poets refer to a Beli in connection with Gwynedd, e.g. CBT I 26.8 *Y am deruyn ma6r meibyon Beli* (referring to the land of Gwynedd); CBT III 21.35 *Cad asgen, ysg6n ysgwyd Veli* (of Cadwallon fab Madog ab Idnerth carrying the ready shield of Beli); CBT V 2.13 *hael o hil Beli* (addressing Dafydd ab Owain); CBT V 17.18 *cedwyr tud Feli* (Llywelyn ab Iorwerth's warriors); CBT V 25.49 *h6nn y6 Beli—Hir* (Llywelyn ab Iorwerth as fulfilling Myrddin's prophecy); CBT VI 20.90 *Bro Veli* (Llywelyn ab Iorwerth's rightful land); CBT VII 1.18 *Angert*

2 Glaswawt Taliessin

ueibyon Beli (Y Prydydd Bychan's praise of Owain Goch, grandson of Llywelyn ab Iorwerth); CBT VII 24.39 *Kymro yw haelryw o hil Beli—Hir* (praise of Llywelyn ap Gruffudd); CBT VII 54.29 *o lin Beli* (elegy for the three sons of Gruffudd ap Llywelyn). The majority of these references, according to the editors, refer to Beli Mawr ap Mynogan, the legendary ancestor (see TYP[3] 288-9), rather than to the grandson of Maelgwn Gwynedd. The latter Beli, son of Rhun fab Maelgwn Gwynedd, and father of Iago (EWGT 95), is mentioned in R578.3 (Cyfoesi) *G6endy[d] g6lat yn anghat Veli*; the same poem also refers to the rule following Serfen Wyn: R579.33-4 *Deu ysg6ydwyn Veli a dyvi y[n]aeth,/ a wnant dyuysgi*. R581.21-6 (Cyfoesi) also approvingly mentions Beli Hir and his numerous brave men while condemning the Scandinavians and the Irish (the *Gynt* and the *Gwydyl*). Beli ap Benlli Gawr in LlDC 18.228 (Englynion y Beddau) is yet another character. In the present example, the kenning might favour Beli Mawr.

4   **yscwyt yscawn** Curiously, *yscwyt* 'shield' is collocated with *Beli* in CA line 449 (on which see above), in CBT III 21.35 *ysg6n ysgwyd Veli*, and in R579.33-4 (Cyfoesi, see n. above).

Yscawn is a variant of disyllabic *yscafyn* 'light' which is perhaps to be restored here, providing a better correspondence (*efn/afn*), though not full rhyme, with monosyllabic *cefyn*; the final vowel in both words is epenthetic. Cf. §8.77 *Nyt yscwyt iolet/ gorescyn Dyuet*; EWSP 438.66 *ys ysgawn gan rei fy ruch*, and (collocated as here with *yscwyt*) CBT II 14.42 (Owain Cyfeiliog) *Lluch y dan ysg6yt ysga6n lydan*; see GPC s.v. *ysgafn*, *ysgawn* for other examples of the variant. *Yscwyt yscawn* can also be interpreted as '[one(s)] bearing] light shields'.

The homonym **ysgafyn* (< L. *scamnum* 'bench, stool') is attested only in the rare compound *marwysgafyn* (also *marw ysgawn*, see GPC s.v.). The *yscwyt/yscafyn* collocation is seen in CA line 5 *yscwyt yscauyn lledan*, and Peirian Faban line 17 *llawer ysgwyt loyw ysgafn lydan*.

4   **ar gefyn yscawt** *Ar gefyn* is most commonly used in the literal sense of 'on the back of' (a horse, etc.), e.g. CA line 1203 *ar geuin e gauall*; CBT VII 30.26), and therefore 'on the back of an apparition' is not impossible (cf. *Táin Bó Cúailnge: Recension I*, edited by C. O'Rahilly (Dublin, 1976), lines 492-500). The meaning 'in addition to, as a consequence of, with regard to' is attested only from the 15c (GPC). *Cefn* is also found in toponyms where it means 'ridge', e.g. Cefn yr Aelwyd, etc. see G. However, if *ar gefyn* is comparable with *cefn nos* (e.g. R1300.40), *cefn dydd*, *cefn gweilgi*, etc., 'midnight' would be more striking. Here *ar gefyn yscawt* is tentatively understood as 'in the depth of the night' (literally 'on the back of the night').

GPC s.v. *ysgod* 'shade, shadow, darkness, night; soul, spirit, apparition', etc. The derived *ysgodogyon*, perhaps under the influence of L. *Scot(t)us* or E. *Scot*, is used in CBT I 5.9 (a piece of prophecy attributed to Meilyr Brydydd) to refer to the Irish 'dark devils,/ Wild (or stealthy) ones, oppressive men', *G6ytyl dieuyl duon,/ Ysgodogyon dynyon lletfer*, transl. Nerys Ann Jones, 'The Mynydd Carn "prophecy": a reassessment', *CMCS* 38 (1999), 73-92, at p. 74.

5   **gwyth ac adwyth** Collocated in CA line 405 *en dyd gwyth atwyth oed e lavnawr*; pl. *adwythein* in PT II.6. *Adwyth* is not used by the court poets, but cf. EWGP 42.12 *adwyth diriaid heb achos*.

2 Glaswawt Taliessin

5   **o yspydawt gaer**   LPBT 8.3-4 *Keint yn yspydawt/ uch gwirawt aflawen*. An unidentified fortress of feasting, hospitality or sojourn which seems to cause anger and destruction.

6   **a naw cant maer marwhawt**   *Maer* 'steward' recalls the frequent mention of the tax-collecting *meiryon* in AP, lines 18, 21, 63, 69 and 100, and note especially the description of the stewards of *Caer Geri* (Cirencester) or else the English forces, 18,000 strong, approaching Aber Peryddon, *naw vgein canhwr y discynnant*, with only four (or four score) returning home: AP lines 73-4. Stewards are mentioned in LlDC 17.47 (Oianau) *Meiri mangaled am pen keinhauc*, and LlDC 17.150 *Ban gunelhont meiriev datlev bichein*.

Maer is collocated with *kaer* in LPBT 24.15-16 *Neu vi a torreis cant kaer,/ neu vi a ledeis cant maer*; LPBT 9.46-7 and elsewhere (see LPBT 305). Other 'nine hundred' locutions, as in line 32 below, are noted LPBT 302-3. GPC tentatively classes *marwhawt* with the vb *marwhau* 'to mortify; die, perish', etc. and it is here treated as 3sg. fut. (like *gwnahawt* line 8, and further examples below; cf. examples in GMW 119); if, more unusually, it is a passive form (GMW 119), 'will be mortified'. There is no clear evidence for an adj. formed from *marw* or *marwhau* (see CA 121 for Ifor Williams's interpretation as adj. of *llewychawt, medwhawt, baruawt, llywyawt, gwaryhawt*).

7   **Atvyd Mei ar Venei**   *Atvyd* signals prophetic discourse, cf. line 23 below; PT XI.39-40 *Atuyd kalaned gwein/ A brein ar disperawt*; CC 20.59-60 *Atuyd triganed/ A chyrn rac rihed*; and line 62; LlDC 17.68 (Oianau) *aduit mab ar warr, a [charr]kychuin*, and again LlDC 17.70, 111, 117, 139, 141; R1052.35-6 (Crist Iesu) *Atuyd kelein wenn heb penn heb perthi/ Atuyd meirch g6eilyd g6ael eu diffodi*.

Mei is understood adverbially. *Menei* is similarly rhymed with *Mei* 'the month of May' in a short poem attributed to Hywel ab Owain Gwynedd, CBT II 12.7-11 *Hawd gwelet goleulosc arnei/ O gaer wenn geir emyl Menei./ Treghissyant trydydyd o Uei—trychanllog/ Yn y llyghes 6ordei,/ A deckant kynran a'y kilyei* 'It was easy to see a blazing conflagration there [Rhuddlan] from the fair fort on the bank of the Menai. On the third day of May there foundered three hundred ships of the ?stately fleet, and a thousand soldiers sent it packing'. This poem appears to celebrate a Gwynedd victory in the struggle between Owain Gwynedd and Henry II, and its editors (CBT II 168) suggest it is more likely to refer to the events of 1157, the year of the Tal Moelfre victory in Anglesey (vividly celebrated by Gwalchmai, CBT I poem 8) and the fall of Rhuddlan, rather than to those of 1167 when Rhuddlan was recaptured. But the same rhyme may have been used in referring to any one of a number of earlier battles fought in or near Anglesey such as those recorded for 853, 874, 877, 918, 989, 993, etc. If the mention of Conwy in line 8 refers to the battle of 881 which avenged the death of Rhodri Mawr (see below), it is likely that the battle in question is the 'Sunday battle in Anglesey' in 877 which may have precipitated Rhodri's flight to Ireland; the place of his subsequent slaying at the hands of the Saxons in the following year is not known.

7   **crei gyflogawt**   Understanding *crei* 'meat, flesh', rather than adj. 'raw, sore, rough' which is also possible, 'a sore place'. *Cyflogawt* 'place' is only attested here and in CBT I 3.7 (Meilyr Brydydd) *glan gyfloga6d* (of heavenly dwelling).

2 Glaswawt Taliessin

8   **atvyd mwy ar Gonwy ◇ (ms creith) gwynyeith gwnahawt** The *gwynyeith* 'vengeance' (< L. *vindicta*) brings to mind especially the Battle of Conwy in 881 described by the Welsh annals, 'in a wholly exceptional departure from their normal succinct and unemotional style' (WaB 490), as revenge by God for the killing of Rhodri Mawr of Gwynedd by the English: *Gueit Conguoy digal Rotri a Deo*. Rhodri had been defeated and killed three years earlier in 878 by the Mercians, under Ceolwulf, who may have been aided by Viking factions prominent in the Great Army. But it was not Ceolwulf but his successor, ealdorman Æthelred (*Edryd Gwallthir*, EWGT 101, WaB 491 n. 109), who was defeated by the sons of Rhodri at the battle of Conwy (WaB 490-1), an event that undermined Mercian authority in Wales for the time being. Charles-Edwards notes that the annalist's interpretation of this as divine revenge stems from 'portraying the hostilities between the Mercians and Gwynedd as a blood-feud', foreshadowing Armes Prydain in the 10c but also reflecting the same attitude towards Æthelred as Asser portrays (*Life of Alfred*, ch. 80), namely a military 'tyranny'. Lloyd, HW 328, gathers that Rhodri's son, Anarawd, blocked a raid on Snowdonia (see on line 16 below) by Æthelred. Further on the context, see T.M. Charles-Edwards, 'Wales and Mercia 613-918', in *Mercia: An Anglo-Saxon Kingdom in Europe*, edited by Michelle P. Brown and Carol A. Farr (London, 2001), 89-105, p. 101; Simon Keynes, 'King Alfred and the Mercians' in *Kings, Currency and Alliances: History and Coinage of Southern England in the Ninth Century*, edited by Mark S. Blackburn and David N. Dumville (Woodbridge, 1998), 1-46, pp. 19-20.

But other battles were fought on the River Conwy, including in the early period, in 954, the battle of Conwy Hirfawr at the place called *Gwrgystu* (cf. the personal name *Gwrwst*, as in Llan-rwst), between the sons of Idwal and the sons of Hywel, in which Anarawd ap Gwri was slain. Ceredigion was then ravaged by the sons of Idwal: ByT (Pen. 20) s.a. 954. Other attacks on sites on the Conwy include the Mercian destruction of Degannwy in 822 (see WaB 477) and later incidents there (see LPBT 283-5 for note on poem 8.23). It is mentioned in the prophecy R1051.6-7 (Llynges Fôn) *llan6 ni6 am Gon6y am gyni/ llithra6t g6yr eryr Eryri*. Perhaps *ni6* should be emended to either *n6y*, or *m6y* (as in our example)?

8   ◇ **gwynyeith gwnahawt** Delete hypermetrical *creith*, wrongly added under the influence of *crei* in line 7 and the ending of *gwynyeith*. *Gwnahawt* is understood here and in line 14 below, with G, as 3sg. fut., cf. LlDC 17.36 (Oianau) *Ef gunahaud ryuel a difissci*; 17.160 *Gunahaud am dyued digiuysci*; R585.19 (Gwasgargerdd) *gwna(ha)6t g6yr G6hyr g6rhydri*. A passive meaning (GMW 119) would also yield sense ('vengeance will be wrought') as in the LlDC examples.

9   **Adoer lleith dyrreith** *Adoer* 'cold' used, for example, of the moon, *lloer* (CBT VI 25.2 and VII 30.48), which our scribe was poised to write, judging by his *lloeith* which he corrected by inserting a deleting point under the *o*. As with the simplex *oer*, *adoer* can mean 'sad, chilling'. CA line 900 *eidol adoer*; CA line 1414 *gwibde adoer a dwyaer*. *Dyrreith*, 3sg. pret. *dyrein*: see note on LPBT 18.10.

9   **anaw barawt** Since *anaw* appears to be a masc. noun, *parawt*, if adj. here, would not be lenited. Thus, 'one ready with wealth/benefit': cf. phrases such as

CBT III 20.46 *rot bara6d*; CBT IV 9.54 *rad bara6d*; CBT IV 9.125 *but bara6d*, etc.; here perhaps an ironic description of the *lleith* 'death'.

10 **o hëyrn erchwyrn** *Hëyrn* here of iron weapons. Rhymed with *chwyrn* in CBT VII 2.1-2 *chwyrn—yg cad/ Yg cadarnwisc heyrn*; with *anchwyrn* and *edyrn* in CBT I 25.12-14 (Einion ap Gwalchmai) *anchwyrn;/ . . . yn llwyth heyrn,/ . . . adwy edyrn*. *Erchwyrn* (< *chwyrn* 'fierce'), unattested elsewhere in early verse, is confirmed by internal rhyme with *edyrn*.

10 **edyrn dyrnawt** CA line 133 *edyrn diedyrn*; LPBT 23.44; CBT IV 10.27 (rhyming with *eurdyrn*) and CBT I 25.14 in note above. See LPBT 5.9 on the personal name *Edyrn* (alongside *Edern*). *Dyrnawt* lit. 'a blow with the fist', then generalised, e.g. AP line 41; CC 22.11 *pimp dirnaud* for Christ's stigmata. *Dyrn* and *hëyrn* are frequently collocated.

11 **Tri dillyn diachor** *Dillyn* 'fair, dear (thing)', rare in early poetry, but cf. CBT V 23.14 *Yn dillin kyuarpar*. Possibly restore *dillyg* (ModW *dillyng* 'liberal, free'), root of vb *dillwng, dillyngio* 'to release, deliver, launch' (GPC), as in LPBT 12.13 *Yn dillig vdunt yn dillat yn* (em.) *da*. A meaning such as 'a launching' for restored *dillyg* would suit the meaning well here, but the ms reading is retained. *Diachor* 'invincible', see LPBT 18.52 *twrwf diachor* (of fire); LPBT 11.35 *Ef yn diachor* (of the wind).

11 **droch drymluawc** If referring to the three fleets of line 12, *troch* 'immersion', as in the vb *trochi* 'to immerse, soak. . . . plunge', i.e. 'the plunging [ships] heavily-laden with hosts', is more likely than *troch*, the fem. form of the adj. *trwch* 'unfortunate, sad, wretched . . . evil; wounded, injured, maimed, shattered, broken' (GPC), which is not grammatically suitable to qualify masc. *tri dillyn diachor*. Could the phrase *droch drymluawc* conceivably be anticipating the fem. *teir llyghes* of line 12? *Troch* is used in CBT V 5.41 *troch aruthyr trachwres*; with *trwm* CBT VII 8.1 *Maredut aestromrut troch*; with *llynges* in Gwalchmai's Gorhoffedd, CBT I 9.74 *Kymynid ar dres droch lyghes lyr*. *Amdroch* 'shattered' is used with *achor* and *llyghes* in Cynddelw's description of a fleet in his list of battles fought by Owain Gwynedd: CBT IV 2.15-16 *Oet amdroch llyghes, aches achor,/ Oet amgen Gweith Uon a Gweith Uangor*.

Trymluawc 'loaded, full heavy; sad . . . ; lethargic', etc. (GPC) is not attested elsewhere in poetry until GDG 92.6 *hun drymluog hwyr*. Adjs. in *-awc* are exceedingly common, especially in the Gododdin and the work of the court poets. Note, however, the predilection for unusual adjectival formations in *-awc* in the work of Prydydd y Moch (see GPC s.vv. *adarweinidog, adfuddiog, anghuddiog, alaog, arffedog, asgethrog, byddinog, cadeiriog, coedog, caerog, cytiriog, cadwychog, estroniog, gorfodog, hyddolog, llawddeog, llueddog, mochddwyreog, meiniog, rhinweddog, sidanog, tafodiog, teuluog, trahaog, ysgwydog*, etc.).

12 **teir llyghes yn aches** On *aches* 'sea-flood, flow, tide', etc. see LPBT 4.168. Cf. especially CBT I 8.32 (Gwalchmai's description of the battle of Tal Moelfre in 1157) *Teir praff prif lyghes wy bres broui*. For collocation, cf. R1053 (Mor yw gwael gwelet) *Ef a ddaw fal diau/ aches llyghesau*; and cf. LPBT 5.18 *dyrehawr llogawr ar glawr aches*. On the 'approaching fleet' topos in prophecy (also in the Afallennau, etc.), see §7.16n and General Introduction, 12.

12 **arymes kyn Brawt** On the range of meanings of *arymes* 'prophecy . . . portent, omen; calamity, destruction, tribulation', see GPC, AP xlv-ix, P. Sims-Williams, 'Some Functions of Origin Stories in Early Medieval Wales', in *History and*

2 Glaswawt Taliessin

Heroic Tale, edited by Tøre Nyberg *et al.* (Odense, 1985), 97-131, pp. 114 and 128-9; LPBT 5.249. The phrase points up the overlap between secular and religious prophecy, bringing to mind *Arymes Dyd Brawt*, the name of the religious poem which foretells the events of Judgment Day (CC poem 20) and which is placed next to *Arymes Prydein Vawr* in the manuscript. With the three fleets compare the Three Hosts (*Tri Llu*) who will be judged (CC 21.132). Various portents (*arwydon*) presage the Judgment (e.g. CBT II 5.7-8 *Meint yr arwydon a vyd/ Pymthecuet dyd kynn Dyd Bra6t*). *Arymes* here could also mean 'tribulation, travail', developed from the original meaning of 'foretelling, foremeasuring, forejudging' (*ar* + *mes*) such trials. Cf. Marwnad Cadwallon englyn 2 *Lloegyr ar dres armes ednaint*; R1051.3 (Moch Daw Byd) *Dygoganaf tyfyrru erymes tra bytha6t*; seven instances of *arymes* in CBT corpus; with *tri* in CBT VI 31.58 *Tri eres armes trachwres trychion*.

13 **teir (ms tri) diwedyd kat** Since *kat* in both meanings, 'battle' and 'army', is a fem. noun, *tri diwedyd* would have to be understood separately, as adverbial, 'at/over [?a period of] three dusks'. It is more likely that *tri* is a mistake for *teir*, arising from anticipating *tri phriawt gwlat* or copying numerals. This provides a more natural diction in the pre-caesura section, as well as correspondence with the preceding line.

   Diwedyd 'evening', 'end of day', CC 12.25; EWSP 454.4 and 455.11 *birr diuedit* (*bir diwedit*); R582.9 (Cyfoesi); it is not found in the CBT corpus, but the hapax compound *godiwedyd* is collocated with *kat* by Meilyr Brydydd, CBT I 3.129-31 *Cad Geredigya6n, gyfya6n gywyt,/ Crenynt wraget g6et6 goddiwedyt;/ Cad yn Iwerton diryon dreuyt*.

13 **am tri phriawt gwlat** *Priawt* indicating a rightful or true ruler, used (like *priodawr*) with *Prydein, tir*, etc. (e.g. CBT I 3.22; V 6.35; 7.7; 18.31; I 1.7).

14 **Gwnahawt bat betrawt** See line 8 above on *gwnahawt*. *Bat* classed as 'boat, ship' by G (< OE *bat*, see EEW 34), but with *bat* 'plague, pestilence, death' by GPC. The latter meaning in CBT I 8.16, and according to G, in GGDT 10.39 *bad—ar doniar* (wrongly translated GGDT 102). *Betrawt* is a variant of *bedrawt* (*-ð-*) 'grave, tomb, vault; cemetery, churchyard', used in CBT II 26.166 *A el ym medra6d mynwent Dewi*. The subject of the vb could be understood as *bat*; but more naturally referring to the three battles of line 13 or else the general cataclysm which will bring about a deathtomb or cemetery (ModW *bad feddrod*), or — with more force — one similar to that brought about by the plague. If the three battles, perhaps read *gwnahawnt* (3pl.) if the scribe's eye was on *betrawt*.

15 **tri o pop tri tri phechawt** Very uncertain. 'Three out of every three [are/were] three transgressions'? Presumably referring to the three fleets or the three dusk battles. *Pop tri* can mean 'in/by threes' (see GPC s.v. *pob*) but this does not seem likely here.

16 **ac Eryri vre varnhawt** 'And it/he will judge (sentence/condemn) the high ground of Eryri', i.e. Snowdonia in Gwynedd. The Battle of Conwy of 881 (see above on line 8) followed an attempted incursion into Snowdonia by ealdorman Æthelred of Mercia (according to later evidence used by HW 328, discussed WaB 490-1) which was foiled by Anarawd.

   Earlier events include the event recorded in the B version of the Annales Cambriae for 816 (and the *Brut*) with the Saxons — Mercians, according to WaB 476 'either led or sent by their king, Cenwulf', who also laid waste Dyfed in 818

— attacking or making incursions into the mountains of *Eryri* and the kingdom of Rhufoniog east of the Conwy. But references to *Eryri*, especially as heartland and refuge, are common in poetry: §5.23-4 *Gynt gwaedvenni:/ galwawr Eryri*; §7.44-5 *diffeith Moni a Lleenni,/ ac Eryri anhed yndi*; §10.4 *ac yn Eryri ymolöi*; R1051.6-7 (Llynges Fôn) *llan6 ni6 am Gon6y am gyni/ llithra6t g6yr eryr Eryri*. Henry I's great offensive attack against Gwynedd and Powys in 1114 precipitated Owain ap Cadwgan's retreat to Eryri, referred to in ByT (Pen. 20), 59: *A gwedy gwybod o Ywein hynny kynullaw y wyr ay holl da gyd ac wynt a mudaw hyd ymynyded Eryri kanys ynyalaf a diogelaf lle oed hwnnw y ffo ydaw*, remembered in R584.19-22 (Gwasgargerdd) *Pan dyuo Henri y holi/ Mur Castell y deruyn Eryri/ galwa6t gormes dra gweilgi*. There are 13 various mentions of *Eryri* in the CBT corpus (see G).

17 **Llu o Seis** For *Seis* 'the Saxon' to represent the whole people as here, cf. AP line 96 *Seis ar hynt hyt Gaer Wynt*; EWSP 457.2c *gelyn i Seis*; EWGP 27.9 *kyfnewit Seis ac aryant*; R1050.16 (Mal Rhod yn Troi) *a g6ander Seis oe jnseileu*; R1051.2 (Moch Daw Byd) *a Seis byd lawen*; R1052.12 (Crist Iesu) *kilya6d Seis o'e dreis dros eluyd*; §10.9 *Ys deubi Seis yna y erchi bwytta*. In the CBT corpus, there are seven occurrences of *Seis*, restricted to vols VI and VII, whereas *Saeson* is used 19 times by 12-13c poets, and is common elsewhere in early poetry.

17 **eil o Ynt** *Gynt* (< L. *gentes*) is used most often of nations harrying the Welsh, especially the Vikings and Danes (sometimes called Gentiles in Ireland), but also the English and the Normans. G notes 'host, people, nation; Scandinavians, Danes'. *Gynt* is used in conjunction with names of other peoples in CA lines 491-2 *a breithell goruchyd y lav loflen/ ar Gynt a Gwydyl a Phryden*; Peirian Faban line 2 *A ddifero di Duw rac Gwyddyl gynt* (also mentioned in lines 3-4 are *Allt Wyddyl, Freinc, Gwydyl*); R581.22 (Cyfoesi) *g6ynn eu byt Gymry, a g6ae Gynt*. Also Moliant Cadwallon line 46 *Aded gynt ethynt yn hydirver* (em.) *hallt*; LlDC 17.60-61 (Oianau) *Ban diholer Taguistil in hir o tir Guinet,/ dybit seith ganllog o Ynt gan wint Goglet*. The word is used in AC 866 *cat dub gynt* (= *nigrae gentes*, Danes), referring to the laying waste of York. Viking attacks on Wales are first recorded in the 850s: in 853 Anglesey was ravaged; in 856 Ormr was killed in battle by Rhodri Mawr. Then, after a lull, there were more attacks from 871. AC 876 (877) records the Sunday battle in Anglesey, *Gweith Diu Sul*, when Rhodri Mawr was defeated in battle and driven to take refuge in Ireland.

17 **trydyd dygnawt** *Dygnawt* 'cruel, grievous, vexatious' (GPC), cf. line 33 below *O bedrydant dygnawt*; CC 9.5 *dignawt annwyt* (see CC 75); Echrys Ynys line 22 *dygnawt eu tra*; LPBT 5.32 *erdygnawt*; CBT II 6.81 *gweith gordygna6d*. The third host is not specified.

18 **yg Kymry yd erhy** *Kymry* either the country or the people. *Erhy* 3sg. pres. of vb *ar(h)os* 'to await; remain, dwell, stay, continue' (the present instance is classed with latter meaning by GPC, but both are possible).

18 **gwraged gweddawt** Understood as 'the widowhood of wives', but if *aros* 'await', then 'wives await widowhood'. The form is derived from *gwedw + -dawt* (abstract suffix), cf. *meddawt < medw + -dawt*. The collocation of *gwraged* with *gwedw* and derivatives is seen in CA line 265 *a gwraged gwydw*; CA line 672 *o gyvryssed gwraged gwydw a wnaethant*; CA lines 273-4 *ef gwneei gwyr llydw/ a gwraged gwydw*; PT V.14 *A uei wedw y wreic*; AP line 118 *Atui gwraged gwedw a meirch gweilyd*; CBT I 3.130 *Crenynt wraget g6et6 goddiwedyt*; CBT V 26.22

2 Glaswawt Taliessin

Neud llwyr wetw y g6raget; R1056.37-8 (Gosymdaith lines 111-12) *bit wastat gwreic, ny erchir/ mevyl, ys gna6t o wedda6t hir*.

19-20 **Kynan ... Katwaladyr** The two heroes who will lead the Welsh to victory, mentioned together several times in Armes Prydain and other prophecies, and once in court poetry (CBT I 6.21-2, before 1160). Because both names were in common use, their identity is not entirely certain. See General Introduction, 10-11.

19 **Rac baran Kynan tan tardawt** *Rac baran* is used by Cynddelw (CBT III 16.140 and IV 16.151. *Baran* with *tan* in CA line 832 *baran tan teryd ban gynneuet*; and cf. §9.17 *baran godeith* 'roar/tumult of a conflagration'. On the vb *tardu* 'issue, emerge, sprout; erupt' see LPBT §5.64. *Tan tardawt* is an unusually short cadence for a long Class 2 line.

20 **Katwaladyr a'e cwyn** Understood as 3sg. of vb *cwynaw* 'to grieve; complain of, bemoan' rather than with G s.v. 'to cause pain to', a meaning not endorsed by GPC; see further EWSP 609. The noun 'complaint, plaint, grievance', with unrealised lenition, is not impossible ('with his grievance'). *Cwyn* is collocated with *brwyn* 'sad' (e.g. EWSP 404.1; CBT IV 5.39; VI 36.44; VII 14.21; VII 48.25); occasionally, as here, with *brwyn* 'bracken', e.g. EWGP 23.15.

21 **briwhawt bre a brwyn** *Brwyn* and *bre* (and synonym *bryn*) are occasionally collocated with forms of vb *briwaw*: e.g. CBT II 5.47 *Pan vo bri6 brynneu*; CBT IV 3.32-3 *brig briwgawn,/ Crynai elorfeirch bre bryd nawn*; LlDC 34.34-5 *kint y sirthei kadoet . . . no bruyn briw y laur*. The idea of heroes being cut down like rushes, as in the last example, is found elsewhere, e.g. CA line 26 *mal brwyn gomynei gwyr nyt echai*; CA line 415 *mal brwyn yt gwydynt rac y adaf*.

22 **gwellt a tho tei ty tandawt** The metre is not regular, but the end-rhyme in *-awt* is present. *Tandawt* 'conflagration, bonfire, ignition' (GPC), also used of a blaze in a house fire in the Welsh version of *Purgatorium S. Patricii*, SC 8/9 (1973-4), 187. The awkward phrasing would be improved by omitting *ty*, but the seven syllables match those of line 16. Another possibility would be to see here a disyllabic *tëi* (a stage in the development from *tegesa* posited by Schrijver, SBCHP 390-3), emending out the *ty* which may have been added in error. But this would go against the evidence of monosyllabic *tei* in all the early poetry examples (e.g. CA line 27 *mordei*; EWGP 26.35 *g6ynn to tei*; and court poetry). Secondary plurals *tyeu, tyoed*, etc. are not attested until the 15c according to GPC. Reading disyllabic *tëi* (or less likely, *tyei*) and omitting *ty* would certainly give a more convincing phrasing and a closer correspondence with the patterning of line 16, but the ms reading is retained since it does make some sort of sense.

23 **Atvyd ryfedawt** See line 8 above on *atvyd*. *Ryfedawt* 'marvel, wonder' is not very common: LPBT 17.18 *Gweles ryuedawt*; CBT VI 29.7 *A'i gweles, gwelynt ryfeddau*. Used of God's wonders in CBT I 3.1 *mor ryuet y ryueta6d*; VII 32.5 *ryued6n ryuedodeu*. Cf. LPBT 17 (title) *Anryuedodeu*; CC 33.65. *Ryfedawt* collocated with *Anarawt* by Cynddelw, CBT IV 9.33-4 *Gweleis-y hael o hil Anara6d,/ A'e gweles, gwelei ryueta6d*.

24 **gwr gan verch y vrawt** Unions were reckoned as prohibited to at least the fourth degree of consanguinity in medieval civil and canon law: Maelgwn was condemned by Gildas for an adulterous and incestuous union with his niece by marriage (his brother's son's wife, *De Excidio Britanniae*, ch. 35). On the social disruption theme in prophecy, see General Introduction, 11-12.

25 **Dyfynhyn durawt** 3pl. pres./fut. *dyfynnu/yaw* 'to summon, call for', with normal loss of final *-t* (see GMW 120). Vb rather infrequent, but perhaps in Gwarchan Maeldderw (CA line 1449, as emended by G.R. Isaac, *CMCS* 44 (2002), 91); CBT I 21.39-40 (Elidir Sais); III 8.41; CC 33.47.

Durawt adj. 'of steel, hard as steel; cruel, severe', used nominally here for 'a harsh or cruel man', is uncommon outside 12c court poetry: CA line 663 *llavyn durawt*; CBT I 2.15 *gretyw detyw duraud*; CBT I 3.24 (Meilyr Brydydd) *ryuel dura6d* rhyming, as in the present example, with *Anara6d*; CBT I 6.4 (Gwalchmai) *pryssur dura6d*; CBT IV 9.52 *bron dewrdor dura6d*.

26 **o lin Anarawt** Which, if any, was our *durawt* 'man of iron' is hard to say (there is no obvious candidate in this lineage for a play on a name here, such as Haearnddur, Haearnwedd, or Peredur). As just noted, *dura6t* is rhymed, as here, with *Anara6t*, by Meilyr Brydydd (early 12c), CBT I 3.23-4. Anarawd (< L. *Honoratus*), a son of Rhodri Mawr of Gwynedd, came to power *c.* 878, and with his brothers is likely to have been victorious against the Mercians at the Battle of Conwy in 881 (see on line 8 above). Subsequently, Powys is likely to have been annexed (WaB 492), and as Asser records in his *Life of Alfred*, Anarawd formed alliances in turn with the Scandinavian kingdom of York, and then with Alfred of Wessex, submitting to his lordship 'with all his people', promising to be obedient in every way, 'on the same conditions as Æthelred and the Mercians' (see WaB 489-90). In 894 Anarawd's attacks to lay waste Ceredigion and Ystrad Tywi were aided by Englishmen (*Angli*), most likely the Mercians, as argued by Charles-Edwards, WaB 495-6. This may have been an opportunistic move precipitated by the recent death in 892 of Hyfaidd ruler of Ystrad Tywi and probably overlord of Ceredigion (see WaB 495). Anarawd's mother, Angharad was later reckoned as being of the Ceredigion line, daughter of Meurig fab Dyfnwal (EWGT 12), and sister to Gwgon, last attested king of Ceredigion (d. *c.* 872). During the second half of Anarawd's reign, Gwynedd suffered a series of Viking incursions — in 892 from the direction of Ireland, and in 894 from the Wirral. It was probably Anarawd who in 902 at Maes Osfeilion, near Llan-faes, unsuccessfully resisted the Viking lord Igmunt (Ingimund), who seems to have arrived in Anglesey after expulsion from Dublin: see WaB 496, and WaB 502 on Ingimund's subsequent move east towards Chester where lands on the Wirral were settled by agreement with Æthelflæd of Mercia. Anarawd died in 916 and was recorded as *rex Britonum* by the B text of the Annales Cambriae.

As noted in the poem introduction, Anarawd was long remembered in poetry as victor at the battle of Conwy: R579.4-6 (Cyfoesi) praises him for his Wednesday battle there: *Ar lann Kon6y kym6y Du6 Merchyr/ etmycka6r y deua6t:/ arbennic anyan Anara6t*. In Englynion y Clywaid (CC 31.19) he is remembered as a skilful soldier, *milwr donyawc, didlawt*. Meilyr Brydydd's elegy for Gruffudd ap Cynan compares his skill at inciting battle to that of Anarawd, using the same collocation with *durawt* as in our poem: CBT I 3.23-4 *Handoet gad gyffro o Anara6d,/ Ac eil o Run Hir, ryuel dura6d*. Cynddelw's reconciliation ode to Rhys ap Gruffudd of Deheubarth (d. 1197) notes the prince's descent from Anarawd, in collocation with *ryfedawt*: CBT IV 9.33-4 *Gweleis-y hael o hil Anara6d,/ A'e gweles, gwelei ryueta6d* 'I saw a generous one of Anarawd's line; whoever saw him would see a wonder'.

2 Glaswawt Taliessin

Anarawd was succeeded by his son, Idwal Foel; other sons were Elise and perhaps Meurig. On Idwal's death along with Elise at the hands of the English in 942 (which WaB 530 suggests was retaliation for Gwynedd siding with Olaf Guthfrithsson in 939-40), his sons, Iago and Ieuaf, were expelled from Gwynedd by Hywel Dda of Deheubarth in south Wales, but from 950-5 they retaliated against Hywel's sons. Rivalry between the brothers led to Ieuaf being imprisoned (and possibly hanged) by Iago in 969. Ieuaf's son Hywel continued the struggle against his uncle, wresting intermittent rule of at least parts of the kingdom during the 970s. A period of instability ensued between Hywel's death in 985 and 999 when his son, Cynan, came to power.

The phrase *o lin*, like the synonymous *o hil* (both common, especially in the court poetry), is most frequently used in conjunction with a figure from the fairly distant past, although some examples are used to refer to the issue of a father or grandfather. The identity of the 'hard man' from the line of Anarawd can only be guessed at: he is perhaps most likely to have been one of the direct Gwynedd line, namely (EGWT 95) Llywelyn ab Iorwerth m. Owain Gwynedd m. Gruffudd m. Cynan m. Iago m. Idwal m. Meurig m. Idwal Foel m. Anarawd.

27 **ohonaw y tyfhawt** *Ohonaw*, either 'from him' or 'because of him'. *Tyfu* 'to grow, sprout; to (cause to) grow, increase; to heal, make, become better', etc., 3sg. fut. (although note GMW 119 for the comment that a few forms in *-(h)awt* appear to be passive). The most straightforward interpretation here is 'from him [i.e. the 'harsh man'] will stem . . .' (cf. EWSP 442 *a dyuynt ual gwyal coll*), followed by mention of another person, a man who 'spares neither kin nor cousin nor brother' (lines 29-30). But not wholly impossible is 'because of him will grow/increase . . . ' or (if passive), 'by his agency will be increased . . . '.

28 **coch** Adj. meaning 'red, scarlet', most frequently used in poetry in the sense of 'blood-stained' qualifying words for weapons, sullied waters, bodies, etc., cf. R1051.18-19 (Llynges Fôn) *Gôr coch yg cochwed gorawen*, and sometimes collocated with *kat* 'battle'. It is also used of people to mean 'red-haired' (and possibly 'florid of face'), as seen in cognomina such as Iolo *Goch*. In the darogan poetry, *Coch Nordmandi* might mean William Rufus: R584.14-15 (Gwasgargerdd) *Pan dyuo Coch Nordmandi/ y holi Lloegyrwys, treul diffôys*. Iorwerth Goch ap Maredudd of Powys, who joined Henry II when he attacked Owain Gwynedd in 1157, was of line of Bleddyn ap Cynfyn back through Cadell to Rhodri Mawr (not of the line of Anarawd). But there are other possibilities — Owain Goch ap Gruffudd ap Llywelyn, and surely many more. Another meaning of *coch*, although somewhat uncommon, is 'redness, red colour': this is adopted by Clare Downham, *Viking Kings of Britain and Ireland: The Dynasty of Ívarr to A.D. 1014* (Edinburgh, 2007), p. 214 n. 92, who translates *coch kat* as 'the redness of battle (i.e. bloodshed)'. *Coch kat* is understood here as 'the florid or blood-stained one of battle', most natural with line 29, although 'bloody' (qualifying *kat* 'battle') with poetic inversion is not impossible.

28 **kattybrunawc (ms kattybrudawt)** As noted in the introduction, this has been associated with the name for the battle of Brunanburh in 937 (*ryfel Brun* in ByT s.a., and *Brune* in AC). Although the Book of Taliesin scribe regularly uses *-tt-* to indicate provection of [d] before [h] (e.g. AP line 68 *attor* (< *ad* + *hor*); LPBT 5.51 *attebwys* (< *ad* + *hebwys*); CC 15.5 *brattäu* (< *brad* + *häu*)), it is unlikely that *hy-* is present here (in the medieval language, adjs. in *hy-* are compounded

with nouns or verbal stems). The combination of -*d* and *d*- is more likely, paralleled before a consonant in Echrys Ynys line 26 *attrefna* (but cf. spelling in §6.18 *atrefnwy*), and cf. the Red Book spellings, *kattarw* 'bull of battle' (*caddarw* < *tarw*), *lletty* (*lled-dy* < *ty*), etc.

In poetry especially, fem. nouns, such as *kat* 'battle; army, throng', very often lenite a following genitive proper noun (cf. *stauell Gyndylan* 'Cynddylan's hall', *bydin Ododin* 'the warband of Gododdin', *hudlath Vathonwy* 'Mathonwy's magic staff', etc.), in which case a name beginning with *Ty* or *Tybr*- might be sought; this would also be the case if *kat* is used as an intensifying (and leniting) element (see GPC s.v. *caterwen*).

A place-name *Tybrudawt is most unlikely because of the unsuitability of the *prud* (ModW *prudd*) element, the lack of early evidence for *brut* (ModW *brud*), and for a word *brud (ModW *brudd). A radical emendation to *Tybrunawc (on which see further below) would, however, yield a plausible formation. The OE personal name *Brun* (or ON *Brunn*) could be the base of a regional name 'the territory of Brun' since the Welsh suffix -*iawc* (ModW -*iog*) is well-attested with personal names (Rhufoniog 'the land of Rhufawn', Anhuniog, Peuliniog, and others, discussed by Melville Richards, 'Early Welsh Territorial Suffixes', *Journal of the Royal Society of Antiquaries of Ireland* 95 (1965), 205-12, at p. 208). The Book of Taliesin is notoriously yod-shy so the lack of the semivowel -*y*- here is not an obstacle. The preceding *Ty* 'house' would refer to a settlement in the region, possibly a caput (very roughly approximating to the *burh* of Brunanburh), or a religious settlement (comparing *Tyddewi*; *esgobty*).

The emendation of the ending from -*awt* to -*awc* is not problematic: the letter forms *c* and *t* are easily confused, and the generic rhyme that would be produced is paralleled in the poem, between lines 1 and 2. Given the poem's dominant rhyme in -*awt*, the emendation has the lectio difficilior principle in its favour. It is more difficult to account for the copying of -*rud* instead of the suggested -*run* since the letters *d* and *n* are not confused (similarly with *t*, used in some orthographies for [ð], and *n*). One answer is that the scribe baulked at writing a segment -*brun*- which for him had no meaning, being unparalleled in the Welsh language; he substituted -*brud*- presumably because *prud* (see below) was the only word known to him in *pru*- (or *bru*-). This implies he had no exact knowledge of the name. On the other hand, his writing of *kattybrudawt* as one word suggests that he was aware of a battle-name which had become merged into one phrase, or at least that he was prepared to follow his exemplar in treating it as such. But it may be worth mentioning the (albeit 15c) degradation of *Cad Gamlan* 'the Battle of Camlan' into a common noun *cadgamlan* 'mixed multitude, rabble, confused mob'. Is it possible that the Welsh name for the decisive encounter at Brunanburh became virtually a term for a major battle, and, for the 14c Book of Taliesin scribe (if not for the Red Book and Hendregadredd copyists), one which was open to corruption because its origin was unknown.

The whole interpretation outlined above (with emendation to *kattybrunawc*) has in its favour, as Lloyd-Jones obviously thought, the alignment with the late 12c forms, R1187.27 *kattybrunawc* and Hendregadredd's *cad dybruna6c* (see CBT II 26.60), addressed by John Bollard in *The Battle of Brunanburh: A Casebook*, edited by Michael Livingston (Exeter, 2010), 205-6; furthermore, it respects the copyist's compound format. It also has the attraction that a reference to Brunanburh (especially if the site is to be equated with Bemborough on the

2 Glaswawt Taliessin

Wirral) sits well with the figures and north Wales battles of the late 9c and early 10c (Conwy, Anarawd). The main problem, as explained above, is accounting for -*brud*- rather than -*brun*-.

We may now turn to another possibility. The -*tt*- could conceivably be the product of *kat* + *dy*- with the unusual merging into one word coming about through scribal error, possibly under the influence of the battle-name already discussed. The only contender here would be the verbal form *dybrud(h)awt*, 3sg. fut. of *prudhau* 'to make/grow wise; to sadden, grieve', a vb first attested in the 14c (GPC), although the adj. *prud* 'wise, prudent, earnest', etc. is commonly used in court poetry (the meaning 'sad, sorrowful' becoming more evident from the 14c onwards). If the latter meaning was already in existence, then 'who will cause grief'. If the primary meaning, then 'who will bring sense/wisdom' or 'who will become wise/grow in wisdom'. Somewhat problematic is the lack of evidence for the suggested compound vb **dybrudhau*, but cf. other hapax verbs in *dy*- such as *dysaethu*, LPBT 23.14. It may be noted that the verbal form is favoured since there is no evidence for an abstract noun formed from *prud* (i.e. ModW **prudd-dod*, MW **pruddawt*). The vb *brudyaw* 'to prophesy' (< *brud/brut* 'chronicle; prophecy', 14c onwards, < OF *brut* < *Brutus*) is attested first in the 16c, according to GPC, and is unlikely to be relevant, especially since no **dybrudyaw* is attested. This second interpretation has the advantage of needing less editorial intervention than the first, and of providing an equally convincing lead-in to lines 29-30. It has against it the compound format and a lack of comparanda for the suggested verbal form, neither of which are insuperable objections, however.

A third possibility with minimal emendation of -*u*- to -*y*- would provide a formation from the productive adj. *dybryt* 'deformed, ugly; hideous, terrible', etc., positing **dybrydawt* alongside the known abstract nouns *dybrydrwyd*, *dybrydwch*. This would give 'a florid one of grievous battle'.

On balance, the first interpretation — the Battle of Brunanburh (more exactly 'the battle for/at the settlement in Brun's territory') — is perhaps the most persuasive. But as stressed in the poem introduction above, the uncertain dating of the poem means that it is not necessarily an early reference to the battle; and if the comments on the scribal treatment of the phrase are correct, then the Book of Taliesin scribe at least was somewhat in the dark about its origin.

29   **nyt arbet na nawt**   The vb *arbet* becomes more frequent in the court poetry. But compare especially AP 116 *nyt arbettwy car corff y gilyd* 'relatives shall not spare each other's bodies' for the vb and the sentiment. Cf. CBT I 14.109; VI 10.81; III 21.161 *ymarbet*; and adj. *diarbet* CBT III 16.237, and Marwnad Cynddylan line 21 *diarbedawg*. *Nawt* (perhaps from L. *natio*, see GPC) is most naturally interpreted as an example of the word meaning 'kin, relation' rather than 'nature, quality, trait', etc. (in which case it may derive from or be influenced by *gnawt*).

31   **Wrth lef corn kadwr**   *Kadwr* 'warrior', cf. CBT IV 9.36. *Wrth lef* 'at the [battle] cry', cf. CA line 148 *gwrth lef agerw* (em.); CBT IV 9.119; VI 7.10; collocated with *corn* and *cyrn* in CBT III 6.1-3 *Balch ei fugunawr ban lefawr—ei lef,/ Pan ganer cyrn cydawr,/ Corn Llywelyn lluyddfawr*; CBT III 22.7 *Llef bon corn blaen cad ehorth*; CBT IV 4.227-8 *Yn t6ryf llu a llef ysglyuyon./ Kyrn cenynt*.

2 Glaswawt Taliessin

32 **naw cant yn afyrdwl** On common nine and multiples, see LPBT 9.22, and on line 6 above.

33 **O bedrydant dygnawt** On *pedrydant* 'perfect (?of sinew), complete, powerful, strong', see LPBT 5.60. See line 17 above on *dygnawt*. The prep. *o* here understood as 'concerning' but 'because of, as a result of' are possible.

34 **dygorelwi lesni o laswawt** *Dygorelwi*, 3sg. imperf. of an otherwise unattested compound vb *dygoralw* (cf. *goralw*). See further on §4.1 for treatment of *dyg-*. While the subject could conceivably be the *llef corn kadwr* of line 31, i.e. 'it sounded forth the verdancy of the fresh/young song', with *glesni* as object, it is more likely to be the *pedrydant dygnawt* of line 33, 'who called out'. Alternatively, if *glesni* is subject (with lenition, TC 214), 'verdancy cried forth from/as a result of a fresh song'. The latter is tentatively understood in the translation.

35 **ef ret (ms efret) wrth a gawd y geudawt** G classes *ef ret* as 'it/he runs'. Cf. perhaps collocation in CA lines 1421-2: *Hu tei en wlyd elwit/ gwr a ret pan dychelwit*. Other possible emendations of *ef ret* include *eniwet* 'harm, injury, damage', or verbal form < *eniwaw*[1] 'reproach, upbraid', i.e. 'Let him reproach he/those who inflame(s) his mind'. Lines 33-5 are uncertain, but the interpretation here is that the Glaswawd prophecy's foretelling of a 'powerful harsh man' emboldens the 'florid/bloodstained one of battle' of line 28 to swoop on those who incur his displeasure.

3 Kychwedyl a'm dodyw o Galchuynyd

This long and involved poem praises the martial and cattle-reaving prowess of two men, Mabon and Owain. Mabon is the rather more prominent of the two, mentioned five times by name. He is an eminent one 'of another region' (line 17), mounted on 'an eager fair-maned horse' (line 25), bringing certain death to enemy raiders in the vicinity of the Rheged cattle — unless they have wings to fly clear away (lines 25-8). His own cattle are lively but not agitated (line 44). He is very likely to be the *mab Idno* mentioned in line 8, the son of Idno ap Meirchiawn, and therefore, according to the thirteenth-century genealogy, Bonedd yr Arwyr, one of the Coeling dynasty and, more importantly, a first cousin of Urien Rheged whose own father was Cynfarch fab Meirchiawn.[1]

The other man is Owain, also mentioned five times by name but first encountered in line 18 fighting for, or defending, the cattle of ?his region. His sphere of activity is indisputably North British, since a battle at *Ryt Alclut*, 'the ford of Dumbarton Rock', follows in line 19, along with battles in two unidentified places (lines 19 and 20 *Ygwen* and *Gossulwyt*) and another battle against a force of the pale *Rodawys* men, also unattested elsewhere.[2] When Owain attacked 'for the sake of his father's cattle' — line 31 is the first of two allusions to his famous father, Urien — shields and staves splintered. These were probably his own, as this is a heroic commonplace which is reprised in line 49-50: Owain's shield did not escape harm, indeed he was to be seen in the tumult of battle fiercely resisting with his dented shield in hand. No cattle would be herded without him causing blood to spill on faces, and gore to flow over heads. Line 60 stresses his 'great cruelty' as his enemies fall in defence of their territory. The final mention of Owain which brings the poem to an end makes it quite clear who we are dealing with: Owain attacked for the sake of the 'blessed land of Erechwydd', a place closely connected with Urien in other sources, both in the praise poems to him in the Book of Taliesin and the englynion cycle attached to his name. It is a name to conjure with in Armes Prydain where the desire is for the Britons to extend their dominion *hyt Erechwyd* 'as far as Erechwydd'. The last line of our poem says that Owain's success resulted in *bud* 'profit' in the shape of dedicated drinking or carousel provided by his father, reminding us of Urien's traditional munificence — his mead and bragget as well as freely dispensed gold and silver — as acknowledged in the title of another prophetic poem, *Anrec Vryen*, 'Urien's Gift',[3] in which material about the old northern leader of the Britons' coalition against the Angles now does duty stiffening and giving lustre to the Welsh *Widerstand* in Wales.

Although some lines are unclear, it seems likely that the two men — Mabon and Owain, his first cousin once removed — are imagined as acting in

---

[1] EWGT 88.
[2] Other probably northern names such as *Cludwys vro*, *tir Gwydno*, *Calchuynyd* and *Rhun* are discussed in the notes.
[3] See General Introduction, 5.

concert in a northern theatre of war, possibly during the dotage of Urien whose grey hair and senior status is made much of in the Book of Taliesin praise poems. Jenny Rowland, however, believes that Mabon and Owain are enemies in this poem, and that Mabon is the main hero, with the cattle of Rheged 'apparently the chief victims'.[4] But the close kinship of the two men, and the evenhandedness of the praise accorded to each seems to suggest, rather, that both are being commemorated for their part in the northern resistance, if not together then as two parts of a common struggle. A significant comparandum in this respect would seem to be the prophetic poem 'Llynges Fôn' in the Red Book of Hergest (R1051.5-29, no earlier than the twelfth century, a copy of which may have been present in the Book of Taliesin when it was complete).[5] It has a similar feel to our present poem with its detritus of northern names, of Armes Prydain phraseology, and above all its conjunction of the two names, Mabon and Owain, in what would appear to be Gwynedd, and more specifically, Merfyniawn propaganda:

> **Penn beird pob eluyd o'th hen ovynnon,**
> *Chief poet of every region on account of your old rights,*
> **mi a'th ogyuarchaf ar ar6ydon**
> *I shall ask you about the signs*
> **py vynych gymhwylly Vabon,**
> *(and) how often you mention Mabon,*
> **Mabon karedic y gyweithyas.**
> *Mabon with his belovéd retinue.*
> **Goruchel awen ar weilgi las**
> *Like the high wind on the blue ocean*
> **llawen** (ms mabon) **oed Brythyon pan delon y6 hurdas,**
> *joyful would be the Britons when they'd come into their own*
> **ac Owein a uyd ryd r6yf [pob] teÿrnas.**
> *and Owain shall be the generous lord of every realm.*
> **G6r coch yg cochwed, gorawen G6yned,**
> *A red-haired man in battle, the delight of Gwynedd,*
> **gwreidyn** (ms gwreid hyn) **hil Meruyn, mur teÿrned,**
> *of the stock of Merfyn's line, defence of kings,*
> **caranna6c Uabon ym bronn g6aret.**
> *belovéd Mabon in the forefront of salvation.*
> **Kyuarwyd y6 Duw, y'm damunet**
> *God is (our) guide (and) I wish*
> **allmyn ar gychwyn, gochwed dyghet.**
> *the foreigners to be sent packing, that bloodshed will be their lot.*

In our present *Kychwedyl a'm dodyw* poem, there is no objection to seeing Mabon as the genuine name of one of the Coeling line. He, or another of the same name, is also mentioned in one of the praise poems to Gwallawg: PT XI.26

---

[4] EWSP 102.
[5] See LPBT 51-3.

kat ynracuydawl a mabon, in a list of nine battles.⁶ The name was known and used throughout the Brittonic world, as evidenced by the place-names Llanfabon and Rhiwabon (< Rhiw Fabon), and Maenor Fabon in Llandeilo Fawr, and by instances in the Book of Llandaf and Breton cartularies.⁷ There is no need to connect our poem character in function with Maponos 'the divine son' or to suppose that Maponos was a 'tribal god' with whom the Rheged ruling dynasty enjoyed a 'traditional association'.⁸

It is clear that we have North British characters and places in the poem, but the mentions of Deheubarth, Dyfed and the men of Gwent (*Gwenhwys*) make it very unlikely indeed that it is a real *Hen Ogledd* production, or that it dates from the time of Owain son of Urien.⁹ As Jenny Rowland says, it is 'a curious mixture of what seem to be remnants of northern tradition and darogan', and she wonders whether Mabon's role has been 'contaminated from prophetic literature'.¹⁰ But it is usually a *M/mab(an)*, not *mabon* that figures in prophecy; this fact has been blurred by the Llynges Fôn example where *mabon* has been taken as a type rather than a personal name as in our present poem.¹¹ And in fact, there is little of the straightforward prophetic mode evident in our text, in contrast, for instance, to the passage of Llynges Fôn quoted above. Our poem is more easily interpreted as Gwynedd propaganda, like others of the prophecies in the Book of Taliesin. The appropriation of the glamorous Old North may have allowed for an imaginative recasting, not unlike the 'back to the future' discourse of prophecy. Here, the old Coeling — Mabon, Owain, and Urien in the background — are refigured to shadow the men of Gwynedd, now presented as the true heirs of the northern heroic age, and thus a force to be reckoned with. The men of Gwent, Dyfed and Deheubarth need to beware. We know that the royal line of Gwynedd claimed the Coeling as their ancestors,¹² but whether this poem was produced to meet the needs of a specific leader, an Owain perhaps, is difficult to determine: the name is far too common to be of any help in this

---

⁶ See PT 125 for the interpretation 'a battle between Gwyddawl and Mabon', followed by H-cd and Clancy, TT 91. For the possibility of an alliance between Mabon and his brother Meurig fab Idno with Gwallawg (and against Urien and Owain), see EWSP 102-3.
⁷ LL 209.8, 75.28, 164.10; and further references in Patrick Sims-Williams, 'Shrewsbury School MS 7 and the Breton lays,' *CMCS* 60 (2010), 39-80, at pp. 58-9.
⁸ John T. Koch, CHAge 348. It is possible, as Ronald Hutton argues, in 'Medieval Welsh literature and pre-Christian deities', *CMCS* 61 (2011), 57-85, at p. 62, that the Maponos/Apollo dedications in Hexham, Corbridge, Ribchester and Brampton were due to Roman soldiers in the second and third centuries A.D. rather than reflecting a cult brought over from the Continent some six hundred years earlier by the Parisii. For full details about Mabon fab Modron, see TYP³ 424-8. Note that *mabon* (rather than *maban*) is used for Christ in C€ 11.34. The noun *maban*, like *mab*, is very common in prophecy for the promised deliverer, and is already present in the Black Book of Carmarthen prophecies
⁹ This was the view, too, of Thomas Jones, 'Datblygiadau cynnar chwedl Arthur', *B* 17 (1956-8), 235-51, at p. 241.
¹⁰ EWSP 102.
¹¹ See n. 7 above. In Pen. 50 there may be confusion of *maban* and *Mabon*: EVW 145.
¹² EWGT 36 and 46.

3 Kychwedyl a'm dodyw o Galchuynyd

regard.[13] Neither is it certain whether the poem was intended in any way as an object lesson in cousinly co-operation, a relationship frequently fraught with violence. The metre is mostly Cyhydedd Naw Ban with the occasional *toddaid byr* (lines 25-6, 48-9, 62-3) and other variations (lines 35-8, 39-40, 45-7). The poem's use of individual awdlau linked by similar opening lines may be compared with Marwnad Cynddylan, Armes Prydain, Edmyg Dinbych and Echrys Ynys, and many twelfth- and thirteenth-century court poems; in this collection, we may compare poems §7 Dygogan awen, and §8 Yn wir dymbi Romani kar.

---

[13] There are well on thirty candidates called Owain indexed in EWGT 207.

3 Kychwedyl a'm dodyw o Galchuynyd
Book of Taliesin 38.11-40.3

Kychwedyl a'm dodyw   o Galchuynyd:
Tidings have come to me from Calchfynydd
gwarth yn Deheubarth,   anreith clotryd.
of disgrace in Deheubarth, (and) of one famed in pillage.
Da a ryd y lew,[1] **dywaled y vedyd:**
Goods he provides for his brave men, (but) ferocity to the world:
llawn yw y ystrat,   lawen gynnyd,
his valley-floor is full — a joyous gain,
5   **llara llued peblet,   llara arallvro,**[2]
generous to the hosts of the people, generous to another region,
kat gormes   tratrachwres   bro.
an oppression in battle (and) fury in the land.
Odit o Gymry   a'e llafaro:
It is an exceptional one of the Cymry who would say this:
'Dyfet dygyrchet   biw mab Idno'
'Let the men of Dyfed attack the cattle of Idno's son'
ac ny llefessit   neb yny[3] **do,**
and nothing would be ventured where he'd come,
10   **yr talu can mu   arofvn**[4] **llo.**
despite the paying of a hundred cattle, (still) desiring a calf.
Goleith dy yscarant   amgant dy vro;
Your enemies avoid your region's border;
mal tan twym   tarth yn yt vo.
like a hot fire, there is a haze wherever it may be.
Pan gyrchassam-ni trwydet   ar tir Gwydno,
When we sought safe passage on Gwyddno's land,
oed kelein veinwen   rwg grayan a gro.
there was a slim white corpse between the shingle and the gravel.
15   **Pan ymchoeles echwyd   o Gludwys vro,**
When the flowing water retreated from the region of the Clyde men
nyt efrefwys buch   wrth y llo.
no cow lowed to her calf.
Gogyfarch Vabon   o arall vro[5]
Prominent (was) Mabon of another region

---
[1] ms *leu*
[2] ms *arall vro*
[3] ms *ny*
[4] ms *yrof vn*
[5] ms *kat*

3 Kychwedyl a'm dodyw o Galchuynyd

      pan amuc Owein   biw y vro.
when Owain fought for the cattle of his area.
Kat yn Ryt Alclut,   kat yn Ygwen,
A battle at the ford of Dumbarton Rock, a battle at Ywen,
20   **kat yg Gossulwyt,   a bann ud*y*n;**[6]
a battle at Gosulwyd, and loudly were they wailing;
kat rac Rodawys,   drych eirwyn:[7]
a battle before the men of Roda, white as snow in appearance,
gwaywawr[8] **du   a lleu lenyn.**
black spears and flashing . . . .
Kat tu man llachar,   *a*erlyw *a*erlin,[9]
A battle near a bright spot, battle leader of a battle-lineage,
yscwydawr yn llaw,   garthan yg gryn.
shields in the hand, an enclosure in the attack/clash of arms.
25   **A welei Vabon   ar ranwyn**[10] **reidawl**
Whoever Mabon on (his) eager fair-maned horse might spot
         rac biw Reget   y kymyscyn —
        (as) they were mingling in front of the cattle of Rheged —
oni bei ac adaned   yd ehettyn
unless they could fly with wings
rac Mabon, heb galaned   wy nyt ëyn.
they would not get away from Mabon without incurring corpses.
O gyfarfot discyn   a chychwyn kat,
Swooping to the fray and inciting battle
30   **gwlat Vabon gwehenyt   anoleithat;**
(came) the inescapable destroyer from the land of Mabon;
ban disgynnwys Owein   rac biw y tat,
when Owain attacked for the sake of his father's cattle,
tardei galch a chwyr   ac yspydat.
shield-lime and wax and thorn splintered.
Nyt yscafael y neb   dwyn biw moel*y*on[11]
It's no plunder for anyone to reave hornless cattle
kyt esclwch rac gwyr   rein, rudyon,
. . . . for fear of stiff, blood-stained men,
35   **rac pedrydan dande,**
for fear of a powerful fiery one,

---

[6] ms *udun*
[7] ms *eirwyn drych*
[8] ms *gwayawawr* with a compressed *a* before a wide form of *w*
[9] ms *derlyw derlin*
[10] ms *ranwen*
[11] ms *moel*

3 Kychwedyl a'm dodyw o Galchuynyd

    rac kadarn gyfwyre,
    for fear of a resolute stirring to arms,
    rac gwyar ar gnawt,
    for fear of blood on flesh,
    rac afar ys taenawt.[12]
    for fear of widespread distress.

    Kychwedyl a'm dodyw o leutired Deheu,
    Tidings have come to me from the open lands of the South,
40   **traeth rieu goreu**[13] **haelon,**
        lauded king, best of the generous ones,
    ny'th yogyfeirch *a*chwynogyon.[14]
    no complainants (need to) importune you.
    Am ryt or, am gwern y gatuaon:
    Around the boundary of the ford, around the marsh (are) his battalions:
    ban berit kat, ri rwyf dragon,
    when battle was brought about, dragon-lord king,
    gw*y*llt[15] **na ow*y*llt**[16] **biw rac Mabon.**
    cattle (were) agitated yet not panicked before Mabon.
45 **O gyfaruot gwrgun,**
    Because of a clash with a band of warriors
    bu kalaned o[17] **rëi yn Run,**
    there were corpses (and) booty in Rhun,
    bu llewenyd dybyd y vrein;
    there was the joy that always comes for ravens;
    ban ymadrawd gwyr gwedy nych*ein*[18] **— kat**
    loud (was) the recounting of men after the torments of battle
        nyt ef dieghis ysgwyt Owein:
        (that) Owain's shield did not escape harm:
50 **ysgwyt uolch wrthyat yg kat trablud.**
    a resister with a dented shield in the tumult of battle.
    Ny reei warthec heb wyneb rud
    He'd not herd cattle without (inflicting) a bloody face

---

[12] ms *ystaenawt*
[13] ms *goleu*
[14] ms *y ogyfeirch ochwynogyon*
[15] ms *billt*
[16] ms *owillt*
[17] ms *ned*
[18] ms *nuchien*

rudyon beuder biw, a mawr *i*rat:[19]
(on) the bloody ones of the cow track, with great cruelty:
gwyar gorgolche*i*[20] gwarthaf iat
blood washed over the top of the head(s)
ac ar wyneb gwyn y*t*[21] yr gaffat.
and was found on white face(s).

55 **Eurobell greulet gen*uein*[22] dullyat;**
Bloodstained (was) the golden saddle of the host's deployer;
preid Wenhwys iolin ○[23] dar*y*sceinat.[24]
the requested herd of the men of Gwent were dispersed.
Preid rac taer urwydyr, taer gyffestrawn,
(There was) a herd before a fierce battle, a fierce alien stock,
preid Pengyfylchi, keig ar yscwydawr,
the herd of Pengyfylchi, (and) spear on shields,
mawr discreinawr llafnawr am iat.
great ?steadfast ones, blades overhead.

60 **Kat y rac Owein mawr, mawr a irat,**
A battle before great Owain of great cruelty,
meindyd kwydynt-wy wyr yn amwyn gwlat.
at mid-day men were falling as they defended the land.
Pan disgynnwys Owein rac gwenwlat — Yrechwyd
When Owain attacked for the sake of the blessed land of Erechwydd
      gorer*y*fein[25] bud oe tat.
(there was) profit (in the form of) carousel from his father.

1 **Kychwedyl am dodyw** Cf. *Moliant Cadwallon* line 16 *Kychwedyl a'm dodyw o Wynedd glawr*; CBT V 2.7 *Kychwetyl a'm dothy6 am dwythualch ri.* Also found in LPBT 15.57-8 '*Henwyn*' *mat dyduc kychwedyl o Hiraduc*; CBT I 25.4 *gychwetyl gychwyrn*; CBT VI 8.24 *Yr pan doeth kychwedyl am l6yth Kichwein*; CBT IV 7.18 *Maurgof ar gychwetyl gychwynn*, the last referring to the slain Ithael fab Cedifor Wyddel, remembered as one who had given rise to favourable reports, presumably of his battle prowess. The much more common simplex *chwedleu*, 'tales', generally refers in poetry to 'tidings', often bearing news of battle, or death or defeat: see LPBT 21.19. *Chwedyl* with vb *dyfot*: CBT VII 30.14 *chwedyl a'm deubyd*; CBT II 23.1 *Chweddl a'm daw, dolur ei gofiain*; CBT VI 15.8 *Llawer chwedel anoeth a doeth Wyned*; CBT VII 15.23-4 *Chwetyl oer y euruab Ywein/ A'e gyfoeth a doeth o'e ddwyn*, etc. LlDC 17.45-7 (Oianau) *Rydibit attam ne chuetil dyfridauc/ penaetheu bychein anudonauc/ meiri*

---

[19] ms *yrat*
[20] ms *gorgolchel*
[21] ms *yd*
[22] ms *genem*
[23] ms *preid a*
[24] ms *daresteinat*
[25] ms *gorerefein*

3 Kychwedyl a'm dodyw o Galchuynyd

mangaled am pen keinhauc, and *passim*, in a tone rather similar to the present poem; CBT VII 5.2 *Ma6r a chwetyl a'm deffry*; CBT V 16.1 *Chwefra6r mis chweiris chweddyl diargel,—ma6r,/ Marw Gruffut uap Howel*; CBT I 24.23 *Chwedyl ma6r a'n deffry, neut ef deffryt*; CBT I 7.85 *Astrus chwetyl rychweirys y Gymry,/ Ystryw chwer6, nyd chweryan y ryle*.

The 3sg. perfect *dodyw* form (= ModW *doddyw*, and see GMW 134 for *dothyw, doethyw*) is reasonably common in prose and verse: found in CA line 1118 *Neum dodyw angkyvwng o angkyuarch*; Moliant Cadwallon line 16 (see above); *B* 26 (1974-6), 407 *Can dodyw pen Edwin lys Aberffraw* (Cadwallon fragment); LPBT 4.34 *neur dodyw ystygat* (recte). There are nine instances in the CBT corpus (including VI and VII, and examples by Prydydd y Moch and Cynddelw, and with infixed *'m*, e.g. CBT III 21.146 *Eilyw a'm dotyw*; CBT V 8.25 *Dy-m-dotyw edliw ac edlid*; GP p. 7, line 11 *dolur gormod a'm dodyw*; ten instances of the variant, *dothyw*, occur in the CBT corpus.

1 **o Galchuynyd** In favour of a northern location of this place is the character, Cadrawd Calchfynydd, reckoned in Bonedd Gwŷr y Gogledd (Pen. 45, late 13c) to be one of the brothers of Clydno Eidin, and one of four (sometimes five) sons of Cynwyd Cynwydion m. Cynfelyn of the line of Coel: EWGT 73 *Clydno Eidin a Chynan genhir a Chynuelyn drwsgyl a Chatrawt Calchuynyd, meibion Kynnwyt Kynnwydyon m. Kynuelyn m. Arthwys m. Mar m. Keneu m. Coel*. Bonedd y Saint and Achau'r Saint (EWGT 61, 70) note him also as ancestor of SS Tegfan and Elian. De Situ Brecheiniauc and Jesus 20 note that Cadrawd was married to Gwrygon (Goddau), daughter of Brychan (EWGT 16, 43), while Cognatio Brychan (EWGT 18) bills him, uniquely, as *Cradauc*, and his wife as *Grucon Guedu* ('widowed'): see further WCD 79-80. Cadrawd is mentioned as a touchstone of generosity by Gwilym Ddu o Arfon in an awdl praising Sir Gruffudd Llwyd ap Rhys *c*. 1316-18: GGDT 6.73 *Myfyr giried ced Cadrawd—Calchfynydd*. But this is the only occurrence of his name outside the genealogies.

No known place-name in Wales corresponds to Cadrawd's cognomen, Calchfynydd. FAB I, 172-3, following Chalmers, identified Calchfynydd with Kelso, south-east of Edinburgh in the Scottish Borders: "'It (Kelso) seems to have derived its ancient name of Calchow from a calcareous eminence which appears conspicuous in the middle of the town, and which is still called the Chalk Heugh'". This was endorsed by CPNS 343, but rejected as illogical by Kenneth Jackson, 'The Britons in Southern Scotland', *Antiquity* 29 (1955), 77-88, at p. 83 n. 13. CHAge 348 favours general south-central England (Cotswolds, Chilterns, Wessex Chalk Downs). For OE *calc* names (mostly in the south, but with exceptions such as Calke, Derbyshire), see David N. Parsons and Tania Styles, *The Vocabulary of English Place-Names: Brace-Cæster* (Nottingham, 2000), 125-7.

2 **gwarth yn Deheubarth** Cf. collocated *gwarth/parth*, AP line 155 *Saesson o pop parth y gwarth a'e deubyd*; LPBT 10.33 *mwyhaf gwarth y marth o parth Brython*; CA line 806 *ny doeth en diwarth o barth Vrython*.

Deheubarth in §8.44 *Arth o Deheubarth yn kyfarth Gwyned*; LlDC 17.142 (Afallenau) *Arth o Deheubarth a dirchafuy*; six instances in CBT, and collocated with *gwarth* in CBT VII 51.11 and 46.31. CA line 318 *Issac anuonawc o barth deheu* is reckoned to refer to an area south of the imagined locus of the Gododdin poet. Line 39 below, *o leutired Deheu*, links the opening of the two

3 Kychwedyl a'm dodyw o Galchuynyd

awdlau, and a south Walian context for this part of the poem is also suggested by the mention of Dyfed in line 8 below.

2 **anreith clotryd** Understanding genitival *anreith*, with commonly used substantival *clotryd* lit. 'one whose fame is free', cf. PT III.5 *gan clotuan clotryd*, discussed in PT 45 (cf. P. Sims-Williams, *B* 28 (1978-80), 402-3); CA line 1415 *clodryd keissidyd kysgut*; EWSP 421.13b *penn Vryen geiryawc glotryd*; Marwnad Cadwallon 9 *clotryd keissydyd kestwy*; Marwnad Cynddylan line 62 *clodrydd pob hael*; LPBT 19.3 *o dyuot clotryd*, etc. The *clotryd* here is understood as the renowned man who has inflicted the *gwarth* 'shame' or 'dishonour', on his enemies. But if *clotryd* is adjectival, as in e.g. Marwnad Cadwallon 4 *Lluest Gatwallawn glotryd*, then 'renowned pillaging' is possible too, cf. CHAge 349 'praiseworthy plunder'.

3 **Da a ryd y lew (ms leu)** Understanding substantival *da* 'wealth, goods, possessions, means; profit, benefit', e.g. CBT II 19.21 *Yr a del o da o dala tir—pressent*; CBT VI 3.1-2 *Kyt del y Ruffud, 6ud gynnan,—o dda/ A ddyglut mor y lan*; CBT VII 26.14 *Nyd etiw heb da ddyn y 6rtha6*. If subject, 'good man'.

Leu is treated here as the lenited form of *glew* (with *u* for [w]), and *y* perhaps an elision of the prep. *y* 'to, for' with the personal pron. *y*. If the reading is retained, then consider GPC s.v. *lleu*, 'light, brightness, bright', with 'open land' noted as a possibility, following *B* 21 (1964-6), 224-6: *lleutired* in line 39 below might favour this interpretation. GPC s.v. *llw* 'oath, vow' notes *llau* as one of many pl. forms. The rare *lleeu* pl. of *lle* (PT 80) seems unlikely here, as does the personal name *Lleu*.

3 **dywaled y vedyd** A hapax abstract noun from *dywal*, according to GPC s.v. *dywaledd* 'fierceness, cruelty' (cf. more common *dywalder*; also *dywalrwydd*). The line points up the contrast between the hero's magnanimity to his own fighting forces and his ferocity to others. Substantival *dywal* 'fierce warrior, brave fighter' is not attested with pl. ending *-ed* (= -edd), although that is not impossible. *Bedyd*, here 'world, Christendom', is very common, e.g. CA line 100 *a llavnawr llawn annawd em bedyd*; PT II.5 and III.1, etc. CHAge 349 offers 'herds of cattle which the violent one of Lleu's world will give to him'.

4 **Llawn yw y ystrat** Referring to the *ystrat* 'valley bottom' owned by the *clotryd* of line 2, perhaps populated by herds taken as booty? Or else an *ystrat* in Deheubarth, such as Ystrad Tywi? Not a common word in poetry outside CBT corpus (but note LPBT 7.11 and LlDC 30.22 and 40.29).

5 **llara llued peblet** *Llara* 'generous' is a disyllabic variant of *llary* (< L. *largus*), cf. CA line 1239 *oid guiu e mlaen llu llarahaf*; LlDC 2.5 *Gueithred llara llyuiau niuer*, and CC 25.3 *llara cloduaur*. This form is used as a personal name, e.g. NLW Mostyn 117 p. 268 (same hand as BT) *mab Llara*; BR 19.26-7 *Llara uab Kasnat* (recte *Kasnar*) *Wledic*. The monosyllabic form would give more regular pre-caesura and post-caesura patterns of five and four syllables respectively. *Llary/llara* is collocated with *llu* etc. in EWSP 420.8b *penn Vryen llary llywei llu*; Marwnad Cynddylan line 37 *a Rygyfarch lary lu pob eithaw*; §8.59 *llary lywyd lüyd*.

Peblet appears to be a form of *pybyl* 'people' (the pl. of *pobyl*, from L. *popul-*) with a pl. ending *-eð* appended. If so, it may have been unfamiliar to the scribe who left it in its orthographic form with *-et* for *-eð* and *e* for the schwa vowel. There are six instances of *pybl* in CBT, four of which are collocated with *pobyl*

3 Kychwedyl a'm dodyw o Galchuynyd

— CBT I 18.23; CBT I 6.3; 26.57; CBT VI 5.4 — as well as CBT VI 14.50; CBT I 9.100. Or is a formation from *pabl* 'vigorous' possible?

5   **llara arallvro** GPC² s.v. *arallfro* 'another country, strange land' (the present example is included with a query), also in §1.45 *keir aralluro*, and CBT II 3.13-14 *Caraf-y neirthyat naf a nerth—vy dull/ Ym dill6ng arallvro*, cf. *arallwlat*, CBT I 17.49 and CBT VII 45.9. 1. But note also *allfro* 'foreign land, foreigner', e.g. AP line 111 *A cherd ar alluro a ffo beunyd*, CBT VI 11.2, see GPC². The compound forms a tolerated rhyme with simplex *bro* in line 6. However, the scribe has written *arall vro* with a space. Koch, CHAge 349, wonders whether this might be equivalent to 'the other-realm'.

6   **tratrachwres bro** Although the form is not attested elsewhere, the final cadence appears regular and it may be an inspired nonce form with reduplicated prefix (one would expect *trathrachwres*). But if dittography is suspected, one might consider emending to *gordrachwres*, cf. CA lines 107-8 *bu truan . . . e neges ef ordrachwres drenghidyd*. *Trachwres* 'fury, wrath' (*tra* + *gwres* 'heat') is common enough, PT XI.13 *prenyal yw y pawb y trachwres*, and PT XI.19 *meidrawl yw y trachwres*; R1050.36-7 (Moch daw byd) *Ma6r trachwres llynghes Lloegyr a gyrchant*; CC 13.2c *llydan y drachwres* (of Christ); and in CBT corpus (three out of eight examples by Prydydd y Moch), sometimes collocated with forms in *troch-, trych-, trech-*, etc. *Trachwres* rhymed internally with *gormes*, as here, in CBT II 2.54 *Eryres ormes, trachwres trechaf*. Other compounds in *gwres* include *lluchwres* (CBT V 5.49). Cf. adj. CBT III 28.29 *Kyflauan trathan, tratherwyn—y haul*. If the initial *tra* is an prep. rather than an intensive prefix, then 'beyond, more than' is possible.

7   **Odit o Gymry a'e llafaro** *Odit* 'rare, singular, exceptional', also substantival, is used most often in hengerdd englyn poetry, especially in gnomic or proverbial statements, e.g. EWSP 426.47 *odit a uo molediw*. But cf. LPBT 4.51 *Odit traethator*; §1.11-12 *Odit a'e gwypwy*; §8.2 *odit o vab dyn, arall y par*. It is less common in the CBT corpus, where two out of three examples are by Prydydd y Moch, CBT V 8.28 and 36; otherwise CBT II 30.1.

A'e llafaro, note the innovative 3sg. subjunct. in *-o* (rather than *-wy*), here confirmed by end-rhyme. See Rodway, Dating 81-3 and LPBT 21-2. The vb *llefaru* is not very commonly used in poetry (though used by Cynddelw twice) with the exception of 3sg. *llefeir*, e.g. AP lines 22-3 *yg ketoed Kymry nat oed a telhyn;/ yssyd wr dylyedawc a lefeir hyn*, which may be compared with the tone of the present line.

8   **Dyfet dygyrchet biw mab Idno** Vb *dygyrchu* 'to make for, attack' is reasonably common, as in LPBT 14.52; AP line 83 *lleith anoleith ry dygyrchassant*; §8.17 *Elyrch dymdygyrch*; LlDC 18.203 (Englynion y Beddau) *dygirchei tarv trin ino treis*; five CBT examples by Cynddelw, Llywelyn Fardd and Prydydd y Moch. Interpreted here as 3sg. imperative. The past impers. is favoured in CHAge 349, despite the disjunction with the end of the line.

Biw 'cattle', a commonly used collective in nature and gnomic poetry; in cattle-raiding and provisioning, PT I.14 *Hac* (recte) *ny rywelet/ y biw rac ffriw neb*; PT V.8 *wyth vgein vn lliw o loi a biw*; LPBT 23.37 *Ry'm afei biw blith yr haf*; seven examples in CBT corpus, including CBT II 25.39 *Am biw Deifr de6r escor yt ysgymu—hael*.

3 Kychwedyl a'm dodyw o Galchuynyd

Dyfet 'men of Dyfed, in south-west Wales', in PT I.13 *Cruc Dymet*; AP lines 99 and 173; Edmyg Dinbych line 24 *noc eillon Deutraeth gwell kaeth Dyfet*; §8.77-8 *Nyt yscawn iolet/ gorescyn Dyuet*; LlDC 17.15, 145, 160, 219 (Oianau); R582.1-2 (Cyfoesi) *P6y g6ascar Lloegyr y ar Dyuet* (ms *diwed*) *mor*. Used especially by Prydydd Bychan who was from the area (but also by Gwynfardd Brycheiniog, Cynddelw, Prydydd y Moch, Dafydd Benfras, and others).

Idno < *iuð* 'lord' + *gno* 'famous'; see LHEB 562 n. 1 on provection [ðn] > [dn]. Idno is an uncommon personal name, with only one individual attested in the genealogies: Idno ap Meirchiawn ap Gorwst ap Cenau ap Coel Godebog in Bonedd y Saint, grandfather of king Elaeth (EWGT 62). His brothers, according to Bonedd yr Arwyr (EWGT 88), were Cynfarch (= father of Urien) and Elidir Lydanwyn. His sons were Meurig and Mabon. Mabon would be the first cousin of Urien, Owain's father. See the poem introduction.

9 **ac ny llefessit neb yny (ms ny) do** See GPC s.v. *llafasaf*: *llafasu* 'to dare, presume, risk, venture', here past impers., cf. LlDC 18.100-101 (Englynion y Beddau) *Pieu yr bet yn y mynyt/ a lyviasei luossit*; LlDC 17.11 (Oianau) *rac kinytion mordei bei llafassed*; CBT II 1.21-2 *Men na lleuessir dir o'e daered,/ Men y llauassaf oes darymred*; CBT II 2.16 *Y liwaw rac llaw ry-s-lla6assaf*; CBT IV 6.179 *Nyd yr lles nyd erlleuessir*; CBT VII 36.34 *Ny lyfassei Seis y ogleissyaw*.

G lists this example *ny do* as rare 3sg. pres. of vb *deuaf*: *dyfot* 'to come'. *Neb* 'someone, anyone; whosoever', and commonly used with neg. 'no-one', e.g. CBT V 28.9 *Nep ny wyr yn llwyr 6y lled6ryt*. The atypically short cadence might suggest restoring *o neb*, perhaps understanding *o* as indicating the agent of the impers. *llefessit*, or more simply *yny do* 'in the place where he comes' (as in the translation). Uncertain.

10 **yr talu can mu arofvn (ms yrof vn) llo** *Yrof* 'for my sake, for my benefit' seems difficult to accommodate unless the condensed diction may be indicating that the speaker would not be prepared to hand over a single calf despite a request for tribute of a 100 cows. CHAge 349 appears to emend > *yr* (which would give an atypical cadence), translating 'to pay a hundred cows for a single calf'. Here, a small emendation is implemented: *yrof vn* is emended to *arofvn*, see GPC^2 s.v. *arofun*, vb 'to desire' and noun 'wish, desire'.

11 **Goleith dy yscarant amgant dy vro** *Goleith* 3sg. pres., according to G (although 2sg. imperative, or noun are not impossible), 'avoid, retreat from'. *Amgant*, like *bro*, can also mean 'region': GPC^2 s.v. Elision between *dy* and *ysgarant* would yield a pentasyllabic first section, a common pattern in this section of the poem. Or else, understanding *goleith-dy* with (optional) emphasising personal pron., 'keep out of the way of the enemies around your region'. The first is more in keeping with the heroic tenor. The modernised text of H-cd seems to imply *dy* 'to'.

Yscarant is one of the pl. forms of *escar* 'enemy, foe, stranger', cf. §7.5 *yscarant*; CC 31.5b, *yn ysgar a'e ysgarant*, and four instances by Prydydd y Moch (CBT V 1.19; 14.16; 23.178 and 206), as well as CBT II 14.109 and CBT IV 4.6. The variant form *yscereint* occurs four times in the CBT corpus too (including CBT V 7.11); also LlDC 18.172 (Englynion y Beddau) *isscereint*. *Amgant* is also favoured by Prydydd y Moch, with five out of 11 CBT examples, otherwise only in LlDC 18.51 and 109 (Englynion y Beddau).

3 Kychwedyl a'm dodyw o Galchuynyd

12 **mal tan twym tarth yn yt vo** *Twym* 'warm' uncommon in poetry, but CC 2.37 *tuim ac oer*; CBT VII 17.8. *Tarth* in CA lines 749-50 *kemre tot tarth/ rac Garth Merin*; PT XII.39 *gwnn gwres. tarth gwres gwres tarth* (rhyming with *gwarth*).

13 **Pan gyrchassam-ni trwydet ar tir Gwydno** On *trwydet*, 'safe conduct, free passage, permit, leave', also 'support, maintenance, sustenance', see J.E. Caerwyn Williams, 'Trwydded, trwyddyd "ymborth"', *B* 27 (1976-8), 224-34; PT XII.31 *chwedlawc trwydedawc*; Edmyg Dinbych line 23 *ar vyn trwydet*; CC 21.90; CC 22.6; *B* 34 (1987), 68 (Pen. 21 Cadwallon fragment) *Neut gweilgi vyn trwydet, gwae vi Duw*; EWSP 414.1a *a elli di drwydded i hen*, and 3b *trwydded a geffi di anwyl*; 13 examples in CBT.

Tir Gwydno here, especially in light of line 14 *rwg grayan a gro*, recalls LlDC 39.3 *maes Guitnev*, the submerged land of the legendary Gwyddnau Garanhir whose loss was remembered by later poets, see WCD 346-8, TYP³ 391-2. He appears as a heroic survivor in a colloquy with Gwyn ap Nudd (LlDC poem 34, edited by Brynley F. Roberts, AH 311-8); his magic food hamper is one of the wedding desiderata in the tale of Culhwch ac Olwen, CO line 618; and in the late tale, *Ystoria Taliesin*, he is the owner of a bounteous weir on the R. Conwy, and father of the protagonist, Elffin, who becomes Taliesin's patron, YT lines 100ff. On this character Elffin, already Taliesin's patron in the Book of Taliesin poems, see LPBT 140-1. Gwyddnau/Gwyddno Garanhir is reckoned to be the son of Cawrdaf in the Bonedd Gwŷr y Gogledd tract, EWGT 73.

The genealogies have others called Gwyddno, listed in EWGT, and there is also the father of the Gododdin hero in CA line 326 *mur greit oed moleit ef mab Gwydneu*. In light of the *Cludwys vro* ('the region of the men of Clyde') in line 15 below, Gwyddno mab Dyfnwal Hen (EWGT 10, Harley 3859 *Guipno*) may be relevant here. His son, Neithon, was a ruler in Clyde and grandfather of the Owain mab Beli who slew Dyfnwal Frych of Dál Riada at the Battle of Strathcarron in 642, CA 969 and 975 (A and B text). *Tir Gwydno* might then be a northern regional designation, cf. *tir Brochuael* for Powys (EWSP 434), *tir Panna* (= Penda) for Mercia (CBT VI 35.68), *bro Dunawt* (EWSP 447), *bro Hiryell* (CBT II 27.10, VI 20.50), etc.

Phylip Brydydd also rhymes *Gwydno* with *gro*: CBT VI 11.15 *Gorwerd tonn tued Porth Gwydno/ Gar6 y llenn a grannwenn y gro*: this place is thought to be Y Borth in Ceredigion, making it not impossible that *tir Gwydno* here could be interpreted as a southern location. The *Porth Wydno* 'in the North' mentioned in the Pen. 50 'Names of the Island of Britain' tract is unlocated, TYP³ 236 and 255.

14 **oed kelein veinwen rwg grayan a gro** The first part echoes the repeated description of Urien's corpse in the englyn sequence, Celain Urien, EWSP 422 *Y gelein veinwen a oloir hediw/ a dan brid a mein*, etc. White corpses occur in CA line 476 *at gu kelein rein rud guen*; R1052.35 (Crist Iesu) *atuyd kelein wenn heb penn heb perthi*. Generally *meinwen* is used only of women in the CBT corpus and thereafter.

Rwg grayan a gro with a pair of alliterating near-synonyms: cf. EWSP 451.27b *y rwng graean a gro*; GC 7.38 *amdo gro a graean*; GIG 15.119 *Bwrw mân raean neu ro*; and further examples noted by G s.vv. *gro, graean*.

15 **pan ymchoeles echwyd o Gludwys vro** See GPC s.v. vb *ymchwelaf, ymchoelaf: ymchwelyd . . . ymchoelyd*, 'to return, go or come back, turn (back), turn over or up . . . upset', etc.; 3sg. pret. form *ymchoeles* also in LPBT 19.1. The vb is used

3 Kychwedyl a'm dodyw o Galchuynyd

in CC 14.80 *ymchueli*; 20.90 and 92 *ymchoelant*; R1049.38 (Anrheg Urien) *Bychan y lu yn ymchwelu*; rather infrequent in CBT, mainly vols. VI and VII.

Echwyd 'fresh water' (sometimes contrasted with *hallt* 'brine') is perhaps preferable, in the light of *tir Gwydno* in line 13 above and other watery references, to the homophone 'noon', see GPC s.vv. *echwyd^1* and *echwyd^2*; but the latter, used adverbially, 'at noon' would give good sense. If so, who then would be the subject of the vb: the fighting leader, or the *buch* 'cow' of line 16? Emendation to *Erechwyd* (CHAge 350) yields an unacceptably long line, although note its use in line 62 below, *gwenwlat Erechwyd*.

Cludwys 'men of Clyde', the region around the River Clyde in Scotland, cf. AP line 11 *Cornyw a Chludwys eu kynnwys genhyn*. Otherwise not found in pre-1283 poetry. There is also a region called Clud in Elfael, central Wales. The ending, derived from L. *-enses*, is seen below in line 21 *Rodawys*, in PT I.10 *Gwenhwys*; CBT II 14.89 *Mochnann6ys*; and *Lloegrwys, Argoedwys, Rhegedwys*, etc. The only other attested example of name + *vro* is by Prydydd y Moch, CBT V 28.3 *Carno 6ro, 6reinya6l addef*, although name + *gwlat*, etc. occur.

16 **nyt efrefwys buch wrth y llo** GPC lists no vb *efrefu* (simplex *brefu*: *brefaf*) perhaps following G s.v. *efrefu* who notes *nyt ef frefwy*s as a likely starting point, comparing *nyt ef* constructions G 443. The meaning remains the same. No cow needed to low to its calf because not a single calf had been taken from the herd by enemy raiders.

17 **Gogyfarch Vabon o arall vro kat** *Gogyfarch* 'to address, ask' (vb noun, also 3sg. pres., and 2sg. imperative), common in the Book of Taliesin and elsewhere, see LPBT 4.63n. If so, here with lenited subject. But G s.v. *gogyfarch*, followed by GPC, classes this as adj. 'certain, clear, obvious, evident', and they are followed here. However, the lenition may be a scribal mistake if 'manifest was Mabon . . . .' is the meaning. *Arall vro*, cf. line 5 above. On the identity of Mabon, see poem introduction. *Kat*, more usually 'battle' than 'battalion', is seemingly hypermetrical and may have been added through scribal anticipation of lines 19-21.

18 **pan amuc Owein biw y vro** See the poem introduction on Owain.

19 **Kat yn Ryt Alclut** Cf. the battle lists in PT I.9, 11-13 and 20; VII.21-3; XI.16-30; CBT I 3.131 and 133. *Ryt Alclut*, the ford of the Citadel of the Clyde, Dumbarton Rock, is mentioned in PT VII.21 *kat yn Ryt Alclut kat ymynuer*, and Thomas Jones, 'Datblygiadau cynnar chwedl Arthur', *B* 17 (1956-8), 235-51, at p. 241, suggested that our line appears to be a textual variant of that. Clancy, TT 355, with further details in 'The Kingdoms of the North: Poetry, Places, Politics', BGod 153-75, at p. 155, identifies *Ryt Alclut* as the medieval ford over the R. Clyde, just east of Dumbarton Rock, at Dumbuck Barrier. It is unclear whether this battle reference is alluding to the events of 870 when the Vikings besieged and overran Dumbarton (see below), or the 945 attack by the West Saxons under Edmund (helped by Dyfed forces, according to later English chronicle sources), or indeed attacks in the early 1030s: the evidence, as it relates particularly to one of the Book of Leinster tale titles, is reviewed by Tim Clarkson, 'The ravaging of Strathclyde: historical contexts for *Argain Sratha Cluada*', forthcoming, *CMCS* (2014).

Cair Brithon in the HB list of cities (Harley 3859 text), sometimes assumed to correspond to Dùn Breatann, Dumbarton, is not used elsewhere in Welsh sources.

3 Kychwedyl a'm dodyw o Galchuynyd

Bede's form *Alcluith* (HE I.i) is Irish, from *ail* 'rock' (Annals of Ulster *obsesio Ailech Cluathe*; Adamnán's *petra Cloithe*). *Arx alt clut* (AC 870), however, implies that it contains the word which became *allt* 'hill' (the Irish cognate of which is OIr *alt* 'cliff, bank'), as does *Aldclud* in some texts of Geoffrey of Monmouth, see HKB 283. Welsh sources use *Alclut*: AP line 151 and note p. 62 where it is suggested that -*l*- here is an older orthography for -*ll*- (see LHEB 400 on -lt > -ll- internally, but > -llt in word final position). However, *o Din Alclud goglet* shows that in the twelfth century the petrified earlier -*l*- form rather than -*ll*- was in use (CBT I 9.145), and this is confirmed by the spelling in chronicles and other prose texts. This might suggest dependence on written sources (and perhaps the influence of the Irish form), with no contact with oral Welsh forms, if any, which had developed to -ll-. See BGod 23-4.

19   **kat yn Ygwen**   Generic proest rhyme with line 20 *udun* (but see below on emendation to -*yn*). Although -*g*- often represents a nasal, *Yngwen* is not a known form; neither is *Ygwyn*, the form favoured in CHAge 350, there interpreted as the country of the *Iceni* tribe in later East Anglia; if *Iceni* had a long *e* it would give a falling diphthong *wy* in Welsh but such an *wy* would not give rhyme or proest in this sequence. *Ygwen* might represent a place- or river-name from *ywen* 'yew tree' (with orthographic -*gw*- for [w], as in *milguir*, etc. see CIB 213-14): see DP ii, 331-3 for Welsh instances. Less likely are *yng*, GPC s.v. *ing, yng* 'strait(s), extremity, press of battle, distress', or *wng* 'near, close; nearness, proximity', the latter more suitable to be qualified by adj. *gwyn/gwen* 'fair'.

20   **kat yg Gossulwyt**   *Gossulwyt* presumably a place-name, not identified by G. CPNS 210 suggests the element *gos*- in a name such as Gospartie (Fife) may derive from W. *gwas* 'abode, dwelling'. Place-names with *gos*- as first element include Gosforth, Newcastle upon Tyne, Northumberland; Gosforth near the coast in Cumbria; Gosforth Valley, Derbyshire; Gosport in Hampshire, etc., all containing the OE 'goose' word. Gossington, Gloucestershire, implies an OE personal name *Gosa*. A trisyllabic word would suit the patterning of the surrounding lines.

20   **a bann udyn (ms udun)**   *Bann* has a multitude of meanings, 'high, noble, splendid, loud' (also substantival), 'horn', 'verse, stanza, song', all possible here. *Udun* 3pl. *y* 'to, for', contrast §7.75 *udu*, but cf. CBT VI 27.92 *Oedd anhawdd iddun ei ddiofryd*; and LPBT 10.23 *vdun*. On this form, more common in poetry than prose, see Sims-Williams, Prepositions 20. The vb *udaw* 'to cry, howl' which gives good sense could only be entertained if emended to *udyn*, as proposed here.

21   **rac Rodawys**   Cf. line 15 *Cludwys*, for inhabitants of a region, but it is difficult to see what the underlying geographical name might be, unless a settlement named for an OE person *Rod(d)a*, or some form derived from the River Roden, a tributary of the Tern in Shropshire on which see §8.38. Is it perhaps a compound of *Tafwys* (written -*auuys*) 'Thames'? Otherwise consider a formation from *rot* 'circle, wheel, ?shield', as in *rodawc, rodle, rodwyd, rodawl*, etc. If medial *ð*, then connected perhaps with *rod* 'gift'. The -*wys* can also be appended to a vb root, e.g. *ffowys*, and to a noun, e.g. *mamwys, tadwys*, etc., see PT 51.

21   **drych eirwyn (ms eirwyn drych)**   G s.v. *drych* 'appearance, image' suggests that emendation is necessary, presumably for the rhyme — *drych eiry wyn* 'with a snow-white appearance'. The cadence suggests that *eiry* 'snow' might have been

3 Kychwedyl a'm dodyw o Galchuynyd

treated as a disyllable (see examples in G s.v. *eiry* including the *Otid eiry* sequence in LlDC 30.13-28). No other close compound *eiry* + *gwyn* is found but collocation with *gwyn* is very common. But consider possibly *erwyn* 'fierce, passionate', or for regular cadence, *drych eiry* (monosyllable) *gorwyn*.

22 **Gwaywawr (ms gwayawawr) du a lleu lenyn** Spears possibly stained with dark blood, as suggested by Day, Arfau 236, comparing Peirian Faban line 62 *A brein ar gelein a chicwein yn du*. *Dur* is a possible emendation, but in favour of *du* is the contrast between *du* and *lleu* 'light'. Could *lenyn* could be 3pl. pres. or imperf. of vb *llynaf: llynu*, GPC 'to infect, defile, corrupt; be infectious, ?smear'. G does not list a relevant form s.v. *glynu* 'adhere'. More extensive emendation might give *lleuueryn* 'were gleaming', with tolerable sense. CHAge 350 appears to connect *lenyn* with *glein* 'gem, pearl, jewel'.

23 **Kat tu man llachar aerlyw aerlin (ms derlyw derlin)** *Tu* is followed by a very faint continuation mark, suggesting that *tu* and *man* either side of the page are one word, an unidentified *Tuman*, although emendation to *lluman* 'banner' would give better alliteration. Nevertheless, *tu man llachar* makes reasonable sense and is undertood here. *Llachar* is also attested as a personal name, as in LlDC (Englynion y Beddau) 18.157 *Llachar mab Run*.

Derw almost invariably used for 'oak' in poetry, although found in some compounds with the meaning 'certain', e.g. *cefnderw*, possibly *Maeldderw*, etc. Cf. also compounds such as *derwgerd*, G s.v. *derw*. While *derlyw* and *derlin* could conceivably be formed from *derw* — true chieftain, true lineage, or chieftain like an oak, lineage like an oak — they would be hapax formations. G's suggestion that there has been scribal confusion between *d* and high-stroke *a* is plausible, especially since *aer* is an extremely productive first element. Cf. CBT II 24.43 *Gwerin aerlyw gwaith gyfeilyw Gwaith Gyfeiliawg*, and CBT III 7.36 *Oet eurllew o aerllin Gadyeith*.

24 **garthan yg gryn** *Yg gryn* CBT I 8.6; CBT III 3.122; V 10.71.

25 **A welei Vabon ar ranwyn (ms ranwen) reidawl** On Mabon, see poem introduction. Here either subject (as in translation) or object. *Ranwen* is emended to *ranwyn* for the rhyme. G s.v. *grann*, 'cheek; ?beard, hair, fur', notes *grannwynn* (fem. *-enn*) 'fair, handsome; ?fair-haired, light-maned', used variously of horses, waves, etc. Cf. PT II.20 *garanwynyon*, recte *granwynyon*, discussed PT 36-7. Most often used, as here, of horses (CBT V 14.36; CBT III 16.239). Note *grannwyn* collocated with *greit* by Cynddelw (CBT III 21.14 *Rad wehyn, grannwyn greid anoga6n*; CBT IV 9.53 *grannwyn greid worgra6d*; CBT IV 9.160 *Na'm g6rthryn, grannwyn greid wolwch*). *Greidawl* 'ardent, eager, passionate, fierce', is used in PT VII.35 of horses, *veirch o genedyl vrych mor greidawl* (see PT 89), of brave heroes in EWSP 420.5a and 420.6a (of Urien Rheged), and eight times in the CBT corpus, three times by Prydydd y Moch.

26 **rac biw Reget y kymyscyn** 3 pl. imperf. vb *kymysgu*, generally straightforward 'mix, mingle' (e.g. blood and brine, in CBT III 21.79, Marwnad Cadwallon 13, and elsewhere; water and jet in LPBT 18.25, etc.). But also 'to confuse'.

27 **oni bei ac adaned yd ehettyn** Strikingly similar to the idea at the close of the poem, Pais Dinogad, that not one of the hunter's prey would ever get clear unless they had wings: CA lines 1115-17 *Or sawl yt gyrhaedei dy dat ty a'e gicwein/ o wythwch a llewyn a llwyuein/ nyt anghei oll ny uei oradein*. The mother's voice portrays the dead father as a successful hunter wielding spear and staff, a form of

3 Kychwedyl a'm dodyw o Galchuynyd

heroism to which the boy Dinogad can aspire: see M. Haycock, '"Deunydd hyd Ddydd Brawd": Rhai Sylwadau ar Ferched ym Marddoniaeth yr Oesoedd Canol', in *Cymru a'r Cymry 2000 / Wales and the Welsh 2000*, edited by Geraint H. Jenkins (Aberystwyth, 2001), 41-70, at pp. 43-4.

28 **wy nyt ëyn** IIMWL 320 compares the syntax of R1035.14 *mi nyt af*, and LlDC 30.24, 36.7 and 40.31 *mi nyd aw*, and compare further CBT II 18.38 *Mi nyd wyf lawen*, and CBT VII 43.12 *Ef ni wnei becha6t*.

29 **O gyfarfot discyn a chychwyn kat** *Discyn* is very common in the Gododdin and throughout martial poetry. *Cyfarfot* 'encounter, battle', with inversion.

30 **gwehenyt anoleithat** G s.v. *gwehenyt* (? -*yð*) suggests a hapax nomen agentis either to be related to vb *gwahanu* 'separate, disperse' or else to vb *gwehyn* 'pull, loose, spill, pour, dispense'. If the latter, cf. *gwehenyawdyr* (GPC s.v. *gwehyniawdr*) 'pourer, dispenser', and later *gwehynnwr*. If -*t* does indeed represent -*ð*, as GPC s.v. *gwehynnydd, gwahennydd* agrees (suggesting 'drawer (of water), carrier (of water); pourer, emptier; destroyer, consumer'), the scribe may have failed to standardise the orthography, also using -*e*- for the schwa vowel. *Anoleithat* 'inescapable, irresistible' is also a hapax, but cf. *anoleithiawr* (GPC s.v.), LlDC 17.50 (Oianau) *anoleithauc*, and CBT I 3.66 *Penn rieu pareu anoleithya6c*.

32 **tardei galch a chwyr ac yspydat** The component parts of the shield — the limewash (*calch* is also used pars pro toto for the shield), the wax used to seal (cf. CA line 1227 *cuir oed arnav ac canet*) and the thorns or splinters of wood (*ysbydat* 'hawthorn(s), thorn bush(es)'). See further Day, Arfau 360. Vb *tardu* 'to split, break forth, crack, burst, jump', used of waters, rivers, springs, the heavens, vegetation, soldiers in battle, and arms.

33 **Nyt yscafael y neb dwyn biw moelyon (ms moel)** *Yscafael* 'booty, spoil(s), plunder, prey', in Marwnad Cynddylan lines 52-5 *Maured gymined mawr ysgafael/ y rhag Caer Luitcoed neus dug Moriael/ Pymtheccant muhyn a phum gwriael/ pedwar vgeinmeirch a seirch cychafael*; CBT III 16.219 (collocation with *Owein*); CBT IV 17.120; CBT VI 35.19 and 24.67. The metre is defective here so the pl. of *moel* is supplied. *Moel* is understood as 'hornless' (CHAge 350's 'speckled' is not possible), but see GPC s.v. *moel*[1] as a noun '(bare) mountain', etc. If so, 'cows from the hilltops'. Or else *moelyon* substantivally for 'bald men'.

34 **kyt esclwch rac gwyr rein rudyon** G has no suggestion for hapax *esclwch*. Could it be some bungled form of vb *ysglyfiaf: ysglyfio* 'to snatch, rob, plunder' or *kyt ef* + some verbal form? GPC s.v. *rhain* 'stiff', often of corpses, e.g. CA line 476 *at gu kelein rein rud guen*; CBT I 9.80 *A chalanet rein a rut uehyr*, etc.

35 **rac pedrydan dande** Adjectival formations in -*ðe* are common in the CBT corpus, and especially favoured by Prydydd y Moch (*tande, ysgarde, angde, eurde, creude*, etc.). *Pedrydan*, also *pedrydant* (as in §2.33 *O bedrydant dygnawt* and LPBT 5.60) is also well-attested in the court poetry, especially as an adj. describing soldiers, thus the suitable cognomen of Arthur's warrior, *Beduir Bedrydant*, LlDC 31.47.

36 **rac kadarn gyfwyre** Both noun *cyfwyre* 'arising, rising (for battle)' and vb noun *cyfwyrein* are found in court poetry, the latter predominating. CBT I 2.9 *kywlaun flamde kywvire vad*; CBT I 13.1 *Kalan Hyture, Kein kyuwyre*, and CBT I 13.4 *Ac*

3 Kychwedyl a'm dodyw o Galchuynyd

auar gyuwyre; CBT V 14.1 *Duw Sulgwyn y6 hynn, hynt gyuwyre—gly6*. Outside that corpus, Moliant Cadwallon line 37 *wrth y gyfwyre gynne Efrawc*. *Cyfwyre* is also attested as a personal name, LL 392-3 *Cimuireg, Comereg*.

37 **gwyar ar gnawt** Cf. §10.15 *Gweleis-i gelein vein a brein ar gnawt*; R1049.24 (Anrheg Urien) *a llauyn ar gna6t*.

38 **rac afar ys taenawt (ms ystaenawt)** *Afar* 'sorrow, grief', CA line 1157 *gwae ni rac galar ac avar gwastat*; CC 27.2 *am y dic a'e awar*; CC 20.71 *Teithïawc afar*; Marwnad Cadwallon 3 *auar anwar yw alon*; LPBT 8.5 *Gweleis treis trydar ac auar ac aghen*. Very common in court poetry; with *cyfwyre* CBT I 13.4 (see above).

Ystaenawt is unlikely here to be connected with *ystaen* 'tin, pewter', and the vb *staeniaf: staenu* (from E. *stain*) is not attested until the 15c. More likely is *taenawt*, an otherwise unattested adj. of the type discussed by CA 121 (cf. *baruawt*) connected with *taenu* 'to spread out', *ar daen* 'spread out', etc. The *-awt* verbal form discussed in LPBT 22 would not suit after the copula *ys*, while our example would be comparable with CA lines 329-30 *lletvegin is tawel kyn dyuot/ e dyd*.

39 **o leutired Deheu** See above on line 1 *Deheubarth*, and line 3 *da a ryd y leu*. On *lleudir* 'cleared, open land', see J.E. Caerwyn Williams, *B* 21 (1964-6), 224-6. Cf. §8.47 *gayaf kelenic yn lleutired*; LlDC 18.118 (Englynion y Beddau) *lleutir Guynnassed*; CBT II 6.3 *lleudir Goglet*; CBT III 3.51 *Breinha6c loc, leudir kyuannhed* (of the clas church of Meifod); CBT III 24.118 *hyt lewdir Trenn*; CBT III 16.53 *yn lleudir Meruynya6n*; CBT V 23.113 *Lleudir teyrn*; CBT VI 20.48 *llewdir Yst6yth ystrat*.

40 **traeth rieu goreu (ms goleu) haelon** Understanding *traeth* GPC 'declaration, statement, account, treatise, spoken, oral', the stem of the commonly used vb *traethu* and noun *traethawt*, see LPBT 4.29n, rather than *traeth* 'shore'. Cf. CBT I 23.17 *O Douyd y traeth tr6y gyhyded*, understood by its editors as a noun, comparing CBT IV 9.14 *Traeth o'm bronn tra thonn, tra thywa6d*; CBT I 21.28 *Traeth uolawt teilygda6t talu*.

Very common *rieu* is used as sg. as well as pl., and to address God as well as earthly kings. *Goleu* 'bright, fair' gives good sense, but may be a misreading of *goreu* in the light of *goreu/rieu* collocations: CBT V 1.123 *Ef goreu rieu hyd y ryduc—heul*; CBT V 1.45; 4.39; 26.95; CBT VI 36.13 and 53; CBT VII 24.87; 25.17. *Haelon* 'generous men'.

41 **ny'th yogyfeirch achwynogyon (ms nyth y ogyfeirch ochwynogyon)** G s.v. *gogyfarch* lists this tentatively with 3sg. pres. and s.v. *dyogyfarch* suggests *nyth (?ryth) (ð)yogyfeirch*. This would solve the seemingly redundant *y*, and yield a pre-caesura pattern of five syllables which appears to be the most regular pattern. G s.v. *achwynawc* 'complaining, whining' (and see *echwynaw*, a variant of *achwynaw*). The initial *o-* was perhaps copied under the influence of *ogyfeirch*, and is accordingly emended. Presumably there are no complaints about this man's generosity!

42 **Am ryt or am gwern y gatuaon** Consider emendation to *amrydar* 'dispute, contention' as in §6.27: 'a contention for/around the swamp of his battalions'. But as it stands, *ryt* 'ford' — 'around the boundary (*or*) of the ford', or 'many a ford'? G s.v. *amrwt* 'uncooked, raw' wonders whether *amryt* is related, but notes also the possibility of a formation from *pryt*, on which see GPC^2 s.v. *amhryd*

3 Kychwedyl a'm dodyw o Galchuynyd

'untimely, unseasonable, at an inappropriate or unlawful time'. *Am gwern* around the marsh' or (less likely) *am* 'many' + *gwern* 'alder stave', either with unrealised lenition.

Three examples of the compound *katuaon* in Cynddelw (CBT III 10.10; IV 4.223; 6.233), and one in LlDC 16.77 (Afallennau). *Gwern* 'alder', also 'alder stave'; 'swamp'. Alder strikes first in the tree-list portion of the poem Kat Godeu, *Gwern blaen llin/ a want gysseuin*, a leader as in Irish, see LPBT 5.75n.

43   **ban berit kat ri rwyf dragon** Cf. §8.43 *Gogwn pan perit kat ar Winued*; AP line 127 *Dygorfu Kymry y peri kat*; R585.19-20 (Gwasgargerdd) *Yn Aber (Per)ydon peritor* (recte) *kat*; CA line 267 *ac ysberi y beri creu*; CBT I 3.21 *peri ffossa6d*. *Ri, rwyf* and *dragon* are all very common. Found together in CBT V 4.32 *Yn moli Rodri, rwyf dragon*; *rwyf* + *dragon* in CBT III 20.43; *ri* + *rwyf*, CBT I 20.3 (of God).

44   **gwyllt (ms billt) na owyllt (ms owillt) biw rac Mabon** G has no suggestion for *billt*, unlisted by GPC. However, it may be an orthographical variant of *byllt*, the pl. of *bollt* 'bolt, dart, quarrel' (< ME *bolt*) although not attested until the 15c. Day, Arfau 346, suggests that bolts of crossbows may be intended. Consider also *pellt* 'wound, injury' (CBT I 8.16 *Cad mal bad aball a phellt ar grut*) and cf. CA line 208 *aessawr dellt anibellt a adawei*.

GPC regards *owillt* as hapax *gowyllt* 'wild, fierce'. Possibly relevant is the syntactic pattern discussed by GMW 232, *brenin na vrenhin* 'a king and (yet) not a king'; *mi na vi* 'I and (yet) not I'; *gwelit na welit*, etc. 'whether he was seen or not seen'. *Gwyllt na owyllt* would give some sense and account for the lenition — 'wild and yet not too wild' were the cattle before Mabon because he had them under control. 2sg. imperative and 3sg. pres. of vb *gwyllt(y)aw* 'to scare, frighten; become scared, wild' are not likely since they end in *-(y)a*. The 6 in 6*illt* may have been misread as *b*.

45   **O gyfaruot gwrgun** G s.v. *gwr* notes this hapax compound with *cun* 'pack, host of dogs', suggesting 'a brave host, band of heroes'.

46   **bu kalaned ned rëi yn Run** If *ned* is simple dittography repeating the ending of *kalaned*, it could be omitted yielding tolerable sense and a line length identical with line 47. The only known *ned* (apart from the River Nedd (< *Nida) in Glamorgan, contrast the River Nidd < *Nido-) is 'nits, parasite eggs'. Is this a way of referring to a multitude of corpses, or else to the corpses as a breeding ground for maggots? The disyllable *rëi* 'wealth, riches, booty' gives a better cadence than *rei* 'some'.

Run here appears to be the name of a place or a region, possibly for Gwynedd, the land of Maelgwn's son, Rhun, or to be associated with the river- or region-name *Run* mentioned in LlDC 16.27-8 (Afallennau), *Awallen peren a tyf tra Run/ kywaethlissvn e in y bon ir bot y wun*, beyond which the north British Coed Celyddon lies (Rhun therefore is not inconceivably Gwynedd if viewed from Wales). On the persons bearing the name, such as Rhun son of Urien, Rhun Rhyfeddfawr ('of great wealth') ab Einion, etc., see EWSP 86-7 and §1.48n.

47   **Bu llewenyd dybyd y vrein** Consuetudinal pres./fut. *dybyd* sits oddly with perfect *bu*; perhaps emend to *dybu*.

48   **Ban ymadrawd gwyr gwedy nychein (ms nuchien) kat** *Pan* 'when', as in line 43, is possible, but here *ban* is understood as adj. 'loud, noisy'. *Nuchien* is not attested, and although a name of a place or a region is possible, an emendation to

3 Kychwedyl a'm dodyw o Galchuynyd

an unattested pl. of *nych* 'torment, suffering, wound', etc. (see GPC s.v.) gives tolerable sense and a rhyme with *Owein*.

49 **nyt ef dieghis ysgwyt Owein** The topos that a true hero's shield is hacked away in the fray: some of the many examples are in GPC s.vv. *ysgwyd, rodawr, calch, tarian, cylchwy*.

50 **ysgwyt uolch wrthyat yg kat trablud** *Bolch* (fem. of *bwlch*) 'dented, full of holes', collocated with *ysgwyt*, CBT III 19.16 *Yn walch balch bolch ei ysgwyd*; CBT VII 18.6 *G6en, lawen ly6, ysgwyd uolch*. With synonym *tarian*, CBT III 20.16; CBT VII 52.27; CBT VII 55.19; CBT V 24.35 *bolcha6c—dy daryan*. *Gwrthyat* 'opposer, opponent, withstander', see CA 184.

Trablud 'confusion, tumult', cf. LlDC 34.16 *kad trablut*; EWSP 458.11 *Yn Llogborth gweleis drablud*, eight examples in CBT corpus. The vb *trabludyaw* in §6.23.

51 **Ny reei warthec heb wyneb rud** GPC s.v. *rheaf: rhe* 'to rise, go, set out, leave; (?dict.) run' includes this example, implying that *gwarthec* would be the subject of the instransitive vb. But a denominative vb *$grëu$ < gre 'herd' is implemented in the translation: this is a homophone of *grëu*, *crëu* 'to croak' generally used of birds. Rowland, EWSP 618, suggests, however, that it is the latter vb that we have here, translating, 'Cattle would not bellow who did not have a red face'. *Wyneb rud* of cattle is possible, or it may be used of an individual with a bloodstained or ruddy countenance, or even one shamefaced. See below on line 54 *wyneb gwyn*.

52 **Rudyon beuder biw a mawr irat (ms yrat)** The collocation with *biw*, also seen in EWSP 448.2a *Llem awel llwm benedyr byw*, favours the connection made with MIr *bóthar* (see GPC s.vv. *beuder^2* and *meidr*). The meaning 'cattle track' is satisfactory. See further EWSP 617-18.

G suggests restoring *yrat* to *irat* 'with great cruelty', in light of line 60 below, *mawr a irat*, a phrase which could conceivably be used twice. *Girat* is not at all common in poetry before the 14c (when it is used very often, mainly as an adj.), but cf. CBT VI 30.12. It is not at all certain whether the 'bloodstained' or 'red' ones refers to cattle (cf. Geraint's blood-reddened horses in EWSP 460.20-6) or to men (as in line 34 above, PT II.17 *wyr lletrudyon*; R1051.25 (Llynges Fôn) *rudyon galaned* — another poem which refers to an Owain and a Mabon: see poem introduction.

53 **gwyar gorgolchei (ms gorgolchel) gwarthaf iat** Cf. CA line 290 *gorgolches e greu y seirch*; AP line 76 *eu crysseu yn llawn creu a orolchant*.

54 **ar wyneb gwyn yd yr gaffat** The blanched faces of the warriors (cf. PT II.20 *garanwynyon*, recte *granwynyon*) or their corpses contrasted with the red blood. It seems possible that *yd yr* should be read *yt yr*, comparing the use of the two preverbs suggested for CBT II 4.14 *yt yr aeth*, and comparing 1.26 *yd yr uolhed*: 1.36 *yd yr lunhyed*. *Yt ry* is also found, e.g. CBT II 14.11 *Llys Ywein ar preid yt ryborthet—eiryoet*.

55 **eurobell greulet genuein (ms genem) dullyat** *Eurobell* 'golden or gilded saddle', a hapax compound. *Gobell* in CA 622-3 *gell e baladyr gell/ gellach e obell*. *Creulet* 'bloody' reasonably common for weapons, flesh (including that of Christ at his crucifixion).

3 Kychwedyl a'm dodyw o Galchuynyd

C/Genem is not attested, nor *c/genein*, and may be a slip for *cenuein* 'host, herd' which would yield good sense with noun *dullyat* 'a musterer, deployer' (this example is not included in G s.v. *dullyat*).

56   **preid Wenhwys iolin** ⇔ **darysceinat (ms preid a daresteinat)** *Gwenhwys* lenited after fem. sg. noun *preid* 'herd, spoil'. *Iolin* is not attested elsewhere but is undoubtedly to be linked with the vb *ioli* 'to entreat, supplicate'. The second part of the line is much too long, and *preid* (and perhaps *a*) may be omitted. The scribe was surely confused by several occurences of *preid*.

   Daresteinat is discussed by G who suggests 'crying, wailing' comparing *darstein* 'resound, cry out', *kystein*, *torstein* and *torsteinyaw*. This is followed by GPC s.v. *darsteiniad*, *darysteiniad* 'ringing or rechoing sound, resounding noise'. G notes however that it may be a corruption of a compound in *ysceinat*, cf. vb *ysgeinyaw* 'to disperse, spread, distribute, scatter', etc. This would certainly give good sense, either as a noun (see GPC s.v. *ysgeiniad*) or as impers. pret. of vb **daryscein/ -yaw*, as understood in the translation.

57   **taer gyffestrawn** G regards *kyffestrawn* as a compound of *kyffest* (< *ffest*) and *rawn* ('with stiff mane/hair') rather than of *kyff* + *estrawn*, the formation favoured by GPC and followed here. Irregular generic rhyme with *yscwydawr*.

58   **preid Pengyfylchi** Examples of *cyfylchi* (fem.) appear to be limited in the main to place-names, listed by G s.v. *cyfylchi*: Dwygyfylchi near Penmaen-mawr, Gwynedd (mentioned in CBT II 10.1), Y Gyfylchi near Pont-rhyd-y-fen, Morgannwg, and Y Gyfylchi between Llandogo and Trelleck in Gwent, the last mentioned in the Book of Llandaf, LL 156 *(y) Ciuilchi*. The lenition in the second element of unlocated *Pengyfylchi* could be due to it being an old close compound in **Penno-* (cf. *Penfro*) rather than due to a missing definite article. GPC suggests *cyfylchi* means 'a kind of circular stronghold or fortress' (< *cyfwlch* 'complete, entire', etc.). If, however, this is not a place-name but a description of the herd, perhaps their heads are fortified (?with horns, cf. *cyfylchig* 'horned' from 16c, see GPC s.v.) or imagined as being perfect or symmetrical.

59   **mawr discreinawr** G regarded *discreinawr* here and in CA line 41 *gwyar dis grein* and 247 *ef disgrein eg cat disgrein en aelawt*, as a vb form (cf. vb *creinyaw* 'wallow . . . fall, cast down; cringe, grovel', rather than a pl., but GPC follows CA 140 where the pl. of *disgrein* 'fearless, steadfast' (etymology uncertain) is favoured over a vb. Understood here as substantival.

61   **meindyd kwydynt-wy wyr yn amwyn gwlat** §7.51-2 *Meindyd brefawt/ meinoeth berwhawt*; LPBT 18.37 *py awr ymeindyd* and 7.8 *meinyd*. *Meindyd* with vb *amwyn*, CBT I 3.103. CHAge 351's 'early in the morning' is a slip.

   Kwydynt-wy 'they fell': redundant *-wy* perhaps through anticipating *wyr*. The intransitive vb is most common in poetry: CA line 377 *kwydei pym pymwnt rac y lavnawr*; lines 1170-2 *kwydassei lafnavr/ ar grannaur gwin*; line 171 *kwydyn gyuoedyon*; line 680 *kynrein en kwydaw/ val glas heit arnaw*; LlDC 31.45 *Pop cant id cuitin*; §8.22 *Cwydynt tyrch, torrynt toruoed taleu*; CBT IV 13.12, etc.

62   **Pan disgynnwys Owein rac gwenwlat Yrechwyd** See poem introduction on Owein and the mixture of northern and southern elements. *Gwyn/gwen* are common elements in the putative northern place-names of early poetry: see BGod 17. *Y/Erechwyd* is found in the Urien Rheged corpus, PT III.1, 18 and 19; VI.13; EWSP 420.19b (Pen Urien) *yr erechwyd oed uugeil*; EWSP 424-5 (englynion 37-39b and 44a); AP line 175 *Llettawt eu pennaeth tros Yrechwyd*. It is not found in

CBT. On its possible location in Swaledale, Yorkshire, see PT xlii, and see now Andrew Breeze, 'Yrechwydd and the River Ribble', *Northern History*, 47, no. 2 (2010), 319-23.

63   **gorerefein bud oe tat**   See G s.v. *goreryfein* on hapax, but cf. *eryf* and common vb *eryuet* CA lines 1144 and 1174; CBT III 24.108 *Yryuassam-ny ued6 uet y Drefwenn*; CBT IV *Ac yryued creu ac eryuein*; CBT II 2.55-7 *Eryueis dy win . . ./ Eryuaf dy 6et . . ./ Eryuant anant o eur*; CBT III 1.18 *Yryueis y'th lys*; CBT V 25.9-11 *yryueis y uet/ . . . / Yryueis y win o'e ualch vuelin*; R584.4-5 and 7-8 (Gwasgargedd) *Eryueis i o win o wydyr g6ynn . . . o ga6c*. If Owein is indeed Urien's son, as suggested by *Erechwyd* in line 62, then the famous 'father' (*tat*) would hardly need to be named.

4 Dygogan awen

Ifor Williams thought that this short poem of 29 lines may have been regarded as the small partner of the 199-line 'Great Prophecy of Britain' that bears the title *Arymes prydein vawr* in the manuscript.[1] This relationship, he thought, was signalled by the fact that the two poems begin with the same four lines. A further reason was that there are other such groupings in the manuscript. He mentioned the three poems *Gwawt lud y mawr*, 'Yn wir dymbi Romani kar' (with small marginal title *[Y]marwar llud mawr* written by the main hand), and *Ymarwar llud bychan*;[2] and the pair, *Kanu y byt mawr* and *Kanu y byt bychan*.[3] But there is no evidence that our poem was ever known as *Arymes Prydein Vechan*. Furthermore, given its unusual length, *Arymes Prydein Vawr* may have been a stand-alone title rather than one of a pair; and since it is partly concerned with the Britons' ancestral right to hegemony over the whole island, as well as current political and practical propaganda, arguably *c.* 927-42, it is not wholly out of the question that the poem's title, which may not be as old as the poem itself, meant or was understood as 'The Prophecy of Great Britain', that is of *Britannia maior*, as opposed to Brittany, *Britannia minor*.

Happily, the special relationship between the two poems perceived by Ifor Williams led him to discuss the present prophecy in some detail in his introduction to *Armes Prydein*, and to provide a fairly full translation.[4] He implies that lines 5-8 complete the first awdl or laisse (in the Cyhydedd Naw Ban metre), and that the second awdl, using a different metre, runs from line 9 to the end. In fact there are different syllabic patterns being used in this second section with the main rhyme in *-on* at the end of each of these groups:

> Lines 9-11 6/6/6[5]
> Lines 12-13 revert to an irregular Cyhydedd Naw Ban with rhyme suspension in line 12 compensated for by internal rhyme; line 13 rhymes in *-on*.
> Lines 14-16 6/5/5
> Lines 17-20 6/6/6/6, an extended group.
> Lines 21-3 5/5/6. This group forms a type of Traeanog in which the first and second units rhyme (*-eb*), and the third is linked by alliteration (*neb/na*). Such patterns are to be seen in the Gododdin[6] as well as in examples by Cynddelw, Gwalchmai and Prydydd y Moch.[7]
> Lines 24-6 5/5/5
> Lines 27-9 5/6/6

---

[1] AP xl-xlv.
[2] Poems §§7, 8 and 9 in this collection.
[3] LPBT poems 25 and 26. The ambiguity of their titles is discussed in LPBT 535. Further conscious pairings such as *Kanu y Med* with *Kanu y Cwrwf*, and *Arymes Prydein Vawr* with *Arymes Dyd Brawt* are not relevant to the argument here.
[4] AP xlii-xliii.
[5] Cf. CA lines 213-15 *a werthws e eneit/ er wyneb grybwylleit;/ a llavyn lliveit lladei*.
[6] E.g. CA lines 112-14 *ny bu mor gyffor/ o Eidyn ysgor/ a esgarei oswyd*.
[7] E.g. CBT V 24.51-2 *A gwaed a bwyd brein,/ a bran ar gelein,/ A galon aduutya6c*, discussed by Peredur Lynch, 'Yr awdl a'i mesurau', in FS Gruffydd 258-87, at p. 267.

The syllabic irregularity suggests that the metre is being driven by a strong pulse of two beats per unit[8] and by the return to the main rhyme at the end of each group of units.

Ifor Williams's comments on the content focus on the portion from line 14 onwards. He connects *Llyminawc* 'leaping one' with the figure from over the sea, also *llyminauc*, who was prophesied by Myrddin according to *Historia Gruffudd ap Cynan*, concluding that the poem alludes to Gruffudd ap Cynan of Gwynedd (d. 1137). The problem here is that such a term may have been used of many different individuals, as was *maban* 'youth' elsewhere in prophecy, or the *Gwr o Gud* 'Man from Hiding' in line 24, or the flexible *Mab Darogan* 'Prophesied Son' of the later medieval period. The author of Gruffudd ap Cynan's biography naturally wished to see his man as fulfilling Myrddin's prophecy and assuming the *Llyminawc* role; but others may have done the same. The *Llyminawc* of our poem as well as conquering Anglesey — which Gruffudd did — will bring devastation or ruin to Gwynedd. Certainly, there were many fierce battles before Gruffudd was able to establish his rule in Gwynedd — at Gwaederw, Bron yr Erw, and Mynydd Carn, for example — and there were great losses sustained by his opponents. 'And so with all his enemies finally routed, and with their lands reduced totally to desert, he was received with honour into his paternal inheritance and began to rule' (VGFC 70, §18). His biographer notes how Gruffudd made a great circuit of his territory (VGFC 62, §12), which could conceivably be matched with our lines 18-19 *oe heithaf oe pherued,/ oe dechreu oe diwed*, but the exploits set out in the poem are not specific enough to allow any certainty. Ifor Williams implies that Rhys ap Tewdwr, initially Gruffudd's ally in the south before the battle of Mynydd Carn in 1081 and the devastation of Deheubarth, is also named in the poem, but without specifying whether Rhys is the 'Man from Hiding' who spills the blood of the *gynhon* (foreigners, i.e. Scandinavians, Normans, or English), or whether he is the shadowy third man in the final section, one who 'will bring joy to the Britons'. Given this uncertainty, Ifor Williams's dating of the poem to the 'last quarter of the eleventh century'[9] on the basis of these identifications can be no more than a possibility.

Margaret Enid Griffiths was rather more guarded, if confused. While allowing that Gruffudd ap Cynan was a possible candidate for the *Llyminawc* of line 14, she suggested that it might refer rather to Cadwaladr, also possibly the Man from Hiding (*Gwr o Gud*) battling against the foreigners (*gynhon*) — unless that figure were identified as Cynan on the basis of the Cyfoesi reference to Cynan as an *Unic o Gud*.[10] The last argument is flawed by assuming a one-to-one correspondence between a historical figure and a prophecy designation or cipher, a correspondence which Griffiths was happy to relinquish in the case of the *Llyminawc,* where her argument was driven by her view that 'there is no

---

[8] Identical with Class 1 lines: see LPBT 36-9.
[9] AP xlii-iii; TYP³ 416.
[10] EVW 121-2. See notes on line 24.

4 Dygogan awen

reference [in the present poem] to the Normans or any events after the Norman conquest'. But this cannot be ruled out since the term *gynhon* 'foreigners' (line 26), not necessarily restricted to the Danes as she assumed, might have included the Normans.[11] In any case, a lack of explicit Normans cannot be a sound reason for placing the poem in the 'period prior to the Norman conquest'[12] especially in view of the considerations discussed in the General Introduction — about the casting of prophetic discourse *as though* it emanated from the past.

As well as foretelling final victory (lines 1-4), and the coming of three martial figures in the section discussed above (lines 14-29), the poem looks back to the 'seven sons of Beli' and the affliction brought about by Caswallon and by Lludd, the brother most drawn in to prophetic discourse. The tale, *Cyfranc Lludd a Llefelys*, where he is presented as a stout defender of the Island of Britain against invaders, and poems §§7 and 9 of the present collection (which bear Lludd's name) are discussed in the introduction to §9. It is interesting how line 7 of our poem introduces another son of another Beli, sliding from the semi-legendary Beli father of Caswallon and Lludd, to a historical, if shadowy, Beli who was the grandfather of Cadwallon of Gwynedd, and therefore living in the late sixth and early seventh century. His may be the *dormitatio* obit of 615 recorded by the Annales Cambriae A text. If he fell at the Battle of Chester, as the Annales Cambriae B text states, then his passing may have been coupled with the political turmoil (cf. line 8 *gwlat uerw hyt Vlathaon*) which may have ensued as Northumbrian influence in the Welsh borders increased. Bede's account (HE II.ii) has no mention of him, only of a *defensor* Brochfael (of Powys) who 'with his men', *cum suis*,[13] failed to defend the massed ranks of the Bangor (on Dee) monks; the Chronicle of Ireland, dating the battle to 613, states that Brochfael's grandson, Selyf ap Cynan, was killed there.[14] The final figure in our poem who arrives to bring 'joy to the Britons' is unknown, but may be coded discourse for a Llywelyn (?ab Iorwerth) whose name is collocated not only with *llew*, but also very frequently with *llawen*, and *llywenyd/llawenyd/llewenyd*.[15]

The first four lines obviously indicate familiarity with Armes Prydain, a text now convincingly argued by T.M. Charles-Edwards to be of Gwynedd provenance, but clearly aimed at the southerners. He would favour a dating *c*. 939-42, at a juncture when Gwynedd, but not Dyfed nor Glywysing, were allied with Olaf Guthfrithsson, arguing that it was the allegiance of the southerners to the English overlord, Æthelstan (and then Edmund) that Armes Prydain was challenging; it was to persuade them to join the coalition of opposition to

---

[11] See notes on line 26.
[12] EVW 122.
[13] Patrick Sims-Williams suggested in an unpublished lecture to the Powysland Club in 2011 that a phrase such as *uir Brocmail* 'the grandson of Brochfael' was misunderstood as 'men of Brochfael'.
[14] WaB 389.
[15] CBT I 7.55-6; III 6.5-6; IV 13.36 *Dydd llawenydd Llywelyn*; CBT VI 18.10; 24.85-6 *Llywelyn . . ./ Lly6 ana6 llywenyd dreulaw6*; 34.8-9 *Llywelyn vrddyn, vrddas hynaf,/ Llawenydd Cymru cymrodeddaf*; CBT VII 36.5, etc.

Wessex which included Gwynedd, the Hiberno-Norse of Dublin, the Gaels of Alba, and the *Cludwys* (understood as Cumbrians).[16] As a supplementary argument, he mentions the present poem's provenance, 'clearly from Gwynedd'.[17] Clearly, however, there is no certainty that the whole of our present poem is to be assigned to the tenth century. The recycled opening lines of Armes Prydain provided a handy general, all-purpose introduction setting the stage for a looser poem running through a succession of deliverers, legendary as well as historical who will repulse the foreigners and 'bring joy to the Britons'.

---

[16] WaB 532-5. See above, General Introduction, 3.
[17] WaB 533.

4 Dygogan awen
Book of Taliesin 70.16-71.6

Dygogan awen   dygobryssyn;
The awen foretells that they will hasten;
maranhed a meuued   a hed genhyn.
wealth and possessions and peace (shall be) ours,
a phennaeth ehalaeth   a ffraeth vnbyn;
and extensive dominion and eager leaders;
a gwedy dyhed, anhed   ym pop mehyn.
and after warfare, settlement in every place.

5   **Seith meib o Veli   dyrchafyssyn:**
Seven sons from Beli had arisen:
Kaswallawn a Llud   achy**studyn;**[1]
Caswallon and Lludd used to cause affliction;
diwed plo coll Iago   o tir Prydyn:
the final ?fateful blow the loss of Iago from the land of Prydyn:
gwlat uerw dyderuyd   hyt Vlatha**on,**[2]
it will become a land in turmoil as far as (Penrhyn) Blathaon,

lludedic eu ho*l***wyn,**[3]
their steeds exhausted,
10   **ymdeithic eu hafwyn,**
their reins abandoned,
gwlat wehyn vargotyon.
with borderers laying waste the country.

Kollawt Kymry   oll eu haelder
All the Cymry will lose their munificence
yn rygystlyned   o pennaeth weisson.
in a great acknowledging of a vassal rule.

Rydybyd Llyminawc
There shall come a leaping one
15   **a uyd gwr chwannawc**
who shall be a man keen
y werescyn Mon,
to conquer Anglesey,
a rewinyaw Gwyned
and to bring ruin to Gwynedd

---
[1] ms *achestudyn*
[2] ms *Valaon*
[3] ms *hoelyon*

4 Dygogan awen

        o'e heithaf o'e pherued,
        from its outermost edge to its centre,
        o'e dechreu o'e diwed,
        from its beginning to its end,
20   **a chymryt y gwystlon.**
        and to seize its hostages.

        Ystic y wyneb
        One of steadfast honour
        nyt estwg y neb —
        who bows to no-one —
        na Chymry na Saesson.
        neither (to) the Cymry or the Saxons.

        Dydaw Gwr o G*u*d[1]
        There shall come a Man from Hiding
25   **a wna kyfamrud**
        who will cause bloodshed
        a chat y gynhon.
        and battle for the foreigners.

        Arall a dyfyd —
        Another shall come —
        pellenawc y lüyd —
        one with hosts ranging far —
        llewenyd y Vrython.
        (bringing) joy to the Britons.

1-4   Exactly the same as AP lines 1-4, with minor variations in the spelling: AP has *maraned* and *ehelaeth*. See notes AP 16-18.

1   **Dygogan awen** The vb again in AP line 13 *dygoganher*; R1051.3 (Moch daw byd) *Dygoganaf tyfyrru erymes tra bytha6t*. Far more common in prophecy is the vb *disgogan/dysgogan*: AP lines 17 *Dysgogan Myrdin*; 107 *Dysgogan awen*; 171 *Dysgogan derwydon*; LlDC 16.68 (Afallennau) *Disgogan hwimleian*; Pen3Afallennau 125.116 *disgogan chwibleian*; CBT III 16.1 *Dysgogan derwyton*. *Disgoganaf* is also very common in the Afallennau and the Oianau (see LlDC 136 s.v. *disgogan*, which agrees with GPC and AP 16 in regarding *dis-* as an intensifier rather than preverb *dy-* + infixed pron.); Pen3Cyfoesi 117.122 and Pen3Oianau 125.137 *disgoganaf*.

     Both vbs are based on the simplex vb *gogan(u)* 'to sing, praise', with secondary pejorative meaning: CC 10.17 *Beird a'th gogan*; CBT I 20.1 *Goganaw i Arglwyd*

---

[1] ms *gwd*

4 Dygogan awen

gogonavl; CBT V 5.61 *Mad gogant molyant*. See also on §7.1 *Kathyl goreu gogant*.
    There are examples, especially in poetry, of the retention of the system of no lenition after the preverb *dy*- but spirantisation of *p, t*, and *c*, as explained by J. Strachan, 'On some mutations of initial consonants in the Old-Welsh verb', *Ériu* 3 (1907), 26-8. At the beginning of his great awdl in praise of Owain Cyfeiliog, Cynddelw uses a startling run of examples, possibly to maintain the vatic feel established by the opening *Dysgogan derwyton*: CBT III 16.7, 8-9, 11 *dygost6g* and *dygwystyl*; 12 *dygwan*; 14 *dyg6asgar*. The status of the *g* after the preverb *dy*- is somewhat clouded by the possibilities of orthographically unrealised lenition (as in OW), or of an invisible infixed pron., or reformation, but it is hard to accept the assertion in AP 16 that -*g*- is merely a survival of OW orthography in all cases: other poetry comparanda include §2.34 *dygorelwi*; §9.3 *dygorescynnan*; AP line 125 *dygorfu*; LPBT 5.59 *dygottorynt*; CA lines 142 *dygollouit* [*recte* -*ei*], 658 *dygoglawd tonn*, 675 *dygodolyn*, 1420 *dygwgei*; LlDC 17.9 (Oianau) *gur digorbit*; R1056.10 (Gosymdaith line 63) *dyg6rthryn gro*.

1   **dygobryssyn** See above on medial -*g*- and -*b*-. No other examples of this vb are attested, but cf. EWSP 454.8 *diuryssint*. With -*n* (< 3pl. -*nt*) in rhyme position, as in line 5 below *dyrchyafyssyn*, cf. CA lines 361 *wy lladassan* and 362 *nyt atcorsan*; LlDC (Ymddiddan Myrddin a Thaliesin) 1.9 *dygan*; 11 *deuthan*; 21 *doethan*; 24 *darparan*; 26 *breuaul vidan*; 34 *dylanuan*; 36 *daruuan*; EWSP 415.9 *llwybryn*; elsewhere CC 1.2 *treithin*; LlDC 1.35 *a aethan ygwllon*; CA lines 1224 *techin* and 1306 *yd aethan*, etc. See further GMW 120 for OW and prose examples, and note rhymed court poetry examples: CBT II 1.166 *nyd ymgelann*; II 5.38-40 *holldan/dangossan/briwan*; V 23.84 *dylochassan*. Non-rhyming examples include CBT I 3.43 *Atgoryn*; 3.111 *tertyn*; 9.18 *Dychysgogan*; II 14.82 *Kerdyn*; 26.235 *aethan*; III 26.51 *Kertoryon kertassan*; VI 31.47 *a borthyn*; 35.18 *a dreissyn*; VII 42.17 *a gredan*. The form without -*t* was clearly a poetic option across the board and not restricted to less formal song: see now Rodway, Dating 58-60.

2   **maranhed a meued a hed genhyn** *marannhed* rhymes with *hed* in CBT III 3.7-8. *Genhyn* common in AP, but not frequent elsewhere in poetry; §8.51 *eu meuoed genhyn*; CC 24.71; 26.8c *Duu genhin*; CA line 689 *aethant e genhyn*; LlDC 16.25 (Afallennau) *nyd ant y kenhin*; CBT III 3.134 *seuit Duw gennhynn*; and V 25.39. See Sims-Williams, Prepositions 11-14.

3   **a phennaeth ehalaeth a ffraeth vnbyn** *Ehalaeth* is common in Black Book, and is used throughout the Cyfoesi (R577.83); *ehelaeth*, as in §1.22 (rhyming with *ffraeth*), is the more common in the CBT corpus, but cf. CBT III 16.65 and V 23.33 *ehalaeth*.

4   **anhed ym pop mehyn** *Anhed* 'settlement', cf. §7.43-4 *diffeith Moni a Lleenni,/ ac Eryri anhed yndi*; §7.46 *anhed yn diffeith*. *Anhed* rhymes with *dyhed* in CBT II 1.71-2; and II 6.7-8. *Mehyn* 'place' is restricted to Book of Taliesin poetry and Pen. 50 prophecy (GPC s.v.: *kat ymob mehyn*): §7.92; CC 20.65; LPBT 4.137; Edmyg Dinbych line 15 *yn eil mehyn*; PT VII.20 *yn eil mehyn*.

5   **Seith meib o Veli** Pl. after the numeral is common, see GMW 47 and R.G. Roberts, 'Arolwg o hanfodion gramadeg y rhifolion mewn Cymraeg Canol Cynnar', *Dwned* 18 (2012), 33-48. Cf. LlDC 1.29 (Ymddiddan Myrddin a Thaliesin) *Seith meib Eliffer, seith guir ban brouher*; EWSP 413.3 *Tri meib*

4 Dygogan awen

Llywarch; 407.24 *Pedwarmeib ar hugeint*; CC 8.12, 13, 17, 19 *Deudec meib yr Isräel*; PKM 76 *Tri meib Giluaethwy enwir*; CBT I 10.27 *a thri meib Gruffut*; IV 16.186; and VII 54 (title) *Trimeib*. On the counting topos in prophecy, see General Introduction.

See on §2.3 *Beli wirawt* where the various figures of that name are discussed. Here, Beli son of Mynogan, presumably, since he is noted in *Branwen* as the father of Caswallon (PKM 45), and, through his daughter Penarddun's two consorts, the grandfather of Brân, Manawydan, Nisien and Efnisien (PKM 29). In *Breuddwyd Maxen*, Macsen emperor of Rome conquered the island from Beli and his sons and drove them over the sea (BMax lines 208-9). The Welsh Bruts make Geoffrey's Heli into Beli (father of Caswallon, Lludd and Nynio). According to *Cyfranc Lludd and Llefelys*, Llefelys was a fourth son. The phrasing *o Veli* suggests that the seven are 'of the line of Beli', which could include descendants as well as the actual sons, Caswallon and Lludd, mentioned here. Another is perhaps to be found in *achestudyn* (see below). After Iago, the remaining three are those figures referred to as the 'Leaper' (*Llyminawc*), the 'Man from Hiding' (*Gwr o Gud*), and an unnamed 'Other' (*Arall*). Iago bridges between the legendary past and future. This would be an alternative to supposing with TYP^3 416 and CLlaLl xiii that some lines are missing after line 6.

o Veli, cf. CBT III 24.160 *O Gadell ener, o Gadellig*; 26.128 *Hwnn oet lew o Leissya6n*; VI 7.21-2 *Handwyd . . ./ O Lary uab Casnar*. Very much more common, however is *o hil/lin* + personal name: CBT I 8.53-5 *Ardwyreaf hael o hil balch Run,/ O Vaelg6n G6ynet . . .,/ O Gadwallawn Lla6hir*; CBT V 2.13 *hael o hil Beli*; VII 24.39 *haelryw o hil Beli*; VII 54.29 *o lin Beli*. Although Beli son of Mynogan is probably meant here, the name may have put the poet in mind of Beli son of Rhun son of Maelgwn Gwynedd who had a son called Iago, on whom see line 7 below.

5 **dyrchafyssyn** Unique 3pl. pluperfect attestation (wrongly modernised from original *-essyn*, according to H-cd) of the vb *dyrchafu/-ael* 'to arise; lift up' (cf. *dydyrchafu*) which is used often in prophecy, frequently of promised deliverers: §8.24 *dydyrchafwy dreic o barth Dehev*; LlDC 16.12 *Dyrchafaud maban in advan y Dehev*; 17.42 *Arth o Deheubarth a dirchafuy*; 17.158 *Dirchafaud dreic faud fau isperi*; 17.180 *Maban dirchavaud mad y Vrython*; R579.19 (Cyfoesi) *Dyrchaua6t unic o gud*; LPBT 9.68 *Dyrchafawt gwledic*; AP lines 82 *Rydrychafwynt Kymry* and 178 *rydrychafwynt Gymry*. Used of raising a standard or cross and weapons, e.g. §6.1 *Rydyrchafwy Duw ar plwyf<> Brython/ arwyd llewenyd . . .* ; AP 129 *A lluman glan Dewi a drychafant*; CC 3.10-11 *Ry drychafom . . . Croes Crist*; PT VI.15 and 17. Other common uses collected by G.

6 **Caswallawn** The present example and Cynddelw's references are the only early poetic mentions of Caswallon. In *Branwen*, Caswallon uses his magic powers to make himself invisible and succeeds in defeating the seven *kynweissyeit* of Britain charged with ruling during Brân's absence in Ireland (but sparing Caradog ap Brân), and is crowned king in London. In *Manawydan* he is mentioned as residing in Kent, then Oxford where he receives Pryderi's homage. He was a touchstone of valour in 12c Powys for Cynddelw as he praised Owain Cyfeiliog (CBT III 16.42 *Kedernyd Kasswallawn*) and Iorwerth Goch, son of Madog ap Maredudd (CBT III 12.25 *Caswallawn eisior*), and a Madog (Rhirid Flaidd's son or Madog ap Maredudd), lauded as the strong defence of *cor Caswallawn* (CBT

4 Dygogan awen

III 24.134). In pitching for Owain Gwynedd's patronage sometime after Madog ap Maredudd's death in 1160, Cynddelw asserts *Nyd keissyaw caled ked Casswallawn* (CBT IV 3.22), understood by its editors as 'Asking for Caswallon's gift/tribute is not a difficult request'. Is this perhaps an oblique reference to the events of the story *Manawydan* (PKM 50-1) where Pryderi does homage to the new sovereign, Caswallon? Or does the *ked Casswallawn* refer to Caswallon's generosity to his comrades after the first successful repulsion of Caesar (HKB ch. 57), or to the vast payment of silver he was ultimately forced to pay Caesar (HKB ch. 64)?

Another poem may be relevant: in an *Ubi sunt?* list, Cynddelw refers to Julius Caesar who had sought out the woman, Fflur, *y gan ut Prydein*, CBT IV 17.69-70. This 'lord of Britain' is likely to be Caswallon since Triad 67 names him, together with Manawydan and Lleu Llawgyffes, as one of the 'Three Noble Shoemakers of the Island of Britain', one who 'went to try and get hold of Fflur in Rome', TYP³ 185-7, 354; the late Triad 71 (TYP³ 199) also connects Caswallon with Fflur. Triad 67 suggested to Bromwich that there was a story about Caswallon going to Rome disguised as a beggar, and that Fflur was contended for by Caswallon and Julius Caesar — the latter possibly even invading Britain to secure her.

The brief mentions of Caswallon in the Four Branches show that he figured in the legendary history of Britain which is the backdrop to *Branwen* and *Manawydan*. Although it is evident that Welsh sources have material about Caswallon not in *Historia Regum Britanniae* — the connection with Fflur, in particular, his horse Meinlas, etc. (see TYP³ 305-6 for details, and WCD 108-9 for a possible reconstruction of the Caswallon 'tale') — it remains uncertain how much the Welsh authors knew of the account of Cassivellaunus in Caesar's *De Bello Gallico*, Geoffrey's *Historia Regum Britanniae* and other Latin sources, and indeed to what extent historical events of the 1c B.C. had become 'the fabric of an original story conceived in the south-east' informing part of the Four Branches, as argued by John T. Koch, 'A Welsh window on the Iron Age: Manawydan, Mandubracios', *CMCS* 14 (1987), 17-52, at p. 51.

For observations on the form *Caswallawn*, see P.-Y. Lambert, 'Welsh *Caswallawn*: the Fate of British **au*', in *Britain 400-600: Language and History*, edited by Alfred Bammesberger and Alfred Wollmann (Heidelberg, 1990), 203-16, but at p. 205 n. 8, note that there are in fact no attested *Caswallon* forms in the early genealogies to exhibit a pre-diphthongised ending *-on*; neither are there any forms (in *-on* or otherwise) of the name in the charters; see *B* 38 (1991), 49. Graham R. Isaac, 'The reflexes of the British diphthong **au*', *Journal of Celtic Linguistics* 11 (2007), 23-47, argues that *Caswallawn* < *Cassiuellaunus* 'cannot be divorced from Latin, i.e. literary, lines of transmission'.

6   **Llud** Although he figures in §§7 and 9 (where his role is fully discussed), other early poetry references to Lludd are rare: LlDC 18.182-4 (Englynion y Beddau) *Bet Tawlogev mab Llut in y trewrud trav/ mal y mae in y kystut;/ a'e clathei caffei but*; LlDC 34.18 *gorterch Creu<>dilad merch Lut*; CC 31.60-1 *Credeilat/ Uerch Lud*; CBT VI 7.4 *Ual Ymarwar Llut a Lleuelys*. CBT III 10.42 *Eil Llutya6n llauyn rutyon* seems to refer to Lludd's people likened to the warband of the sixth *gwelygordd* of Powys, the lords of Caereinion: see CBT III 126. In Triad 37 Lludd is remembered for burying the dragons in Dinas Emrys in Snowdonia, and

4 Dygogan awen

is grouped with Bendigeidfran and Gwerthefyr whose buried remains acted as a protection for the island.

6 **achystudyn (ms achestudyn)** Without emendation, *aches* 'flood, surge, tide' + *tudyn* (3pl. pres. or imperf. vb *tudaw* 'to cover, conceal, envelop', as G suggests s.v. *aches*. The vb is occasionally found with words for sea, LlDC 18.52 and 55 (Englynion y Beddau): *a'e tut mor*. Since Caswallon and Lludd are unlikely to be covering the tide, a loose compound meaning 'to cover as does a high tide' would be more promising, especially since prophetic discourse often talks of deliverers advancing over the sea. Alternatively, a 3pl. (imperf. or pres.) of a vb **achystudyaw* would give good sense (< *cystudyaw* 'to scourge, cause pain, grief'), comparing formations such as *achwynaw*, *athechu*, etc., as well as *dygystudyaw* and *dychystudyaw*. This emendation is adopted here for the time being. G but not GPC notes a second possible meaning for the vb *cystudyaw*: 'cover, protect'.

While G s.v. *kestuδyn* allows a possible connection with *cystudyaw*, he does not favour a personal name *Cestudyn*. Nevertheless, reading *cystudyn* as a noun, 'one who causes tribulation', or as a nickname *Cystudyn* is not impossible.

7 **diwed plo** It is indeed extraordinary that the only other extant example of the rare word *plo* is used by Prydydd y Moch who also rhymes it with *Iago*: CBT V 23.137-9 (of Llywelyn ab Iorwerth of Gwynedd) *Llwyr y dyd y uryd ar uro— Gadwalla6n/ Uab Caduan uab Yago,/ Llary ysbar, ysbenyt y plo* 'He concentrates his mind entirely on the territory of Cadwallon son of Cadfan son of Iago, generous with his spear, splendid his fate' (as per the Welsh transl. by Elin Jones). This lends further support to a connection of some sort between Prydydd y Moch and some of the Book of Taliesin poems, proposed in LPBT 27-36. This particular poem, CBT V 23, has a number of other correspondences such as Dygant, Nefenhir, etc.: for details see LPBT 8.23 and 5.41.

CBT V 233 refutes the connection with Bret. *diblo* made by CA 380 and deduces 'fate, course' from these two examples, although the Prydydd y Moch example is made more problematic by the other crux *ysbenyt* in the line (also in CBT V 6.11). Could one venture that *plo* is a loan word from ME *bloue/blawe* (with devoicing *b* > *p* as W. *ploc*, *potel*, *ponc*, etc.), although ME [bl-] was often retained, and that *diwed plo* means something rather like 'the final utterance or blowing'? Unfortunately, although ME *blouen* 'to blow' has a range of meanings such as blowing away, sounding a horn (including the Last Trump), proclaiming a name, uttering, etc. there is no evidence cited by OED that the meaning 'a blow, striking' was established before the 15c. *Diwed* can be adj. 'end, final, last' or advb 'at the end, at last'. On *plo* cf. CBT II 21.19n.

7 **coll Iago** Iago son of Beli, grandfather of Cadwallon of Gwynedd (d. 634), is the Iago referred to by Prydydd y Moch (above), and by Prydydd Bychan CBT VI 11.24 *Hil Catuan kynnan vab Iago*. Also R578.7 (Cyfoesi) *wedy Beli y uab ef Iago*. The death of a Iago fab Beli is noted AC 613 *Iacob filii Beli dormitatio*, a locution interpreted by Lloyd, HW 181, as implying his passing in a monastery. AC ms B notes the Battle of Chester where *Seysil filius Chinan et Iacob filius Beli moriuntur cum multis aliis*.

Other notable figures called Iago include Iago son of Idwal Foel (d. 979), in power in Gwynedd with his brother Ieuaf from *c.* 950, expelled on 974 captured by the Vikings 979 and defeated by his nephew, Hywel ab Ieuaf. He may have

4 Dygogan awen

been based in Llŷn and Arfon (see WaB 545-8). Another Iago, son of Idwal ap Meurig (of the northern Merfynion line), gained the kingdom of Gwynedd after the death of Rhydderch ab Iestin at the hands of the Irish, and was killed *a suis* 'by his own men' in 1039, according to the Annals of Ulster, the Chronicum Scotorum and Annals of Tigernach (see WaB 560-1).

TYP³ 403 notes the report of Edward Lhuyd, *Archaeologia Britannica* (Oxford, 1707), 256, col. 3, that the lost manuscript Hanesyn Hen (Hengwrt 33) contained a poem described by Lhuyd as *marunad Iago' ab Lhodhi [ne Iago ab Beli] o waith Taliesyn*. This item stood before genealogies of Llywelyn ab Iorwerth and followed on from two prophetic texts, an awdl by Adda Fras, and *Anrheg Yrien Reged*. It is not impossible that Lhuyd saw in Hanesyn Hen a prophetic poem such as our present text, with its mention of *coll Iago*, and ventured that it was an elegy (*marwnad*) of some sort.

7 **o dir Prydyn** *Prydyn* has a north British (but possibly vague) location in PT XI.7-8 *o Brydein* [recte *o Brydyn*] *gofein/ o berth Maw ac Eidin*; R581.13-14 (Cyfoesi) *ym Mana6/ a chat ym Prydyn geirllaw*; LlDC 16.21-2 (Afallennau) *kad im Prydin,/ in amvin ev terwin a guir Dulin*; and perhaps in the listings CA lines 492 *ar Gynt a Gwydyl a Phryden*, and 475 *at gwyr a Gwydyl a Phrydein* (?recte *prydyn*, with proest-rhyme, -*en* rhyming with -*enn*: for further examples of 'trwm ac ysgafn rhymes' (if -*yn* rather than -*ynn*), see EWSP 336 and refs.); AP line 10 *Gwydyl Iwerdon Mon a Phrydyn*; §7.78 *Kymry, Eigyl, Gwydyl, Prydyn*. Elsewhere in poetry, it might be taken as a synonym of *Prydein* rather than a designation for Pictland or its inhabitants, e.g. AP line 67 *ryfel heb dychwel y tir Prydyn*; AP 105 *trwy eiryawl Dewi a seint Prydeyn* (recte *Prydyn*), see Eric P. Hamp, 'Notes to Armes Prydein', *B* 30 (1981-3), 289-90, for correction to AP 21-2. The form is not used by the court poets, but has some currency in the 14c: GMD 1.66 *hyd Brydyn Llyn Llumonwy*.

8 **gwlat uerw** Either 'a tumult of the land' or 'a seething/boiling land'.

8 **dyderuyd** Also in LPBT 13.28, otherwise uncommon in poetry: the simplex *deruyd* is the norm.

8 **hyt Vlathaon (ms valaon)** The dimensions of Britain, of interest since the classical writers, and witnessed in Gildas and Bede, were reckoned at 900 miles from tip to tip in the story included in some Welsh law texts, not the 800 of the Latin tradition: see Morfydd E. Owen, 'Royal Propaganda: Stories from the Law-Texts', in WKC 224-54, at 229-32 and 250. As well as the law-text story (see Ior. 59), a few other sources use 'the promontory of Blathaon' (*Penrhyn Blathaon*) for the northern extremity located by Bromwich, TYP³ 251, at either John O' Groats or Duncansby Head in Caithness: BD 292, line 25 *Penryn Blathaon yn y Gogled*; 'Enwau Ynys Brydain', TYP³ 246 *o Benryn Blataon ym Brydein* (White Book of Rhydderch text; *o benn Blathaon Pen.* 50; *o bryn Bladdon* Pen. 240). Arthur's lookout (CO line 262) could spy from Cornwall 'a fly rising in the morning' on *Pen Blathaon*. The chroniclers reported an attack in 1114 by King Henry I on Gwynedd and Powys when he gathered a host from the whole island, 'from Penwith in Cornwall to Blathaon promontory in the North': ByT (Pen. 20) 59a *hyt ym Mhenryn Blathaon*: cf. *Pen Blathaon, Brenhinedd y Saesson*, edited by Thomas Jones (Cardiff, 1971), 120 (the Red Book of Hergest and Pen. 19 have *Blataon*; Pen. 18 has *Balathawon*). *Blathaon* is also found as the name of a son of one Mwrheth (Ir. *Murchadh*) in the tale *Breuddwyd Ronabwy* (BR 18, lines 29

and 59), and Dafydd Benfras (CBT VI 31.12) compares the assault of Llywelyn ab Iorwerth of Gwynedd to 'the blow of Blathaon'.

The emendation in the present text to *hyt Vlathaon* was first suggested by G 54 and 57, cautiously endorsed in AP xlii. *Blathaon*, may be based on a Cambricisation or adaptation of an Irish first element, such as *blad* 'fame', *bláth* 'flower', *b/mlaithe* 'smoothed, eroded', etc. Or if totally Welsh, and a personal name, < **blatto-* (cf. hypocoristic personal name *Blattius*, 'flower?', discussed by Wolfgang Meid, *Keltische Personennamen in Pannonien* (Budapest, 2005), 256) and the element *-aon* as in the name *Addaon*, etc.: CIB 209. There is perhaps influence from *blaidd* 'wolf' and/or *balaon* 'pine-martens'.

However, Iwan Wmffre, 'Penrhyn Blathaon ac amgyffred yr hen Gymry o eithafion Gogledd Prydain', *SC* 38 (2004), 59-68, at 63-6, takes a different view, maintaining that *blathaon* cannot be derived 'from any form in Welsh or Celtic for that matter' (63). He would regard the Book of Taliesin *hyt valaon* as preserving the original *balaon*, a plural of *beleu* 'marten', and that such a name may have predated the Ir. *Cataibh* (Caithness) with which it (very) broadly corresponds. He further postulates that a form **blawaon*, bungled from *balawon*, was further altered through transmission in a text where the letter *wynn* was misunderstood as a *thorn*. But it is hard to believe that the numerous instances of *blathaon* (including the court poetry attestations and the forms of the personal name Blathaon cited above, all ignored by Wmffre) derive from the ignorance of a single scribe. Our scribe may have mistaken *Blathaon* for *balaon*.

9 **lludedic eu holwyn (ms hoelyon)** *Lludedic* 'tired, exhausted' perhaps playing on the name *Lludd* in line 6.

The manuscript reading *hoelyon* 'rivets, nails' is possible literally, or figuratively perhaps for 'leaders' (cf. ModW use of *hoelion wyth* 'eight-inch nails' for worthies). But *haelyon* 'generous ones' is an obvious emendation following EWV 121 'tired knights', and AP xlii. For the sense, cf. PT II.16 *gwyr llawr lludedic*. But note B 26 (1974-6), 406 (NLW 9094 Cadwallon fragment) *Kymry gan hoelion [ ]yfo morde*.

The metre changes here to shorter sections of six syllables, the first and third rhyming in *-on* which is atypical for the second portion of the poem. The lack of rhyme with *hafwyn* is therefore a problem. I suggest emending *hoelyon* to *holwyn*: *olwyn* 'hoof', also used for a horse, e.g. R584.9; CBT V 14.3; VII 29.8. The scribe may have been confused by the change of metre here and substituted a word ending in *-on*. See below on line 10 for the different solution suggested by Ifor Williams.

10 **ymdeithic eu hafwyn** *Afwyn* 'rein' < L. *habena*, collocated with *lludedic* in Marwnad Cadwallon englyn 11 *llaw lludedic ar awyn*. GPC s.v. *ymddeithig*, adj. 'fast, swift' (of horse in a prose example), and nominally of a person 'wanderer, traveller'. The interpretation assumes that we have here the topos of the riderless horse whose reins have been abandoned, and are flapping about ('rein' *pars pro toto*). Cf. AP line 118 *Atui gwraged gwedw a meirch gweilyd*; R1052.36 (Crist Iesu) *Atuyd meirch g6eilyd*. See further General Introduction, 12. AP xlii suggests emending *hafwyn* to *kaffon* 'horses' for rhyme with *hoelyon*; see PT 38-9 on this problematic word, uniquely attested in PT II.22 *rawn eu kaffon*. I prefer to emend *hoelyon* to *holwyn* as noted above on line 9.

4 Dygogan awen

11 **gwlat wehyn vargotyon** *Gwehyn* has a range of meanings including 'to pull, pour, dispense, scatter, dispose', etc., see AP 20 for sense 'destroy utterly, to lay a country bare of everything', cf. §7.93-4 *Yt vi brithret a lliaws — gyniret/ a gofut amwehyn*; AP line 8 *gwnahawnt goruoled gwedy gwehyn*; R584.8-9 (Gwasgargerdd) *Pan del g6rthryn y ar olwyn du/ Y lad Lloegyr llwybyr wehyn*; LlDC 17.14-15 (Oianau) *A mi disgoganaf e rac ton navfed/ Rac vnic bariffvin gvehin Dived*; 17.71 *In Aber Dulas gvanas guehin*. See also on §3.30 *gwlat Vabon gwehenyt anoleithat*. *Gwlat wehyn* qualifies *bargotyon*.

GPC² s.v. *bargod* (b) 'edge, border', etc., and in pl. 'inhabitants of the borders or marches'; note that G suggests the additional possible meaning 'mongrel, mixed blood'. Very unusual in poetry, but cf. R579.10-11 and 13 (Cyfoesi) *Ys bargodyein ny biss6ys* and *p6y wledych wedy bargotyein*.

12 **Kollawt Kymry oll eu haelder** LPBT 22 lists a number of examples of 3sg. in *-(h)awt*, forms which continue into the 13c in verse. There are 12 examples of the abstract noun *haelder* in the CBT corpus, but none elsewhere in early poetry although it is very common in prose. *Oll* with peoples: PT IX.15 *it oll yd ynt geith*; §8.51 *Lloegyr oll ymellun*; R577.17 (Cyfoesi) *a Chymry oll y dana6*; LlDC 17.7 (Oianau) *Kimry oll inyeu kyfluit*. Irish rhyme with *rygystlyned* in line 13.

13 **yn rygystlyned o pennaeth weisson** GPC s.v. *cystlynedd* notes 'relationship, kindred, affinity, alliance; claim (of kinship, etc.)', as in GMD 1.40. The vb *cystlynu* can be used with *o*, as in CBT III 21.166 *Yd gystlynei pa6b o'e gystlyned* 'everyone acknowledged his claim'. Intensifying *ry-* rather than prefix *ryg-* = ModW *rhyng-*, although neither is found elsewhere with *cystlyned*.

EWV 121 suggests 'Wales will lose her nobility through alliance with servitors'. *Pennaeth weisson* is most naturally interpreted as 'vassal sovereignty' (qualifying noun lenited after fem. noun *pennaeth*). The Welsh will lose all their ability to be generous by swearing alliance to a regime ruled by vassals — the upside-down world of prophecy where churls will occupy thrones. On this topos, see General Introduction, 11-12. *Yn* is understood as prep. but could be particle or 1pl. possessive pron.

14 **Rydybyd Llyminawc** See on LPBT 14.44 *llyminawc llumoes*, 15.48 *llemenic*, and 18.19 *Lleminawc*. *Llyminawc* 'leaper, leaping' (VGFC 135) or if (as in GPC) derived from *llym* rather than a form in *llam-*, then 'keen, eager, ready'. It seems to refer to a prophesied deliverer or attacker in the quotation attributed to Myrddin given in HGK 5 *Llyminauc lletfer a daroganer*, where the Latin *Saltus ferinus praesagitur (venturus de mari)* indicates it was understood as to do with 'leaping', and where *ferinus* might echo the ending of the compound *lletfer*, a word also used in AP line 38. See further AP xliii-iv; HGK 58; and VGFC 134-5. Gruffudd's uterine brother, Ranuldus, was admired for his speed of foot and skill at jumping, and also had a leaping horse, Isliniach (VGFC ch. 6); on Irish leapers, see IIMWL 179 and 312. Ifor Williams's identification of the *Llyminawc* with Gruffudd ap Cynan of Gwynedd is discussed in the poem introduction.

15 **chwannawc** Adj. from *chwant* 'desire, keenness', cf. possibly CA 884 *oed mor guanauc i dinin*; and EWSP 438 *gauyr galet/ chwannac y gelyn*; EWGP VII.7 *Bit mab llen yn ch6ann6c*; VII.12 and 18; R1055.28 *chwanna6c vyd llen llwyda6c lla6 diuo* (Gosymdaith line 20 is emended); CBT 24.41 *Ac aur ac aryant wrth chwant chwannawc*; VII 33.11.

4 Dygogan awen

16   **y werescyn Mon**   The form *gwerescyn* is very common in prose texts, though not in poetry; note however, LPBT 21.15 *gorescyn*.

17   **a rewinyaw Gwyned**   Several examples in this manuscript: AP line 150 *rewinyawt y gat*; LPBT 6.42 *rewinyaw*; 11.86 *rewinyat*; Echrys Ynys line 4 *rewinetor*; CC 20.85 *rewinywys*; cf. LlDC 16.41 (Afallennau) *Ryrewineis y mab a'e merch*.

18-19   **o'e heithaf o'e pherued/ o'e dechreu o'e diwed**   The second *oe* in both lines is more naturally interpreted (with AP xlii) as 'to its' (ModW *i'w*): see GMW 53. With the collocation, cf. CA line 1238 *ef ladhei a [pher]uet ac eithaf*; LPBT 5.104-5 *Ef lladei a pherued/ ac eithaf a diwed*. For *perued* rhymed with *Gwyned*, CBT III 8.65-6. *Dechreu* is found with *diwed* and *Gwyned* in CBT VI 29.69.

21   **Ystic y wyneb**   Understood by Ifor Williams (AP xlii) as 'Angry his face' (= ModW *ys dig*), but not followed by GPC where this example is given s.v. *ystig* 'diligent, industrious, persevering, persistent . . . willing, ready', cf. the collocation with vb *y/estyngu* seen in CBT VI 12.21 *Ys yng yn yst6ng ystic uara— Rys* 'It is hard for us to assuage Rhys's persistent wrath'. GPC is followed, understanding *wyneb* as 'honour' rather than 'face', while noting that the former meaning tends to be found most often with vbs *cadw* and *colli*. H-cd implies an emendation to *ystyg* (ModW *ystyng*), the same vb as in line 22: this has in its favour the poets' doubling tendency, as in, e.g., CBT VI 6.18 *Na cheis vy ystvg, o'm estygyt,— vr*.

24   **Gwr o Gud (ms gwd)**   Emending with AP xliii; Ifor Williams's identification of this figure with Rhys ap Tewdwr is discussed in the poem introduction. The phrase *Gwr o Gud* may be compared with other prophetic texts: R1049.32 (Anrheg Urien) *Kyuyt o gud g6r a uyd bud y Wyndodyd* 'there will arise from hiding a man who will be of profit to the men of Gwynedd'; R1052.8-9 (Crist Iesu) *G6r o Gud para6chrud wythuer/ A da6 y lywya6 y la6er* 'a Man from Hiding — with a ready red-bladed spear — will come to lead his host'; R579.19-20 (Cyfoesi) *Dyrchaua6t unic o gud . . . Kynan y k6n Kymry bieiuyd*. Of the dead rising: IGE^2 281 *Cyfyd pawb i gyd o gudd*.

25   **kyfamrud**   Cf. EWSP 436 *cyuamrud* [recte] *kat*; CBT IV 6.15 *[c]yuamwyn gyfamrut*; CBT VI 17.12 *Cad gyfamrudd*.

26   **y gynhon**   G s.v. *gynt* 'tribe, people, nation; Scandinavians, Danes, also English, Normans'. Often used in name lists in poetry, as in §2.17 *Llu o Seis, eil o Ynt*; AP line 176 *Attor ar gynhon Saesson* (near *Gwydyl*, *Kymry*); CA line 492 *ar Gynt a Gwydyl a Phryden*; CA line 197 *gogyuerchi Ynhon* (rhymed with *Brython* as here); and in prophecies LlDC 17.61 (Oianau) *Dybit seith ganllog o Ynt gan wint Goglet*; Peirian Faban line 2 *A ddifero di Duw rac Gwyddyl gynt*.

28   **pellenawc y lüyd**   *Pellynn(h)ic* (also *-enn(h)ic*) 'coming from afar' or 'ranging afar' is the more common adj. based on *pellynt* (*pell* + *hynt*): see GPC s.v. *pellennig* and PT 46 for examples. EWSP 421 *pellynnyawc y luyd* and the spelling of our form with one *-n-* alerts us to identify it as a different orthography (*e* for schwa) for *pellyniog*, with GPC s.v. (also *pellennog*). The Book of Taliesin scribe has a tendency to omit yod, although note line 11 *vargotyon*; line 17 *rewinyaw*; see LPBT 2, 7, 325, 512. In the Cyfoesi series (R579.23-4) a *G6r pellennic o dramyr* follows the *unic o gud* (see on line 24 above). *Llu*, pl. *llüyd* is collocated with *llewenyd*, as in §6.2 and 30 *arwyd llewenyd llüyd o Von*. Cf.

4 Dygogan awen

EWSP 419 *llewenid lluyd*, and CBT I 14.38 and 31.10-11; III 13.3; IV 16.79; VI 18.115; VII 32.60. The pl. *lluoed* gains ground but the pl. *llüyd* persists in 13c poetry.

29 **y Vrython**   Cf. §7.40-1 *Y Vrython dymbi/ gwaed gwned ofri*; LlDC 17.180 (Oianau) *Maban dirchavaud mad y Vrython*; B 26 (1974-6), 407 (Pen. 120 Cadwallon fragment) *Neus duc Gwynedd gorvoled i Vrython*; PT VIII.25 *mawr gwrnerth ystlyned y Vrython*. Lines 24-5 and 27-9 are recycled in Pen. 50, 17-18.

5 Kein gyfedwch

The first section of this poem (lines 1-7) uses a tripartite line in the manner of the rhupunt metre, used in Echrys Ynys, although lines 1-4 are all irregular.[1] The first five lines set a scene of carousing and drinking from golden horns in a strong fort, with reinforced stone ramparts, and a surrounding wall. This is a fort (*caer*) which appears to have been written about (*rysycrifyat*), or perhaps one which contains writings. If it is in the vicinity of two lakes, as *deulwch* suggests, and if it refers to a Welsh location, there are many possibilities, most obviously Dolbadarn, situated dramatically between Llyn Peris and Llyn Padarn. It might be suggested that Llywelyn ab Iorwerth, creator of Dolbadarn Castle, is being praised indirectly for his innovative castle-building in stone, which he had recently trialled in the early 1220s in Castell y Bere. He may be compared indirectly with the character Beli son of Mynogan mentioned in lines 6-7, or his son Lludd who built and gave his name to London. In the *Historia Regum Britanniae*, Lud, the eldest son of Heli, is renowned as a town-planner and fortifier: 'He surrounded the city [of Trinovantum, later renamed Kaerlud "London"] with fine walls and wonderfully built towers', and 'commanded its citizens to build homes and houses there, so that no foreign city could boast finer palaces'. He was famous as 'a warrior and a generous feast-giver'. After his death, since his two sons were minors, his brother, Cassivellaunus, was 'crowned in their place'.[2] The fifteenth-century Lewys Glyn Cothi, one of many later authors who drew extensively on the Geoffrey material via the *Brut* translations, compares the architectural prowess of his patron, Ieuan ap Phylip Cefn-llys, to that of Beli *fael y weilgi las,/ a ordeiniodd roi dinas*, and to Lludd *a g'weiriodd rhag llaw/ Caer-ludd a'r cweryl iddaw*.[3] Lludd, also mentioned in poem §9 in our collection, and in the title of poem §7, may be the 'one having a dragon's qualities' in line 4 (prolepsis in line 3), but that line may describe Beli, his father, certainly mentioned in lines 6-7.

There are problems with ambiguous *llwch*, and *pleit* and *ysci*, and a further complication in this section is the metre which lacks final end-rhyme (unless the frequent antistrophe compensates for this, which is possible).[4] Lines 1-3 have final consonantal correspondence -*t*.

Line 6, beginning a more regular section of short Class 1 lines, introduces Beli son of Manogan (or a figure in his mould), the *teithïawc* or rightful ruler of 'the Honey-Island of Beli', *Ynys vel Veli* (the only example of this locution, as

---

[1] This metre is adhered to strictly in Echrys Ynys, in the religious poems CC nos. 3, 9, 10, 11, 22, and in the two earliest attested of the twelfth- and thirteenth-century court poems, CBT I nos. 1 and 2.

[2] HKB chs. 22 and 53. BD 44 *ac a atnewydhavys muryoed Llundein a'e thyroed. A chet bei llaver ydav o dinassoed ereill, hvnnv eissoes a garei yn wy no'r vn, ac vrth hynny ygelwit Caer Lud*. BD 20 *y cadarnhavs ynteu y dynas o geyryd a thyroed anrydedus*. Similarly, RBB 59, 82.

[3] GLGC 170.31-4.

[4] Cf. PT IV.

5 Kein gyfedwch

opposed to *Y Fel Ynys*). This glorious dreamtime past contrasts with the turmoil of the second part of the poem and the arrival of waves of five dominions (*pennaeth*): the first five (lines 11-14) include the Gwyddyl Ffichti, and 'hostile sinners' and a 'swift nation' (or scum!) — although the last two designations may refer to the Gwyddyl Ffichti themselves. A further five (lines 15-16) will come from Normandy (see note on line 15), followed by a sixth, 'ruling from sowing to harvest' (lines 17-18), perhaps implying a short period such as Richard I's ten-year reign (1189-99) when only seven months were spent in England. The seventh will be a ruler whose burial ground is 'over the sea'. The eighth is a 'Lynx' (perhaps Henry III, see note), 'not a protector to the old' (but see note on line 22); there will be great clamouring as the region of *Eryri* (Snowdonia) is called upon to thwart the invader. There are similarities with *Historia Regum Britanniae* and its *Brut* versions in the animal symbolism (the *Linx* in particular), and with the numbered groups of five and the mention of Eryri (see note on line 21 for comparisons with material in Pen. 14 and 16).

The poem ends with an entreaty for entry to Heaven. The poem is clearly later than the arrival of the Normans, and a good deal later if five rulers or reigns are envisaged, succeeded by three more. *Modrydaf*, 'chief bee', as a figure for a ruler is paralleled in the work of the court poets as are many other features of lexis and diction. There is some apparently wilful playing around with words, e.g. *Nordmynmandi*.

5 Kein gyfedwch
Book of Taliesin 72.9-22

Kein gyfedwch y am deulwch, llwch am pleit,
Fair carousing around two lakes, a lake (?of drink) around the throng,
pleit am gaer, kaer yn ehaer ryyscrifyat,
a wall around a fortress, an impregnable fortress which has been written about,
Virein ffo racdaw — arlleg[1] kaw mwyedic uein.
a wondrous retreat before him — the one who has a well-wrought protection of reinforced stones.
Dreic amgyffreu oduch lleeu llestreu llat,
He with a dragon's quality, above the places of the drinking vessels,

5 **llat yn eurgyrn, eurgyrn yn llaw, llaw yn ysci,**
drink in golden horns, golden horns in the hand, a hand (deep in) foam.
Ys ʢ[2] modrydaf — nu ry'th iolaf[3] — budic Veli
It is the lord — I now beseech you — a victorious King Beli
aMhanogan ri
son of King Manogan
rygeidw y teithi.
who will defend his entitlements.
Ynys vel Veli:
The Honey-Island of Beli:

10 **teithiawc oed idi.**
he would be her rightful ruler.
Pymp pennaeth dimbi —
Five dominions will come —
o Wydyl Ffichti
of the Irish-Picts,
o pechadur kadeithi,
of hostile sinners,
o genedyl ysci.
of a race of scum.

15 **Pymp ereill dymgöi**
Five others will come

---

[1] ms *ar lleg*
[2] ms *ysci y*
[3] ms *nur yth iolaf*

5 Kein gyfedwch

     o Nordmynmandi.
     from Normandy.
     Whechet ryfed ri
     Sixthly will rule a king
     o heu hyt vedi.
     from seed-time until harvest.
     Seithuet oheni
     Her seventh (shall be)
20   **y weryt dros li.**
     one whose burial-ground is over the sea.
     Wythuet, Linx a dyui:
     The eighth, a Lynx will come:
     nyt llwyded escori.
     not protecting the elderly.
     Gynt gwaedvenni
     (At) the clamourings of the people
     galwawr Eryri;
     Eryri will be summoned;
25   **anhawd y deui.**
     not easily will he (the Lynx) come.
     Jolwn Elöi
     Let us implore God
     pan y'n bo gan Geli
     there may be for us with the Lord
     adef Nef dimbi.
     a home in Heaven to come.

1   **Kein gyfedwch** *Cyfedach* is more common than the variant *-wch* form found in Diffaith Aelwyd Rheged, EWSP 427.57. Both are used together by Cynddelw, CBT IV 9.140; the *-wch* form is used twice by Prydydd y Moch, CBT V I.58 and 77.

1   **y am deulwch** *Deulwch* is written as a compound in the manuscript. 'Two lakes' perhaps refer to a spot where there are two distinct bodies of water such as Talyllychau (north of Llandeilo), or (formerly) Llyn Nantlle Uchaf and Isaf at Baladeulyn; Llynnau Mymbyr near Capel Curig; Llyn Penrhyn and Traffwll near Llanfihangel yn Nhywyn, north-west Anglesey (south of Daronwy, and Aber Alaw, on which see §1); or the two lakes, Llyn Crafnant and Llyn Geirionnydd, to the west of Llanrhychwyn, which are separated by Mynydd Deulyn. The pair which most comes to mind, however, are the two great lakes Padarn and Peris where Llywelyn ab Iorwerth erected his commanding castle at Dolbadarn on a previously occupied site, probably during the 1220s. The castle, noted for its sophisticated masonry, its huge hall 50 feet by 27 feet, and high tower, controlled the Llanberis pass westwards into North Wales. Together with the early stone part

5 Kein gyfedwch

of Pen-y-bryn, Abergwyngregyn, identified in 1997 as the lost residence of Llywelyn ab Iorwerth, and later of his grandson, Llywelyn ap Gruffudd, Dolbadarn constitutes the first appearance of domestic building in stone, albeit within a defensive site where timber was also used. As part of the programme of disinheritance following the conquest of 1282/3, Edward I ordered Dolbadarn's timbers (like those of Aberffraw and Conwy) to be moved to Caernarfon, just as the wooden hall of Ystumgwern was moved to Harlech. Llywelyn ab Iorwerth's ambitious stone-building, as evidenced in Dolbadarn, and in many stone castles, may conceivably have some bearing on the interpretation of the phrase *mwyedic uein* in line 3 below.

While the hapax *deulwch* is here understood as *deu lwch* 'two lakes', we may note how *deu* sometimes has an intensive force, as in the examples *deuliw*, *deulwyr*, *deune*, and *deuryw* cited by G 315. If this were the case, 'a great stretch of water or lake', or even metaphorically, in the light of what follows, 'a great amount of drink', comparing the use of *llyn*.

1   **llwch am pleit** Since *cyfeddwch* is mentioned, this instance of *llwch*, too, may be used figuratively for drink (cf. *llyn*, and note above), although in late medieval sources, *llwch* is often used of stagnant, dirty or murky water. *Llwch*, *lluwch* 'dust' does not seem likely here.

On *pleit* see PKM 184 'wall, partition; party' and GPC's much wider range of meanings including 'hurdle, side; row, rank, company; throng, faction; support, succour'. *Pleit* is attested frequently in the court poetry, usually in the sense of 'host, throng', also possible here.

2   **kaer yn ehaer** G connects this hapax with *aer* 'battle', suggesting 'martial, military, warlike', and this would be consonant with the very common poetic collocation of *kaer/aer*. GPC adds the possibility 'immovable, strong' < *haer*. The prefix *ech-*, *eh-* can mean 'free from' (as in *ehofyn* 'fearless'), or 'out of' and is used in verbal and pronominal contexts: if from *haer*, perhaps from the nominal use 'angry threat, challenge' cited by G 760, and thus *ehaer* 'impregnable', as in the translation.

2   **ryyscrifyat** No noun *ysgrifiad* 'writing, written document' is attested until the 18c, nor is the vb *ysgrifyaw*, according to GPC, until 1803; *(y)sgriffio* is attested from the 16c. However, in light of OIr *scríbaid*, Corn. *scrife* 'to write', and Bret. *skriva*, we may assume the past impers. of *ysgrifyaw* with perfective *ry*, or else a nomen agentis in *-yat* (cf. OW *grefiat* (ModW *greiffiad*) 'title-deed, written document' < L. *graphium*) preceded by intensifying *ry-*. Thus either 'which has been written (?about)' or 'inscribed/planned out (on parchment)'; or 'having a great [amount of] writing' or 'of a great writing/written works'. The description of the writings pertaining to Britain in Edmyg Dinbych line 45, *ysgriuen Brydein bryder briffwn*, comes to mind. Prydydd y Moch favours preverbal *ry-* especially with impers. past, as in *rygreat*, *ryerchit*, *ryanet*, etc. (see CBT V 338), as does his older contemporary, Cynddelw (CBT IV 431-2). If *ryyscrifyat* is a vb form rather than a noun, then it is more natural to take *yn ehaer* as an adverb qualifying it — 'which has been written confidently.

3   **virein ffo racdaw** The reason for lenition of *mirein* is not clear; the five-syllable first section is atypical, as is line 2 with three syllables.

3   **arlleg kaw (ms ar lleg)** Understood as *arlleg*, see GPC s.v. *arlleng* 'defence, refuge' (four occurrences in CBT corpus, three by Cynddelw) although *ar lleg*

5 Kein gyfedwch

'over a host' with unrealised lenition is possible, cf. the same ambiguity in LlDC 31.56-7 *Oet hyneiw guastad/ ar lleg ar lles gulad* (of Cai, Arthur's soldier, see AW 43). *Kaw*, adj. 'consistent, skilful, ordered; harmonious' [often of poems, poets]; bound', as a noun 'knot, band' (see PT 135) or, as G suggests, the personal name Caw, as in the name of the giant, Caw of Prydyn. Three syllables in this unit might suggest corruption.

3 **mwyedic uein** GPC s.v. *mwyedig* 'increased, augmented', possibly here referring to defences around the fortress. Although *mwyedic* is not attested elsewhere in early poetry, the alliteration with *mirein* and *mein* argues against emendation to *hwyedic*. *Mein* understood as pl. of *maen* 'stones', used especially of masonry and graves.

4 **Dreic amgyffreu** *Dreic* is extremely common in the CBT corpus, and in prophecy. GPC s.v. *amgyffrau* suggests '?faculty, attribute' for this hapax following G; both suggest < *cyffreu*, attested only in CC 2.24 *duyuaul y kyffreu* (of God) where *kyfreu* 'utterance' could be meant, or, with G, *ryffreu*: see further CC 21. For common *ffreu* 'stream', see on LPBT 4.116, 6.52; on *ryffreu* cf. LPBT 23.46; §8.15 *mynut ryffreu*; Pen3Oianau 127.195 *a rwyf o wynt a ryfreu o law*. *Amryffreu* 'wealth, possessions; ?flow, flood': CC 2.22 *a fop amriffreu*; CBT VII 40.12, etc.

4 **oduch lleeu llestreu llat** The prep. is common *inter alia* with drinks, feasts, vessels (*llestri*), etc. and cf. *oduch llat* in Edmyg Dinbych line 55. *Lleeu*, presumably pl. of *lle* 'place', is very rare, cf. PT VII.5 *lleeu gowy gwyn gwylein yMathreu* hence the view in PT 80 that it may be for *lleueu* (ModW *llefau*) 'cries' or *lleiseu* 'voices'. *Llestreu* is another unusual pl. formation unparalleled in poetry or prose; the normal form is *llestri*, whether for 'drinking vessels' as here, or 'ships'. Although *llat* is generally 'drink', it is sometimes used of a gift or bounty; however, there is no evidence for a figurative usage 'sea' as in English. The form *lleeu* is presumably driven by the needs of the internal rhyme, but not so *llestreu* which could be a dittography mistake. If the reading stands, the use of two such internal rhyme-words in a passage where the end-rhyme has been suspended suggests a poet not afraid to break the rules.

5 **llat yn eurgyrn** Cf. CBT III 16.203 *Drud la6n y eurdyrn o lad yn eurgyrn*; CBT III 17.12 *Yn lla6 llew cad, kyrn llad llawn*. In early poetry the compound *eurgyrn* is restricted to the CBT corpus.

5 **llaw yn ysci** GPC is uncertain as to the meaning of *ysci* which occurs also in the problematic text 'Dydd dyfydd' printed by Ifor Williams, 'Dalen o Femrwn', *B* 4 (1927-9), 41-8, line 66 *ar ysci asceini ascellurith/ llestri lly ar heli tuth eleurh* [= *eleirch* 'swans']. Ifor Williams, *B* 11 (1941-4), 83, posits a variant form of *ysgai*, 'foam, froth, scum', which would give good sense in line 14 below (comparing *cri/crai*), and be reasonable here if we imagine a brimming vessel dousing the hand with foam ('hand in the foam'); a noun would maintain the pattern set by the first two units of the line. 'Foam, scum' gives rather less good sense in line 6 ('leader [over the] foam[ing drink]', or 'foam of the leader', but is tolerable.

This translation follows this option but with caution in the light of GPC s.v. *ysgai* where the primary meaning is 'fat, lard, dripping, tallow' and the meaning 'scum, foam, froth', it is suggested, may be a dictionary meaning. The 14c satire example, GPB 8.14 *Gwyw lugorn ysgai*, is interpreted as 'a dull *worthless* lantern' by its editor who notes further examples of *ysgai* as a general derogatory

5 Kein gyfedwch

adj. 'scummy', GPB 121; however, 'tallow' is also possible with *llugorn*. GIG 38.15 *Cymwrn burm ysgai*, again used derogatively in a satire, is a more certain example, where yeasty froth or scum is clearly meant. In CDG 31.34 *baw estynwefl ysgai*, 'greasy' is suggested.

Otherwise, *ysgïen* 'knife' (cf. Ir. *scían*) might have produced a seeming collective 'knives', etc. which would give tolerable sense in both lines 5 and 14. Or is there some mistake, repeated *twice more*, for the common adj. *gwisgi* 'ready, swift; mature' which occurs in collocations with *llaw* (GLlG 6.2 *Yn llaw egored, weisged wisgi*) in contexts of gift-giving, e.g. CBT V 23.57 *Gwisci eur ac aryant*; CBT VII 23.13 *g6r gwisgoet gwisgi*; CBT VII 24.50 *eurwisgoet wisci*. This would also fit all three lines ('a ready hand', a 'ready leader', 'ready/swift nation').

6   **Ys (ms ysci y) modrydaf** See above on *ysci*. The line section is two syllables too long, and *Ysci y* may simply be be a mistake for *ys*. The figurative use in poetry of *modrydaf* 'queen-bee' for a leader (twelve instances in CBT corpus, two by Cynddelw and four by Prydydd y Moch) is discussed by Elin Phillips, 'Modrydaf', *B* 25 (1972-4), 119-20.

6   **nu ry'th (ms nur yth) iolaf** GPC s.v. *nur* (following G s.v. *casnur*) suggests *nu + ry* for this example, followed here. If, however, = *nur* 'lord', then vocative perhaps. GPC also suggests that *nur* may be from a personal name (comparing *Casnur, Cawrnur*, on which see LPBT 9.12; 24.10), following G's suggestion, 'hero, champion', etc.

6   **budic Veli** On Beli, see §2.3; rhyming with *ri* as here in CBT V 17.18-19. Common adj. *budic* EWSP 420.5 *ryuel godic budic uael*; §8.13 *blwydyned budic*; CBM IV 6.25 *Grut vutic wledic*, etc. Very commonly compounded with *gweith, cet*, etc., e.g. PT II.2 *am wledic gweituudic gwarthegyd*; EWSP 445.113 *gwaithfuddig*, especially so in court poetry.

7   **aMhanogan ri** Beli's father, Manogan, is not otherwise mentioned in early poetry. Some (Zimmer, followed by Rhys, Gruffydd, Wade-Evans) regarded HB §19 *Minocannus* father of *Bellinus* as a ghost name derived from misreading Orosius's *Minocynobellinus Britannorum regis filius* while TYP³ 288-9 sees it as a genuine Celtic name, comparing *mynawc*, OB *Monocan*, and ogam [MI]NNACCANNI. The *-a-* form in our poem shows a common variation (cf. *mynach, manach*) also found in the White and Red Book texts of *Cyfranc Lludd a Llefelys* (CLlaLl 1, line 1), and the Pen. 16iii text of *Breuddwyd Maxen*, see BMax 7, line 209, *vab Manogan*. Also VGFC 52 *filiu[s] Manogani*; EWGT 206; but PKM 29 *Mynogan*.

The use of the contraction of *am* (< *mab*) + personal name in *M-* is well-established in court poetry, for example, in CBT I 7.53 *ma6r Amada6c*; CBT IV 12.17 *Run—am Maelg6n*; CBT VII 27.13 *Hywel Ammawda6c*; cf. LlDC 18.209 *Ebediv am Maelur*; LlDC 31.13 *am Mydron*; 31.23 *am Melld*; R584.8 (Gwasgargerdd) *Myrdin y6 vy en6 Amheid6c*.

8   **rygeidw y teithi** *Ceidw* attested in LPBT 4.158 *py geidw*, otherwise in early poetry restricted to CBT corpus (18 examples). *Teithi* 'rightful characteristics, attributes', common in prophetic discourse, as elsewhere: e.g. LPBT 8.13 *teir kenedyl gwythlawn o iawn teithi*; LlDC 16.87 (Afallennau) *Kaffaud paub y teithi, llauen vi bri Brython*; LlDC 17.189 (Oianau) *Kertorion allan heb ran teithi*. With the compound vb *achadw* in R528.34-5 (Cyfoesi) *nyt achatuo y deithi*.

5 Kein gyfedwch

9 **Ynys vel Veli** In the White Book of Rhydderch section on Enwau Ynys Brydain (TYP³ 246), the three successive names of Britain are given as *Clas Merdin*, then 'after its getting and settling' *Y Vel Ynys*, then after it had been conquered by Prydain son of Aedd Mawr, *Ynys Prydein*. TYP³ 248-9 wonders whether *Y Vel Ynys* comes from *Ynys Veli*, but both *vel* and *Veli* are needed for length of the present line, and there is no reason why *mel* 'honey' should not have formed part of a traditional name, perhaps on the model of the 'land of milk and honey' so frequently mentioned in the Old Testament. HB ch. 30 notes that 'the Romans . . . deprived Britain of . . . all her precious raiment and honey'. The form *Y Fêl Ynys* is used by several of the Cywyddwyr from the 14c, e.g. GGGryg 9.42, GSCy 1.29, and later, as noted in TYP³ 249.

Other names for Britain are used in the present collection: §9.3 *prif van ynys*; §9.12 *y Wen Ynys*. Prydydd y Moch is exponent of *Prydein ynys*, *ynys Prydein*, etc. (3 examples); he uses *rhagynys* as well, and alludes possibly to *Clas Merdin* in addressing Llywelyn ab Iorwerth, CBT V 18.31 *Wyt priawd tir Prydain a'i chlas*. The anonymous poem in praise of Cuhelyn Fardd, CBT I 1 *Medel visci mel vartoni mynogi guyth*, contains a number of words and ideas also used here: *mel*, *modrydaf*, *llat*, drinking vessels etc. and possibly *gwisgi* (see above on line 5 *ysgi*).

10 **teithiawc oed idi** Common adj. used in a similar context of rightness or fitness to rule in §8.34 *teithiawc Mon*; CBT I 8.29 *Teithia6c Prydein*; CBT I 11.34 *wlad teithia6c*; CBT II 26.36; CBT V 24.25. CA lines 1072-3 *mab teyrn teithiawc/ yng Gwyndyt* and 1095-6 *mab brenhin teithiauc/ ud Gwyndyt*. See Rhian M. Andrews, 'The nomenclature of kingship in Welsh court poetry 1100-1300, Part I: the terms', *SC* 54 (2010), 79-109.

11 **Pymp pennaeth dimbi** See on §1.20 *pedeir prif pennaeth*. Understood here, too, as 'dominion' rather than 'leader' which is also possible. This manuscript, unlike the modern standard, sometimes uses *pymp/pump* before a noun, as in LPBT 5.215; 12.21 *pump*; §7.16 *pymp llong*, etc. *Pum* is generally used in the CBT corpus.

Dimbi here and in line 28 below is irregular orthography (*i* for schwa); *dymbi* in §7.23 and 40, §8.1, etc. On other fut. forms in *-bi*, see §1.24. See on line 12 below for the five dominions.

12 **o Wydyl Ffichti** Lit. Irish-Picts. Cf. Edmyg Dinbych lines 7-8 *Dydybyd gwanec ar vrys dybrys idi,/ Adawhwynt y werlas o glas Ffichti* (for *clas* 'people', see above on line 9), where *Ffichti* is for 'sea-raiders' or pirates in general and perhaps Vikings, as explained by Gruffydd, *Cerdd Lys Gynnar* 24. Similarly, CBT II 26.176 *Pan del ryfel a rwysc Fichti* refers to either the Irish or Picts or simply sea-raiders attacking the cantref of Rhos in Pembrokeshire. See further on LPBT 1.68 *Ffichti* [recte] *lewon*, and G s.v. *Ffichti*.

More relevant to the present poem is the use of the term *Gwydyl Fychti* for the second *gormes* 'oppression' which came to the Island of Britain according to Triad 36: the first was the Coraniaid who came during the time of Caswallon son of Beli, and the third was the Saxons led by Hors and Hengist (TYP³ 93). Even more telling is the correspondence between our poem and the description of Britain, loosely based on Bede, which precedes Book I of Geoffrey's *Historia Regum Britanniae*, HKB ch. 5: 'It is finally inhabited by five peoples, the Normans, the Britons, the Saxons, the Picts and the Scots', rendered in the *Brut*

5 Kein gyfedwch

as *Nordmannyeyt, a Brytannyeyt, a Saesson, a Gvydyl Fychti, ac Yscoteyt*, BD 2, with a note making more explicit that the last three constituted a *gormes* sent by God to avenge their sin and pride (BD 3); Geoffrey implies that divine retribution caused the Britons to give way not to three peoples, but to two, the Picts and the Saxons. BD 60 indicates clearly that the *Gvydyl Fichti* are the mixed-race descendants of the Picts (imagined to be from Scythia, as in Bede) and Irish women.

The distinction between the five dominions and the three *gormesoedd*, made explicit in the *Brut*, seems to be matched in lines 11-14 here. Only the *Gwydyl Ffichti* are named, but it is more than likely that the 'hostile sinners' and the 'scummy people' are the others of the *Brut*'s triad, the Saxons and the Scots.

13 **pechadur kadeithi** Collective *pechadur* here, with *kadeithi* 'war, enmity, wrath', used in CBT V 2.11 *6ur kadeithi*; CBT V 25.58 *lyw kadeithi*; CBT II 16.13 *lyw kadeithi—bro*, and in CC 14.70 *llin Kaïn kadeithi* of the wrathful line of sinners back to Cain.

14 **ysci** See on line 5 above.

15 **Pymp ereill dymgöi** See G s.v. *dyouot* noun 'profit, luck' (as in CBT V 8.37 *Neud llei dyouod*), and vb *dyouot* 'to befall, happen, come', cf. CA line 1184 *Dim guoiu* [recte *guoui*]; CA line 606 *dyouu*; LPBT 1.86 *dygofi*; 1.99 *A gwedy hynny digoui*; 3.34 *dy-m-gofyd*; CC 8.21 *deudec dymgofu*. G explains the *-m-* as a second preverb (i.e. *ym*), or else a relative marker. The five rulers or dominions are presumably the first five of the Norman kings — William I, William Rufus, Henry I, Stephen, and Henry II. Matilda was not crowned but may have been counted.

16 **o Nordmynmandi** The Oianau prophecy (LlDC 17.33) talks of the need for prayer in the face of the five leaders from Normandy, *pimp penaeth o Nortmandi*, the fifth crossing the sea to conquer Ireland. This is clearly Henry II who landed in Waterford in 1171.

The hybrid tautological form *Nordmynmandi* is not paralleled anywhere else, whereas the forms *Nordmandi* 'Normandy', *Nordmyn* 'Normans' are common enough (in poetry R584.15 *Pan dyuo coch Nordmandi*; LlDC 17.116 (Oianau) *Ban diffon Nortmin y ar llidan llin*; CBT I 8.35 *dros for o Nordmandi*, etc.), together with *Nordmein* (CBT IV 1.20; VI 18.46), *Normadi*, *Nordmannyeit*, etc. See EEW 46. Again one has the sense of a poet at play, capriciously lengthening the form for a better line; this seems more likely than a simple scribal error.

17 **Whechet ryfed ri** Note the orthography of *whechet*, generally considered a southern or mid-Walian symptom (like *hw-* of the Black Book of Carmarthen): see 'Llyfr Taliesin', *NLWJ* 25 (1988), 357-86. *Ryfed* is understood as *ry + med* 'he rules' (vb *medu*) rather than 'wonder' or 'wondrous', which is also possible — 'a wondrous king'. The sixth if there is a chronological sequence from the five Norman kings in lines 15-16 would be Richard Lionheart who reigned from 1189-99.

18 **o heu hyt vedi** Cf. Genesis 8:22 'As long as the earth endures, seedtime and harvest, cold and heat, summer and winter, day and night will never cease'; also many biblical pairings of sowing and reaping, reaping what is sown (Galatians 6:7), etc. The force is unclear here, but it may imply a comparatively short reign, or an intermittent presence such as Richard Lionheart's, although his styling as an absentee king is a modern development. The vb noun *heu* is used uniquely in

5 Kein gyfedwch

early poetry by Prydydd y Moch, CBT V 8.13 and 14, although its conjugated forms are more common.

19 **Seithuet oheni** Lit. 'the seventh of hers', referring back to *Ynys vel Veli* line 9. *Oheni* CC 14.82, also occurs in a rhyme-block with *Normandi* in LlDC 17.38 (Oianau) *a doant oheni*; otherwise rare in poetry, but common in southern prose texts, including those copied by the Book of Taliesin scribe. See Sims-Williams, *Prepositions* 10-11.

20 **y weryt dros li** *Gweryt* understood as noun 'earth, land,' rather than 3sg. vb *gwaret* 'to save', both common in early poetry. The noun is particularly used for 'earth, burial-ground', see G s.v. *gweryt¹*. Richard Lionheart (if not the sixth, see on line 17 above) was buried at Fontrevault near Chinon, next to his father, Henry II; his heart was buried in Rouen Cathedral. His successor, Henry III, was buried in Westminster Abbey.

21 **Wythuet Linx a dyui** The learned spelling (< L. *linx*, with very occasional *lynx*) is consistently employed in the prose texts, contrasting with later poetry, GLGC 12.20 *bual a lings, oen a blaidd*. The lynx was famous for its sharp sight, and was thought to be a kind of wolf in medieval times (the Vocabularium Cornicum *commisc bleit hahchi* 'mixed wolf and dog' follows the OE gloss on L. *linx*: see Alderik H. Blom, 'The Welsh glosses in the *Vocabularium Cornicum*', *CMCS* 57 (2009) 23-40, p. 25). The animal is not mentioned elsewhere in early poetry, but the Prophetiae Merlini (HKB ch. 115) assert that, following the *sixth* 'crowned with the lion's head', a Lynx shall emerge, 'which will pierce through everything and threaten to destroy its own people. Because of it Normandy will lose both islands and be stripped of its former honour'. Then follows a native resurgence, the diversion of the River Periron, the summoning of Conanus by Cadualadrus, and the slaughter of the foreigners, rivers flowing with blood, and rejoicing in Wales, Cornwall and Brittany. The Pen. 16 text of the Welsh translation (f. 36^{r-v}) is similar but mentions (as does our poem) the rejoicing of the mountains of Snowdonia (*Eryri*):

> O hvnnv e kerda e linx a erchyrvyna pob peth, er hvnn a emdengys en gwymp y'u briaut genedel, canys trwy honno e kyll Normandi e dwy ynys ac o'e hen deilyngdaut yd yspeilir. Odena yd emchvel y kiwdautwyr e'r ynys, canys aglyvundeb er estronyon a emgyuyt. Er hen gwynn y ar varch gvelw a drossa avon Peryron ac a gvyalne wenn a vessur melyn arnei. Kadwalader a eilw Kenan ac a gymer en e gedymdeithas Ysgotlont. Ena e byd aerua o'r estronyon, ena e llithrant er avonoed o waet. Ena a llawenhaant menyded Eryri ac o deyrnwyalen Vrutus e coronheir. Ena e llenwir Kemry o lewynyd ac yd irhaa kedernyt Kernyu.

The Welsh version of the commentary on the Prophecies from Pen. 16 does not elaborate on the identity of the Lynx, but Pen. 14, 143 (14c) notes *y linx a gerda dros bob peth, nyt amgen Henri gam yw hwnnw*, Brynley F. Roberts, 'Esboniad Cymraeg ar Broffwydoliaeth Myrddin', *B* 21 (1964-6), 277-300, p. 278. This agrees with Matthew Paris (in his *Flores Historiarum*, edited by H. R. Luard (London, 1890), I, 208) who takes Geoffrey's Lynx to be Henry III. See further, Lesley Coote, *Prophecy and Public Affairs in Later Medieval England* (Woodbridge, 2000), 66-8. Henry III's Welsh epithet *cam* may refer to his drooping left eye. Proffwydoliaeth yr Eryr (edited by Henry Lewis, *B* 9 (1937-9), 112-15, p. 113) has *Linx a daw o hat y llew* (cf. the Latin version printed in J.J.

5 Kein gyfedwch

Parry, *Brut y Brenhinedd, Cotton Cleopatra Version* (Cambridge, Mass., 1937), 225).

22   **nyt llwyded escori**   *Nyt* suggests following a noun or adj. rather than vb form < *llwyddaw*. *Llwyded* could represent ModW *llwydedd* 'pallor, greyness, being grey-haired', and if so, with no emendation as in the translation, the Lynx is one who has no regard or care for the old, unlike the commendable Urien, praised in englynion as a *dinas henwred*, 'a refuge for the old' (ESWP 421, englyn 12, but see note 555-6 for Rowland's reservations about the reading). If Henry III is the Lynx, note that he was crowned very young and might be imagined to have no interest in the old.

However, *llwyd* (ModW *llwydd*) 'success' is very productive in compounds and *llwydget* (*llwyd* + *cet* 'gift') is a possibility, cf. CBT VII 7.2 *Llyw llwytged*, perhaps more likely than a back formation from adj. *llwydedig*.

Escori is an extremely rare variant of vb *esgor* 'to expel, get rid of; rid, defend', otherwise attested only in Edmyg Dinbych line 1 *Archaf y wen y Duw plwyf escori*, assigned the meaning 'to rid, to defend' by G, and translated as 'protector of the people' by Ifor Williams and R. Geraint Gruffydd. One might wonder in light of the EWSP 421 example cited whether *esgori* might not be linked, rather, with *ysgor* 'citadel, defence', as suggested by GPC s.v. *esgoraf: esgor* 'to gather into a fold, enclosure; or fortress' (but cf. CBT III 274).

23   **Gynt gwaedvenni**   *Gynt* 'tribe, people', as in §2.17 *eil o Ynt*, but note that G s.v. *gynt²* suggests emendation to *gwynt* in our example, possibly suggested by CBT IV 16.210 *Dychyrch hynt dychre g6ynt gwaeduan*, and EWSP 455 englyn 21 *goruchel awel guaet vann. Gwaedvann* < *gwaed* 'cry' + *bann* 'high, loud'.

24   **galwawr Eryri**   See note on §2.16 *ac Eryri vre varnhawt*; and cf. §7.43-4 *diffeith Moni a Lleenni,/ ac Eryri anhed yndi*; §10.4 *ac yn Eryri ymolöi*.

25   **anhawd y deui**   G s.v. *anhawd* suggests emending to *anhawr* 'fame, praise' which is the *lectio difficilior* certainly. But this is not implemented here since *anhawd* gives reasonable sense — the Lynx attacking will give no quarter to the old; people will be agitated and Eryri will be called upon for its protection which will mean that the attacker will find it hard to invade. *Deui* is understood as *dyui* 'he will come'.

26   **Jolwn Elöi**   Hebrew *Elöi*, CC 33.3 *Eli, Elöi ac Adonäi*; CC 2.12; CC 25.4.

27   **pan y'n bo gan Geli**   Cf. CBT I 30.1 *A'm bo y gan Du6, a'm bo—trugared*. For *pan* 'that', see on LPBT 3.2 *pan vyd Duw dy-m-gwaret. Pan + y*, cf. CBT V 10.85 *Pan y'm gwnaeth vuled. Celi* is very common, especially in the CBT corpus.

28   **adef Nef dimbi**   See on line 11 above *dimbi*, and *dymbi* §2.41; §7.23. Collocated *Nef* and *adef* 'home' are exceedingly common throughout early poetry, particularly handy as internal and end-rhyme partners: see G s.v. *aðef¹*.

6 Rydyrchafwy Duw ar plwyff Brython

This is a rare instance of a Book of Taliesin text which can be compared with another of medieval origin. In this case, we can turn to a copy made by John Jones, Gellilyfdy in Peniarth 111 (*c*. 1610), 378-80: there it is entitled *Kywrisset Gvynet a Dehevparth*[1] 'The Contention between Gwynedd and Deheubarth'. It follows on from 'Dydd dyfydd, trengi deweint', a poem with religious and prophetic elements, attributed to Meugan.[2] Some lines of 'Dydd dyfydd' appear to have been lifted from other poems, including phrases and words found in the Book of Taliesin.[3] John Jones's source was a copy by Sir George Owen Harris who had copied it out of a piece of vellum at the request of Sir George Owen (*c*. 1552-1613, historian, and squire of Henllys, Pembrokeshire), who could not understand the old poetry nor copy it correctly on account of the many corrupt letters therein. Another copy was seen and copied by Dr John Davies, Mallwyd in the early seventeenth century, and this was consulted by the editors of the *Myvyrian Archaiology* in 1801. According to Dr Davies's note, it had came out of a book belonging to Thomas Gruffudd, the squire of Lampeter, in Ceredigion. Ifor Williams felt confident that the piece of vellum contained two poems written in orthography and script very much like those of the Black Book of Carmarthen. The texts in the Book of Taliesin and Peniarth 111 are essentially the same, although there is one line missing after our line 25 (see textual footnotes): also at the end of the Peniarth 111 text there are a few confused lines in a different metre.[4]

As Ifor Williams noted, the poem appears to favour the Gwynedd forces,[5] perhaps especially those of Anglesey. These seem to be acting in concert with the men of Powys who are praised as 'keen ones', 'proud men triumphing against false laws or customs'. Echoing the diction as well as the Cyhydedd Naw Ban metre of Armes Prydain, the two forces are said to be in harmony, 'with one instinct, one utterance, orderly and disciplined'. Further south, in the Vale of Aeron, along the Rivers Tywi and Teifi, the men of Ceredigion, too, are ready to play their part well as the action moves further south to *llys Lonyon*, 'the court of Llonion', just to the west of present day Pembroke Dock.[6] The enemy, unnamed

---

[1] Ifor Williams, 'Dalen o femrwn', *B* 4 (1927-9), 41-8. Only significant variants are noted below.

[2] Whether this has anything to do with Moucan whose prayers survive in the 8c Mercian manuscript, BL MS Royal 2.A.XX is uncertain: see David R. Howlett, '*Orationes Moucani*: early Cambro-Latin prayers', *CMCS* 24 (1992), 55-74.

[3] A new edition of this text is in preparation.

[4] Williams, 'Dalen o femrwn' 48: *kae kert nis guipo// trychan cant talho/ ei gil guin ar y to/ duhuit ae girro/ llu bid ae guyppo* 'he who knows not the chaplet of song should pay 300 . . . . . the host of the world knows it'.

[5] PT xxvii.

[6] This region was connected in Triad 26, *Tri Gwrdueichyat Enys Prydein*, with the progeny of the sow Henwen, one of whom was Palug's Cat, one of the three oppressions emanating from Anglesey, with Daronwy and Edwin (see on §1).

here, will find no refuge — not in *Dynclut, Dyn Maerut* or *Dyn Daryfon* or even *Dyn Riedon*, wherever these last three may be. By contrast, in lines 17-18, we have the return of Cadwallon over the sea from Ireland to re-establish a base or refuge at Ardd Nefon. An obvious candidate here is the seventh-century Cadwallon fab Cadfan, foe of Edwin of Northumbria, a figure who seems to have become vaguely associated with sea-power and maritime travel in the various pieces of poetry about him.[7] There are two medieval references to his exile in Ireland. In Triad 29 *Tri Diweir Deulu*, 'The Three Faithful Warbands', the first on the list is the warband of Cadwallon son of Cadfan 'who were with him in Ireland for seven years; and during that period of time they asked nothing of him in case they should have to leave him'.[8] The second reference concerns Geoffrey of Monmouth's Caduallo, who figures very large indeed in *Historia Regum Britanniae*: there, after his quarrel with the Anglian king, Edwin, and their subsequent clash of arms beyond the Humber, Caduallo marches through Scotland, and retreats to Ireland for a period leaving Edwin to burn the cities of the Britons and to torture town- and countrymen (HKB ch. 191-3). His attempts to return to Britain are foiled by Edwin, aided by the skilled augur, Pellitus, who understood the significance of bird flight and the movements of the stars. With the ports closed to him, Caduallo journeys to seek help from Salomon in Brittany. Rachel Bromwich maintained that these two references to Cadwallon's exile in Ireland may have had an historical basis, perhaps as a consequence of what Bede reports as Edwin's conquest of the Menavian islands (HE II.ix) — if these are Man and Anglesey. Other possible candidates called Cadwallon are discussed in the notes to line 17.

Cadwallon fab Cadfan may have been thought of as a figura for the next-mentioned ruler, Idwal Foel, also ousted from power in Gwynedd, in his case by Hywel Dda. In our poem the Welsh cavalry force in the vicinity of Chester play football (or polo?) with the Saxon heads as they avenge Idwal's death at the hands of the English in 942. This brings to mind the Annales Cambriae description of Rhodri Mawr's death in 878 being avenged by God at the Battle of Conwy in 881. They, or else the unnamed and unassuming young man of line 25, will ravage the Specked Cat and her foreigners from Taradr Ford in Gwent as far as Porth Wygyr, the latter extremity in the poet's probable home patch of Anglesey. Resisting the foe will bring its own satisfaction, as intimated by the honey and clover representing the good times to come.

T.M. Charles-Edwards notes that Ifor Williams dates the poem to 942-50 on the basis of the Idwal reference, but comments that the period should include the following decade, to 960.[9] Williams clearly thought it should be dated to the period 'when such a prophecy . . . . would be most relevant to the needs of

---

[7] See details in note on poem line 17.
[8] TYP³ 62. The other two warbands were those of Gafran son of Aeddan 'who went into the sea', and Gwenddolau's warband at the battle of Arfderydd. The earliest ms of this triad is Pen. 16iv, saec. xiii², TYP³ xvi.
[9] WaB 661: PT xxvi-vii.

Gwynedd . . . when the land was in dire distress and in the depths of despair',[10] but it is possible that events from the past — such as avenging the death of Idwal, or some successful Gwynedd and Powys attacks on Ceredigion and beyond, or even the dimmer memory of Cadwallon's return to Wales, could continue to have a live charge to inspire and encourage long after those events had happened.

---

[10] Referring to HW 337-8 and 343-4.

6 Rydyrchafwy Duw ar plwyff Brython
Book of Taliesin 72.23-73.19

Rydyrchafwy Duw   ar plwyff Brython
May God raise up over the people of the Britons
arwyd llewenyd   llüyd o Von.
the emblem of joy of the hosts of Anglesey.
Kyfryssed[1] Gwyned,   brys gorchordyon
The battle of the men of Gwynedd, swift forces
ffaw claer, o pop aer   kaffael gwystlon.
of radiant fame, taking hostages from every fight.

5   **Powys dybydant[2]   dwys yg kyfleudon,**
The men of Powys shall come, (praised as) keen ones in eulogy,
gwyr goruyn[3]   gorynt   ar eu deduon.
proud men who shall triumph over false laws.
Deu lu yd ant,[4]   bydant gysson,
In two hosts they shall proceed, they shall be in harmony,
yn vn redyf, vn[5] eir,   kyweir kymon.
with one instinct, one utterance, orderly and disciplined,
Kyfranant yn iawn   Keredigyawn vaon.[6]
The men of Ceredigion shall play their part well.

10   **Pan welych wyr ryn   am Lyn Aeron,**
When you may see fierce men around the Vale of Aeron.
pan vo trwm Tywi   a Theiui Afon,
when the Tywi and the River Teifi shall be saddened,
wy gwnant aer ar vrys   am lys Lonyon.
they shall make battle in haste around the court of Llonion.
A gennis[7] a dewis   yn orllwython:[8]
Those who held out fell silent in great numbers:
ny nothwy dinassoed rac y rwython:
citadels shall not protect (them) from their swift men:

15   **Dynclut, Dyn Maerut,   Dyn Daryfon;[9]**
(whether) Din Clud, Din Maerud, Din Daryfon,
nyt oed lwyr degyn   Dyn Riedon.
not (even) Din Rhieddon/Rhiyddon would be entirely impregnable.

---

[1] BT *Kyffryssed* with deleting point below first *f*.
[2] Pen. 111 *dybitaut*
[3] BT *goruyn*, Pen. 111 *gorvuit*
[4] Pen. 111 *itaut*
[5] Pen. 111 *vu eir*
[6] Pen. 111 *karedigiaun* (no *vaon*)
[7] BT *a geunis*
[8] BT *A geunis adewis orllwython*, Pen. 111 *a kimis a tewis morlluthion*
[9] Pen. 111 *da rywon*

6 Rydyrchafwy Duw ar plwyff Brython

Pan dyfu Gatwallawn dros eigyawn   Iwerdon
When Cadwallon came over the Irish sea
yd atrefnwys nefwy   yn Ard Nefon.[10]
he re-established a court in Ardd Nefon.
Keinyadon moch clywyf   eu gofalon:
Soon shall I hear the tribulations of the singers/poets:
20   **marchawc lu mor taer   am Gaer Llion,**
how fierce the cavalry force around Chester,
a dial Idwal   ar[11] **ranwynyon,**
and the avenging of Idwal on the white-cheeked ones,
a gware pelre   a phen Saesson.
and playing ball with the heads of the Saxons.
Ys trabludyo y Gath Vreith   a'e hagyfieithon
May he wreak havoc on the Speckled Cat and her foreigners
o Ryt ar Taradyr hyt ym Porth Wygyr yMon —
from the Ford on the Taradr as far as Porth Wygr in Anglesey —
25   **jeuanc didwynas   dinas maon.**[12]
(he), the unassuming young man, the people's refuge.
O'r pan amygir   mel a meillon
From (the time) when honey and clover shall be seized
gadent eu hamrydar   a'e hamrysson:
their contention and their dispute will vanish:
nyt diwystyl godi   dic wrth alon.
enmity towards the foe is not an unhappy inciting.[13]
Rydyrchafwy Duw   ar plwyf Brython
May God raise up over the people of the Britons
30   **a[rwyd] ll[ewenyd   llüyd o Von.]**
the emblem of joy of the hosts of Anglesey!

---

1   **Rydyrchafwy** *Dyrchafu* 'to raise up', used of the banner of St David in AP line 129 *A lluman glan Dewi a drychafant*, with *stondardd* in GIG 20.121, here with *arwyd* 'ensign, banner' (and cf. WM 136.17 *dyrchafel ar6yd ymwan*). *Oduch* (as in PT VI.15 *dyrchafwn eidoed oduch mynyd*) might be thought more natural for 'over, above, over the heads of' than *ar*. Other meanings such as 'facing, before' are possible, and since *dyrchafu ar* can mean 'to augment' (GPC s.v.), 'may God augment the peoples of the Britons. The hosts of Anglesey [shall be] a sign of joy'. But Ifor Williams's more straightforward interpretation, PT xxvii, 'God will

---

[10] In the Pen. 111 text, lines 17-18 occur after line 25.
[11] BT *ac aranwynyon*; Pen. 111 *ar aranwinion*
[12] In Pen. 111, three lines follow line 25: viz. *tetru tut ner a thad tad alltudion/ ba dyfy kaw* llaun dros eigaun Jwerton/ i tachref inis n*vuy in art nevon*; the last two correspond to lines 17-18.
[13] Following line 28, Pen. 111 ends *ryd ael etauc hiruv// periw ae parvy/ kae kert nis guip// trychan cant talho/ ei gil guin ar y to/ duhuit ae girro/ llu bid ae guyppo*.

6 Rydyrchafwy Duw ar plwyff Brython

raise over the Britons the sign (banner) of joy of a host from Anglesey', is followed here.

1 **plwyff Brython** The occasional doubling of *-f-* for intervocalic [v] is found in the Black Book of Carmarthen: CC 14.28 *vffyldaud*; CC 22.72 *vffil*; LlDC 16.78 *affon*; 5.148 *goffalon*; 17.78 *duffyr*. In final position, as here, LlDC 6.10 *godvff* ('neck'), 16.48 and 54 *tiff*, as well as in other 13c manuscripts, e.g. Cotton Caligula A.iii f. 186^v, col. 1 *a dyrcheyff arna6*; Pen. 29, p. 19 *eff* (3 examples); Pen. 30, col. 2 *dywaethaff*; col. 109 *heneyff* (= ModW *hynaif*); col. 150 *tyr kyfryff*; *tref gyfryff*; col. 151 *tref gyfryff*; col. 163 *ryff*; col. 324 *turyff*; col. 325 *adeff*. 14c examples are also seen, e.g. NLW 3035 (Mostyn 116) has many. LPBT 3.35 *araff hirdyd* appears to represent devoicing before *h*-, as perhaps in Pen. 10, f. 42^r *yn araff heb neb*. Rhyming the commonly collocated *plwy(w)/Dwy(w)* may have been intended, cf. CC 9.3 and 20.12-13; LPBT 3.31; Edmyg Dinbych line 1 *Archaf y wen y Duw plwyf escori*; Marwnad Cynddylan line 30.

Brython is common at the end of a line: e.g. PT VIII.25 *mawr gwrnerth ystlyned y Vrython*; PT XII.5 *ny golychaf an gnawt beird o Vrython*; LPBT 10.33 *mwyhaf gwarth y marth o parth Brython*; CA line 806 *ny doeth en diwarth o barth Vrython*; §4.29 *llewenyd y Vrython*; §8.35 *ffaw dreic, diffreidyat y popyl Brython*; LPBT 1.86 *Dygofi dy hen Vrython*; AP line 12 (before caesura) *Atporyon uyd Brython pan dyorfyn*, and lines 42 and 90; B 26 (1974-6), 407 (Cadwallon fragment) *Neus duc Gwynedd gorvoled i Vrython*; LlDC 17.180 (Oianau) *Maban dirchavaud mad y Vrython*.

2 **arwyd llewenyd llüyd o Von** *Arwyd* 'sign, portent; banner' used in political prophecy contexts in LPBT 1.63; R1051.14, etc. *Llewenyd llü(yd)* collocations are noted in discussion on §4.28. For common and proper nouns + *o* + name of region, see on LPBT 14.26.

3 **Kyfryssed Gwyned** The Pen. 111 text is entitled *Kywrisset Gvynet a Dehevparth*, and has *kywrisset vynet* (with lenition) in line 3. See CA 240 on *kyfryssed*, fairly common in hengerdd (with *lluyd* in CA line 1160) and prose, but limited in the court poetry corpus to CBT I 2.43.

3 **brys gorchordyon** *Gorchordyon*, in hengerdd used of heavenly hosts: PT XII.1; CC 11.42; CC 21.149; LlDC 16.65 (Afallennau); those under God's aegis, in Moliant Cadwallon line 14 *As am[n]odwy Duw y dewr orchordon*. Common of temporal hosts in CBT corpus, and rhymed with *Mon* in CBT IV 5.2-3, and also collocated with Gwynedd, CBT VI 5.31-2 *Gwae ni, Wynet orchordon,/ Gwelet lla6r ar llyw ma6r Mon*.

4 **ffaw claer o pop aer** Cf. CA line 947 *an gelwir ny faw glaer fwyre*; *aer/claer* are commonly collocated in the CBT corpus.

5 **Powys dybydant** Both readings give good sense. 3pl. fut. *dybydant* also in §7.3 *Duw Llun dybydant* and §7.15 *diheu dybydant*; LPBT 5.190 *wrth urwydrin dybydant*; cf. LPBT 13.20 *A chyn dybydyn*. Pen. 111's *dibitaut* (= dybydd(h)awd), 3 sg. fut., cf. CBT IV 9.26 *Gvrth ur6ydr crwydyr creula6n dybyta6d* (and see note p. 199), CBT VI 20.63 *dybyda6t dyd*. WaB 552 notes that Powys is not mentioned in annals between 854 and 1069.

5 **dwys yg kyfleudon** *Dwys kyfleudon* would yield a more regular cadence, but pentasyllabic cadences also occur in lines 11, 23 below. G s.v. *kyfleudon* suggests a pl. meaning 'hosts, armies' for this hapax, but GPC s.v. *cyfleuddon* ventures that

6 Rydyrchafwy Duw ar plwyff Brython

it is it is a variant of *cyflawddon* (*eu* ~ *aw*), a rare word, seeming to mean 'praise, eulogy', used only by Prydydd y Moch: CBT V 4.23 *Ym o'm da6n y'm da6 kyfla6don*; CBT V 25.17 *Yg Caer-yn-Aruon yng kert gyfla6don*. The base is *llawd* (= llawdd) from L. *laud-*, cf. vb *llawddaf: llawddu*, and the poet's name *Llawdden*. *Yg* understood as prep. *yn* 'in', but if it is the pron. *(f)y*, then 'intense my praise'.

6 **gwyr goruynt (ms goruyn)** Pen. 111 *guir gorvuit. goruit ar ev decuon* may be due to minim confusion, as suggested by G s.vv. *goruyn* and *goruot* (G 565). The Book of Taliesin's *goruyn* 'passionate, fierce' may have been substituted for its near synonym *goruynt* 'proud, eager', restored here for internal rhyme; cf. its use with *gwr/gwyr* in CA line 125 *gwr gorvynt*, line 145 *gwyr goruynnaf*; R581.21-2 *Beli hir a'e wyr goruynt*; CBT IV 5.83 *Llas llary vrodyr, g6yr goruynt*; CBT VII 25.62-3 *Goruynt chwetyl kenetyl . . . / Gwr. . .* ; etc.

6 **gorynt** Rare 3pl. pres. of vb *goruot* + *ar* 'defeat, triumph over'.

6 **ar eu deduon** *Geu* 'false', or 3pl. pron. as in LlDC 31.18 *in amuin ev detvon*. The pl. *dedueu* is on the rise in the CBT corpus, but *deduon* is still being used by Dafydd Benfras in 1248, CBT VI 31.59.

7 **Deu lu yd ant** Cf. EWSP 420.7 (Pen Urien); LPBT 24.2 and 8; PKM 29 *y rwg y deu lu*, and innumerable other prose examples. Pen. 111 *i taut*, emended by Williams to *i cat*, but the present reading seems preferable for internal rhyme.

7 **gysson** *Kysson* collocated with *kyweir* (as here) in AP line 126 *yn gyweir gyteir gytson gytffyd* (referring to the Cymry imagined as prevailing in battle); LPBT 8.27 *teir kadeir kyweir kysson*; CC 21.146-7 *Myn y mae kertorion/ In kyveir kysson*.

8 **yn vn redyf vn eir kyweir kymon** *Vn eir* 'unanimously', cf. examples of *o vn eir* in *Brut y Brenhinedd* texts (e.g. NLW 3035, the Red Book of Hergest, Philadelphia Public Library Company ms 8680.O, etc., as accessed via the rhyddiaithganoloesol.caerdydd.ac.uk website). *Kymon* (< *bon*) 'orderly, tidy, compact; regular, seemly, becoming, noble, worthy', according to GPC s.v. *cymon*; poorly attested in the medieval record, but cf. vb *cymoni*, and *cymondeb, cymoned* 'as noble', etc.

9 **Kyfranant yn iawn** Vb *kyfran(nu)* 'to contribute' also 'to share with, apportion, distribute', here implying that the host of Ceredigion will pull their weight in battle: cf. the martial usage by Owain Cyfeiliog in CBT II 14.47 *Teleir6 'yg kygrein yn kyfran—br6ydyr*.

9 **Keredigyawn vaon** The final cadence is typically four or five syllables, implying that if *vaon* (not present in Pen. 111) is to be retained, then *Keredigyawn* might have been syncopated (> *K'redigyawn*), as in Dafydd y Coed's example (14c) noted by G, now edited in GDC 1.15. In Pen. 111, *Karedigiaun* may have been thought to give a tolerable rhyme with *-yon*. For examples of the variant *Karedigiaun*, as in the Pen. 111 text, see G s.v. *Keredigyawn*. Ifor Williams, PT xxvii, regards this as an allusion to the events of 894 when Anarawd came with the English and laid waste Ceredigion and Ystrad Tywi: see poem introduction.

10 **Pan welych wyr ryn** *Gwelych* 2sg. pres. subjunct., perhaps expressing possibility, as in CA line 660 *ny welych weyelin*; R1053.5-6 (Crist Iesu) *edrych a welych wael anreith*; CBT II 30.1 *Pan welych llewych lliw gwawr*; and perhaps in CBT VII 33.6 *Sal6 ymgelu pan y g6elych*. See CA 93 on *ryn* 'stiff, rigid' of

corpses, 'stout' of weapons, 'tough, rough' of soldiers, as here; LlDC 31.18-19 *Oet rinn vy gueisson/ in amuin ev detvon*. With *gwr*, CA lines 442-3 *anthuim cim mruinauc/ o goll gur gunet rin*.

10   **am Lyn Aeron** Glyn Aeron, the valley of the River Aeron that flows to the sea in Aberaeron, Ceredigion (there is no *llyn* 'lake' of that name, Llyn Eiddwen being the only water of any size, at its upper reaches). The house of Glyn Aeron — its precise location as yet unidentified — in the commote of Anhuniog, near Llangeitho, was the home of several generations of important patrons in the 14 and 15c, including Rhydderch ab Ieuan Llwyd. GBLlH 7.12 *Hyder gloyw nêr Glyn Aeron*; GDC 1.30 *Glyn Aeron da ddragon diddrygedd*; GLlBH 19.72 *Ceinion glan Aeron a'i glyn eurog*; GGG 89.9 *Pôr glân oror Glan Aeron*. Mentions of Aeron are common, cf. LPBT 14.27 *ae Dyfyd o Aeron* and n. The commonly mentioned North British *Aeron*, see G s.n. (1), can be discounted here.

11   **pan vo trwm Tywi a Theiui afon** The two rivers, Tywi and Teifi, which rise some nine miles apart, flow to the sea in Carmarthen Bay and in Cardigan respectively. They are mentioned together in connection with a raid by Cadwaladr: LlDC 16.77-80 (Afallennau) *iny del Kadwaladir oe kinadil kadwaon/ y erir Tywi a Teiwi affon,/ a dyuod gra[e]nde o aranwinion,/ a guneuthur guar o willt, o gwallt hirion*. 'Until Cadwaladr comes to/from his battle-troops to the eagle of Tywi and the River Teifi, and the coming of fierce ones with white faces, and the taming of the savages, of the long-haired ones'. And singly, in other prophetic texts (Tywi): R581.37-8 (Cyfoesi) *Pan disgynno Kadwaladyr yn Dyffryn Tywi*; LlDC 17.196 (Oianau) *Ac imlat in taer am dvylan Tywi*; R580.30-1 (Cyfoesi) *Pan uo pont ar Daf ac arall ar Dywi/ y da6 ar Loegyr [lwyr] dyuysgi*; LlDC 17.218 (Oianau) *ban vo pont ar Taw ac arall ar Tywi/ y dav y Dyved ryvel iti*. These last examples show how lines can be reused at will, cf. Armes Prydain's first lines recycled in poem §4. Teifi is seen in LlDC 17.156 (Oianau): *Ban diffon brodorion o amtiret Mon/ y holi Brithon, brithuid dybi./ Dirchafaud dreic faud, fau isperi,/ gurt kyuan uaran o lan Teiwi./ Gunahaud am Dyued diygiuysci,/ bit itau in aelau eilon indi*. It also occurs in Marwnad Cadwallon englyn 13 along with scores of other river- and place-names: *Lluest Gatwallawn ar Deiui/ kymysgei waet a heli*. On the affiliations of the territory of Ystrad Tywi, first attested in AC 893 coupled with Ceredigion, see WaB 19-20.

12   **wy gwnant aer ar vrys** CBT III 5.86 *Ni'm hu vrys o'e llys*. *Ar frys* 'in haste' (and *ar ofrys*) are occasionally used in poetry, see GPC s.v. *brys*.

12   **am Lys Lonyon** The name survives as L(l)anion, Pembroke Dock, mentioned seemingly as a region in Pembrokeshire in LL 124, 255 *Din guennham* (*guennhaf*) *in Lonion*; *Llonyon ym Penvro* TYP³ 45. B.G. Charles (PNP 721) identifies this *Din Guernham* with Golden Hill to the south-east, with the original second element — the personal name *Gwenha(f)* — subsequently anglicised. As to Llonion, he posits a territorial suffix *-ion* attached to an unrecorded personal name, Llon (cf. saint's name, *Llonio, Lloniaw*), adding, PNP 722, that our line should be understood as 'towards (*am*) the court (*llys*) of (the district of) Llonion'. However, *am* in poetry most often means 'around', or 'because of', 'concerning', or else 'for' (to get, possess, etc.), which is also possible here: see G. s.v. (a)-(d). It is possible that *Din Guenham* was the *llys* referred to by our poet. T.M. Charles-Edwards, WaB 661, cites DP ii, 421, for a legal text, no later than 1093, that mentions Llonion (along with Tenby, Lawrenny and *Amiteil* (cf. *Amithieil* in LL

6 Rydyrchafwy Duw ar plwyff Brython

124, probably around Monkton)) as a royal site. He notes also the complex of important sites to the south-east of Llanion: Tenby itself with its promontory fortlet, together with Longbury Bank inland to the west, and the two important ecclesiastical sites, Penally (Penalun), and Caldey Island (Ynys Bŷr).

In Triad 26 *Tri Gwrdueichyat Enys Prydein* (Pen. 16iv text, saec. xiii^2), stories are included about the three swineherds, Drystan, Pryderi, and Coll fab Collfrewy. Details are given of the wanderings of the sow, Henwen, first in Cornwall (Penrhyn Austin), then Aber Tarogi, Gwent, and thence to Llonion where she brought forth a grain of barley and a bee. From there she continued to Rhiw Cyferthwch in Eryri (Snowdonia), leaving a wolf-cub and a young eagle, and thence to Llanfair in Arfon where she brought forth a kitten thrown by Coll into the Menai (the cat was known subsequently as Cath Balug).

A similar text in the White Book of Rhydderch notes that Henwen, sow of Dallwyr Dallben in Cornwall, was the subject of a prophecy that said 'that it would get worse for the Island of Britain because of her litter': *a darogan oed yd hanvyde waeth Ynys Brydein o'r torll6yth*. In this version she brings forth a grain of barley and a grain of wheat in Llonion, and 'because of that there is a saying about the swarm of Llonion': *Am hynny y diharhebir o heid Llonyon* (TYP^3 51). Trouble came from the other progeny too: Cath Balug was reared by sons of Palug in Anglesey 'to their own harm', becoming one of the three oppressions reared there (*Ac a uu vn o Deir Prif Ormes Mon a uagwyt yndi*) together with Daronwy and Edwin (*A'r eil oed Daronwy. A'r dryded, Edwin vrenhin Lloegyr*, TYP^3 52).

13   **A gennis (ms geunis) a dewis yn orllwython**   Pen. 111 has *a kimis a tewis morlluthion*. G suggests that Pen. 111 *kimis* might be a mistake for *kinnis* (an orthographical variant of either *kennis*, *kennys* or *kynnis*, possible 3sg. pret. forms of vb *kannu* 'to maintain, keep, hold, collect, take possession of', as in CBT I 8.20 *A gennis dra chas dra Chors Vochno*; CBT I 10.34 *Tranc a'e kennis kyn no mi*; CBT VI 30.45 *Cyn angeu Dafydd, cynnydd cennis*; CBT I 2.37 *Rychedwis detyf, rychynis gretyw rac lletyw ogyrven*; CBT V 4.40 *Ef cynnis tud forion*, and cf., with *dewis*, CBT I 11.67 *Dechennis dewis deurut goeluein*. The BT reading *geunis* could have started from such a form (with minim confusion leading to -*eu*-). But G does not rule out *agennis*, although the vb *agennu* 'to split, gape open' is not attested until the 16c according to GPC^2 s.v.

Another way forward is suggested by H-cd's modernised and emended *ac efnys a dewis — yn orllwythion*. *Dewis* could be understood as 'chosen, elite' with nominal force, with *efnys a d(d)ewis* displaying the 'da a ddwy ynys' construction. But Isaac's non-lenition suggests that he understands the 3sg. pret. of vb *tewi* 'to fall silent', perhaps 'and the fierce ones fell silent in great numbers'.

G suggests connecting *gorllwython* with *llwyth* (comparing OIr *forlucht* 'excessive load, number'), although GPC s.v. *gorlwyth*, *gorllwyth* has attestations from the late 18c only. It would correspond broadly with the meaning of Pen. 111 *morlluthion*, recte *morlluithion* if *morllwyth* were an old compound of *mawr* (compare *mordei*) rather than from *mor*. But it would seem more economical to take the Pen. 111 *m* as a misreading of *in*.

If -*th*- in both forms were understood as [ð], consider pl. of *gorllwyd* (GPC s.v. *gorllwydd* 'increase, prosperity'), or with more radical intervention, *gorlludyon 'hindrances, obstructions' < *lludd* (which forms its plural in -*on*), comparing vb *gorlludyaw* (see GPC s.v. *gorlluddiaf*) and attested *golludyon*. For the sense, cf.

6 Rydyrchafwy Duw ar plwyff Brython

PT II.19-20 *Vnynt tanc gan aethant golludyon* 'they wanted peace since they had got into difficulties'. The translation is very uncertain: 'those who held out (*a gynnis/gennis*) fell silent (*a dewis*) in great numbers (*yn orllwython*)'. For *tewi* as falling silent in death, cf. (in battle) Moliant Cadwallon line 11 *Tewynt rieu krawn rac proystlawn*; CBT I 9.81-2 *Gweleis yno ym mro yn arygyr:/ Tewi gan llyw a wyr o anystyr*.

14 **ny nothwy dinassoed** Cf. §1.7 *Nyt wy a'm nodwy*; LPBT 8.20 *a'n nothwy rac gwyth llwyth agh*ymes. The -*wy* rather than -*o* 3 sg. subjunct. of this vb is used by Prydydd y Moch, CBT V 23.2 *A'm notwy rac auar*, the sole example in CBT. Compound in Moliant Cadwallon line 14 *As am[n]odwy Duw y dewr orchordon*.

14 **rac y rwython** Pen. 111 *rac y ruython*. GPC lists no *rhwyth*, and *grwyth* is late. If the exemplar was like BBC with *th* for [ð], perhaps *rwyd* 'bountiful; easy, quick, ready, unimpeded', etc., here used substantivally in the plural (= -*ion*) although this is uncommon.

15 **Dynclut** Pen. 111 *dinclud*. The only example of this particular locution for Dumbarton Rock: cf. CBT I 9.145 *Dygwystlir itaw o Din Alclud goglet*; see on §3.19 *Kat yn Ryt Alclut*. AC 870 *Arx Alt Clut a gentilibus fracta est*. Each of these names in lines 15-16 is spelt *dyn* rather than *din*. GPC s.v. *dyn(n)* 'hill, height, fortification' suggests that *dyn(n)* is a cognate of or a borrowing from Ir *dinn*; it is found as a second element in place-names such as Creuddyn, Treuddyn, etc.

15 **Dyn Maerut** Unknown. One might canvass similar names such as *Dinmael* (Powys Fadog), *Dinmawr* and *Dinmeir* (a *Gueith Dinmeir* is noted AC 906 (A text), the same year as Mynyw 'fracta est', but this is probably a mistake for *Dineirth* on the River Arth, Ceredigion; but see ByT (Pen. 20) 140). Although Ifor Williams hints at a correspondence between *Dyn Maerut* and Dinmeir, both *Dyn Maerut* (perhaps based on *maer* 'steward') and *Dyn Daryfon* may be imagined names.

15 **Dyn Daryfon** Pen. 111 *din da rywon*. Otherwise unknown: it almost looks like a hybrid of Rhyd ar *Dar*adr and Per*yddon*/Per*yfon*.

16 **lwyr degyn Dyn Riedon** Cf. LlDC 17.66 (Oianau) *a guneuthur Dyganhuy dinas degin*. No fortress of this name is known. *Riedon* may be based on *ried*, pl. of *ri* 'king', or *ried* 'majesty, kingship, sovereignty' (see GPC s.vv. *rhi*, *rhiedd*, *rhiydd*).

17 **Pan dyfu Gatwallawn dros eigyawn Iwerdon** Lines 17 and 18 do not stand here in the Pen. 111 text, but after line 25. On Cadwallon ap Cadfan and Ireland, see poem introduction. EWSP 169-73 surveys the strands of Cadwallon's historical and legendary career, referring to the fragments edited by Graham C.G. Thomas, and evidence for lost englynion, as well as the surviving englynion, 'Marwnad Cadwallon'. The awdl, Moliant Cadwallon, is regarded by its editor, R. Geraint Gruffydd, and by Bromwich, TYP[3] 300-1, as a piece composed at the height of Cadwallon's career before 634; some doubt has been expressed about this by Graham Isaac, H-Cd (who classes the poem as a prophecy), and by Alex Woolf, 'Caedualla rex Brettonum and the passing of the Old North', *Northern History* 41 (2004), 5-23, who also questions the identity of Bede's Caedualla. Cadwallon fab Cadfan was revered by the poets. Prydydd y Moch's awdl to Llywelyn ab Iorwerth, composed *c*. 1215, styles the king as a second Urien, as 'the sovereign of Britain' whose fame runs as far as Carlisle and beyond, and it is

6 Rydyrchafwy Duw ar plwyff Brython

against a northerly backdrop and the memory of the momentous struggle against Edwin for the imperium of Britain in the 7c — as well as Llywelyn's recent triumphs in north-east Wales — that we should read the poet's two references to Cadwallon: CBT V 23.88-92 *Lloegyr diwreit . . . ./ Ll6r6 da6n Cadwalla6n uab Caduan,/ Y mae am Brydein yn gynnan* 'Ouster of the men of Engand . . . complete with the ability of Cadwallon son of Cadfan, he is intent on the whole of Britain'; CBT V 23.136-8 *Lloegyr gychwyn, a uynn a uynho./ Llwyr y dyd y uryd ar uro—Gadwalla6n/ Uab Caduan uab Yago* 'One who disturbs the men of England, who gets what he desires, who sets his sights entirely on the region of Cadwallon son of Cadfan son of Iago'. Cf. CBT V 1.36 *Cad walla6, Cadwalla6n amhad*, and see note CBT V p. 18. Since dynastic struggles in Gwynedd at many periods might involve tactical retreats to Ireland, there may be other possibilities, such as Cadwallon ab Ieuaf (d. 986) fighting for power struggle against his first cousin, Ionafol ap Meurig (WaB 547-8). But there is no particular reason to prefer over Cadwallon fab Cadfan characters such as Cadwallon son of Gruffudd ap Cynan (perhaps referred to in CBT I 8.67), or much earlier figures such as Cadwallon Lawhir, the father of Maelgwn Gwynedd.

18 **nefwy** The word (cf. poem §1.1) is not listed in GPC, suggesting that Ifor Williams's suggestion 'court, hall, citadel' (*B* 7 (1933-5), 30, presumably < *nef*) was not supported, but cf. LPBT 1.7 *gwlat nefwy*, where a meaning similar to *nef* 'heaven' seems likely. There is no attested formation from *neu* 'need, want, paucity' (as in *neuaf, neued(d)*). In other examples, including possibly §1.1 *Dvw differth Nefwy* and §1.8 *amgylch Balch Nefwy*, as well as CBT IV 16.184 *g6erinualch Nef6y*, a personal name is most likely, for Biblical Noah in these instances, and as a Biblical name used by the Welsh, certainly in CBT I 1.22 *arpennic peir o blant Nevuy*, referring in all probability to the descendants of Nowy ap Gwriad, the mid-10c king of Gwent: see David Stephenson, 'Mawl Hywel ap Goronwy: dating and context', *CMCS* 57 (2009), 41-9.

18 **Ard Nefon** Moliant Cadwallon line 22 *Ossid art y Mon ryphebyllas/ Maelgwn hevelit haylon o gwas*. *Ard* 'hill, high land' is very rare in poetry, but cf. EWSP 450.16a *Gordyar adar ar Edrywy ard*; and perhaps LlDC 16.19-20 *Awallen . . . a tyw inhal art heb art in y chilchin*. In place- and regional names, Pennardd, Ar(dd)llechwedd, etc. *Nefon* is unknown, and may be related to *nef* 'heaven, refuge'. Since OW *e* can represent a diphthong, *neif(y)on* may be considered, either connected with *naf* 'lord' or *nef*, as discussed in connection with LPBT 5.47 *gelwysit ar neifion/ ar grist o achwysson*, where it might seem to be for God (or Heavenly one).

19 **keinyadon** Pen. 111 reads *reiniaton*, with which cf. perhaps GPC s.v. *rheiniad* 'giver, distributor, sharer', as in CBT III 20.3 *Ha6l wa6l wastad reinyad reid*; CBT VI 30.32 *Neud Duw a'i rhannws yr hael reiniad*; however, no pl. in *-yon* is attested, and the *-t-* would imply *rheiniaddon. The pl. of *keinyat* is *keinyeit*, hence G's query about this example; but it seems to give reasonable sense, and the formation can be compared with the seemingly one-off *deiliaid ~ deiliadon*, CBT V 12.29 *Deilyadon dyfrynt a'm defry—hiraeth*, and with the alternation *beidadon ~ beidyeit* (see G s.v.). The syntax is inverted.

20 **Caer Llion** Chester (Caer Lleon < *castra legionis*) presumably, rather than Caerllïon ar Wysg (with G 96), and if so perhaps referring to the events of 924, discussed in n. on line 21 below.

6 Rydyrchafwy Duw ar plwyff Brython

21   **dial Idwal** Cf. *digal Rotri a Deo*, discussed in §2.8n. Idwal Foel (d. 942), king of Gwynedd, 916-42, son of Anarawd and grandson of Rhodri Mawr. In 918 according to the A text of the Anglo-Saxon Chronicle, scions of the Gwynedd Merfynion line, Idwal Foel son of Anarawd and his southern kinsmen, Hywel Dda son of Cadell, and his brother, Clydog of Deheubarth, made submission to Edward the Elder, son of Alfred, at Tamworth. In 921 Edward built a fortification at *Cledemuþa* on the mouth of the River Clwyd, possibly at Rhuddlan, perhaps as a defence against Viking attack. AC 921 record a battle at *Dinas Neguid*, possibly this 'new' *burh* at the mouth of the Clwyd (WaB 499). Although not strong evidence in the view of D.N. Dumville, 'Brittany and "Armes Prydein Vawr"', *Études celtiques*, 20 (1983), 145-59, p. 149 n. 26, William of Malmesbury suggests that Edward was in Chester in 924, shortly before his death at Farndon-on-Dee (Cheshire) and that he was there to put down an insurrection of its townsmen in alliance with the Welsh. This may have involved Idwal but this is not certain. WaB 503 wonders whether the *Gueith Dinas Neguid* could 'as well have been fought between Welsh allied with Edward (the Elder) against Vikings as between the Welsh and the English'.

Idwal visited Æthelstan a number of times, witnessing at least eight of his charters from 928-37. Whether Idwal rebelled outright against Edmund, Æthelstan's brother and successor, after 939 is not certain. But the Annales Cambriae 942 record the death of Idwal and his son Elise at hands of the English, and that may have been connected with the reconquest of Mercia in that year by Edmund.

Idwal's sons, Ieuaf and Iago, were ousted on the death of their father, as Hywel Dda assumed the rule of Gwynedd. It was not until Hywel's death in 949/50 that Idwal's sons (Iago, Ieuaf, Meurig, Cynan, Idwal Fychan) were able to return to power, despite the claims of Hywel Dda's sons: Iago and Ieuaf fought them successfully at the battle of Nant Carno in 951, and in 952 conducted two raids into the heartland of Dyfed. In 954 Owain ap Hywel Dda and his brothers joined battle on the River Conwy at Llanrwst, probably losing the day to the northern troops who killed Edwin son of Hywel. This was followed up by the sons of Idwal ravaging Ceredigion.

Idwal was mentioned in verse down to the 15c: he was remembered as 'yr hen Idwal', and as ruler of Gwynedd — Wiliam Gruffudd of Penrhyn was hailed as a 'shield protecting the lands of Idwal', GLGC 223.31. Lewys Glyn Cothi refers to Idwal in connection with traditional prophecy attributed to Hinyn Fardd: GLGC 15.29-32 *O dir Gwynedd y darogenid/ i dyrau Idwal y dôi rhydid;/ dywod Hinyn Fardd doe tynnid — Sacson,/ wedy un estron y'u dinistrid*. There are earlier mentions of his name in the Cyfoesi (R578.25, 27 and 28), in CBT IV 6.133 *hil Idwal*, and CBT I 8.65 *A'm kyhut am ut ya6n essillit Idwal/ Nyd el heb dial mal galanas*, 'and my assertion concerning a lord of the true lineage of Idwal who does not forgo vengeance as punishment for slaying', with the same rhyming collocation *Idwal/dial* as in our instance.

21   **ar ranwynyon (ms ac aranwynyon; Pen. 111 ar aranwinion)** Emended with G s.v. *grann* 'cheek' for the sense and the cadence, cf. PT II.20 *garanwynyon*; AP line 62 *blaen wrth von granwynyon kyfyng oedyn*; CBT III 16.239; CBT V 14.36. Cf. also *brychwyn* for the English in §8.52.

22 **gware pelre a phen Saesson** Cf. LlDC 16.9-10 (Afallennau) *Aer o Saesson ar onn verev,/ a guarwyaur pelre ac ev pennev* (describing the carnage at the battle of Cyminawd). The word *pelre* is used, uniquely in the court poetry corpus, by Prydydd y Moch as he addresses a horse messenger, CBT V 14.6 *Dossa6c, hytola6c, ha6t y belre* 'foaming, stately, of easy gait' where *pel* 'ball' in the compound is used in a similar way to *olwyn* to describe the horse's hooves; the same poet also uses the hapax compound *dibelre*: CBT V 9.25 *fynnyant dibelre* 'immutable flourishing'. See also CA line 710 *mal pel ar ryre* (em.).

23 **Ys trabludyo y Gath Vreith a'e hagyfieithon** The Speckled Cat could be the subject of the vb, or the object (as in the translation), with the *marchawc lu* of line 20 as undertood subject. *Agyfieithon* are either foreigners (possibly foreign allies) or enemies. The Speckled Cat invites comparison with the Anglesey monster cat, Cath Balug, indirectly associated through Triad 26 with Llonion in Pembrokeshire, discussed in note to line 12 above. But in 15c prophecy, there are various references to a speckled cat, e.g. GLGC 12.33-4 *Tair iaith y gath fraith fu rodd,/ trychant a losgant Caer-ludd*; GLGC 138.29-30 *Pan ddêl y gath vraith i lan Ieithon,/ pan fo'r Gwyddelod ym margod Mon*; Hafod ms 5 (*c.* 1586), 213 *Ef a gyfyd gath fraith yn y dwyrain*. The origin of such an animal symbol may be Biblical, e.g. Daniel 7:6 (lion, bear, four-headed leopard, horned beast) and Revelation 13.2 (composite of leopard and bear, with horns). The Lynx in some manuscripts of Geoffrey's Prophecies of Merlin (HKB ch. 115, but 'light' in others) may have been influential, and see Michael A. Faletra, *The History of the Kings of Britain* (Peterborough, Ontario, 2008), 134 n. 1 on the confusion between L. *lux* and *linx*).

24 **Ryt ar Taradyr** The stream Taradr (OW *Taratir/-yr*), whose name means 'auger', is frequently mentioned in the Book of Llandaf as running into the River Wye on the very eastern border of the parochia of Llandaf; Tywi was the corresponding western limit. Ekwall was uncertain what stream was meant, suggesting 'one of the brooks that falls into Wye between Hereford and Sellack', ERN 392. Jonathan B. Coe, 'The Place-Names of the Book of Llandaf', unpublished PhD thesis, University of Wales, Aberystwyth, 2001, pp. 800-1, places it in the general area between the source of the Worm and the Wye, following Gwenogvryn Evans's lead that the name might survive in Tar's Brook, or that Taradr might be identified with the small stream which flows into the Wye at the site of a mill called *Abbertaret* in 1230 (and various other forms). Both of these are modern parish boundaries. It is mentioned elsewhere in prophecy: LlDC 17.5-9 (Oianau) *A mi discoganaf e a gwir uit/ hid in Aber Taradir rac trausev Prydein/ Kimry oll inyeu kyfluit./ Llyuelin y env o eissillit Gwinet,/ gur digorbit* 'And I prophesy, and it shall be true, as far as Aber Taradr before the oppressors of Britain, all of the Cymry in the days of the army (?). Llywelyn his name, of the stock of Gwynedd, the man who will triumph'. Aber Taradr is found partnering nearby Porth Ysgewin in a length-and-breadth topos with Porth Wygyr in Anglesey at the conclusion of Gwynfardd Brycheiniog's propaganda ode to Lord Rhys ap Gruffudd of Deheubarth, composed perhaps after the death of Owain Gwynedd in 1170. It mentions 'darogan Myrddin' and names several other rivers — the Severn, the Dee and the Tern (W. *Tren*) before reaching a crescendo: CBT II 25.47 *Am hyfryd, kymryd Kymry benn baladyr,/ Am Aber Taradyr yn tremynu,/ Am Byrth Ysgewin yn goresgynnu,/ Am Borth Wygyr y Mon yn menestru*.

24 **Porth Wygyr yMon** In Cemais Bay, Anglesey, at the mouth of River Gwygyr, also called Porth Cemais. Frequently referred to, usually as northern point, by Giraldus Cambrensis (*portu Yoiger in Monia*), in Gogynfeirdd poetry (CBT I 9.91; CBT II 2.52; CBT II 25.50 (quoted above); CBT VII 50.36), in prose and in triads (see TYP³ 255). Line 24 is rather long as it stands: it could be shortened by emending to *Ryt Taradr*, and perhaps *bet* 'as far as' rather than *hyt ym*.

25 **jeuanc didwynas dinas maon** Pen. 111 reads *Jeuaut cliduyuas dinas maon*. G has this as the sole example s.v. *diðwynas* 'unassuming, gentle', not listed by GPC. *Dinas maon* 'people of the citadel' or 'citadel of the people'. The poet seems to be referring to a young leader whose presence (after his martial triumphs?) heralds a period of peace and prosperity. Whether this is an oblique reference to Christ or to a Christ-like Cadwallon or other deliverer is uncertain.

26 **O'r pan amygir mel a meillon** On *o'r pan*, see GMW 242. The range of meanings of vb *amwyn* includes 'fight for, seize, possess; defend'. *Mel* 'honey' and *meillon* 'clover' are united in sweetness, cf. LPBT 7.67-9 *a gofrwy hinon/ a mel a meillon/ a medgyrn medwon*. Clover denotes fertility and prosperity in CBT II 26.96 (Henfynyw) . . . *Hyfaes y meillyon, hyfes goedyt*; CBT III 3.138 *Tiryon Mon, meillon y morbenn*; and Heavenly bliss in CC 21.144-5 *Myn y mae meillon/ A gulith ar tirion*. In Canu Heledd, the bloodied clover of Eglwysau Basa points to the destruction of all that was fair in the land before its conquest by Mercia, EWSP 435.48b *ys gwaedlyt eu meillyon*.

27 **gadent eu hamrydar a'e hamrysson** G s.v. *gadu* 3pl. pret. queries this example. *Amrydar*, a hapax, GPC² 'contention, uproar' (with *tar as in *clochdar*, *trydar*), here used in a pair of near synonyms, it would seem.

28 **nyt diwystyl godi dic wrth alon** On *diwystl* see G s.v. *diwestl* 'cheerless, sad', a somewhat uncommon word, but cf. CBT V 13.15-16 *Ner trymder tromgad ddiwestyl,/ Neu'n gwneir uegys Gweir uab G6estyl*; CBT VI 4.29 *Diwestyl y ysgor, ys k6yneis—nat by6*; R1056.35 (Gosymdaith line 107) *diwestyl alaf dirmygjr*; GPB 6.80 *Lle diwe, lle diwestl mennig*. GPC does not specify whether this is from < *gwestl*¹ 'din, confusion' or *gwestl*². G initially suggested a different range of meanings, 'stubborn, persistent', but s.v. *gwest(y)l* amended this to 'quiet, peaceable', comparing *gwestlawc*, *hywestyl*, etc. A compound with *gwystl* 'pledge, assurance, security ... hostage', etc. is not canvassed. The lenition of vb noun *codi* 'to inflame, anger' indicates that it is qualified by the preceding adj. I understand *dic* as noun 'wrath' rather than adj.

29 The final couplet, here abbreviated, repeats lines 1-2 as in other poems, e.g. PT X.

7 Gwawt Lud y mawr

This long poem of 117 lines contains some of the most familiar elements of political prophecy,[1] yet has some puzzling aspects. Although it is entitled 'The Great Song concerning Lludd', Lludd himself is not mentioned at all in the body of the poem. As discussed in the notes, the poem has a 'lesser' partner poem, *Ymarwar Lud bychan*, poem §9 in this collection, which alludes to him and his brother Llefelys. For convenience, the present poem has been divided into numbered sections, some of which begin with variants on the formulaic phrase *Dysgogan . . .* , as found at the beginning of the individual awdlau of Armes Prydain and other poems.[2] Their content may be summarised as follows:

¶1 (lines 1-25) The first two lines announce 'the best song' in praise of eight defending hosts. Lines 3-15 are framed by the listing of the days of the week, a structural device found in the Gododdin and elsewhere. They tell of unidentified hosts who will come, who will cause suffering to 'our enemies', who will raise victorious shouts. Line 16 mentions five hundred and five ships, but is followed by a very difficult passage between lines 17 and 23: there are mentions of *brithi brithöi*, and *brithi Brithanhäi* — Britons and/or Picts — and snatches of dog Latin as found elsewhere in the poem. The section ends with what seems to be a reference to the power of the Lord (*Adonäi*), possibly redeeming the evil here symbolised by the fruit tree in the Garden of Eden.

¶2 (lines 26-31) A new section is signalled by *Darofum darogan* and the recalling of the 'long-renowned' partnership of the promised deliverers Cynan and Cadwaladr. Their help is presumably being called up because the world is in turmoil: even the heat of the sun has been destroyed.

¶3 (lines 32-44) This section also begins with a formulaic line referring to the prognosticatory power of the *deruyd*, the wise man or wise poet who knows what has been and what will be. The following uncertain lines appear to refer to the *kerdawr*, the poet or crafter who perceives the significance of the cloud's torrent of rain as it moves over the high ground. The marten with its shrill cry (*ban bel*eu, recte) and the well-nourished stag (*llawn hyd*) may accord with the mention of the Britons acting according to counsel, perhaps in the summer months. After gold and ornaments (see notes) there will follow the laying waste of Anglesey and Llŷn (the curious Latinate forms, *Moni a Lleenni*, are used), and refuge will be sought in the mountain fastnesses of Snowdonia (*Eryri*).

¶4 (lines 45-103) The core of the poem is concerned with extensive tribulation, already alluded to in the second section: inhabited regions will become waste, the Cymry, the Welsh people 'of perfect language' (or having four languages, or peoples), will change or alter their language (*symudant eu hareith*).[3] The 'Speckled Cow' will wreak vengeance, bellowing at mid-day and plotting at midnight. The land will be seething and the *llogoed* (consecrated

---

[1] See General Introduction, 11.
[2] See introduction to poem §3.
[3] Or 'move their assembly': see note on line 48.

places) will be devastated (see notes for other possibilities). This section has a number of impersonal verbal forms, some of which may be nonce. A song of woe will encompass Britain, but the natives will come together to repel the threat and possibly (line 59) to reinstate joy, or *gwir venhyt*. Lines 61-3 are obscure. Lines 64-70 return to imagining a world turned upside-down, a world where there shall be no horse-raiding, nor cattle-reaving (or perhaps animal management — *eppa* and *henuonha* are infrequently attested), no protection nor food. This passage may be compared with the tale, *Cyfranc Lludd a Llefelys*, built around three 'gormesoedd' or oppressions: (1) the race of the Coraniaid, who could hear everything going on; (2) a scream causing the land and animals and women to be barren (cf. perhaps *heb eppa, heb henuonha*); (3) food becoming scarce (cf. §10.9-10), so that only the food of the first night could be eaten.[4] Lines 67-8 foretell a world laid waste, so wretched that even the cuckoos are fated. 'Small men' will have base natures. However, a swift man with hosts will emerge to be a tamer, a leader. The cryptic lines 73-4 declare that 'Knives cannot pierce the swords of cowards'. In line 77, there is a reference to a transgression or wrongdoing (*kared*) perpetrated in Creuddyn, possibly an encounter in the commote of Creuddyn in Rhos on the River Conwy. Line 78 recalls the listing of Welsh, Angles, Irish and Picts seen in Armes Prydain and other prophecies. Loss accompanies the Cymry. Lines 80-1 seem to refer to the coming of wooden horses (i.e. ships), with harmful Northerners, referred to as *hermyn* (cf. AP lines 40 and 184 *cechmyn*, line 27 *kychmyn*), etc. (if *herw* + *myn*, see notes). Lines 82-3 are obscure, possibly elaborating on their ancestry. Lines 84-95 talk about a starling being brought forth to startle or arouse (*cychwyn*) a flock of ravens — possibly a figure for the Welsh v. Vikings. Line 86 refers to a sluggish host and perhaps the personal name *Seithin* (Lloyd-Jones suggested restoring *Seithenhin*); the following line mentions Cristin, possibly the notorious second wife of Owain Gwynedd, but the connection with the rest of line is unclear. There follows a series of *vch o* . . . (familiar from PT V) and more general commotion and tribulation, including acts of vengeance which seem to have arisen through the angering of God (line 96). This leads into the penultimate section foretelling ultimate victory, to be proclaimed (*darlleawr* 'read out') some time before the Day of Judgment. There will be a resurgence for Britain, in the shape of a Briton or Britons from the stock of Rome.

¶5 (lines 104-17) The last section says that the *sywedydyon*, 'the wise men', will prophesy to the bereft, and that the wise poets (*deruydon*) forecast poor summer weather. The oppressive *breyron* 'nobles' who have come from over the sea will be enfeebled. In the final lines the poet appears to see the Day of Judgment with a thousand-strong host present, and the wrongdoers (likened to the race of Cain) consumed by a fiery swamp in the nether reaches of Hell. Sections 4 and 5, then, are a good example of the seepage between secular and religious apocalypse discussed in the General Introduction, and pointed up in the

---

[4] See CLlaLl.

7 Gwawt Lud y mawr

manuscript's arrangement which sets the great Prophecy of the Day of Judgment next to the great Armes Prydain.

Much of the poem uses the short Class 1 line and the sense units tend to move by couplet.[5] Lines 42-4 are irregularly long. From lines 75 onwards, the lines are longer, with a tendency to a patterning of three strong stresses, typically seven syllables, with occasionally recognisable *toddeidiau*, e.g. lines 91-2, 93-4, 96-7, but there are many instances where the rhyme patterns break down.

---

[5] On metrics see LPBT 37-9.

7 Gwawt Lud y mawr
Book of Taliesin 74.11-76.14

1

Kathyl goreu gogant
The best song has praised
wyth nifer nodant:
the eight hosts who defend:
Duw Llun dybydant;
On Monday they shall come;
peithiawc yd ant.
they shall go ravaging.
5   **Duw Mawrth yt rannant**
On Tuesday they shall distribute
gwyth y'n yscarant.
suffering to our enemies.
Duw Merchyr medant
On Wednesday they shall possess
ryodres rychwant.
desired pomp.
Duw Ieu escorant
On Thursday they shall let out
10   **eidyolyd anchwant.**
eager shouts.
Duw Gwener, dyd gormant,
On Friday, a day of triumph,
ygwaet gwyr gonofant.
they shall wallow in the blood of men.
Duw Sadwrn[1] . . . .
On Saturday . . .
Duw Sul, yn geugant,
On Sunday, for certain,
15   **diheu dybydant**
they will definitely come.
Pymp llong a phymcant
Five ships and five hundred
o ranant o niant
. . . . .
o brithi brithöi.
of mixed-race ones in turmoil.
Nuoes nuedi
. . . . .

---

[1] The text breaks off at this point and part of the next line in the ms has been left blank.

7 Gwawt Lud y mawr

20 **brithi Brithanhäi,**
Britons in turmoil,
sychet eurröi[2]
thirst for the giving of gold
eil coet condigni[3]
like ?worthy trees
antared dymbi;
enemies will come;
pawb y Adonäi
(and) everyone (else) to the Lord
25 **a'r weryt pwmpäi.**
who has redeemed ?the (evil which emanated from) the apple-tree (of Eden).

2

Darfu[4] **darogan,**
A prophecy has come to pass,
gwaed hir rac gorman:
a long cry in the face of oppression:
hir kyhoed kyghan
a long, manifest, fitting (prophecy)
Katwaladyr a Chynan.
concerning Cadwaladr and Cynan.
30 **Byt budyd bychan**
The world (is) of little profit
difa gwres huan.
with the warmth of the sun having been destroyed.

3

Dysgogan deruyd
The wise man foretells
a uu, a uudyd.
what has been and what will be of avail.
Wybyr gerd geironyd
The cloud which scuds over the high ground
35 **— kerdawr ry kenuyd**[5]**—**
— it is the poet who sees/interprets it —
wylhawt eil echwyd
will lament like a torrent

---

[2] ms *sychediedi euroi*
[3] ms *cogni*
[4] ms *darofum*
[5] ms *kerd awn ygenhyd*

yn torroed mynyd.
on the slopes of the mountain.
Ban be[le]u,[6] llawn hyd,
Loud the marten, replete the stag,
Brython ar gyghyr.
The Britons (acting) according to counsel.

40 **Y Vrython dymbi**
There shall come to the Britons
gwaet gwned ofri;
blood through splendid combat;
guedy eur ac eurynni,
after gold and gold ornaments,
diffeith Moni a Lleenni,
the laying waste of Anglesey and Llŷn,
ac Eryri anhed yndi.
and (taking) refuge there in Eryri.

4

45 **Dyscogan perffeith**
A perfect one foretells
anhed yn diffeith.
settlement in a waste place.
Kymry pedeirieith
The Cymry of perfect language
symudant eu hareith.
will change their speech.
Yt ⌐vi y Uuch Vreith[7]
There shall be the Speckled Cow
50 **a wnaho gwynyeith.**
who will wreak vengeance.
Meindyd brefawt,
At mid-day it shall bellow,
meinoeth berwhawt,
at midnight it shall plot,
artir[8] berwhodawr,
the arable land shall be rendered seething,
yn llogoed yssadawr.
our consecrated places shall be destroyed.

---

[6] ms *beu*
[7] ms *Yt yvi yuuch y uuch vreith* ~~vreit~~ (strikethrough and deleting points beneath *vreit*)
[8] ms *ar tir*

7 Gwawt Lud y mawr

55 **Kathyl gwae canhator**
A song of woe will be sung
kylch Prydein amgor.
around Britain's border.
Dedeuant vn gyghor
With one counsel they shall come
y wrthot gwarth*f***or.**[9]
to repel a sea of shame.
Boet gwir venhyt
May there be true joy
60 **dragwynawl byt.**
in the sorrowful world.
Dolwys dolhwyckyt
....
Dolaethwy eithyt.
to Dolaethwy he went.
Kynran llawn yt gyfarch:
The leader makes sweeping demands:
kynut heb eppa,
(just) herding with no horse-breeding,
65 **heb henuonha.**
with no reaving of breeding cows,
heb ofur byt.
with no certainty of food.
Byt a uyd diffeith direit,
The world will be a wretched wasteland,
kogeu tyghettor
cuckoos shall be fated —
hoywwed trwy groywed,
splendour mixed up with simplicity —
70 **gwyr bychein bron otwyllyd.**
small men with treacherous natures.
Toruenhawl tuthiolyd,[10]
A swift-pacing one with hosts,
hy**wedyd,**[11] **arvedyd.**
a tamer, a leader.
Ny wan cyllellawr
Knives cannot pierce

---

[9] ms *gwarthmor*
[10] ms *tuth iolyd*
[11] ms *hwedyd*

7 Gwawt Lud y mawr

cledyfawr meiwyr.
the swords of cowards.

75 **Nyt oed udu y puchysswn**
I would not have wished on them
anaw angerdawl trefdyn,
the one passionate for the wealth of the homestead,
ac y wyr kared Creudyn.
nor on men the wrong perpetrated at Creuddyn.
Kymry, Eigyl, Gwydyl, Prydyn,
The Cymry, Angles, Irish, Picts,
Kymry kyfret ac ascen.
the Cymry keeping pace with loss.

80 **Dygedawr gwydueirch ar llyn:**
Ships shall be brought forth on the sea:
Gogled o wenwyn ◦[12] o hermyn ,
the men of the North, of (a line of) slayers, of raiders,
o echen casnur[13] caslyn,
of the line of wrathful ones of persistent enmity on the hostile sea,
o echen Adaf henyn.
of the line of Adam they (too) are sprung.
Dygedawr trydw y gychwyn
A starling will be brought forth to incite

85 **branes o goscord gwyr◦in.[14]**
a host of ravens from a blessed retinue.
Meryd milet Seithenhin[15]
Sluggish the host of Seithennin
ar vor agor ar Gristin.
at anchor on the sea, against Cristin.
Vch o vor, vch o vynyd,
An attack from the sea, an attack from the mountain,
vch o vor, ynyal ebryn,
an attack from the sea, the uninhabited region in tumult,

90 **coet, mäes, tyno a bryn.**
the wood, the plain, the hollow and the hill.
Pop arawt heb erglywaw — nebawt
Every supplication going completely unheeded

---

[12] ms *wenwynuyd*
[13] ms *echlur caslur*
[14] ms *gwyrein*
[15] ms *seithin*

7 Gwawt Lud y mawr

o vynawc ○¹⁶ pop mehyn.
by the lord of every place.
Yt vi brithret a lliaws — gyniret,
There shall be turmoil and tumult in the host,
   a gofut amwehyn:
   and spreading tribulation:
95 **dialeu trwy hoyw gredeu bresswyl.**
acts of vengeance mixed with constancy of fair promises.

O godi Creawdyr kyfoethawc, Duw vrdin
Because of angering the all-powerful Creator, holy God,
   pell amser kyn no Dydbrawt
   a long time before the Day of Judgment
y daw diwarnawt,
shall come the appointed day,
a dwyrein darlleawr
and (an account of) a resurgence will be read out,
100 **teruyn tiryon tir Iwerdon.**
and an end to the territories of the land of Ireland.
Y Prydein ○¹⁷ **y daw datwyrein:**
A resurgence shall come to Britain:
Brython o vonhed Rufein.
a Briton of the noble stock of Rome.
A'm bi barnodyd o aghygres dieu.
I shall have a judge as a result of these days of travail.

5

Dysgogan sywedydyon
The sages foretell
105 **ygwlat y colledigyon;**
in the land of those bereft/condemned;
dysgogan deruydon
the druids foretell
tra mor, tra Brython,
as long as there's a sea, as long as there are Britons,
haf ny byd hinon;
there'll not be fine weather in the summer;
bythawt breu breyryon
feeble will be the lords

---

¹⁶ ms *o pop*
¹⁷ ms *yna*

110 **ae deubyd o gwanf/et,**[18]
who come to them through deceiving the weak,
tra merin tat ket.
from beyond the sea . . .
Mil ym Brawt Prydein vrdin,
A great host (will be present) at the Judgment of noble Britain,
ac y am gyffwrn[19] **kyffin**
and around the region of the furnace.
Na chwy*d*af[20] **y goglyt gwern**
May I not fall into the lurking swamp
115 **gwerin gwaelotwed Uffern,**
of the inhabitants (who are) in the very depths of Hell,
ergryna*w*[21] **kyllestric Käen**
the fiery (line) of Cain made to tremble
gan wledic gwlat anorffen.
by the Lord of the eternal realm.

title *Gwawt lud y mawr* has been written in red by the scribe in the middle of the page above the first line of the text; the same words in a smaller size stand to the left of the striking capital K. Another fourteenth-century hand has written . . . *colof(yn c)erdd* alongside lines 3 and 4 of the poem: see GPC s.v. *colofn* 2: '(a) main division or category and (b) principal metre, division' etc., variously four, five, seven, etc. Taliesin was associated with some of these metres in the bardic grammars (GP 117 *pvmp kolofn kerdd Daliessin*), and the scribe may have been noting that the short-lined metre used at the beginning of the poem was one of these. The main title declares the poem to be a *gwawt* 'song', perhaps prophecy, concerning Lludd, although he is never mentioned in the body of the text. Its designation as *y mawr* 'the big one' is presumably contrastive with poem §9 *Ymarwar Llud bychan*, as with the pair *Kanu y byt mawr* and *Kanu y byt bychan*, LPBT poems 25 and 26, and the pair of poems — one of 208 lines and the other 60 lines — that Prydydd y Moch sang to Llywelyn ab Iorwerth: CBT V poems 25 and 23, see further LPBT 535. On the use of the definite article in *Gwawt Lud y mawr*, cf. Proinsias Mac Cana, '*Húas mo lebrán ind línech*: Welsh and Irish Cognates', in *Saltair Saíochta, Sanasaíochta agus Seanchais*, edited by Dónall Ó Baoill *et al.* (Dublin, 2013), 117-23. The character Lludd is discussed in the poem introduction.

1 **Kathyl goreu gogant** *Kathyl* 'song' used of poetry, birdsong, etc., is treated by Cynddelw as synonymous with *gwawt* (CBT IV 6.70-1 *caffa6d an gwa6deu,/ Cathleu cleu, kerteu caw*). Cf. LlDC 16.88 (Afallennau) *kathil hetuch a hinon*;

---

[18] ms *gwanfret*
[19] ms *gyffwn*
[20] ms *nachwyaf*
[21] ms *ergrynaf*

7 Gwawt Lud y mawr

and of the heavenly choir, CC 20.79-80 *Kyrd a cherdoryon,/ A chathleu egylyon*. Its root links it to vb *canu* and its compounds.

The vb *goganu* appears to be used in a favourable way 'to praise, eulogise' (rather than 'to satirise, mock, disparage'), as in CC 10.17 (addressing God) *Beird a'th gogan; wynt a'th garan yn tragywyd*; CBT I 20.1-2 *Goganaw i Arglwyd gogonavl,/ Gogoned Vrenhin, Dewin d6ywawl*. Here we have the rare 3sg. pret. of *goganu* (cf. *kant*, *darogant*), uniquely used in the court corpus by Prydydd y Moch, CBT V 5.61 *Mad gogant molyant rwy moles/ Mal Mertin ym marteir kyffes* 'Fortunately did the one who praised him sing his praise like Myrddin in skilful verse'. On the possible instance in CA line 1040 *kyvedwogant ef a'n dyduc ar dan adloyw*, see CA 318. In our instance, *kathyl goreu* is understood as the subject of the vb, rather than object (with *wyth nifer* in line 2 as subject). For *gogant* as a noun, cf. CA line 1040 *kyved wogant*.

2   **wyth nifer nodant** Understood as 'eight' rather than a lenited form of *gwyth* 'wrath', etc. which occurs in line 6 below. The eight hosts do not quite correspond to the seven days of the week listed in the following lines, but cf. the concept of a week as *wyth nos* 'eight nights'. Lines 1 and 2 could also be interpreted as two independent sentences.

3   **Duw Llun dybydant** The days of the week structure is found in CA lines 833-9 (and 846-52), starting with Tuesday, and also in Gruffudd ab yr Ynad Coch's awdl to God, CBT VII 40.1-25 (starting on Sunday). Wednesday and Thursday only in Edmyg Dinbych lines 62-3; Sunday and Thursday only in LPBT 10.30. A Holy Week schema (Tuesday to Easter Sunday) is used by Elidir Sais, CBT 24.1-22. There may also be seepage from the portents preceding the Day of Judgment, arranged in a week schema in the Apocalypse of Thomas (see CC 174-8 for details) and derived material. *Dybydant*, see on §6.5.

4   **peithiawc yd ant** Rather uncommon outside CBT corpus, but cf. EWSP 432.28a *Stauell Gyndylan ys peithiawc heno*. Nine examples in CBT, four by Prydydd y Moch (CBT V 10.50; 19.7; 20.47 *Tyreu poeth, peitha6c pob un*; 24.50 *A gwaedlenn am penn yn peitha6c*) as well as CBT I 11.39 *wallt peitha6c*; CBT IV 17.124 *peitha6c drwyted*. GPC s.v. *peithiog, peithog* suggests 'desert, desolate, uninhabited, laid waste, destroyed; bruised, wounded', but also 'devastating, ravaging, destroying'. The latter meanings are most suitable here if the poet is talking about the triumphing Welsh hosts.

6   **y'n yscarant** Understood as prep. + possessive pron. *Ysgarant*, pl. of *esgar/ysgar* 'enemy', see on §3.11 for its use by Prydydd y Moch and others.

7   **Duw Merchyr medant** Common variant of *Mercher*, used, for example, in CA line 834; Edmyg Dinbych line 62; LlDC 16.4 (Afallennau) *In Diffrin Machavuy Merchyrdit crev*; Elidir Sais, CBT I 24.9, etc. Elsewhere, the 3pl. of *medu* is found uniquely in CBT V 23.146 *Mam Gymry y metant*.

8   **ryodres rychwant** Cf. CA line 158 *e rihyd ryodres*. CBT comparanda are restricted entirely to Prydydd y Moch: CBT V 5.70 *O voli Rodri ryodres*; CBT V 7.1 *Hael Rodri, rodres edneint*; CBT V 26.93 *A'm rotes ryodres riued*. GPC s.v. *rhychwant* (b) suggests '?covetousness, desire', and this is followed in the translation.

9   **escorant** Cf. AP line 86 *oes oesseu eu tretheu nys escorant*, and see the n. where it is treated as a denominative vb from *ysgor* 'fort, refuge', comparing Edmyg

7 Gwawt Lud y mawr

Dinbych line 1 *plwyf escori*. But by far the most common meaning in poetry is to 'push, expel, get rid of', etc. and that is the interpretation here (with G).

10 **eidolyd anchwant** Cf. LPBT 23.3 *bedyd rwyd rifedeu eidolyd*. *Eidolyd* may mean 'praises, praise-songs', and GPC s.v. *eidol, eidiol, ?eidd(i)ol* suggests a range encompassing 'shout, cry, praise'. On *anchwant* 'eager', see LPBT 5.80n.

11 **gormant** PT VII.26 *ar ormant gwaet*; very common in CBT corpus (13 instances).

12 **yg gwaet gwyr gonofant** On the very common collocation, *gwaet gwyr*, see LPBT 5.68n. The phrase is collocated with the same vb *g(w)onofi/gwynofi* 'to wallow in, roll around in' in EWSP 433.35b *ygwaet gwyr gwynn novi*; with *gwyar*, CBT IV 4.194 *Ar donnyar gwyar gwonofyei*.

13 **Duw Sadwrn** This is written at the end of a normal line and most of the subsequent line has been left blank as though to be filled in later, perhaps when a more legible or better text came to hand.

14 **yn geugant** Cf. LPBT 10.30 *Dyf Ieu, yn geugant, yd aethant Von*; CA line 99; PT IV 11-12 *racwed rothit y veird y byt./ Byt yn geugant itti yt wedant*; LPBT 26.14, *Etwa, yn geugant*; CBT I 31.4; V 23.196.

16 **Pymp llong a phymcant** Cf. the cumulative counting in the Gododdin and elsewhere, used of ships in the Afallennau and Oianau, LlDC 16.23-4 (Afallennau) *Seithlu y deuant dros lydan lin/ a seith cant dros mor y oreskin*; Pen3Afallennau 121.8-9 *Seith long y deuuant a seith gant dros donneu,/ disgynant ar draeth a dan saetheu*; LlDC 17.61-2 (Oianau) *Dybit seith ganllog o Ynt gan wint Goglet/ ac in Aber Dev eu kinatlet*. Cf. also CBT II 12.9-11 *Treghissyant trydydyd o Uei—trychanllog/ Yn y llyghes 6ordei,/ A deckant kynran a'y kilyei*, and the numbering of the fleets in CBT I 8.31-2 *Teir lleng y doethant, liant lestri,/ Teir praff prif lyghes wy bres broui*. Of hosts present at Senedd Frefi, CBT II 26.28 *Yg g6yt seith mil ma6r a seith ugeint*; of time, R582.13-14 (Cyfoesi) *Tri mis, teir blyned teithyawn/ a thrychant mlyned kyfla6n*.

17 **o ranant o niant** The text appears corrupt, and perhaps *riuant* might be suggested for the last word, given the numbers in line 16, and collocations of *riff/rann* as in CA lines 1395-6 *Etmygir e vab Tecvann/ wrth rif ac wrth rann*. T. Gwynn Jones (EVW 125) suggested a drastic emendation to *tra naw ton lliant* 'over the nine waves of the sea' which not surprisingly (!) gives good sense. With less intervention, *(g)orannant nwyfiant* 'they will spread joy' (although no vb *gorannu* is attested); or is *anant* 'poets' relevant? *Anant a rifant* 'poets will recount/exalt'?

18 **o brithi brithöi** Seemingly based on *brith* 'speckled, variegated; mixed', although line 20's *Brithanhäi* suggests a 'Britain' word (L. *Britannia, Brittania*) as G notes s.v. The abstract noun *brithni* is attested from the 14c onwards, and *brithi* could conceivably be an alternative (cf. *coegni* v. *coegi*; *bryntni* v. *brynti*, etc.). It may have the same force as the *brithfyt* or 'world in turmoil' of prophecy, discussed LPBT 1.100n. Otherwise a Latinate plural *-i*, indicating 'speckled ones, people of mixed stock', or 'Picts' (Juv. 16^v *brith* glosses *pictam* 'painted', cf. VVB 59). *Brithöi* is equally problematic, and brings to mind the endings of Hebrew *Elöi, Adonäi* (as in line 24 below) used occasionally by the medieval Welsh poets. The translation of lines 17 and 18 is extremely uncertain.

7 Gwawt Lud y mawr

19 **Nuoes Nuedi** Small capital at the beginning of each word. *Nu* 'now', GMW 221, is not very common, but there are examples before a conjunction, CBT II 18.46 *A nu bei gallón ymgeryt—a Duw*; before a preverbal particle, LlDC 17.30 *nv neud araf*; CBT II 2.39 *A nu neut ethy6 lly6 gly6 gle6haf—yn rin*; CBT I 8.75 *A nu neud adwen*; CBT I 3.83 *A nu neud g6eryd yn warweidya6c*; or a negative particle, LPBT 5.228 *a nu [n]y'm gowy*; CBT I 3.154 *nu ni bu gelwyt*. Emendation to *nyt oes* (or *nys oes*) is possible — the majority of occurrences of *oes* in poetry occur with preceding *nyt*. *Nuedi* could be a miscopying of some form such as *riuedi/rifedi* 'number'.

20 **brithi Brithanhäi** See on line 18 above. The first *i* in *Brithanhäi* is either because this is a seemingly Latinate form (note that the scribe has inserted the first *h* after writing *Britanhai*) or else the exemplar's *i* represented the schwa vowel.

21 **Sychet eurröi (ms sychediedi euroi)** Another difficult line, unusually long. Read perhaps *sychet* (*y*) 'thirst for' or *sych(y)edic*. For *sychet* with *eur* 'gold', cf. BD 45 (Caswallon's reply to Julius Caesar) *A ryuedu meint sychet a chuant gvyr Ruuein y eur ac aryant, mal na adan dynyon . . . hep gymhell teyrnget arnadunt*. Could the second word contain *eur* + the disyllabic vb noun *röi* 'to give', i.e. the giving of gold, or, if *eur* is intensive, 'splendid giving'. Very uncertain.

22 **Eil coet cogni** G s.v. *codigni* suggests that *cogni* be emended — presumably for the length of the line — to *condigni*, from *condignus* 'wholly deserving, worthy', as found in another obscure line, R1054.34, edited LPBT 1.78 *Co[n]digni cota gosgord mur cornu amandur*.

23 **antared dymbi** G has no suggestion, but *an careð* is a possibility: G s.v. *careð* 'wrongdoing, sin; desire, greeed; love'. *An* 'our', common variant of *yn*. Or else, an otherwise unattested pl. of the rare *angar* 'hostile, cruel', used substantivally (as in translation) or an abstract noun. *Dymbi* with prefix *dym-* (~ *dam-*) as in *dymunaw*, etc.) is a signature 3sg. fut. form in prophecy, cf. §5.11 and 28; §8.1, 11, 26, 34, 57, and line 40 below. Otherwise rare in poetry. *Dybi* is also common, e.g. AP lines 149, 151 and 153; LPBT 8.17 *dybi dylles*; LlDC 17.157 (Oianau) *brithuid dybi* and 17.217 *brithwyd dybi*; CBT II 5.56 *Ar wyneb daear dybi* (Signs before the Day of Judgment); CBT V 25.18 *Ac yg Caerllion uy lly6 dybi* (in a poem which alludes to Myrddin's prophecy).

24 **pawb y Adonäi** Cf. CC 2.16 *On Adonäy*; CC 33.3 *Ely, Elöy ac Adonäy — ac O ac Alpha*. One of the Hebrew names for God. See on line 18 above.

25 **a'r weryt pwmpäi** *Ar weryt* could mean 'on the ground/grave of. . .', following G who notes this example with a query. Another possibility, adopted here, would be *a* (rel. pron.) + *ry* (consuetudinal perfect pres., or else expressing possibility, see GMW 168) + *gweryt*, 3sg. pres. of vb *gwaret* 'to deliver, save, redeem, sustain'. Although *gweryt* is common, its use with *ry* is otherwise only attested in the instance by Prydydd y Moch, CBT V 6.24 *Ef ry6r ryweryd digreid*, of Rhodri son of Owain Gwynedd as 'a man able to sustain the weak'.

Pwmpäi may be related in some way to *pwmpa* 'large apple, ?fruit(-tree)' (pl. *pwmpâu, pwmpae*), commonly attested from 15c and a borrowing from ME *po(u)me* or OF *pome* according to GPC who note, however, the discussion by J. Lloyd-Jones, *B* 11 (1941-4), 122-3, connecting the word with MIr *popp* 'pap, shoot, tendril', pl. *pappe, pupa* and L. *papula*. In the West, the fruit tree of Eden (Genesis 2 and 3) was often imagined as an apple tree, and it may be that we have ellipsis, 'God who has/is able to redeem the (evil which emanated from) the apple-tree (of the Garden of Eden)'. If *pwmp* is a mistake for *pump*, it would be difficult to compound one of the usual fives — *pum oes byt* 'five ages of the world', Christ's five stigmata, five zones of the world, etc. — with an ending in *äi* as required by rhyme. Another possibility would be a nonce formation for the rhyme from a Latin form such as *pompa* 'solemn procession', perhaps from the genitive sg. *pompae*? With the third of these possibilities, perhaps *gweryt* 'ground, burial ground'. Very uncertain.

26 **Darfu (ms Darofum) darogan** G notes the hapax *darofum* and doubts whether an emendation to *darofun* 'request, wish, to request, wish for, aim for' yields suitable sense here. Yet, 'the 'desired prophecy' seems reasonable (with inversion). With more intervention, *darfu* is very likely (with *daro-* having been written under the influence of following *darogan*). This is what is implemented in the translation.

27 **gwaed hir rac gorman** *Gorman*, fixed by rhyme, and regarded by G, followed by GPC, as a hapax variant of common *gormant* 'excess, supremacy, pomp, bravado' (comparing *darogan* v. *darogant*, *goruyn* v. *goruynt*).

28 **hir kyhoed kyghan** G s.v. *kyngan* 'suitable, complete, even, consistent, harmonious', used of even-gaited horses by Cynddelw (CBT III 1.27, III 16.160, and IV 4.54); not witnessed by GPC as a noun until the late 16c. Therefore, it does not seem that the poet is describing the long-standing (*hir*) and well-known (*kyhoed*) harmony between the traditional deliverers, Cynan and Cadwaladr. Rather, the three adjs are qualifying the *darogan* 'prophecy' of line 26-7 which gives hope when all the signs bode ill (lines 30-31).

30 **Byt budyd bychan** Understood as a nominal sentence, with *budyd* taken as a synonymous here with *bud* 'worth, profit', possibly played off against a homophonous verbal form in line 33 below. For a review of the problematic verbal form *budyd*, see Simon Rodway, 'What was the function of 3rd sg. prs. ind. "*-ydd*" in Old and Middle Welsh?', *Studi Celtici* 2 (2003), 89-132, at p. 96; Dating 118-21; and LPBT 125-6.

31 **difa gwres huan** On the theme of the world in turmoil, see General Introduction, 11-12.

32 **Dysgogan deruyd** *Deruyd* = ModW *derwydd*, 'wise man' (the Magi appear to be described as *derwydon* in CC 11.33). Other Book of Taliesin examples indicate a particular connection with singing prophecy — LPBT 5.238-9 *Derwydon doethur/ darogenwch y Arthur*; line 106 below; AP line 171 *Dysgogan derwydon* — as does Dydd dyfydd line 23 *derwrtion* (recte *deruition*) *darogant*. Another possible occurrence is PT XII.36-7 *bint bydi derwyt bryt haf/ pryt mab Lleenawc lliawc*. Otherwise the word is not found in hengerdd, and is significantly less common than words such as *syw, sywyd, sywedyd*, etc. (discussed LPBT 5.174n). A prophetic link is made by Cynddelw (CBT III 16.1 *Dysgogan derwyton*), and twice by Prydydd y Moch: CBT V 11.45 *Kynan, darogan derwyton—dyda6*; V 25.43-4 *Dywa6d derwyton dadeni haelon/ O hil eryron o Eryri*. Gwalchmai ap Meilyr, however, appears to use *derwydon* simply for 'poets' in CBT I 7.82 *Derwyton 6einiuiad* (of Madog ap Maredudd giving supplies to poets).

G suggests this instance of *dysgogan* may be a noun, i.e. 'the prophecy of the wise man', rather than 3 sg. pres. of vb *dysgogan*. Cf. the same ambiguity in line 45 below.

7 Gwawt Lud y mawr

33   **a uu a uudyd** See above on line 30 for *budyd*. Here it is understood as 3sg. vb form perhaps meaning 'to succeed, to be of avail', although it would be natural to expect a synonym of *bydd* (comparing tense topoi such as PT III.22 *o'r a uu ac a uyd*; CC 24.100 *Nifer a uu ac a uyd*; CBT II 5.16 *Nad ym men yt uu yt vi*, etc).

34   **Wybyr gerd geironyd** *Cerd* could be understood as 'movement, walking, moving' with G s.v. *kerð*, or (as in translation) 3sg. pres of vb *cerdet* ('the cloud which traverses the high ground') rather than *cerd* 'song, craft'.
    GPC s.v. *ceirionnydd* '?lord; height, heaven' following G's lead. Cf. R1050.4-5 *Minneu Dalyessin o ia6n llyn* (?recte *llin*) *geirionnyd*; CBT VI 20.62 *Argerdd gerdd geirionnydd* 'taith foliannus dros ucheldir', in an anonymous poem to Llywelyn ab Iorwerth and his warband. Prydydd y Moch uses it unequivocally for 'Lord God' in CBT V 26.6 *Keiryonnyt, kyrcheist uym buchet*. Already in 1803, Sharon Turner had interpreted the R1050 reference cited above as 'of the banks of lake Ceirionydd' (*A Vindication of the Genuineness of the Ancient British Poems of Aneurin, Taliesin, Llywarch Hen and Merdhin* (London, 1803), 171), and this was followed by others including J. Morris-Jones (Tal 194). Thus the lake near Trefriw was claimed to be connected with Taliesin, and in due course a monument was erected on its shores in 1850 by Lord Willougby d'Eresby of nearby Gwydir Castle. The mention of the cloud in this instance, at least, seems to favour 'high ground' (as in translation) or 'heaven'.

35   **kerdawr ry kenuyd (ms kerd awn y genhyd)** G emends > *kerdawr ergenhyd*, suggesting 'sustainer, patron' for *ergenhyd*, connected possibly with vb *arganuot*. Here a different emendation > *kerdawr ry kenuyd* (< vb *canfod*) or *kerdawr a'e kenuyd*. But very uncertain. H-cd suggests it is to be modernised as *cerdd a wn ei genydd*. It may imply that the poet — or prophet in this case — assesses the weather, and sees signs of the disruption of nature (the sun's warmth retreating) and its participation in the lament caused by the current woes.

36   **wylhawt eil echwyd** As it stands, 'it (the wandering cloud of line 34 rather than the *kerdawr* of line 35) will weep/lament like a torrent'. There is no particular justification for emending to *gwylyaw* 'to watch, guard' with H-cd.

37   **yn torroed mynyd** See GPC s.v. *tor²* (c) 'breast, slope, flank, or side (of mountain, hill, &c.); river-bank'.

38   **Ban be[le]u llawn hyd** G suggests emending *beu* to either *beleu* 'pine-marten', or else to *bereu* 'spits, spears, lances'. *Ban* 'high' or 'loud' is often used of birdsong, but note CBT I 11.50 *Ban bref biw yn riw rac e deon*. The marten is characterised by its sharp, shrill cry, and its valuable pelt reserved for the king, according to the Welsh lawbooks: Dafydd Jenkins, *The Law of Hywel Dda* (Llandysul 1986), 187-8. The *llawn hyd* 'full, replete stag' is in stark contrast to the starved animals of winter in EWSP 454.4b *cul hit caun barywhaud*; 455.17b *oer callet cul hit*; EWGP 28 *Kalan gayaf, cul hydot*. This suggests that this interlude is more propitious, a period when the Britons are debating the next move or acting according to counsel.

39   **ar gyghyr** *Cyghyr* is pl. of *cyngor*, but can be sg. according to G s.v. (not endorsed by GPC). *Ar gyngyr* suggests that the Britons are waiting on advice or counsel, or else are acting according to such advice.

40   **Y Vrython dymbi** On *dymbi*, see on line 23 above.

7 Gwawt Lud y mawr

41 **gwaet gwned ofri** Disyllabic *gwned* 'ferocity, anger, battle, fighting', common in hengerdd, e.g. PT XII.32; CA line 219 *o wyr gwychyr gwned*; line 777 *sengi wit gwned*; line 794 *gwr gwned divudyawc dimyngyei*; line 1018 *en dyd gwned*, etc. Six CBT examples. *Gofri* 'splendid, praiseworthy', also abstract noun 'good sense, wisdom, dignity' also well-attested in hengerdd and CBT.

42 **guedy eur eurynni** Atypical *gu* rather than *g6*. The metre changes here to a longer line with a four-syllable, two-stress cadence. *Eurynni*, pl. of *euryn* 'jewel, (gold) ornament, precious thing (or person)', according to G (followed here), or possibly a compound of *rynn* ('stiff, stout') or *ynni* 'vigour, energy'. *Eur* can mean 'splendid' in compounds as well as 'golden'.

43 **diffeith Moni a Lleenni** See below on line 67 for *diffeith*. Seemingly Latinate genitive forms for *Môn* 'Anglesey' and *Llëyn*, or their inhabitants. However, one would not expect *-nn-* in the latter, in what appears to be an attempt to represent *Lleÿni*. The disyllabic is generally spelled *Llyyn*: also *Llein* in CBT I 1.13 (Black Book of Carmarthen). Llŷn is a more likely identification than Leominster (*Llanllieni*). There may be an allusion to the events of 961 when 'the sons of Olaf' (i.e. Amlaibh Cuarán or Olaf Guthfrithsson) sacked Holyhead (Caergybi) and ravaged Llŷn (see WaB 539), and again those of 962 when 'the son of Olaf' attacked Gwynedd (Annals of the Four Masters), or to later events initiated by others of the same Uí Ímhair dynasty. In 971 Maccus son of Harald sacked Penmon in Anglesey; and in 972 his brother Guthfrith Haraldsson ravaged Anglesey exacting a large tribute. In 978 Gwrmid (Guthfrith) again ravaged Llŷn (see WaB 547). Later still, in 980, Custennin ab Iago, together with Guthfrith Haraldsson, attacked Anglesey and Llŷn. Custennin was killed, allowing Hywel ab Ieuaf ab Idwal Foel (Iago's nephew) to flourish, perhaps with help from the English, although he was subsequently killed by them in 985 (WaB 547-8). Hywel, with English aid, had attacked Clynnog in 978, perhaps because it was a power base for Iago. The various Gwynedd factions may have had different Viking backers (WaB 547).

44 **ac Eryri anhed yndi** *Anhed* is 'dwelling, habitation, settlement' (see AP line 4 *anhed ym pop mehyn*), perhaps here 'a place of refuge' for the Cymry in the mountain fastnesses of Snowdonia, as in §10.4 *ac yn Eryri ymolöi*, CBT I 3.59 *Ni yn Eryri yn reia6c*, etc.

45 **Dyscogan perffeith** Understood as 'a perfect one foretells' rather than a noun 'prophecy' and adj. (as G favours here and for line 32 above). The adj. *perffeith* is poorly attested in poetry outside the CBT corpus, but see LPBT 3.23 *reith a pherpheith neithawr*.

46 **anhed yn diffeith** The poet reprises the words used in lines 43 and 44. The *anhed* 'settlement' becomes a waste, or else settlement now has to be made in the normally waste place. Perhaps the latter is preferable, indicating how the Cymry will be confined to marginal or inhospitable land.

47 **Kymry pedeirieith** *Pedwar/pedeir/pedry-* can indicate perfection rather than literally 'four': see LPBT 442 on *pedryfan* and *pedrychwelit*. If so, 'the Cymry of perfect language' as in the translation. There is a half space between the elements in the manuscript. The close compound *pedeirieith* is used by Cynddelw, CBT III 7.26 and 13.6 *ysgwyd pedeiryeith*, where *pedeir* is understood literally, and *ieith* as 'people, nation, kin' rather than 'language' with J. Loth. What four nations or peoples these are is debatable: J.E. Caerwyn Williams suggested they were the

7 Gwawt Lud y mawr

four parts of Wales — Dyfed, Gwynedd, Powys (the last first mentioned as an independent entity in 1102, WaB 552) and Gwent — or else Scotland, England, Wales and Ireland (or Cornwall): details in CBT III 90. On Bede's 'four languages' + Latin, see the comments on §1.20. CBT IV 2.51-2 *A'th uolant ueirtyon, derwyton dor,/ O bedeiryeith d6fyn, o bedeiror* is understood by its editors as 'four languages of the world'. Four nations ('pedair cenedl') is the translation of Llygad Gŵr's example in CBT VII 24.116 *(l)lyw pedeiryeith*, but no further qualification is offered. In the present instance, there may be some play on the dual meaning of *ieith*, indicated perhaps by the use of *areith* in the following line. Inversion with unrealised lenition could be understood here, but *pedeirieith* could equally well be genitive.

48 **symudant eu hareith** As well as 'to move; remove', the vb *symud* (not at all common in early poetry) can mean 'to change, alter, exchange', as understood here, with *areith* 'speech, way of expression', GPC^2 s.v. *araith*. This is possibly a reference to language shift, or a change in register brought about by social unrest. But a comparison with OIr *airecht* (as well as the semantic development of words such as *dadl* and *cyfranc*) might suggest an original meaning 'assembly or meeting', IIMWL 135 n. 11.

49 **Yt vi y Uuch Vreith** The ms has *Yt yvi yuuch // y uuch vreith vreit*, with deleting points under *vreit*, and red strikethough. The scribe was evidently tired. *Bi* (and *Yt vi*, as restored here) are naturally found in prophecy: e.g. line 94 below; §1.24 and 25 *gwraged a ui ffraeth,/ eillon a ui kaeth*; R577.14 (Cyfoesi) *pa ri a'n bi ni gantha6*, R577.15 and 579.24; R585.16-17 (Gwasgargerdd) *yt vi a gnaho g6dic,/ a g6edy cat kyuarlluc*, and R585.18 *Cat a vi ar Vyrri* (recte) *auon*; LlDC 17.126 (Oianau) *A'n bi ni inaeth guared guyd(i gu)aeth* and LlDC 16.87 (Afallennau) *llauen vi bri Brython*; CBT II 5.54 *Rac aryneic Bra6t bra6 vi*. Not so common in other contexts, but cf. CBT V 10.53 *Glyned Duw trined y'm trugardawn—ui/ O uawrnen Meruynyawn* where *bi* is interpreted as 'a fydd'; see note CBT V 106.

The Brindled Cow may be analogous to the mysterious *Ych Brych* in Preiddiau Annwfn, the Triads and *Culhwch ac Olwen*. The mention of the *Ych Brych* in LPBT 18.39 is in close proximity to the word *meindyd* 'mid-day', as is the *Buch Vreith* here.

51 **Meindyd brefawt** See note above. The battle of Mynydd Carn is described as being at mid-day, CBT I 3.103 *Amuc a'e dragon, ut Mon, meindyt,/ Men yd las trahaearn yg Karn 6ynyt*. Further on this text, see Nerys Ann Jones, 'The Mynydd Carn "prophecy": a reassessment', *CMCS* 38 (1999), 73-92. With *meinoeth* in LPBT 7.8 *ar veinyoeth veinyd*; also LPBT 18.45 *py awr ymeindyd y ganet Perchen*.

52 **meinoeth berwhawt** The sinister connotations of midnight may have been augmented by Exodus 11 where the tenth and most severe plague, the slaying of the firstborn, happens around midnight. Cf. Echrys Ynys line 8 *meinoeth tymhor*. The vb *berwi* 'to boil' (here understood as 3sg. fut., with G) is used in a number of figurative senses, include 'to plot, incite, throw into turmoil'.

53 **artir (ms ar tir) berwhodawr** Understood as *ardir* 'arable land': although attestations before 16c are uncertain (see GPC^2 and cf. *tir âr*), it yields a marginally stronger line than *a'r tir*, which is also possible. *Berwhodawr*, fut. impers. hapax form, seemingly based on *berwhawt* in line 52.

7 Gwawt Lud y mawr

54   **yn llogoed yssadawr**   The orthography is ambiguous — pl. of *lloc* 'place, consecrated place' (GPC s.v. *llog²*), *lloc* 'tax, rent' (GPC s.v. *llog¹*) or *llog* 'boat' (GPC s.v. *llong*; the usual pl. is *llogeu*).
   A fut. impers. < vb *ysu* 'to consume, devour; destroy' would give good sense, partnering line 53 although both formations are problematic. A form of the vb *sadiaw* (with prosthetic *y-*) is thought by GPC to be unlikely, possibly since it is attested only from the 17c and is based on *sad* 'firm, solid', borrowed from ME. Nevertheless, 'is made secure, steady' would suit ships and holy sites alike. Uncertain.

55   **Kathyl gwae canhator**   *Kathyl*, see on line 1 above. A number of examples of the *-(h)ator* endings are found in the Book of Taliesin, especially in prophecy: LPBT 1.54-5 *prouator eneit/ rac llwyth eissyffleit*; and 1.63 *Gwelattor arwydon*; §9.16 *dullator petrygwern llugyrn ymdeith*; CC 20.163 *Kayator y dyleith*; LPBT 4.51 *Odit traethator* and 4.226 *traethattor*. Elsewhere: CA line 950 *mynawc am rann kwynyator*; CBT II 1.83 *gwelhator*; 1.84 *edrychator*; 5.3 *g6elhattor*; III 16.63 *g6astator*; IV 2.26 *eiryachator*; 2.27 *gwelhator*; 2.31 *gweinidator*; 2.48 *golychator*; 2.55 *kyfurdator*; V 8.43 *magator o'm dlid*; 23.126 *g6elhator*. Note especially Moliant Cadwallon line 44 *Canator cathyl*, one of several 'prophetic' symptoms in that text (see §6.17n).
   Endings in *-etor*, *-itor*, and *-otor*: line 68 below *tyghettor*; LPBT 9.61 and 62 *keissitor*; 18.25 *kymyscetor*; 23.16 *cwynitor*; Echrys Ynys line 4 *rewinetor*; 15 *kyrbwylletor*; 17 *cynwyssetor*; LlDC 16.88 *kenhittor kirrn eluch*; 17.203 *megittor*; EWSP 430.12c *kwynitor*; 457.35b *ryt rewitor*; R585.13 *treulitor*; 585.20 *peritor* (em.); Peirian Faban line 44 *klywytor*; LlDC 8.4 *brithottor*; CBT I 8.7 *g6elitor*; 14.68 *treithitor*; II 1.81 *clyhwitor*; 1.97 *molidor*; 16.19 *klywitor*; 24.3 *draethawd a draethitor*; III 3.43 *keritor*; 10.38 *keritor*; 10.46 *eu traetha6d traethitor*; 10.58 *kenitor*; 16.185 *honitor*; 21.183 *treithitor 'yg kert*; IV 2.20 *clywitor*; 2.23 *dilochitor*; 2.24 *ergrynitor*; 2.28 *telitor*; 2.29 *aruollitor*; 2.32 *kenitor*; 2.56 *pwyllitor*; 6.206 *keffitor*, etc. See GMW 120-1 and Rodway, Dating 102-5 for further examples. Clearly, these forms continue to be used in the 12c, especially for vbs *gwelet*, *caru*, *clybot*, *canu*, *traethu*, etc.

56   **kylch Prydein amgor**   Uncommon *amgor* GPC² 'border, boundary, periphery' but used by Cynddelw, CBT IV 2.30 and IV 6.126.

57   **Dedeuant vn gyghor**   Cf. AP line 48 *vn gor vn gyghor vn eissor ynt*; AP line 109 *Vn cor vn gyghor a Lloegyr lloscit*. *Cyghor* with *gwarthfor* in LPBT 1.60-2 *Dydoent gwarthuor/ gwydueirch dy ar uor/ Eingyl yghygor*. *Dedeuant* is the 3pl. indic. form used in §1.18-19 (Daronwy) *Dedeuant etwaeth/ tros trei a thros traeth* (with §1.28 *Dedeuho*, §1.32 *dydeuho*).

57   **y wrthot gwarthfor (ms gwarthmor)**   If the emendation is correct, cf. LPBT 1.60-2 *Dydoent gwarthuor,/ gwydueirch dy ar uor,/ Eingyl yghygor*, and especially the triple collocation our lines share with CBT IV 2.10-12 *Kadarn gyuaruod g6rthod gwarthuor:/ Oet dygygh6et Eigyl, oet digyghor/ Lloegyr a llu Predein yn ymatcor*. GPC emends Echrys Ynys line 13 *ny bu werthuor* to *ny bu warthuor*, 'disgrace, shame; foreign army', followed by Gruffydd (FS Mac Cana 46) who cites the suggestion in CBT IV 2.10 'sea of shame' (*gwarth + môr*), cf. CA 297, understood here as being a kenning for seaborne raiders. However, Gruffydd translates the Echrys Ynys example as 'he was no mercenary', and John T. Koch derives the second element, rather, from **bor*, FS Mac Cana 46-7,

7 Gwawt Lud y mawr

translating 'bearer of disgrace'. The hapax GPB 1.12 *gwarthfar*, presumably from *gwarth* + *bâr* 'wrath', GPC 'disgrace', may also be relevant.

59 **Boet gwir venhyt** GPC s.v. *mynwyd, menwyd* 'joy, bliss', etc < ?*mynw*. This would give rhyme and good sense, and is in common use by the poets, normally in the *menwyd* form. Is there a suggestion in our instance that the medial -*w*- had weakened, cf. *marwnad* > *marnad*, etc. If not a noun, conceivably the vb noun *mynnyt*, 'to claim, demand' (see GPC s.v. *mynnaf: mynnu, mynnyd*): again the lack of early attestations is a problem, cf. Bret. *mennout*? An abs. form in -*yt* would not be expected in this position.

60 **dragwynawl byt** G s.v. refers to *tragwynawl*, but this is not attested elsewhere. Presumably G would relate this adj. to noun *cwyn*, and vb *trachwynaw 'to lament, complain', and this is tentatively followed here. Also possible is an emendation to adj. *dragonawl, draganawl* or *dragwnawl (used substantivally, possibly as pl.), 'dragon-like one(s); ferocious one(s)'. This formation is reasonably common: EWSP 421.15(b) *pen Vrien vdd dragonawl*; CBT I 11.56; III 14.15; IV 5.5; 9.208; V 1.153, and the *draganawl* form in Echrys Ynys line 20, emended to *dragonawl* by Gruffydd, FS Mac Cana 44.

61 **Dolwys dolhwyckyt** Although the text seems hopelessly corrupt (even G s.vv. offers no guidance), the rhyme and length of lines 61 and 62 are more 'normal' than lines 63 and 66-7. The -*wys* suffix can be somewhat empty of meaning when attached to nouns, or else lend an adjectival force, e.g. *mamwys, dragonwys, ffynhonnwys, ffowys,* ?*caerwys. Dol* '(water-) meadow', also 'loop, ring, bow, snare', etc. but the second word defies any meaningful segmentation.

62 **Dolaethwy eithyt** If *Dolaethwy* is a place-name, it may be that the strange forms in line 61 are troping the *dol* element. *Daethwy* rather than *Aethwy*, possibly a tribal name in origin, is reckoned by Lloyd-Jones (G s.v. *din*) to underlie Dindaethwy and Porthaethwy. Cf. CIB 100, 178-9 and 192. It may have already been thought to come from *aethwy* (note forms in poetry such as CBT IV 13.20 *Porthathwy*; CBT V 22.24 *Porthaethwy*; CBT V 23.39 *Porthathwy* where Prydydd y Moch appears to refer to a battle there following victory at Aberconwy, *c*. 1194, but see details in CBT V 208 on the date and context). On abs. form *eithyt* 'he went', which survives sporadically into the 13c, see LPBT 5.83n and 17.9n. Here used with accusative of destination which persists into the 14c, see GMW 227-8.

63 **Kynran llawn yt gyfarch** Following G, 3sg. pres. vb *cyfarch* 'to ask, beseech, claim, demand' with *llawn* adverbial rather than adj. qualifying *kynran*, GMW 171. No end-rhyme.

64 **Kynut heb eppa** G wonders whether *kynut* is a mistake for *kynnut* 'firewood, fuel' or whether it should be connected with *ut*, and *udaw* 'to howl, wail': the latter would suggest a state of disquiet. But see GPC s.v. *cynudaf: cynudo* (2) 'to gather, collect', followed by GGM I 3.138 *A chynudaw glaw gloewddeigr lleufer*.

The hapax *eppa* < *eb*, as in *ebol* 'foal', *cyfeb* 'with foal', the mountain-name, *Epynt*, etc., with -*ha* causing provection. Similar denominative formations such as *yta* (< *yt* 'corn'), *blota* (< *blawt* 'flour'), confirm the meanings of infrequently attested *eppa* and *henuonha*. The idea being expressed here may be that there is herding and collecting up stock, but no breeding, or perhaps no raiding.

65 **heb henuonha** Another hapax, a vb from *henfon* 'old cow, breeding-cow'.

66 **heb ofur byt** G relates this hapax to *mur*, suggesting 'defensive place, compound; safety'. I understand *byt* here as 'food' (see GPC s.v. *byd²*) rather than 'world; life', although that is also possible.

67 **Byt a uyd diffeith direit** *Diffeith* is used for desolate or uninhabited regions, the ocean, the mountains, as well as for places laid waste, as in line 43 above: EWSP 430.4c *yn amwyn Tren tref diffeith*; R1050.13-14 (Mal Rhod yn Troi) *a diffeith eluyd heb aelwydeu*; LlDC 17.81 (Oianau) *Ac escib lluch lladron diffeith llannev*, etc. *Direit* 'wretched', see EWSP 30-1, 197-200, 284. Our line is too long, and one of the two last words probably needs deleting. There is no end-rhyme in either case.

68 **kogeu tyghettor** 'Cuckoos' rather than 'cooks', indicating perhaps the disruption of the seasons. They are closely linked with the cuckoo's appearance and disappearance in the literary texts as in folk tradition: see LPBT 4.157n and 4.177n. As in the present instance, R584.36-7 *Mei mar6 cogeu rac ann6yt* prophesies a world upside-down: cuckoos will die in May, the very month of their annual floruit, e.g. LPBT 3.21 *Atwyn Mei y gogeu ac eaws*, and cf. Whitsuntide birds in CBT V 14.23 *Neud adneu cogeu, coet neud atre*.

69 **hoywwed trwy groywed** *Hoyw* 'magnificent, splendid, fine, lively' is productive in compounds, here with *gwed* 'appearance, condition', CBT I 1.34 *Caffaud Hyuel urth ei hoewet wy rhybuchvy*; CBT II 15.45 *Patha6r—eu hoywet*. See LPBT 9.30n on problems of *ban vyd hyn hoywed*. *Croywed* 'purity, clarity, brightness', possibly referring to spiritual virtue, or an ascetic mode of life contrasted with opulence or magnificence. These two conditions are mixed up (*trwy*) — a commonplace of prophetic discourse (see General Introduction, 11-12) — rather than the first being achieved through the second. Proest rhyme with line 70, but see below.

70 **gwyr bychein bron otwyllyd** G *godwyllyd* 'deceitful, treacherous', a hapax, but cf. the hapax vb *godwyllaw* < *twyll* 'deceit'. *Bron* 'breast' is often used for 'nature, disposition'.

71 **Toruenhawl tuthiolyd** *Toruenhawl*, if with medial [v], appears to be a hybrid < *torment* 'host, army' with adj. suffix, but influenced by *toryf* 'host'. It is not listed by GPC. The usual adj. from *torment* is *tormennawc* (with variant *tormynnawc*), as seen in CBT I 11.41; III 21.87; V 24.69; VI 6.39 and VII 28.4. Another possibility is *torwynnawl* 'bulging-eyed?' < *torwyn(n)* (cf. GPC s.v. *torwynnaf*).

Tuth ~ *tith* + adjectival *-yawl* + agent suffix (GPC only notes *tuthiog*, 'trotting, moving fast', not *tuthiol* nor *tuthiolydd*). *Iolyd* 'suppliant, petitioner', etc. seems less easy to accommodate.

72 **hywedyd (ms hwedyd)** Emended to *hywedyd* = ModW *hyweddydd* 'tamer, trainer, instructor' (< *hywedd*), attested first in 1592 according to GPC (though the vb is attested early). This would link with the *tithiolydd*, most likely a horseman.

72 **arvedyd** If two words, 'on, over the world' (= ar fedydd), which would give reasonable sense. But if from vb *arwein/arwed(u)* 'to lead, carry, take off', etc., then an agent noun, although 1502 is the first attestation noted by GPC² of *arweddydd* 'leader, guide; maintainer, supporter; carrier, bearer, porter'.

7 Gwawt Lud y mawr

73 **Ny wan cyllellawr** Lines 73-4 have a gnomic feel. Even cowards (*meiwyr*), if well armed, will be defended from attack by a lesser weapon. *Cyllellawr* is an otherwise unattested analogical pl., rather than the ablaut pl. *cyllyll* (or *cylleill*).

74 **cledyfawr meiwyr** *Meiwyr*, lit. 'half-men,', 'cowards' is fairly uncommon; but CA lines 831 and 1444; CBT III 3.52 and CBT VI 19.8. The abstract noun occurs in LlDC 2.6 *meiuret*.

75 **Nyt oed udu y puchysswn** *Udu*: see GMW 60 on *udud, udu, ydu* and *udunt*, forms of 3pl. conjugated prep. *y* 'to'; and Sims-Williams, Prepositions 15-20 and 43-4. The form *udu* is used in EWSP 410 *dangossei Byll bwyll udu*; CC 8.24 *A their mam udu*; and cf. CC 1.4c (Juvencus 9) *oimer didu (ỏy* 'to'). *Vdunt* in LPBT 12.13 *Yn dillig vdunt*. *Udud* is the most common form in pre-1283 poetry, however: e.g. LlDC 16.38 (Afallennau) *Oet aelav vtvt dulloet diheueirch*, used eight times in the CBT corpus. On problematic *udun*, see §3.20n and LPBT 10.23n. CBT VI 27.92 *iddun* is from the late ms NLW 4973B.

    Puchaw 'to wish, desire', 1sg. pluperfect, cf. CBT I 29.5 (Einion ap Gwalchmai) *Ar eu pechodau puchs6n* (R text has *puchysswn*) *arwyt—croc*. Other forms of the vb are fairly common, often with preceding *ry* as in OW Juv example CC 1.7 *rit pucsaun mi*.

76 **anaw angerdawl trefdyn** Since *angerdawl* 'passionate, ferocious; wrathful' is used substantivally (e.g. in LPBT 8.33 *kigleu gyfarfot angerdolyon*, following G's emendation), *anaw angerdawl* is understood as 'one passionate (to gain) wealth', rather than 'passionate wealth/profit' or 'wealth of the ferocious dwelling'. *Trefdyn*, cf. AP line 53, where it precedes, as here, a list of peoples.

77 **ac y wyr kared Creudyn** *Y wyr* 'to/for men' or perhaps *y'y wyr* 'to his men' referring to the *angerdawl* of the previous line. Uncertain. *Cared* 'transgression, sin, crime', is common, especially in CBT corpus; also LPBT 10.2 and CC 18.7. Creuddyn is a region, perhaps the one in Rhos with its caput at Degannwy (HW 239-30), but there are two other *cymydau* of that name, one in Powys Fadog and one in Ceredigion. The 'wrong-doing at Creuddyn' might refer to a defeat or slaying brought about by treachery. Several disasters took place at Degannwy, e.g. its sacking by the English in 823 (AC), King John's siege in 1201-11, and Henry III's activities in 1245.

78 **Kymry, Eigyl, Gwydyl, Prydyn** Lists are common in prophetic discourse, see General Introduction, 12-13.

79 **Kymry kyfret ac ascen** *Kyfret* 'jointly moving, accompanying; as swift as', cf. PT I.3 *kant gorwyd kyfret*; LPBT 5.220 *cyfret a gwylan*, etc.

80 **Dygedawr gwydueirch ar llyn** *Dygedawr*, impers. of vb *dwyn* 'to bring (forth)', also in line 84 below, and in Day of Judgment poem, CC 20.29 *Dygetawr Llawethan*; 20.45-6 *Gwynt rud dygetawr/ ech ei gadwynawr*; also CC 21.132 *Dygettaur y Tri Llv*. The compound vb *dydwyn* has a similar formation, *dydyccawr*, e.g. LPBT 13.33, 34. *Gwydueirch* 'wooden horses' is a kenning for ships (see LPBT 5.29n), used in a comparable prophetic passage about sea-raids in LPBT 1.60-64 *Dydoent gwarthuor,/ gwydueirch dy ar uor,/ Eingyl ygygor./ Gwelattor arwydon/ gwynyeith ar Saesson*. *Llyn* 'lake, water, drink', here for sea, as, e.g., in LlDC 16.23 (Afallennau) *Seithlog y deuant dros lydan lin* (in a rhyme block with *Prydin*).

7 Gwawt Lud y mawr

81 **Gogled o wenwyn (ms wenwynuyd) o hermyn** The line is longer than the norm here. *Gogled* is almost always north Britain in early poetry: BGod 7-39, p. 11. Here, however, the term might correspond to *Llychlyn*, the homeland of the *Nordmyn, Nordmein*, 'Scandinavians, Vikings; Normans'.

Gwenwyn 'poison; man or thing which slays; jealousy; enmity'; as adj. 'cruel, bitter', etc., is productive in compounds, and G notes *gwenwynuyd* tentatively as one word, presumably *gwenyn* + *gwŷð* 'wood'. GPC lists no such compound. The repetition of *o* might suggest textual corruption, but taken with *o* in the following lines, would seem to indicate a listing pattern.

Hermyn has a punctum delens under *i* (*heirmyn*), perhaps copied from *heruin* or *herumyn*. The context suggests *her(w)myn* 'raiders, outlaws', etc. < *herw* + *myn* (pl. of *mon* borrowed from English), perhaps for Vikings? But *hermon/myn* is not noted by GPC (*herwllong*, etc. and others occur however, as does *herw*). Another possibility might be *her* 'challenge' (cf. vb *heriaw*), reckoned by GPC to be influenced by or borrowed from ME *herian* 'to harry': this would give 'defying or challenging men'. In OF, *Hermins* is used for 'Armenians' see *CMCS* 60 (2010), 62. With more intervention, emendations to *erwyn* 'fierce, passionate' or *goerwyn* 'fierce' (i.e. *gogled wenwyn goerwyn*) might be suggested, although the latter is not attested. The whole line is very uncertain.

82 **o echen casnur (ms o echlur caslur) caslyn** Emended to *echen* 'line, lineage, stock, nature' in the light of line 82. The scribe seems to have anticipated -*ur*. G s.v. *caslur* suggests emending to *casnur* 'wrathful' (understood here), also arguably a personal name in LPBT 24.10 *yn difant a charant Casnur*. Casnar (Wledig) is frequently mentioned in the prose tales (PKM 1, CO and BR), and in court poetry, CBT II 22.44; III 12.24; IV 9.158; VI 12.30; VII 52. In genealogies, he appears to be connected with the line of Powys, and in Achau Brenhinoedd a Thywysogion Cymru (EWGT 96) he is a son of Lludd ap Beli Mawr. G s.v. *caslyn*, either 'persistent in enmity/wrath' (cf. vb *glynu*), or 'sea/water of enmity' (cf. line 57 *gwarthuor*).

83 **o echen Adaf henyn** *Echen Adaf* 'race of man', one of several similar phrases, e.g. *plant A.; llin A.; gwerin A.; A. feibion*. *Henyn*, 3pl. vb *hanfot* 'to come from, originate from' (with loss of -*t* confirmed by rhyme). A curious parallel is found in the Cyfoesi, R582.23-4 *A chiwta6t plant Adaf a henynt oe g6a6t*.

84 **Dygedawr trydw y gychwyn** *Trydw/drydw* 'starling'. The most famous of Welsh starlings (*ederyn drydwen*) carried Branwen's message to her brother Bendigeidfran (Brân) in Caernarfon (PKM 38); this initiated (?*cychwyn*) the movement of Brân's troops over to Ireland to save his sister.

85 **branes o goscord gwyrin (ms gwyrein)** The most famous flock of ravens is that associated with Owain son of Urien Rheged in *Breuddwyd Ronabwy*: see BR 12.28 where he calls them *vy mranos*. *Branes* not otherwise found in early poetry outside the CBT corpus where it is very common, often collocated with *Bryneich*. *Gwyrein*, the pl. of *gwyran* 'barnacle-goose', would be an attractive avian partner to *branes* and *trydw*. Another *gwyrein*, also not attested until 15c, means 'grass, pasture'. But the rhyme would be defective. Emend to either *gwerin* 'crew, men' (cf. R1333.13 for the same mistake), or (as in the translation) with G to *gwirin / gwyrin* (-*yn*) 'pure, holy, chaste'. However, the precise import of these line is unclear to me.

7 Gwawt Lud y mawr

86 **Meryd milet Seithenhin (ms seithin)** *Milet* 'warband, host'. Ifor Williams suggested a personal name *Seithin* < L. *Sanctinus*: on this known name, see CIB 143 n. 846 and 178 n. 1076. G s.n. *Cristin* suggests emending to *Seithenhin*, which would give a heptasyllabic length as in line 85, and is followed here. With different emendations, possibilities might include *seithnyn* 'seven men', bringing to mind the seven *cynweisiad* 'officers, stewards' who allowed the Island of Britain to be overrun by Caswallon son of Beli who became king in London (PKM 45). But there may be some other word here, connected with *seith* 'seven', or with *seith* 'saint, holy', a rare learned borrowing < L. *sanctus*.

If *meryd* means here 'stagnant (of water); humid, moist' rather than more general 'slow, sluggish, slow to move' (the latter in EWGP 24.19, 26.5, 30.14 and 16, 42.11; CBT I 3.132), that might support some connection with the drowned land of Maes Gwyddnau, as Lloyd-Jones intimates, although Mererid, not Cristin, is clearly the culpable figure in the version of the Seithennin story in the Black Book of Carmarthen (LlDC poem 39 passim). Could *meryd* be a mistake for, or derive from an abbreviation of, *Mererid*?

87 **ar vor agor ar Gristin** Since *wrth agor* is the usual way of expressing 'at anchor', as in AP line 191 *Saesson wrth agor ar vor peunyd*, it would seem that *ar vor agor* means 'an anchor at sea; a sea-anchor'. The vb *agor* 'to open' ('to/before the opening of the sea') is possible, especially if *Seithenhin* is to be restored in line 86. It is hard to see how *Cristin* could refer to Cristin ferch Goronw ab Owain, the second wife (and first cousin) of Owain Gwynedd (d. 1170). Their consanguinity incurred excommunication for the king. After her husband's death, her championing of her sons, Dafydd and Rhodri, over their half-brother, Hywel ab Owain, was condemned by Peryf ap Cedifor. The elegy he sang for Hywel and his own brothers accuses Cristin and her sons of having hatched treachery: despite her pious name, Cristin is part of the faction he styles as the *Brython anghristiawn*. This *ad feminam* treatment is unprecedented in court poetry, and she may have been reviled and linked with various calamities. But there were undoubtedly other women of that name, e.g. Cristin (or Efa) daughter of Bledrws ap Ednywain Bendew, and mother of Iorwerth Goch (brother of Madog ap Maredudd, ruler of Powys, d. 1160), EWGT 103. G notes how the form *a Christyn vanaches* in RBB 393.29 (Brut y Saesson, for the year 1015) is used to denote the name of Christina, daughter of Edward the Exile, d. 1057. Pen Cristin (1840) is on the south-east side of Bardsey and it is the name of a farm in the middle of the island.

88 **Vch o vor vch o vynyd** *Vch* occurs in a similar, but more extended, run in PT V.20-5 *Ossit vch ymryn,/ neut Vryen a'e gryn./ Ossit vch ym pant,/ neut Vryen a'e gwant./ Ossit vch ymynyd,/ neut Vryen a oruyd./ Ossit vch yn riw,/ neut Vryen a'e briw./ Ossit vch yg clawd,/ neut Vryen a blawd./ Vch hynt vch as,/ vch ym pop kamas*. PT 69-70 suggests 'an enemy, someone or something to be attacked, to be pierced, wounded and overcome'. The fact that it occurs as *vch* in our instance and throughout the PT V passage throws some doubt on the suggestion in PT 69-70 that it is a scribal error for *hwch* 'pig, sow; ?attack' (with the initial [h] of the word wrongly interpreted as an orthographic *h*). On the other hand, there is no other evidence for *uch*. The single instance of *hwch* where it appears to mean 'attack' is by Prydydd y Moch, CBT V 1.79 *G6yr hoetylwydyr, g6r hydyr yn y h6ch—a'e uar* translated by its editor as '(attacking) men whose lives are fragile

7 Gwawt Lud y mawr

as glass, a strong man in his attack and his wrath'. This meaning can be compared with *hwrdd* 'ram', also 'a shove, thrust'. The syntactical repetition may compensate for the lack of rhyme which resumes in line 89.

89 **ynyal ebryn** Rare *ebryn* 'ferment, agitation', found only in prophecy: AP line 101 *na chynhoryon Saesson keffyn ebryn*; CC 20.57 *Ebryn pop dyhed*. *Ynyal* is here understood as a noun rather than adj. *Ynyal* (as opposed to *anyal*) is the usual medieval form, see CA 241-2.

90 **coet mäes tyno a bryn** Disyllabic *mäes* perhaps (giving seven syllables), as in PT II.8; AP line 87; EWSP 414.2; CC 9.10 *ffrwyth coet a mäes*; LPBT 5.135; 8.21; 13.15; LlDC 17.135; 39.3; Tymhorau line 11 *Segites ar vaes a buches lawn*; PKM 90, and see discussion, PKM xviii-ix.

Or else emend to *coet a maes* (diphthong, as in LlDC 18.137 and 226; EWSP 443.102 and 103; 445.111, and in all 18 CBT instances). A very common pairing, e.g. PT II.8-9 *Ny nodes na maes na choedyd,/ tut achles, dy ormes pan dyuyd*; AP line 87; CC 9.10; LPBT 11.17 *Ef maes ef yg koet*; 13.15 *bud coet a mäes*; CBT II 26.96-7 *Hyfaes y meillyon, hyfes goedyt*; CBT III 23.3-4 *Nyd bleit coed coll y auael,/ Namwyn bleit maes moessauc hael*; CBT IV 18.5 *A wnaeth coed a maes a mesur iawn*; CBT V 1.97-8 *Ef y uaes, y uaws gadarn6ch:/ Chwi y goed—y gad nwy beit6ch*, etc.

Tyno and *bryn* are also partners: LPBT 9.56 *na bryn na thyno*; CC 16.9 *Ym brin, in tyno, in inysset mor*; CBT V 23.119 *Hyd yt el y doryf ar dyno—a brynn*; CBT VII 25.54 *Dywyssa6c breinyawc brynn a thyno*.

91 **Pop arawt heb erglywaw nebawt** *Arawt* < L. *oratio* 'prayer, utterance' in CC 1.7 (Juvencus 9) *in haraut celmed* (emended for rhyme), and in Juv colophon *araut di Nuadu*; multiple instances in CBT III 10, CBT VII 40, etc. and increasingly used in the 14c, e.g. GSRh 6.75 *Tafawd un arawd Aneirin—gwawtglaer*. *Erglywaw* 'to listen to, to hear'. *Nebawt* 'anything, something, nothing', with generic rhyme with *mynawc* as part of the metrical arrangement in the *toddaid* formed by lines 91 and 92.

92 **o vynawc pop mehyn (ms o pop)** If the second *o* were deleted, then 'lord of every place' (*mehyn* relatively uncommon), perhaps used of God, comparing LPBT 12.2 *arglwyd pop tra*; CBT I 4.17 *Rwyf pobua*, etc. However, common *mynawc* is used exclusively of a secular ruler in poetry, as understood here.

93 **Yt vi brithret a lliaws gyniret** *Brithret*, cf. LPBT 16.28 *digonynt brein gwneint pen brithret*; CA lines 775 (A) and 783 (B), *ri guanaid brit ret*; *ketwyr am Gatraeth a wnaeth brithret*; EWSP 459.14 *gweleis i vrithret*. It is synonymous with more common *brithuyt*, as in LPBT 1.100 *brithuyt a byt dyuysci*, and see note. The lenition here following *lliaws* would indicate inversion, i.e. 'tumult of a host', but note that GPC s.v. *lliaws* (b) lists several examples of lenited nouns following *lliaws* 'many a'.

94 **a gofut amwehyn** G notes *amwehyn* as hapax vb noun 'spread, spread out', and see also LPBT 4.171n.

95 **dialeu trwy hoyw gredeu bresswyl** Unusually long line with nine syllables. Pl. *dialeu* attested but rare (see G s.v. *dial*); *credeu* is understood here as 'promises, pledges'. See above on line 69 *hoywed trwy groywed*. *Presswyl*, as well as being a noun 'abode, home' and adj. 'constant, inhabiting, ready to hand', etc., could

7 Gwawt Lud y mawr

also be 3sg. of vb *presswylyaw* 'to dwell, inhabit', as in CBT I 11.33 *Hyd yd bresswyl hwyl heul Ueheuin*.

96   **Kyfoethawc Duw vrdin**   The usual form *vrdyn* (< L. *ordin-*) gives internal rhyme with *kyn* in line 97. Of God, CC 13.4 *Meckyt Meir mab ac urdyn y arnaw*; adj. as here in CA line 236 *urdyn deuawt*, and in six CBT examples. *Kyuoethawc* of God, as in CC 12.33 *kyvoethauc Duw vab Meir*; CC 21.10 *a oruc kyuoethauc*; and CC 21.122 *Kywoethauc Duw a wet*; CC 20.61, etc.

97   **kyn no Dydbrawt**   *Kyn no* 'before' + noun, cf. CA line 54 *kyn noe argyurein*; (in Signs of Day of Judgment by Llywelyn Fardd) CBT II 5.57 *Eil dyd kyn no dyd dilyw*; LPBT 9.4 *kyn no Cherituen*; CBT I 10.34 *kyn no mi*; CBT II 26.9 *kyn no heneint*; CBT VII 53.21 *Kyn no llat Dauyt*, etc. But the form without *no* which becomes the norm is also in use, CA line 101 *kyn kystlwn kerennyd*; line 339 *kynn kysdud daear kynn affan*; line 552 *kynn gwawr dyd dilin*, etc.; CC 21.41 *Kin kyues argel*; CC 14.12 *O pechaud kin Braud pryderaw*; LlDC 17.210 (Oianau) *kin gorffen bid*; etc. This needs further investigation.

98   **y daw diwarnawt**   *Diwarnawt* 'day' in R577.42 (Cyfoesi) *g6ae Brydein o'r diwarna6t*; CC 14.29 *diwarnaud*; CC 20.50 *Dayar diwarnawt* (the appointed Last Day, see GPC s.v. *diwrnod*); CBT VI 17.14 *Llangollen ddiwarnawd*, etc.

99   **a dwyrein darlleawr**   *Dwyrein* is ambiguous: a 'rising up, resurgence' seems most likely in the context, especially since line 101 uses the related vb *datwyrein* (< *dat-* + *dwyrein*). However, 'the east' is not impossible. The idea of a text being read may be adapted from Scriptural treatments of the Day of Judgment, notably in Revelation 20:12 'And I saw the dead, small and great, stand before God; and the books were opened: and another book was opened, which is the book of life: and the dead were judged out of those things which were written in the books, according to their works', and 20:15 'And whosoever was not found written in the book of life was cast into the lake of fire'. It is referred to in poems on the Day of Judgment, e.g. CC 20.157 *a deu lyfyr yn ach llaw/ yn eu darlleaw* (addressing John the Evangelist and John the Baptist); CBT VII 38.11-12 *Nyt digewilyd pan welher—Dydbra6t/ Darllein pob pecha6t ual y pecher*. The point here is that a weighty proclamation is going to be read out in the same way, but a while *before* the Day of Judgment. G s.v. *darlleaw* queries the hapax *darlleawr* fut. impers., presumably because of the lack of full end-rhyme with preceding *-awt* (?emend to *darllehawt*), although the meaning is fine.

100   **teruyn tiryon tir Iwerdon**   *Tiryon*, either adj. 'pleasant, fair', or a formation from *tir* (see GPC s.v. *tirion* 'lands; territory, plain, grassland'), the former in comparable collocation, CBT I 3.131 *Cad yn Iwerton diryon dreuyt*; the latter in CBT II 26.143 *Ac Iwerton tiryon, tir Gwytelec*. *Teruyn* 'boundary, border, bordering land', but also 'end, termination, limit', etc. see GPC. Ir. *termonn* appears to have a stronger sense of 'sanctuary, protection' within the bounds of a church, etc. If *teruyn* is used adverbially here, perhaps 'at the bounds of the fair land of Ireland'; but since the Irish were generally reviled by the medieval Welsh, the prophecy might rather be foretelling an end to their territories. Uncertain, however.

101   **Y Prydein ⇔ y daw datwyrein (ms yna)**   Delete *yna* for a reasonable line length. *Datwyrein*, vb noun, used of 'resurrection' in eschatological contexts, e.g. CC 21.120 *A daduirein o bet*; Peirian Faban line 65 *datwyrein o vedd*; CBT I 4.34 *G6rthrych dadwyrein, ys kein yndi*; CBT II 27 *Dadwyrein o uein, o uet—a'n*

7 Gwawt Lud y mawr

dybyt, as well as for the sun rising, and resurgence of might. Cf. LPBT 5.45 *Datwyrein y Vrython* (recte).

102 **Brython o vonhed Rufein** On the Roman connection, see §8.1n, LPBT 8.39n, and General Introduction, 12. For mentions of *Brython*, which could be pl. as well as sg., see on §8.35.

103 **A'm bi barnodyd o aghygres dieu** The *a* + dative pron. + *bot* mode of denoting possession is still going strong in late 13c court poetry, with some 14c examples, e.g. GC 5.15 *a'm bu dâl*. While *a'n bi* might be more natural, the ms reading is retained. The line is long and could be divided into two lines of 5 and 6 (or 5) syllables; if so, G's suggested *barnodeu* 'judgments', a hapax, or emended *dyd* (rather than synonym *dieu*) to rhyme with *barnodyd* 'a judge'. G suggests 'confused, troubled' for otherwise unattested *aghygres* (< *kygres*).

104 **Dysgogan sywedydyon** *Syw* 'sage' is treated as a borrowing from OIr *suí* by GPC s.v. following Lexique S-199 which compares the pair *dryw*, OIr *druí*, see LPBT 5.174n. The Book of Taliesin has a concentration of words formed from *syw*: LPBT 1.90 *wyf syw amrysson*; 2.9 *wyf dryw . . . wyf syw*; 4.4 *sywedyd yn yt uo*; 4.65-6 *doethur, prif geluyd,/ dispwyllawt sywedyd*; 4.98-100 *mawrhydic sywyt* (em.)/ *Pan dyfrensit/ awel uchel gyt*; 4.165-6 *Talhayarn yssyd/ mwyhaf sywedyd* (em.); 7.5 *Hard bron sywedyd*; 7.40 *sywyon synhwyr*; 7.41 *sewyd amloer*; 8.44 *pensywet*; 11.91 *Seon sywedyd*; 15.60 *bum syw, bum swch*; 25.21-2 *Seith awyr yssyd/ od uch sywedyd*; PT XII.6 *Ryfed hael o sywyd sywedyd* (see note, PT 130); CC 24.10 (BT) *sywedyd llyfreu*.

Elsewhere in poetry: CA lines 212-14 *Mab Sywno sywedyd a'e gwydyei/ a werthws e eneit/ er wyneb grybwylleit*; CC 12.14 *a'r sir syweditiaeth*; LlDC 31.11-12 *Vythneint Elei/ a ssivyon ell tri* (viz. Mabon m. Modron, Cysgaint m. Banon, and Gwyn Godyfrion); R577.2 (Cyfoesi) *sy6 pob tut*; Tymhorau line 22 *pen sywedydd*; CBT II 26 (Gwynfardd Brycheiniog of St David), lines 11 *syw gormant*, 85 *syw sywedyd*, 205 *seint sywedyd*, 231 *syw synhwyreu*; CBT V 4.13-14 (Prydydd y Moch) *Marc6lf a Chad6 . . ./ A Selyf, benn sywedytyon*; Dydd dyfydd line 27 *Selyf suinedic syuedit*; CBT VII 41.30 *Geyr bronn Dofyd a Ssywedyd*; GC 4.2 *Sywedyd, Douyd* (of God), etc. See further GPC s.v. The poetry examples noted here illustrate the range of meaning: 'sage, learned man, instructor', one who has insight and foresight including prophetic powers. Some indicate a particular connection with the celestial bodies and the heavens and CC 24.10 connects the *sywedyd* with books.

105 **ygwlat y colledigyon** *Colledigyon* may be understood as ones suffering a *collet* 'loss', or 'lost souls' astray (see GPV s.v. *colledig*).

106 **dysgogan deruydon** This vb and noun are collocated by Cynddelw (CBT III 16.1) and cf. Prydydd y Moch (CBT V 11.45 *darogan derwyton*; CBT V 25.41-3 *Darogan Mertin . . . Dywa6d derwyton*). See LPBT §5.238n ('uniquely' in LPBT 29 is to be corrected).

107 **tra mor tra Brython** See GPC on *tra¹* 'beyond, after; in addition to, as well as', and *tra²* 'while'.

108 **haf ny byd hinon** *Hinon* 'sunshine, fine weather', rhymed with *Brython*, and collocated with *tra*, as here, in LPBT 10.32 *Aranrhot drem clot tra gwawr hinon*. See General Introduction, 12 on bad weather.

7 Gwawt Lud y mawr

109 **bythawt breu breyryon** On *bythawt*, see §8.64n. Collocation *breyr-/breu-* found in CBT II 4.7 *Hoedyl breyr breua6l a beth*; 4.15-16 *breuolyaeth . . ./ Breyr*. The pl. form *brehyr(y)eit* 'lords' is used in R579.15 and 19 (Cyfoesi), *breyreu* in CBT I 9.142.

110 **o gwanflet (ms gwanfret)** No *gwanfret* is attested. It looks like a miscopying of *gwanflet*, as H-cd implies, with rather uncommon noun *fflet*, as in AP lines 31 and 52, understood AP 31 as 'deceit, falsehood', followed by GPC s.v. *ffled*. This word is used twice by Prydydd y Moch, CBT V 26.87 (to Rhys Gryg in Deheubarth) *Yssym eur ac aryant, nyd fled*; and again V 26.111 *Ac o'r pryd y prouaf nad fled/ Na'th ad6s Yessu eissywed*, also CBT VII 42.2 *na phlet na phla*.

111 **tra merin tat ket** *Tra* ambiguous as in line 107, but the phrase occurs elsewhere: CA line 591; §8.80-1 *tra Merin Reget;/ perif perchen ket*, collocated, as here, with *ket*; CBT I 17.23 (emended). There is also the possibility of compound *tramerin*. WaB 90 cites Gildas's idea (*De Excidio Britanniae*, ch. 14) that the Picts were regarded as 'a transmarine nation' like the Irish, intrusive and separate; see Neil Wright, 'Gildas's Geographical Perspective: Some Problems', in *Gildas: New Approaches*, edited by Michael Lapidge and David Dumville (Woodbridge, 1984), 85-105, at pp. 88-92. Is *tat* a slip for *tra*? 'The father of a gift'— for a generous one, perhaps — seems odd. A radical intervention, in the light of §8.80, would be to emend to *Merin Reget*.

112 **Mil ym Brawt** *Mil* can be used for a 'great host' as well as a thousand.

113 **ac y am gyffwrn (ms gwffwn) kyffin** *Cyffwn* is not attested, but a compound of *ffwrn* 'oven' would suit the context of Hell, as noted in H-cd, cf. CBT VII 40.44 *A'r ffeir yn hirdr6c a'r ff6rn dywyll6c*; CBT VII 40b.82 *Satan sutiwr ffyrnau* and 40b.88 *A phob cog ffyrnig o'r coeg ffyrnau*. Also for 'furnace; conflagration' in CC 20.52 *Dayar yn vn ffwrn* (one of the signs before Judgment). *Kyffin* 'region, border, edge' rather than a region or river, but if the latter, the River Cyffin flows into the Conway near its mouth at Conwy, just up-river from Degannwy; another Cyffin is near Llangadfan, Montgomeryshire.

114 **Na chwydaf (ms nachwyaf) y goglyt gwern** Although G s.v. **cwy²* cross-references *nachwyaf* (no such vb is listed in GPC) and *gorchwy* 'sustenance, provision', the easiest course here might be to understand *na chwydaf*, from the vb *cwydaw* 'to fall, fell', or else (with H-cd) *na chwynaf* 'may I not lament, be dolorous'. If the latter, *y* meaning 'in' rather than 'to, into'. GPC s.v. *gogelaf: goglyt* (b) 'to care for, keep, guard, defend, protect, secure, ward off, avoid, evade'. *Gwern* 'swamp' and its compounds (*crawnwern, hagrwern, mignwern*, etc.) are frequently collocated with *Uffern*, and used with *gweglyt* (a variant of *goglyt*) in CBT I 24.30 *O oerwern uffern, wern weglyt. Cethern* 'rabble' is another favourite collocation.

115 **gwerin gwaelotwed Uffern** *Gwerin* 'inhabitants, crew', with *Cain* in CBT VI 24.35-6 *A lle yd oed druan, dr6y ada6—Cain,/ Y werin wirin y waranda6*.

116 **ergrynaw (ms ergrynaf) kyllestric Käen** The vb *ergrynu* 'to tremble in fear; to fear' is reasonably common: e.g. CA line 608 *Er kryn*; LlDC 16.62 (Afallennau) *ergrinaf wy nragon*; LPBT 23.4 *Ergrynawr*, and 23.7 *ergrynawt*; CBT I 3.166 *Ergrynei vym pwyll e bell gerded*; III 24.105 *Ergrynynt eu bar seirff saffar senn*; IV 2.24 *Grym afyrd6l Erk6l ergrynitor*; 6.184 *Tr6m yt ergryner crynoder y uar*; V 26.108-9 *Mal g6rhyd Ercwlf ergrynhed/ A Sams6n (gwytg6n gogoned—acha6s)*.

Also CBT I 4.16 *Rydyergryneis o'e gymhelri*; PT XII.9 *yn y wlat yd oed ergrynic* 'one who is feared'. Here, the final *-af* appears to be a false modernisation of *-aw*, and the vb noun is understood in the translation.

Kyllestric 'fiery, flaming, bright' (GPC) as well as primary 'flinty, hard' (G), cf. its use in other Hell descriptions, e.g. CBT I 13.24 *Yg kyllestric dande*; CBT VII 52.5 *Yn y may mawrway marwar—kyllestric*. On the adj., used by Prydydd y Moch (CBT V 1.133) to describe the raiment of light in which Adam and Eve were clothed, according to apocrypha, see Elin M. Phillips, 'Callestrig(i)awl', *B* 25 (1972-4), 118-19, and CC 14.49 *o gyllest(r)ic gwisc*.

Käen is understood as the Biblical Cain, the evil brother of Abel. There are many variants of the spelling of Cain in MW, most disyllabic — CC 14.79 *Käi*; CC 10.28 *Käim*; CC 10.28 and 14.70 *Käin*; GGDT 10.56 *Käi* — and this would seem to be yet another. It was a medieval commonplace to denote evil men and monsters alike as 'the race of Cain', and he himself was a byword for sin: CBT IV 17.127 *Yn yt aeth Cain can y weithred—cam*; CBT I 11.29; 33.101 *Yn rewin Kayn can Sathanas*; CBT VI 24.35 (see n. above); CBT V 15.17 *Cain a'e glas*; CBT V 4.4 *Vu Cain ac Afael wirion*, etc. However, G suggests emending to *kenn* 'skin, scale(s)': one wonders whether perhaps the synonym *kaen* had come to the scribe's mind as he was writing. If Lloyd-Jones is right, translate 'the fiery-scaled ones made to tremble by God . . .'.

8 Yn wir dymbi Romani kar

The poem has eight individual awdlau, each beginning with *Yn wir dymbi*, or *Yn wir dyrehawr/dedeuhawr*, and is broadly similar in this respect to Armes Prydain and other poems in this collection.[1] Line 42 *Dysgogan delwat* is also treated as the start of a discrete section since variations on this opening line are found in Armes Prydain and in poem §7. The metre in sections 1-7 is consistent Cyhydedd Naw Ban with a clear caesura and a two-stress, generally four-syllable cadence, in good order, like Armes Prydain which is over double the length with 199 lines. However, the final awdl in the present poem uses the short line, perhaps signalling the end by a change of metre, and perhaps deliberately quickening the tempo for effect as happens in poem §2. Although there is no comparable metrical change in the final section of Armes Prydain, it does have a very clear sense of an ending signalled by its syntactical repetition and extended imprecation to God. The sections of the present poem may be summarised for convenience.

¶1 (Lines 1-10) The poem foretells the coming of an unnamed, but exceptional man who will cause great confusion, noise and bloodshed to his enemies. He, or those he delivers, are kin or allied in some way to the Romans: there may be a reference to the legendary descent from Trojans held in common by the Romans and Britons, or perhaps an allusion to Caswallon or another semi-Romanised figure. The stock battle description uses collocations found elsewhere — *lluch a llachar*; *triganed kyrn* (also used of the Final Trump on the Day of Judgment); *brein ac eryron*, etc. The last three lines appear to use repetition (cymeriad llythrennol) of *ar-* in a manner particularly associated with the twelfth- and thirteenth-century court poets. The reference to Cadwaladr in line 9 might be taken as 'one having the honour of Cadwaladr', but given the frequency of the references to him in the other awdlau, probably 'splendid Cadwaladr' himself, 'dazzling and brilliant'.

¶2 (Lines 11-25) Cadwaladr is again mentioned towards the end of the awdl, and he may be one of those mentioned earlier. Possibly if *dranoneu* in line 11 is to be emended to *drathonneu* (see notes), there is deliverance from over the sea, or by sea. Ships are certainly mentioned here (*llogeu* and *balcheu*), and the *elyrch* 'swans' may refer to them, or to the deliverers or their horses disembarking. The deliverer as well as having sea-power is likened, in familiar fashion, to the sea-flood, implying boundless and limitless liberality: *mynut ryffreu*, etc. Line 18 mentions a Bear and 'a worthy Lion'; also a dragon from the 'southern region' who will be accompanied by a 'youth' (*gwas*) who fought (*rydadlas*) on a Thursday, recalling other Thursday battles including the renowned battle of Cyminawd, mentioned in the Black Book of Carmarthen Oianau and other prophecies (see notes).

---

[1] See introduction to poem §3.

¶3 (Lines 26-33) This section does not end with an explicit mention of Cadwaladr, presumably because he is so evidently the main character in this unusually focused piece of praise. His name will resound in poems as 'wide-coursing', possessed of many followers and wide dominion. There are correspondences here with the imagery and diction of the twelfth-century court poets (e.g. line 29 *hyt pan uwynt seith ieith y ri Gwyned*). He will cause the Angles (*Eigyl*) to slide through the sea, and to return to a condition of *alltuded*, the state of exile from one's homeland, as used three times of the Germanic invaders in Armes Prydain, where the same, rather uncommon verb *llithraw* is also used to express the hope that these undesirables be sent packing back across the sea. This section is using the same stock of discourse as Armes Prydain, or else is intended as a deliberate echo.

¶4 (Lines 34-41) This foretells the coming of a rightful ruler of Anglesey (*teithiawc Mon*) who will be the deliverer of the Britons. Forces, possibly enemy forces, will strike camp on the Tren and the Trannon, two rivers on the eastern borders of Powys, in mid Wales, and will have Anglesey in their sights. An uncertain passage follows which seems to concern a long journey from Ireland (*pell debet byhyt o Iwerdon*) possibly by a fair renowned one who will release the *Cesarogion* — perhaps those like Caesar, or Romanised, or perhaps the Britons themselves.

¶5 (Lines 42-9) Line 43 introduces a 1st person verbal form, rare in our present collection, but reminiscent of the know-all Taliesin discourse elsewhere in the manuscript. Using a signature Taliesin locution, *gogwn* 'I know', the poet says he knows why battle was caused on *Winued*, possibly a reference from a written source to the Battle of the Winwæd, fought in 655 on a river near Leeds: the form *Winued* is not unlike that in Bede's account of the battle,[2] in which a tiny force faced overwhelming odds, and in which Penda of Mercia was defeated (his death in the Peniarth 98B version of Englynion y Beddau (EyB 134) corresponds to LlDC 18.30 *in ergrid avon*). However, the next line reverts to Gwynedd v. Deheubarth rivalry: the bear of the Deheubarth challenging Gwynedd, and fighting for Rhosedd (if a place-name), or possibly for pomp and wealth in general: a lavish Calend-tide feast is described. Swords and shields will be ranged in readiness for Cadwaladr's confrontation with an unnamed, perhaps usurping, lord of Gwynedd.

¶6 (Lines 50-6) Like parts of the third section, this concern the appropriation of wealth from *Lloegyr* (*meuoed*, ?*ymellun*) and the forcible expulsion of the English, the 'pale mottled ones' (*brychwyn*). They will be sent over the sea, so that they will be bobbing in the ocean, and have only islands under their sway. This section again is very reminiscent of Armes Prydain.

¶7 (Lines 57-66) This section foretells the coming of an honoured or invested one 'from beyond the River Severn', a leader of hosts of more than one origin,

---

[2] HE III.xxiv *Uinued*. According to Henry of Huntingdon the slaughter 'in Winwed amne' was proverbial (see note by C. Plummer in *Venerabilis Baedae Opera Historica*, II (Oxford, 1896), pp. 183-4).

8 Yn wir dymbi Romani kar

who will bring universal happiness so that 'all the people of the world shall indeed be content' (line 61 *Gwerin byt bydawnt lawen*). The Gwynedd deliverer, Hiriell, will blaze 'above the Severn'. Again the phrase *y kynnif Katwaladr* ('in Cadwaladr's struggle') occurs near the end, with a brief mention of the acclamation accorded by poets.

¶8 (Lines 67-86) The poem moves into a shorter more urgent line as it foretells a deliverer who will come with ships and a shield-bearing host, one who will put himself 'around Britain' (*kylch Prydein*), who will be its famous one (*y gno*), a dragon who will not go into hiding however much may befall him. The verb *fflemychit*, 'let him blaze', already used in the preceding section, may imply it is Hiriell again, or else Cadwaladr who is mentioned in the final line. The poet declares that he will praise (or entreat) him 'to the skies' (if that is what *wrth awyr* means: see notes). The aim of defeating Dyfed is not easy, says the poet. The hero will carry suffering beyond the 'sea of Rheged' (*tra Merin Reget*), perhaps the Solway Firth, and will rule in Elfed.[3] This aspirational hyperbole may preserve some memory or tradition of Cadwallon, Cadwaladr's father, and his exploits in Northumbria *c.* 633-4. It seems very likely that some of the father's fame has devolved to the son.

---

[3] Charles-Edwards, WaB 10, wonders whether Morecambe Bay might not have been Merin Rheged but warns that we know little about the exact whereabouts of the original Rheged. On Elfed (Elmet in West Yorkshire) see ibid. 10, 13-14 and 344.

8 Yn wir dymbi Romani kar
Book of Taliesin 76.15-78.18

1

Yn wir dymbi   Romani kar,
Indeed there will come the friend of the Romans,
odit o vab dyn,   arall y par.
exceptional among mankind, different in kind.
Racdaw ryglywhawr   maw[r] gyfagar,
In front of him will be heard a great cry/lament,
a bydin, a gwaetlin   ar y escar,
and an army, and blood flowing on his enemies,
5   **a thriganed kyrn   a gwerin try*d*ar:**[1]
and the sounding of horns and the clamour of a host:
rythrychynt rygyrchynt   yg cledyfa*l* —[2]
they would pierce those they attacked in sword-play —
brein ac eryron   gollychant wyar.
ravens and eagles craving for blood.
Arllwybyr gwrit ar*th*[3]   **gwrys diarchar,**
A course with a bear's ferocity, invincible might,
ardyrched Katwaladyr,   lluch a llachar,
splendid Cadwaladr, dazzling and brilliant,
10   **arwyneb bydinawr   brooed ynyal.**
a defence of battalions in remote regions.

2

Yn wir dymbi   dy dra *th*on[n]eu[4]
Indeed there shall come from beyond the waves
gofunet dysgogan   yg kynechreu:
the desire (expressed in) prophecy at the beginning:
blwydyned budic rossed   rihyd reitheu.
the successful years of ?luxuriance, the rights pertaining to sovereignty.
Gayaf gyt, llyry llym   llywit llogeu,
(Making) a winter alliance, on a hard course he will steer ships,
15   **keith iawn**[5] **eilyassaf   mynut ryffreu.**
a true leader to bondmen, generous as the great (sea-)spring.

---

[1] ms *trygar*
[2] ms *cledyfar*
[3] ms *arch*
[4] ms *dydranoneu*
[5] ms *keithiawn*

8 Yn wir dymbi Romani kar

Prit myr ryuerthwy   ar warr tonneu
At the seas' high-tide on the crest of the waves
elyrch dymdygyrch ◇⁶ o glawr balcheu.⁷
he will bring (horses like) swans from the ships' decks.
Arth a Llew derllys   o leu⁸ bylleu —
A Bear and a worthy Lion from the shining pools —
ef dibyn y teruyn   orud vereu.
their brave soldiers will pierce with very bloody javelins.

20 **Rwy keiss*ynt*⁹ kystud,   rybud rac geu,¹⁰**
They will be asking for suffering, a warning against falsehood,
rac y varanres   a'e vawr vedeu.
in the face of his tumult and his great powers.
◇¹¹ Cwydynt tyrch, torrynt   toruoed taleu,
The boars will fall, they will fell the hosts of the ramparts,
y kynnif, Katwaladyr   clot lathyr leu;
in battle, it is Cadwaladr who is the bright-famed radiant one;
dydyrchafwy Dreic   o parth deheu
may a Dragon arise from the southern region,
25 **gan was rydadlas   yn dyd Dyf Ieu.**
with a youth who fought by day on Thursday.

3

Yn wir dymbi   hael hywred,
Indeed there shall come a generous one of valour,
tyruawt molut   mawr edryssed,
there shall resound the praise of one (possessing) great glory,
llwybyr tew lluossawc,   llydan y wed,
wide-coursing, with many followers, broad his subjugation,
hyt pan uwynt seith ieith   y ri Gwyned,
until there'll be seven peoples under the king of Gwynedd,
30 **hyt pan traghwy   traghawt trydar.**
until commotion may cease and come to an end.
Ri eidun   duhun duded —
The benevolent king of united peoples —
treis ar Eigyl a[r] hynt   o alltuted,
the scourge of the Angles, on (their) course from exile,

---

⁶ ms *tam*
⁷ ms *balcheeu*
⁸ ms *oleu*
⁹ ms *keissut*
¹⁰ ms *rageu*
¹¹ ms *credeu*

trwy vor llithrant eu heissilled.
whose progeny will slink back through the sea.

4

Yn wir dymbi teithiawc Mon,
Indeed there shall come the one with the right to (rule) Anglesey,
35 **ffaw dreic, diffreidyat y popyl Brython,**
a famous dragon, a deliverer for the people of Britain,
penllüyd perchen[12] llurygogyon.
a commander of hosts, controlling (warriors) clad in breastplates.
Dwfyn darogan dewin drywon
The sage's wise men foretell profoundly
pebyllyawnt ar Tren a Tharanhon,
that the (hosts) will strike camp on the Rivers Tren and Tarannon,
gorllechant gor<>fynt[13] y geissaw Mon
that they will harbour a desire to seize Anglesey
40 **pell debet byhyt o Iwerdon,**
until (that) long journey from Ireland
tec ffaw dillygyaw Kessarogyon.
(undertaken by) a fair, famed one, releasing the followers of Caesar.

5

Dysgogan delwat <> a*r*grat[14] dyhed
The shaper foretells the terror of war
(Gogwn pan perit kat ar Winued),
(I know why battle was joined on the River Winwæd),
Arth o Deheubarth yn kyfarth Gwyned,
a Bear from Deheubarth challenging Gwynedd,
45 **yn amwyn rihyd ryfed rossed:**
fighting for the glory of the riches of pomp:
y che*i*n *y*fet *ll*at, rat[15] darmerthed
its honourable drink, a generous dispensing
gayaf kelenic yn lleutired.
(as) a gift at the winter Calend-tide in the open lands.
Kyflewynt aessawr yg gawr yg cled
May they arrange shields in battle, in sword-fighting,

---

[12] ms *perchyd*
[13] ms *gordyfynt*
[14] ms *o agarat*
[15] ms *ycheiric altirat y*

    8 Yn wir dymbi Romani kar

  y gynnif Katwaladyr ar ior Gwyned.
for the struggle of Cadwaladr against the lord of Gwynedd.

6

50 **Yn wir dydeuhawr   dyderbi hyn:**
Indeed this will be brought about, this will happen:
Lloegyr oll ymellun   eu meuoed genhyn,
all the English in turmoil, their riches ours,
gwelet ar tebet   y gwyr brychwyn
seeing their pale mottled men taking flight
rwng saeth vereu   a hayarn gwyn.
between flying shafts and pale iron lances.
Galwhawr ar vor,   gwaywawr a'e gryn,
They will be summoned onto the sea, javelins will drive them out,
55 **nuchawnt yn eigawn, tra llydan lyn:**
they will bob in the ocean, over the wide flood:
hallt ac ynyssed vyd eu budyn.
brine and islands will be their refuge.

7

Yn wir, dymbi   dy dra Hafren
Indeed there shall come from beyond the Severn
vrthenedic Prydein,   brenhin gorden,
the ordained one of Britain, a powerful king,
llary lywyd llüyd   lliaws ○[16] echen,
a generous leader of hosts of many lineages,
60 **teyrnas kyfadas   cas oiaen.**
one worthy of a kingdom, unperturbed by enmity.
Gwerin byt yn wir   bydawnt lawen:
The inhabitants of the world shall indeed be content:
medhawnt ar peiron   berthwyr echen.
a lineage of fine men shall possess dominions.
Fflemychawt Hirell   t*u*[17] uch Hafren;
Hiriell shall blaze in the region above the Severn;
bydhawt Kymry kynnull   yn discowen,
the muster of the Cymry shall be fearless,
65 **y kynnif Katwaladyr   bythit llawen,**
let it go joyfully to Cadwaladr's battle,

---

[16] ms *y*
[17] ms *ty*

8 Yn wir dymbi Romani kar

banieri [18] **cerdoryon clot a gweithen.**
(by) the loud acclamation of poets, a battle of renown.

8

Yn wir dedeuhawr
Indeed there shall be brought
a'e lu a'e longawr
both his host and his ships
a'e taryf yscwytawr
and his repulsing of shields
70 **a'e newityaw gwaywawr.**
and his clashing of spears.
A gwedy gwychyr awr
And after a fierce battle
y uod ef gwnelawr.
his will shall be imposed.
Kylch Prydein bo,
May he make a circuit of Britain,
flemychit ygno —
may the famous warrior blaze —
75 **dreic nyt ymgelho**
a dragon who will not go into hiding
yr meint y do.
however much may befall him.
Nyt yscawn iolet
It is not an easily achieved aim
gorescyn Dyuet.
to defeat Dyfed.
Dydyccawt *eniwet* [19]
He will carry suffering
80 **tra Merin Reget;**
beyond the Firth of Rheged;
perif perchen ket
a lord (who is the) owner of gift(s)
gwledychawt yn Eluet;
shall rule in Elfed;
hael hydyr y dylif,
a generous one, strong his strategy,

---

[18] ms *peneri*
[19] ms *ynwet*

8 Yn wir dymbi Romani kar

goruawr y gynnif.
mighty his struggle.
85   **Wrth awyr yolif** [20]
To the skies shall I praise
Katwaladyr gweith heinif.
Cadwaladr, energetic in battle.

1   **dymbi Romani kar** On *dymbi*, see §5.11n. Geoffrey of Monmouth in his account of Julius Caesar and Cassivellaunus (brother of Lud) shows the British ruler reminding Caesar how the Briton and the Roman 'share the same blood-line from Aeneas, a shining chain of common ancestry which ought to bind us in lasting friendship', HKB ch. 55, an aetiology which comes to light in the *Historia Brittonum*. The Roman topos is discussed in the General Introduction, 12.
   Romani, lit. 'Romans', but perhaps used in prophetic poetry for a category of Britons or allied people, cf. LPBT 8.39 *Gwydyl a Brython a Romani/ a wnahon dyhed a dyuysci*, and the same couplet in LlDC 17.193-4 (Oianau). Cf. §1.32-3 (Daronwy) *Dydeuho kynrein/ o amtir Rufein*; §7.101-2 *Y Prydein <> y daw datwyrein:/ Brython o vonhed Rufein*; perhaps §9.13 *rac pennaeth o Rufein*. In GEO 1.66-7 *Pen-cun llys yw Rhys rhysedd Beli—Mawr,/ Amherawdr Romani*, the last part is regarded simply as 'emperor of the Romans', praise hyperbole rather than a phrase describing Beli Mawr (p. 167). R1050.13 (*Mal Rhod yn Troi*) *a diffeith eluyd heb aelwydeu/ ac allwed Rufein gan r6yueu*; LPBT 7.57-9 *a mynych adneued,/ a gwin talgibed/ o Rufein hyt Rossed*; CBT IV 1.12-14 *gwaed ar ddarwein,/ Kyuarfu ddreigieu, rieu Ruuein,/ Ac essillyt Run rut y gigwein*. *Rufein* is used in a distance topos 'as far as Rome', etc., e.g. CBT I 11.69; II 3.5; II 23.10; VI 8.32 and VI 18.72.
   Cadwaladr is praised in lines 9-10 below (see note), and it is reasonable to assume with EWV 126 he is the *Romani kar* of our line. Keeping back the full identity of the object of praise is a common poetic technique — in the Gododdin, the poems to Urien Rheged, and many other examples.

2   **odit o vab dyn arall y par** The caesura generally comes before the final 4 syllables (but contrast line 5 *a gwerin trygar* — possibly corrupt — and line 7 *gollychant wyar*). The *mab dyn* 'son of man' is understood as a term for any human being, 'human being, living soul' (like *mab mam* in the contested CA line 366 *nyt mab mam a'e maeth*); it is often contrasted with *Mab Duw*. Examples of the phrase include CBT I 24.39 *Ny byd dadwodeu detwydyt—mab dyn/ Gan Uab Du6 o'e wynuyt*; CBT IV 16.51-2 *Mab Du6/ Yr mab dyn dirparaeth*; CBT IV 16.171 *G6ae uab dyn dilit y gamd6y*; CBT VI 1.26 *Ef goreu o 6ab dyn*; CBT VI 24.49 *Pam na char mab dyn Du6 a'e geissya6*; CBT VII 24.103-4 *Nys plyga6t mab dyn, bu donyaw6c fyt,/ Nys plyko Mab Duw yn dragywyt*; CBT VII 25.19 *Ti freiscaf mab dyn o dir Cred—a wn*; CBT VII 17.14 *Gan vab dyn da6n ym pressent,/ Mab Du6 o nef, drwy nerth seint*. This is attested somewhat earlier in Welsh than as a term for Christ (14c). *Mab* is used in darogan from the 15c (GPC).

---

[20] ms *awyryohif*

8 Yn wir dymbi Romani kar

Internal rhyme could be restored by emending *arall* > *arab* 'lively' which would give good sense here. *Pâr³* 'spear, javelin' also used figuratively (rhymed with *escar* in PT V.29 *eil agheu oed y par/ yn llad y escar*), or else *pâr⁴* 'created, ready; ?condition, state', the latter yielding the better meaning: *y par* 'his state, kind'. Cf. LPBT 4.35 *trydyd par ygnat*, CBT V 23.59 *goruynt par*, and CC 21.102 *Pan im roted par* 'when I was given being'.

3   **Racdaw ryglywhawr maw[r] gyfagar** The final word is written *gyfargar* with a punctum delens under the first *-r-*. The word here is rare *cyfangor* '?wail', on which see Lloyd-Jones, *Celtica* 3 (1956), 201, and for the other attestation, CBT I 7.63 *Gwae Gymry gymri gyuagar*. *Maw* has been emended to *mawr* although there is some slim evidence for *maw* (or *Maw*), see PT 120-1 on PT XI.8 *o berth maw ac Eidin*; **maw* (? < **mawf*), as in *mawaid* 'cupped hands full, handful', is unlikely.

4   **a bydin a gwaetlin ar y escar**   *Gwaetlin* in CA lines 311, 663, 773, 992, Gosymdaith line 57, and five instances in CBT corpus, but the precise collocation occurs in AP line 64 *Eu bydin ygwaetlin yn eu kylchyn* referring to the reviled Saxon stewards bathed in the blood of battle. *Ar y escar*, CBT III 24.50.

5   **triganed kyrn** The *-i-* may suggest that the scribe was not familiar with the word, and had not harmonised the orthography with his usual system. GPC notes *tryganedd* as an abstract noun (< *trygan* 'voice, song, chorus'), '?poetry, song, sound; consistency', or else the pl. of *trygan*. It is used for the songs or sound 'with horns' preceding the Day of Judgment CC 20.59-60 *Atuyd triganed/ A chyrn rac rihed*; elsewhere, CBT I 2.18 and CBT III 3.10.

5   **gwerin trydar (ms trygar)** Although full correspondence with *triganed* is lost, emending to *trydar*, frequently used of commotion of battle seems preferable to unattested **tryar* (< **gar* 'shout', etc.) or *trugar*.

6   **rythrychynt rygyrchynt yg cledyfal (ms cledyfar)** The vbs *trychu* 'to pierce, gore', and *cyrchu* 'to attack, make for' (both 3pl. imperf., with *ry* perhaps having little force, GMW 167). The second, with *ry* + lenition rather than spirantisation, would appear to be relative with no realised object antecedent, see GMW 62. Common *cledyfal* 'sword-play' (Irish rhyme *-ar/-al*) is restored, following G: Lloyd-Jones does not include *cledyfar* (or *trygar* in line 5) as **gar* compounds in his treatment in *Celtica* 3 (1956), 198-210. A scribe may have instinctively created a full rhyme, cf. the treatment of *gwyarlyt* as *gwyarlet* in PT I.10 according to Ifor Williams.

7   **brein ac eryron gollychant wyar**   Cf. LPBT 24.26 *poet y gan vrein ac eryr ac wytheint* (and see n.). Both ravens and eagles are found throughout early poetry gorging on corpses after battle and wallowing in blood. Both are used extensively as metaphors for warriors; the eagle, especially, is a very common figure for a leader or lord, e.g. CBT V 25.44 *O hil eryron o Eryri*, etc.

Gollychant treated by G as 3pl. pres. of vb *g(w)olwch* 'to praise, worship, pray, crave', very common in the Book of Taliesin and see LPBT 8.1n. GPC also notes the meaning 'to assuage', seen in CBT V 2.19 *G6ollycha dy uar, ueirtyon westi*, which uses (as here), the alternative *-ll-* form.

8   **Arllwybyr gwrit arth (ms arch) gwrys diarchar**   *Arllwybyr* 'path, track' is understood here as one word to match the *ar-* compounds at the beginning of lines 9 and 10. As G notes, *gwrit* is likely to be variant orthography for *gwryt*

8 Yn wir dymbi Romani kar

'bravery, valour; battle, strength, might', and the emendation *arch* > *arth* also follows G. The deliverers, Cynan and Cadwaladr, are referred to in AP line 170 as *deu arth nys gwna gwarth kyfarth beunyd* 'two bears whose daily attack brings no shame upon them'. *Gwrys* 'battle, attack, wrath', etc. *Diarchar* 'invincible' is also used in the same passage of the two deliverers: AP line 168 *deu diarchar barawt vnffawt vn ffyd*. Limited elsewhere, to LPBT 23.17 and 45 (of Cunedda) *diarchar dychyfar dychyfun*, and *Ef dywal, darchar, deidig*, and eight instances in the CBT corpus.

9 **ardyrched Katwaladyr lluch a llachar** Somewhat uncommon abstract noun *ardyrched* 'splendour, excellence', with inversion here. CA line 918 *eillt Wyned klywet e arderched*; LPBT 5.100 *Onn goreu ardyrched*; CBT II 6.21-2 (Hywel ab Owain Gwynedd) *gweith ardderchet/ Y r6g glyw Powys a glwys Wynet*. Cadwaladr is discussed in the General Introduction, 10-11.

Lluch/llachar are collocated in LPBT 5.203-4 *Llachar y enw, llawfer/ lluch llywei nifer*; CBT I 9.19 (Gwalchmai) *Llachar uyg cleteu, lluch yt ardwy—glew*; II 22.27 (Seisyll Bryffwrch) *Cyfiaith gar llachar, lluch ryfig—Arthur*; III 3.156 (Cynddelw) *cas llachar lluchnawt*; 12.22 *Brwysc luchyad, breisc lachar*; 17.17-19 *llachar ei derfysg . . . yn llaw lluchfar*.

10 **arwyneb bydinawr brooed ynyal** LPBT 9.21 *arwyneb yg kat* 'a defence in battle'; R579.38 (Cyfoesi) *arwyneb keda6l*. Four of the five CBT instances are by Prydydd y Moch, each followed by *Prydein*: CBT V 3.10, 13.9, 25.45 and 30.15; cf. also V 12.9 *arwyna6l arwynebet—glyw*. Otherwise limited to CBT I 3.69 *Arwyneb neuat yn amniuera6c*. *Brooed* is less frequent than *broyd* in poetry: *brooed* was still being used by Dafydd Benfras, CBT VI 35.29. *Ynyal*, Irish rhyme with rhyme block in *-ar*, cf. emended *cledyual* in line 6.

11 **dy dra thonneu (ms dydranoneu)** G 405 suggests *dy* 'from', as in line 57 *Yn wir dymbi dy dra Hafren*, and other examples cited by G s.v. The ms reading might suggest a connection with *nawn* 'noon, afternoon', and indeed H-cd has the attractive suggestion, *dyd tra noneu*, i.e. presumably 'there shall come a day, beyond the ?noons, following days' (*nawn*, pl. *noneu*), perhaps by analogy with the formation of *trannoeth* (*tra + noeth*). But the pl. is *nawn(y)eu* according to GPC, noting *nonau* 'nones' as a late borrowing from English. LPBT 21.8 *delleinw nonneu* poses a similar problem, and it was suggested that *nonneu* is perhaps a mistake for *nanneu* or *nanheu*, a (rare) pl. of *nant* 'stream, flow', but used elsewhere in the manuscript, CC 20.95. In the case of LPBT 21.8, the scribe may have been led by *ffynhawn* to think of its pl. *ffynhonneu*. In the present instance, emendation to *tonneu* is somewhat tentative. In its favour are *tra + ton* collocations such as EWSP 454 2a *Ton tra thon toid tu tir*; CBT II 26.241 *draw dra thonnau*; CBT IV 9.14 *Traeth o'm bronn tra thonn*; in either case, cf. *tra + mor, moroedd, myr, merin, mordwy, gweilgi, gwanec, llyn, llyr*, etc. There is no evidence for a plural form (**Tranonnau*) of the river-name Tarannon (Trannon, EANC 126 and 197), comparable with Clydogau (< Clywedogau).

12 **gofunet dysgogan yg kynechreu** *Gofunet* 'vow, promise; entreat, desire', possibly in the Cyfoesi prophecy for 'that/whom is desired or promised', R579.39 *kyn no'r gorunnet* (recte *gofunet*), and R581.32 *pa da6 yn y deu ouunet*. Of Christ in CBT IV 17.120 *Bro oet ysgauael, ys gofunet*; CBT IV 18.44 *Dyfu y'n gofwy an gofuned*; CC 11.9 *Gofunet gwas* 'Son of promise'. *Dysgogan* is understood as

noun here, rather than 3sg. of vb (as in line 42 below), an ambiguity found elsewhere, e.g. §7.32n.

Yg kynechreu 'in the beginning', rather rare, CBT VII 24.1 *Kynnechreu donnyeu* (of God as wellspring of talents). GGDT 7.1 *Neud cynechrau Mai*.

13 **blwydyned budic rossed rihyd reitheu** The first part of line is too long. Perhaps read *blwydyned bud rossed rihyd reitheu*; or *blwydyned budic, rossed reitheu* (with *rihyd* emended out); or *blwydyned budic rihyd reitheu*; or *blwynyded rossed rihyd reitheu*. Suggestions 1 and 4 are perhaps preferable (given collocations with *rihyd*, cf. line 45 below).

The problematic form *rossed* was discussed in connection with LPBT 7.59 *o Rufein hyt Rossed* where a place- or a region-name seems most likely, as possibly below in line 45 *yn amwyn rihyd ryfed Rossed* 'defending the great glory of R.' (but see note) and perhaps CA line 1275 (Gwarchan Tudfwlch) *eil dal rossed* ('a place famous in the past for pomp and luxuries?', according to the suggestion in CA 353). Instances where a place-name rather than the pl. of the common noun *rhos* might be suitable include CBT IV 4.119-20 *As dygaf (ys dygyn atchwetlet)/ Y ua6rglod hyd Ua6rgluyd rosset* 'I will carry his great fame (it is a grievous story) to the great gate of Rhosedd', if not 'to the moorlands of great Clwyd'. R. Geraint Gruffydd suggested that *Yr Orsedd*, the older name for Rossett, north-east of Wrexham (Clwyd), near Trefalun on the present-day border, may have been a learned back-formation from Rhosedd (*Bardos* 16 n. 2); but *le Orseth Goch* is attested in 1473, having apparently replaced the Domesday *Radenoure* 'at the red bank' (DPNW 426), with *Rossedh* by 1700, anglicised to *Rossett*, perhaps under influence of E. adj. 'russet'. In CBT IV 76 *Ua6rgluyd rosset*, while the place-name is not entirely ruled out, is treated as pl. of *rhos*: this, however, would be a unique pl. formation, as GPC^2 indicates s.v. *rhos*, pl. *rhosydd*.

Note also CBT VI 20.65-6 (praise of Llywelyn ab Iorwerth and his warband for their victories *c*. 1208, possibly by Prydydd y Moch) *Tremyn6ys ryssur Rossed— Diabret/ Am diebryt G6yned*, identified tentatively (p. 315) with the Rhos Ddiabred area on the southern bank of the Severn, between Llandinam and Penstrowed. There are the sites here of two Norman motte-and-bailey castles, at Moat Farm and Bronfelin, probably late 11c. This fertile area is just south-east of the important Roman fort at the confluence of the Carno and the Severn and near the Roman road from Caersws to Castell Collen.

Andrew Breeze, 'Early Welsh poetry and Rossett, Cumbria', *Northern History*, 49: 1 (March 2012), 129-33, argues with no very firm evidence that the place in LPBT 7.59 *o Rufein hyt Rossed* 'was hardly in Wales' (p. 131), and seeks a North British candidate, settling on Rossett high in the Lake District — where there is a house, two peaks (Rossett Pike is 2136 feet) and Rossett Gill nearby. Breeze derives the name from *rhos* 'moor' and *sedd*, and proposes that PT XI.30 *kat yn ros terra gan wawr*, may conceal a garbled form of the name. August Hunt, in his March 12, 2012 entry at stagspirit.wordpress.com (accessed 24.5.13), points out that the Cumbrian Rossett has been connected rather, with ON *hross* 'horse' + *saetr* 'hill pasture, shieling'. He suggests instead that Rossie Law (earlier Rosyth), the Iron Age hill fort in Perth and Kinross, might be a more plausible candidate: following others, he reckons it also as a contender (among many others) for the site of the Battle of Mons Graupius.

8 Yn wir dymbi Romani kar

In the discussion of problematic §10.10 *o ryfyr* (recte *ryswyr*) *rosseda*, it is argued that *rosseda* is most naturally explained as *ryssedā*. If this is the case, can a similar alternation be postulated for *ryssed* 'pomp, luxuriance', i.e. *rossed*? This is the interpretation followed tentatively here.

14 **gayaf gyt llyry llym llywit llogeu** *Cyt* 'union, joining, alliance', qualified by *gayaf* 'winter'. *Llyry*, understoood here as pl. of *llwrw* 'track, path; manner, mode, form, semblance' rather than pl. of *llory* 'staff, cudgel, club; (?shaft of) spear or javelin'. Cf. the description of a fleet, CBT I 8.34 *llwrw hiryon lli*. *Llywit* understood (with some uncertainty) as abs. 3sg. pres./fut. of vb *llywyaw* 'to steer, pilot' rather than past impers.

15 **keith iawn (ms keithiawn) eilyassaf** G lists hapax *keithiawn* 'captive, bound' while Ifor Williams CA 237 suggests emending to *keithyawr* 'prisoner', understanding that 'the nobleman is captive' because of the winter weather. Here it is taken as *keith* 'captives, bondmen', with *iawn eilyassaf* 'a true splendid one' or 'true leader', cf. PT IX.4 *ydan eilassaf*; PT XII.35 *ygan llu eilassaf*; CA lines 659 and 411; CBT VI 13.3 *bron eilyassaf*.

15 **mynut ryffreu** *Ryffreu*, cf. LPBT 6.52 *rywynt a ryffreu* 'the great wind and the great stream'; Pen3Oianau 127.195 *a rwyf o wynt a ryfreu o law*. For common *ffreu* 'stream' and related words, see §5.4n. For generosity like sea flood, etc. see CA line 1045 *molut mynut mor* and line 319 *tebic mor lliant y deuodeu*.

16 **Prit myr ryuerthwy ar warr tonneu** If *prit* 'dear, costly, expensive; valuable, precious', then used nominally; if *prit* is an orthographic variant of *pryt¹* either 'time, occasion' or *pryt²* 'appearance, aspect', both of which give good sense.

17 **elyrch dymdygyrch ⋄ (ms tam) o glawr balcheu (ms balcheeu)** The line is somewhat long and *tam* 'morsel . . . bit, part' seems difficult to accommodate and has been emended out, although with little justification. The vb *dygyrchu* 'go, make for, attack, bring' is common enough (e.g. LPBT 4.51-2 *Gweleis wyr goruawr/ a dygyrchynt awr*, and note that emendation of our line's *tam > (g)awr* 'battle' would give another internal rhyme). However, there are no other instances with an extra *dym* prefix (although *ymdygyrchu* occurs). *Elyrch* 'swans', although *eleirch* is the usual medieval pl. The swan is a common figure to convey female beauty and purity. In CA line 1165, horses are likened to swans, *meirch eiliv eleirch a seirch gwehin*, hence the interpretation as 'he will bring horses like swans . . .' or else 'swans [i.e. horses] will disembark from the ships'. A figure for 'ships' might also be considered in this context, comparing the OE double kenning for the sea as the 'swans' road', but it would not yield sense before *o glawr balcheeu*. *Clawr* seems to mean 'deck, board' here, not a common usage, but cf. MIr *clárad* 'planking'. *Balcheu*, presumably the pl. of *balch* 'ship' (cf. §1.8), has a small *e* inserted in faint ink above the other letters, cf. sporadic spellings of this sort, as in CA line 1304 *breeych* 'arm'.

18 **Arth a Llew derllys o leu (ms oleu) bylleu** See General Introduction, 11 on animal ciphers. Both *arth* 'bear' and *llew* 'lion' are very common metaphors for warriors and rulers, and see line 8 above. G classes *derllys* as adj. 'worthy' rather than 3sg. pret. of vb *derllyd* 'to merit, deserve'. *O leu bylleu* 'from shining pools (?of blood)' does not convince entirely. H-cd restores *pill(i)eu*, pl. of *pill* (also *pillion*), GPC 'trunk, stock, log, branch, pole; stronghold, sanctuary, fortress, strength, force (14c); snatch of song (14c); cradle'. Very uncertain.

19   **ef dibyn y teruyn orud vereu** (*G*)*orud vereu* 'very red/ bloody javelins' could be understood as the subject of vb *dibynnu* 'strike, cut, pierce'. *Teruyn* = *terwyn* 'fierce ones', rather than *terfyn* 'border'. The pron. *y* presumably refers to the hosts of the leaders styled as the Bear and the Lion.

20   **Rwy keissynt (ms keissut) kystud** G emends > *rwy keissint* 'they (will) seek it it'. But if *kystud* were subject, 'suffering will seek them/it', we could consider emending to *keisswy*.

20   **rybud rac geu (ms rageu)** *Rybud* 'warning', with emended *rac geu* 'against falsehood/wrongdoing'. If *rageu* (= rhangau) is retained, then it is possibly to be connected with vb *rhyngu, rhanc/g bodd*, etc.

21   **rac y varanres a'e vawr vedeu** Generic alliteration with *baranres* might favour *bedeu* 'graves' (with G) rather than *medeu* (noted as a possible pl., GPC s.v. *medd* 'power, dominion, authority', etc.). *Baranres* is relatively common, indicating martial fury (e.g. Echrys Ynys line 13) or the raging of the sea (e.g. LlDC 39.2 and CC 20.40). It continues in use by Cynddelw and Prydydd y Moch, CBT III 16.105 and 21.82; CBT V 5.18. In CA lines 1304-5 *Breeych Tutvwlch/ baranres dost; benn gwaed gwin*, G suggests reading *dwrch* instead of *dost* for the rhyme, cf. line 22 below.

22   **◇ (ms credeu) Cwydynt tyrch** The line as it stands is significantly longer than its neighbours, and it may be that *credeu* ('beliefs, vows, certainties') has been spawned by the preceding *vedeu*, or that it is the end of a missing line. G suggests that *cwydynt* here is not 3pl. imperf., but pres./fut., see GMW 120. *Tyrch* is understood as pl. of *twrch* 'boar', a figure for warriors: although they will fall, they will fell others, cf. CA line 361 *cet ledessynt wy lladassan*, and CA 164 for other examples of this topos. However, in CBT V 1.101 *aerdyrch* is treated (following G) as a compound of *aer* + *tyrch*, a sg. variant of *twrch*. The use of *twrch, tyrch* is otherwise restricted in the CBT corpus to CBT IV 6.207; it is reasonably common in the Gododdin, and there is a density in Canu Heledd (EWSP 429.3b; 430.10c; 442.90c).

22   **torrynt toruoed taleu** Vb *torri* collocated with *tal* 'shield front/boss' in CBT II 14.48 *Tal ysg6yt eurgr6ydyr torrynt yn vuan*. But *tal*^{2} can mean 'end, edge; rampart', etc., and *tal*^{1} 'payment, tax' is not impossible.

23   **y kynnif Katwaladyr clot lathyr leu** *Y kynnif* perhaps for regular orthography *yg kynnif* 'in battle' (see also line 49 below, *y gynnif*). But *y* may be the prep. 'to'. *Clot lathyr leu* may suggest tmesis, since *clodleu* is a known compound, e.g. LPBT 8.7 *vd clotleu*; R578-83 (Cyfoesi); Peirian Faban line 52 *Aedan clotleu*. Cf. also CBT V 1.110 *clodluc*. *Llathyr* is normally one syllable, so the cadence is atypical. Perhaps read *hylathyr*?

24   **dydyrchafwy Dreic o parth deheu** See below, line 44 *Arth o Deheubarth*. The vb is paralleled only in §9.21 *dydyrchefis*. See General Introduction, 16 on vbs with preverb *dy-*. See also §1.17n on *-wy* v. *-o* pres. subjunct. forms.

25   **gan was rydadlas yn dyd dyf Ieu** *Rydadlas* in Tymhorau line 8 *mors rydadlas*; rhymed with *gwas* in Moliant Cadwallon line 24 *ny ry dadlas*; and in CBT I 1.8 (describing the young Hywel ap Goronwy) *Nev rydadlas am luith eurgvas Euas lyvuy* where the vb is interpreted as 'congregate, meet'. In the present instance, perhaps rather 'meet in battle or combat'.

8 Yn wir dymbi Romani kar

Compare the Thursday battle of Cyminawd mentioned in the Afallennau prophecy LlDC 16.6-9 *Oian a parchellan dydau Dyw Iev/ gorvolet y Gimry goruaur gadev/ in amuin Kyminaud clefytaud clev*; this section of the poem concludes by prophesying the rising up of a deliverer in the south: LlDC 16.12 *Dyrchafaud maban in advan y dehev*. The battle of Cyminawd is mentioned again in the Oianau, LlDC 17.177 *A chad Cors Mochno a chad im Mon,/ a chad Kyminaud, a chad Caerlleon*, and in a 14c addition to the Black Book of Carmarthen, LlDC 16.17 *ac am gylch Kyminawd kymyn leas Eingyl/ gan pendeuic Eryri eri attkas*, echoing CBT III 21.133 *Am gylch Kymina6d kymynei—Saeson*, as noted in CBT III 275. See G s.n. for the emendation and CBT III 275 where Phillimore's identification of Cyminawd with the Montgomery location (DP iv, 662-3) is accepted. R. Geraint Gruffydd says it is 'on the eastern border of Powys': 'Why Cors Fochno?', *THSC*, N.S. 2 (1996), 5-19, p. 7. DP iv 665 also cites Jonathan Williams's *Radnorshire* for a stream *Caeminod* north-east of Rhaeadr Gwy, not otherwise known. But GDGor 89-90 favours an identification with Cymunod near Trefdraeth in Anglesey for the instance in GDGor 6.64.

In the Oianau prophecy another Thursday encounter is associated with fighting around the two banks of the River Tywi: LlDC 17.195-6 *Ac y kywenv Dyw Iev divod iti/ ac imlat in taer am dvylan Tywi*. A further Thursday encounter is described, or rather prophesied post eventum, in the poem attributed to Meilyr about the Battle of Mynydd Carn, CBT I 5.10-14 *A Thrahaern a later/ A Mab Rywalla6n, rwyf myr,/ O'r gyfergyr nyd aduer./ Difyeu ym penn teir wythnos! (Tru a nos!) yd ith later*, on which see Nerys Ann Jones, 'The Mynydd Carn "prophecy": a reassessment', *CMCS* 38 (1999), 73-92, where n. 47 on p. 85 can be modified given the 'battle-day' motif in prophecy and elsewhere. Yet another is in Peryf ap Cedifor's elegy for Hywel ab Owain Gwynedd, d. 1170, CBT II 21.5 *Difiau in dieu leas/ Yn y Penrhyn vch Penrhos,/ Ym Mon, y mewn ei hynys,/ Ydd ym lleddir a llafn glas*. Many later instances of Thursday mentions are listed by G s.v. *diw*. There are possibly overtones of the apprehending of Jesus (sometimes called *gwas*) on the Thursday before his crucifixion on the Friday; or else a reference to Ascension Thursday (*Difieu Dyrchafael*) as in CBT I 27.63. See further on §7.3 for the 'days of the week' scheme.

26 **hael hywred** Abstract noun *hywred* rare, but cf. CA line 1285 (Gwarchan Tudfwlch) *vur heywred* (in rhyme block with *edryssed*, as here); CBT II 6.17, and CBT II 26.282 *bro hy6ret* (also in rhyme with *edryssed*). *Hael* with *hywr* in CBT IV 6.151.

27 **tyruawt molut mawr edryssed** 3sg. fut. of vb *tyruu* 'to roar, resound: clamour', see GMW 119 on the form, surviving into the 14c in GBDd 2.31-2 *ddiwarnawd—cyhoedd,/ Diwedd yr oesoedd, torfoedd tyrfawd*. See note above on *edryssed* (also *adryssed*, with adjacent *Gwyned*, CBT V 21.24).

28 **llwybyr tew lluossawc** CA 302 *y ar llemenic llwybyr dew*, 'wide-tracked, i.e. prancing' of a horse. *Llwybr ehag* is used of armies, CBT VI 5.50 and VII 24.130. Here *llwybyr tew* of the deliverer, the *ri Gwyned* 'Gwynedd king' of line 29, who has many hosts under him (common *lluossawc*).

28 **llydan y wed** *Gwed^1* 'appearance', marginally favoured by G over *gwed^2* 'yoke, subjugation'. *Med* 'dominion' as (possibly) in CC 1.9a (but see CC 16) is preferred here.

8 Yn wir dymbi Romani kar

29 **hyt pan uwynt seith ieith y ri Gwyned** Vb *bot* + *y* to indicate possession, GMW 198, e.g. in poetry, CBT I 29.17 *Kyn bod ym oerglat, boed ym Arglwyt*; CBT VI 24.11 *yr bot ida6—da*. See above on §7.47 for the ambiguous *ieith* 'people, nation, kin' as well as 'tongue, language'. Seven here may indicate completeness or perfection rather than a literal tally, rather as Gwalchmai hopes that seven score tongues will unite to praise Owain Gwynedd, CBT I 8.52 *Yn seith ugein yeith wy ueith voli*.

    Ri Gwyned is not found elsewhere in early poetry, but synonyms such as *brenin, rhwyf, llyw, llew, gwawr, argynnan, llywiawdr*, etc. are very common with *Gwyned*, especially in the CBT corpus. But conceivably a mistake for *er(h)y* 'very brave, courageous': then 'so long as the brave men of Gwynedd may (?still) be seven peoples'.

30 **hyt pan traghwy traghawt trydar** Unrhymed line, with common *trydar*, and two forms of the vb *trengi* 'to fail, cease, pass away, die', cf. CBT I 10.32 *A'm dyurys eu treghi;/ Traghaf truaf trueni*. The subject of *traghwy* may be *ri Gwyned*, 'until he dies, (all) commotion will cease', or *trydar* may be the subject of both. Uncertain.

31 **Ri eudun duhun duded** The final word = ModW *tudedd*, pl. of *tud* 'people, nation; country, territory', etc.

32 **treis ar Eigyl a[r] hynt o alltuted** Lines 32 and 33 (with line 29 *Gwyned*) strongly recall Armes Prydain, especially AP lines 27-8 *Pell bwynt kychmyn y Wrtheyrn Gwyned/ ef gyrhawt allmyn y alltuded*, line 43 *poet kynt eu reges yn alltuded*, and line 189 *Allmyn ar gychwyn y alltudyd*, the last echoed in CBT V 26.30 *Y gychwyn allmyn alltudet*. *Alltuted*, lit. the condition of an *alltud*; see GPC s.v. *alltudedd* 'exile, banishment . . . captivity', etc., and also CC 16.13; EWGP VI.8; CBT II 6.24; III 3.21. Atypical *t* for intervocalic [d] as in LPBT 12.16 *y dillwg Elphin o alltuted*. *Eigyl* can denote English in general (see G s.n.), not just Angles.

33 **trwy vor llithrant eu heissilled** Cf. AP line 68 *Attor trwy law gyghor mal mor llithryn*. *Llithraw* 'slide, retreat, slink', as in R1051.7 (Llynges Fôn) *llithra6t g6yr eryr Eryri*; R1050.32 *am lithra6 mab Henri anryuedant*. *Eissilled* is a variant of *eissillyd/eissyllyd* 'progeny, descendants'.

34 **teithiawc Mon** *Teithiawc* '(one) fit or qualified to rule': see on §5.10 for CBT I 8.29 *Teithia6c Prydein* and other comparanda.

35 **ffaw dreic diffreidyat y popyl Brython** *Ffaw*, and again in line 41 below (< L. *fama* via **ffawf*) 'fame, reputation; honour', EWSP 441; LlDC 17.158; 15 examples in CBT corpus; *ffaw* and *dreic* in CBT VI 13.9 *dreigwawr ffawr ffaw*.

    Brython is very common at the end of a line: e.g. PT VIII.25 *mawr gwrnerth ystlyned y Vrython*; PT XII.5 *ny golychaf an gnawt beird o Vrython*; LPBT 1.86 *Dygofi dy hen Vrython*; LPBT 10.33 *mwyhaf gwarth y marth o parth Brython*; CA line 806 *ny doeth en diwarth o barth Vrython*; §4.27-9 *Arall a dyfyd —/ pellenawc y lüyd —/ llewenyd y Vrython*; §6.1 *Rydyrchafwy Duw ar plwyff Brython*; AP line 12 (before caesura) *Atporyon uyd Brython pan dyorfyn*, and lines 42 and 90; *B* 26 (1974-6), 407 (Cadwallon fragment) *Neus duc Gwynedd gorvoled i Vrython*; LlDC 17.180 (Oianau) *Maban dirchavaud mad y Vrython*. But towards the beginning of the line, e.g. in §7.40-1 *Y Vrython dymbi/ gwaed gwned ofri*, and §7.102 *Brython o vonhed Rufein*.

8 Yn wir dymbi Romani kar

Diffreidyat, PT III.14 *Reget diffreidyat*; PT IV.15-16 *diffreidyat gwlat/ gwlat diffreidyat*; CA line 1059 *Rywonyauc diffreidyeit* (but see CA 318 for emendation to *diffret*); EWSP 456.28b *diffreidad kad Kynuid*; and seven examples in CBT corpus, including CBT IV 9.85 *Cymry difreidyad* and CBT VII 46.23 *Kymry ddiffreityat*.

36   **penllüyd perchen (ms perchyd) llurygogyon** *Penllüyd* is apparently unattested elsewhere, cf. CC 30.34 *pen kadoed* (of Arthur). *Perchyd* could conceivably be 3sg. rel. of the common vb *parchu* 'keep, defend, honour' (GMW 119), but it is not cited as such by Simon Rodway, 'What was the function of 3rd sg. prs. ind. "*-ydd*" in Old and Middle Welsh?', *Studi Celtici* 2 (2003), 89-132, nor in Rodway, Dating. Rel. *-yd* may originally have obviated the need for rel. pron. *a*. An agent noun, from *parchu*, is not impossible, though unattested. But it is more likely to be a mistake for very common *perchen*, perhaps written under the influence of the common internal rhyme pattern.
Llurygogyon, pl. of adj. *llurigawc* 'wearing a breastplate', cf. CA line 184 *tri llu llurugawc*; line 690 *llurugogyon*; LlDC 15.11 (Bedwenni) *Ac a wil y Freigc in lluricogion*, and see prose examples in GPC s.v. *llurigog*. Used (with *perchen*) in CBT V 24.62 *Amhera6dyr, llywyawdyr llurycawc,/ Llywelyn, llary rwyf, Rywonya6c—berchen*. For variant name *Llud Lluryga6c* in the White Book text of Triad 18 (rather than *Llyr*), see TYP^3 lxxxvii and 35.

37   **Dwfyn darogan dewin drywon** The Taliesin persona claims to be a *dryw*, either a 'wren', or more likely a 'wizard': see LPBT 2.9n on this very rarely attested cognate of OIr *drui*; OE *dry* is thought to be a borrowing from Irish. *Darogan* is either 3sg. pres. (as in translation) or else a noun.

38   **pebyllyawnt ar Tren a Tharanhon** Vb *pebyllyaw* in Moliant Cadwallon line 22 *Osidd art y Mon rhyphebyllas*; LlDC 17.65 (Oianau) *Pan bebillo Lloegir in tir Ethlin*; CBT II 24.27 *yn pebylliaw*; CBT VI 20-45 *pebyll(y)wys* (× 5). The Tern, a Shropshire tributary of the Severn, is frequently mentioned (as a river, sometimes paired with R. Trydonwy, and as a regional or township name) in Canu Heledd (see EWSP 576), also in Marwnad Cynddylan, and six instances in CBT corpus (*tra Thr., ger T., oduch T.*, etc.). *Taranhon* is most likely the River Trannon which joins the Severn near Caersws, in Powys: see EANC 126, 197; ERN 415-18; CLlH 194; HB §67 (where the form is *Trahannon*); LHEB 504, 524-5, 688. It is mentioned as *Trennon* in a charter of Hywel ab Ieuaf of Arwystli in 1143 × 1161, *The Acts of Welsh Rulers 1120-1283*, edited by Huw Pryce with Charles Insley (Cardiff, 2005), 145-7. Less likely candidates for the latter < *Trisantona* include Trent in north-east England and Trent in the midlands, as well as two Tarrants on the south coast, east and west of the Isle of Wight: see PNRB 476-7.

39   **gorllechant gorfynt (ms gordyfynt) y geissaw Mon** *Gorfynt* 'desire, longing' gives a much better meaning than *gordyfynt* ('perverseness, repugnance, displeasure, opposition', etc.), and brings the line into metrical regularity (generally five syllables). The vb *gorllechu* somewhat uncommon, but used by Gwalchmai, CBT I 7.39 *Gorllecheis-y*.

40   **pell debet byhyt o Iwerdon** *Tebet* 'retreat, flight, journey', again in line 52 below; PT XII.25 *hwyrwedawc Gwallawc ar tebet*, see PT 133, CA 304, CC 26.4a, CBT I 9.46. *Byhyt* is regarded by G as a form of the prep. *bed, fed* (variants *behet, bihit*, etc.), 'as far as, up to, until': these are discussed by Jon Coe, 'Dating the boundary clauses in the Book of Llandaf', *CMCS* 48 (2004), 1-

44, at pp. 13-16. G s.vv. *bet¹* and *behet* suggests that in R1337.41 *bet myn* (= GPB 6.59), we have a different word, 'plea, cry'; thus GPB 78 interprets *bet myn* as a compound *bedmyn*, a pl. form of *bedman* 'entreater, one who prays for the souls of others', comparing OE *bed* and ME *beodeman, bedeman*.

41 **tec ffaw dillygyaw Kessarogyon** This would be pl. of *Kessarawc. *Tec ffaw* is understood as describing the deliverer, but it could describe the 'fair and renowned' freeing of the followers or successors of Caesar. G notes *Kessaryeit* as a comparable term to the unique *Kessarogyon*. It occurs in the Red Book of Hergest version of *Pann aeth llu y Lychlyn* 'When a Host went to Llychlyn' (cited by G), referring to the *Kessaryeit* 'of this Island' whom Caswallon pursued with the third of the Three Silver Hosts of the Island of Britain who remained in Gascony: see Triad 36, and also Triad 35 (*Tri Chyuor a aeth o'r Enys honn* 'Three Levies that departed from this Island'), TYP³ 81-9. TYP³ 87 understands *Cesaryeit* as 'Caesar's men'. Cf. General Introduction, 12.

42 **Dysgogan delwat** *Delwat* is discussed in CA 387 'shaping, forming' (with clear examples from the law texts) where it is suggested that if *delwat* were older orthography for *deilwat* it might mean 'shaper, former, creator'; however, GPC lists *delwad²* 'maker, creator' (understood in my translation as a description of the prophet-poet). But note that GPC favours *delwad¹* 'form, shape, effigy . . . impression', etc. for our example, which is possible if the line is referring to prognostication by portent.

42 **argrat (ms o agarat) dyhed** G's emendation, which gives a regular cadence, is endorsed by GPC² s.v. *argrad* 'terror, commotion', used six times in the CBT corpus, but not otherwise in early poetry. *Dyhed* is very common, with many instances in prophecy.

43 **Gogwn pan perit kat ar Winued** *Gogwn* 'I know' is used extensively in the poem Angar Kyfundawt, LPBT 4.88, 122, 124, 169, 175, 180-5, 187, 196. Otherwise rather infrequent: CA line 1054 *gogwn e* (em.) *eissyllut*; EWSP 424.36a; CBT I 9.89; V 2.47. *Pan* can mean 'how, why, whence' or 'when'.

Ar winued could conceivably be construed as *ar* 'on' or 'before' + *gwinfedd* 'wine-feast', understanding *perit* as 'was/would be urged [to fight]' and *kat* as 'host, army', i.e. 'I know how a host was urged [to fight] on/before a wine-feast'. However the prep. *uwch* would be more typical than *ar* to mean 'on', and the diction appears forced.

More natural would be 'I know how a battle was caused on . . . .' with a river-name. It might be ventured that we have here a form of the name *Winwæd*, noting that it is not dissimilar to *Uinued*, the Latin spelling in HE III.xxiv (sometimes identified as the River Went but see ERN 449). The battle, recorded in AC 656 *Strages Gaii campi*, was fought between the small army of Oswiu and his son Alhfrith, pitted against the Mercians and their allies, a force thirty times as great as the northern army. Nearly all the thirty ealdormen were killed. There were great mortalities because of the swollen river (see WaB 394-5). This may be the event referred to in LlDC 18.30 (Englynion y Beddau) *Bet Run* (recte *Panna*) *mab Pyd in ergrid avon* (though LlDC 141 notes *Ergryd* could be a proper name, rather than adj. 'swollen, turbulent-waved'): see §1.48n and poem introduction. If our *Winued* is connected with *Winwæd* (Bede's *Uinued*), it could be derived from a written text, although note that Andrew Breeze, without knowledge of the rhyme in our poem, has argued that *Uinued* has [-ð] ('The Battle of the *Uinued*

8 Yn wir dymbi Romani kar

and the River Went, Yorkshire' in *Northern History*, 41, no. 2 (2004), 377-83). The poet appears to validate his prophecy by asserting his knowledge and insight into past events, here one of the decisive battles of the mid 7c at a period when Cadwaladr, son of Cadwallon, was active: see General Introduction, 11.

44 **Arth o Deheubarth yn kyfarth Gwyned** Note the mention of the *arth* 'bear' in lines 8 and 18 above.

45 **yn amwyn rihyd ryfed rossed** See above on line 13 and §10.10 for *rossed*, interpreted here as a common noun 'luxuriance' rather than a place-name though that is not impossible. *Ryfed* could be a form of the vb *medu*, or — more likely — *ry* + *med* 'great mead, large amount of mead', or the common *ryfed* 'wealth, excess; host, throng' (cf. *reufed*) as well as 'wonder, miracle', etc.

46 **y chein yfet llat rat darmerthed (ms ycheiric altirat y darmerthed)** The first part of the line is corrupt, and the emendation draws on comparanda such as CA line 321 *a chein yuet med*; and *llat/rat* rhymes. Other possible emendations include *y cheinmic lat rat darmerthed*. G suggests *llat a rat darmerthed*, but without regard to the cadence. H-cd suggests a modernisation *ych eirig a [llad a] rhad i ddarmerthedd*, with *ych* 'oxen' and *eirig* 'warlike', although the second word is very rare, and the line would be somewhat long. The *darmerthed* 'provisions' is certain: cf. verbal forms, CA line 1068 *cann calan a darmerthei* (matching the *darmerth/kelenic* association in our example); LPBT 11.81 *darmerthat*; and sg. noun CBT III 12.55 *Aerwalch balch, b6lwch y darmerth*; CBT V 26.140 *Y'th gannerth kyn darmerth daruod*.

47 **gayaf kelenic yn lleutired** The *kelennic* is a gift given at a Calend-tide, here at Calan Gaeaf, the beginning of November, as opposed to January (mentioned as a time of gifts in CA line 295 *diw calan Yonawr*) or Calan Mai. See §3.39 on *leutired Deheu*.

48 **Kyflewynt aessawr yg gawr yg cled** G s.v. vb *kyflëu* 'put, place, arrange' lists *kyflewynt* as subjunct. 3pl. while wondering, s.v. *kyflew*, whether it may not be connected with the common vb *llewa* 'to eat, drink voraciously'. The first (from *lle*) yields the better sense with *aessawr* 'shields'. G s.v. *cleð* 'sword' suggests *yg = fy(g)* 'my' which seems unlikely — 'in battle (will be) my sword' — but not impossible. If, as GPC suggests, *cledd* can also mean 'champion, defender', then 'in the battle of my champion' is possible. The translation here is very tentative, understanding *cled* rather as 'swordfighting', the same as *cledyual*.

49 **y gynnif Katwaladyr ar ior Gwyned** *Kynnif* 'contention, battle, struggle'. 'In battle' would be realised as *yg kynnif* in the usual orthography of the manuscript, so *y* is understood as 'to, for'. *Ar* 'over' the lord of Gwynedd is odd, not least if Cadwaladr — as we suppose — is connected with Gwynedd, more particularly Anglesey (see General Introduction, 11). Possibly understand as 'against, facing', an older meaning of the prep. (*yn erbyn* is the usual locution for facing an enemy in battle, however), or emend to *am*, translating 'ready for the contention of Cadwaladr, around the lord of Gwynedd', describing the troops mustering and arranging their shields in formation around their leader. Uncertain.

50 **dydeuhawr** G s.v. *dyuot* 'to come', impers. fut., paralleled only by *dedeuhawr* in line 67 below. On the use in prophecy of verbs with the prefix *dy-*, as well as *-(h)awr* forms, see General Introduction, 15-16.

50   **dyderbi**   3sg. fut. of *dydaruot* 'to happen, to come to pass', cf. AP line 157 *dyderpi agheu yr du gyweithyd*; R578.2 (Cyfoesi) *Run y en6 ryuel ovri/ a oganaf y dyderbi*; and other forms of the same vb noted by G s.v. including the proverb *pob darogan dydderpid* (cf. Diarhebion 119.554 etc.).

51   **Lloegyr oll ymellun**   G s.v. *emellun* refers to Mellun, interpreted by P.K. Ford (cited LPBT 203) as a place or a region (= *ym Mellun* 'in Mellun') in the Kat Godeu instance (LPBT 5.67 *Ny'n gwnei emellun*), but otherwise unknown. The *e* rules out *Mellun* < *mall* of a wet or unwholesome spot (cf. Malltraeth) or < *ma-* 'plain', etc. Names such as Melltun (Churchstoke) and Mellteyrn (Botwnnog), discussed by ELISG 55-6 and Ifor Williams, 'mell', *B* 10 (1939-41), 41, are not likely for the present instance where a meaning such as 'despoiled, destroyed, enervated' or 'destruction', etc. seems likely, possibly connected with OIr *mell* 'destruction, ravage' (see Lexique M-33) or other words discussed by E.P. Hamp, 'Celtic and Indo-European words in *mVL-', *Celtica* 10 (1973), 151-6. The matter is complicated by LPBT 4.7-8 *Trwy ieith Taliessin/ budyd emellin*, on which see now Rodway, Dating 119. GPC s.v. *ymellin* cites only one certain medieval example of *ymellin* 'manna', with *nef.*

51   **eu meuoed genhyn**   The sole attestation of pl. form of *meu* 'possession, property', unless it is a mistake for very common *meued*.

52   **ar tebet y gwyr brychwyn**   *Tebet* above, line 40. Rare *brychwyn* 'with white spots, mottled-white, freckled' (and *brychwen*) in CBT VII 38.41-2 *Ny byd brychwenn llenn lla6 a nycher,/ Ny byd brychwyn dyn dyd y cladher*. The medical text Hafod 16 (cited in GPC) confirms it to be a good colour in the living (*Da yw lliw brychwynn*), but *brych* 'freckled' and its compounds can often have a perjorative meaning, e.g. CBT II 19.20 *O'r Brochuaelyeid brychuoelyon*. The pale-skinned or fear-blanched English are found elsewhere, e.g. §6.21 *a dial Idwal ar* (recte) *ranwynyon*; 6.21; PT II.20 *granwynyon* (recte); CBT III 16.239 *Granwynnyon trychyon*, and see nn. PT 36-7 and CBT III 219.

53   **saeth vereu a hayarn gwyn**   Cf. CBT 4.27 *Glas uereu heyrn heassant*; CBT VII 40.43 *A'r llech las hayarn a'r sarn saetheu*. *Saeth vereu* could refer to 'arrowed shafts' of some sort, or else (as in the translation) flying or darting shafts. Day, Arfau 342-3, notes the rarity of poetry references to shooting arrows in combat, suggesting that they may reflect the Norman (or possibly Scandinavian) modes of fighting, citing as a possible reference, Pen3Afallennau 121.6-9 *dydaw ar Wyndyt brithvyt diheu/ a llyghes dros vor ac angoreu./ Seith long y deuant a seith gant dros donneu,/ disgynant ar draeth adan saetheu*. See further §3.44n. It is difficult to know precisely what weapon is denoted by *hayarn* and whether *gwyn* refers to pale wood or metal.

54   **Galwhawr ar vor gwaywawr a'e gryn**   *Galwhawr*, 3sg. fut. impers. *Grynnyaw* 'push, drive, expel'.

55   **nuchawnt yn eigawn tra llydan lyn**   The context suggests that the vb is a variant of the poorly attested vb *nugiaw* 'to shake, quiver', although not mentioned in GPC s.v., or *nuc* + *-hawnt*. The ending *-hawnt*, not attested in CBT or 13c prose mss (Rodway, Dating 62), may have been conventional in the prophetic genre (see General Introduction, 15-16). The idea would be similar to that in Armes Prydain when the foreigners are sent packing over the channel, or remain at anchor out at sea, AP lines 190-1 etc. The kenning *llydan llyn* is used for the sea, e.g. in LlDC 16.23-6 (Afallenau) *Seithlog y deuant dros lydan lin*; Edmyg

8 Yn wir dymbi Romani kar

Dinbych line 11 *Aduwyn gaer yssyd ar llydan llyn*; LlDC 17.116 (Oianau) *Ban diffon Nortmin y ar llidan llin*; and cf. Peirian Faban lines 5 and 10 *Aedan a dyuyd(d) o dramwy mor llydan*, and LPBT 21.1 *Dy ffynhawn lydan*.

56   **hallt ac ynyssed vyd eu budyn**   Cf. Moliant Cadwallon line 46 *Aded gynt ethynt yn hydirver hallt*. In CBT II 477, Henry Lewis's suggestion that *ynysset* in CBT II 26.278 *Seint Mana6 ac Ana6 ac Ynysset* refers to the Hebrides is adopted. In the present instance, something less specific is likely, more like the islands of the sea in CC 16.9 *Ym brin in tyno, in inysset mor,/ im pop fort it elher*. See CA 105 on *budyn* (< *bu* 'cow') 'fold; refuge, stronghold'.

57   **dy dra Hafren**   See above on line 11 *dy dra thonneu* (em.); cf. CBT V 22.23 *O Lydaw, o draw, o drwy—Mor Hafren*. The River Severn is mentioned in a portion of another prophecy in LPBT 1.71-2 *a medi heon/ am Hafren auon*; and in Golychaf-i Gulwyd (LPBT 8.7) where the Taliesin persona boasts of having sung before his lord *yn Doleu Hafren* — there, as here, it is in a rhyming block with *echen*, *llawen* and *gorden*. The latter collocation is seen, too, in a list of names, in CBT II 25.46 *Am Hafren, am orten, 6rt luestu*. See further 58n.

58   **vrthenedic Prydein brenhin gorden**   Understood as atypical orthography for *urdenedic*, a word not attested elsewhere but < *urden* 'dignity, honour, praise', etc. (or < *urdyn* if the first *e* represents the schwa vowel), or more likely as a mistake — triggered by anticipating *brenhin* — for the synonymous and commonly used *urdedic* (six instances in CBT corpus, along with over fifty words in *urd-* < forms of L. *ordo* and its derivatives). However, G does not mention this s.v. *gwrthenedic* where he suggests tentatively *gwrth eredic* 'ploughing' (used figuratively). He rejects as unlikely **gwrtheni* (< *geni* 'to be born') and **gwrthenni* (< *genni* 'to be contained'), suggesting instead an emendation to **gwrthuenedic* (= gwrthfynedig) < *gwrthfyn*, a well-attested vb in poetry, 'to receive, accept, meet, welcome; challenge, oppose'. If so, 'the welcomed one, the ?awaited one' rather than 'the ordained, invested one of Britain'.

The weighty title is one of many such designations, e.g. LPBT 5.27 *Prydein wledic*; PT VII.31 *vd Prydein pen perchen broestlawn*; Moliant Cadwallon line 29 *y luydawc Prydain*; R584.19 (Gwasgargerdd) *penndeuic Prydein*. *Prydein* is extremely common in court poetry, often with other terms for a ruler, such as *priawt* and *priodawr, teithiawc, dreic, rwyf, llyw, ud, peir*, etc. It is especially favoured by Prydydd y Moch (37 examples, and two of *Ynys Brydein* (see CBT V 347), compared with 20 examples in the work of Cynddelw). Does this *brenhin* (a word used only once elsewhere in this manuscript, LPBT 3.44) denote someone in the same mould as Hiriell and Cadwaladr, the two redeemers mentioned in lines 63 and 65 below? Without knowing the poet's location, it is not clear what territory is denoted by 'beyond the Severn' — Wessex, Ergyng, Mercia, or indeed northern Powys or Gwynedd seen from the south, or the centre and the south-east viewed from the north.

59   **llary lywyd llüyd lliaws ⇔ echen (ms y echen)**   A richly alliterative line, cf. runs on *ll-* with *llywyd* in CBT II 26.97-8 and CBT I 33.30-2, and many paired *llary* and *llu* instances. *Lliaws*, noun and adj. frequently precedes a sg. noun ('many a') in poetry. The phrase *lliaws y* 'many his' is found, uniquely in the court poetry corpus, in CBT V 23.142 *Llywelyn, llia6s y Uranuro* 'Llywelyn, numerous his [forces from] the region of Brân', and also in LPBT 4.10 *lliaws y gyfolu*. But cf.

the 3pl. pron. in LPBT 21.21 *lliaws eu teruysc am eu teruyn*; LlDC 1.28 *llyaus ev hymchuel in eu hymvan*. In our present instance, the cadence is more regular without the *y*, and the meaning is better. It refers to the hosts from different lineages, but one would expect *lliaws y hechen* if the 3pl. pron. were present.

60   **teyrnas kyfadas cas oiaen** With the first phrase, cf. CBT VI 2.4 *Teyrnas adas idaw*; CBT VII 46.3 *Teyrnas adas idaw boed mad*. *Kyfadas* is commonly rhymed with *cas*, as here: EWSP 418.15c *neu nat mi eu kyuadas*; CBT I 2.6 *ked kywatas*; CBT I 8.68 *ced gyfadas*; CBT III 19.26 *Llugyrn gyrn gyuadas*.

Goiaën 'freezing, frosty, icy, shivering' (G), sparsely attested, and possibly to be understood in CBT V 30.8 *oes o yaen*. GPC's suggested additional meaning, 'cool, unperturbed', is suitable here as adj. qualifying *cas* 'enemy'. The translation understands *cas* 'enmity, hostility', throughout which the hero maintains his equilibrium. It may be that the meanings 'sad, grave' also assigned by GPC are relevant (cf. *oer* 'sad' as well as 'cold'): the hero is saddened by enmity.

61   **Gwerin byt yn wir bydawnt lawen** 3pl. fut. *bydawnt*, not attested elsewhere. If it were not for lines 38 *pebyllyawnt*, 55 *nuchawnt* and 62 *medhawnt* (and comparable *cuinhaunt*, JuvTC f. 29^r, 10; AP line 8 *gwnahawnt goruoled gwedy gwehyn*), it might be regarded a slip for *bydant* or *byd(h)awt* under the influence of *lawen*. On the *-(h)awnt* 3pl. ending see note on line 55. There is a glancing similarity here to PT III.4 *llawen beird bedyd/ tra vo dy uuchyd* and PT VIII.47 *ef gwneif beird byt yn llawen*.

62   **medhawnt ar peiron berthwyr echen** There is a lack of artistry here — or textual corruption — with the same rhyme word *echen* being repeated, as *llawen* is in line 65. See n. above on vb ending. *Berthwyr echen* 'lineage of splendid men' is understood as vb subject, with obj. *peiron* the pl. of *pair^2* 'lordship, dominion' rather than *pair^1* 'cauldron'.

63   **Fflemychawt Hirell tu (ms ty) uch Hafren** Vb *fflemychu* 'to blaze, flame' (< *fflam* < L. *flamma*), also in line 74 below, is used of the prophesied Christ, CC 11.9 *ffest fflemychawt*; three further instances in CBT corpus (of Owain Gwynedd, CBT I 8.21 *flemychws*; CBT II 12.5 *flemychei—hyt nef*; and CBT VI 35.56 *flemycha*). Since *fflemychu* appears to be an intransitive vb in the medieval period, *ty* is emended to *tu*.

The hero Hiriell, discussed by Ifor Williams, *B* 3 (1925-7), 50-2, is referred to in the Oianau prophecy about a Tuesday battle between Powys and Gwynedd when he will arise from his long sleep to defend the boundary of Gwynedd against his enemy: LlDC 17.89-92 *Rydybit Div Maurth dit guithlonet,/ kywrug glyu Powis a chlas Guinet,/ a chivod Hirell o'e hir orwet/ y amvin a'e elin terwin Guinet*. Several of the seven instances in the CBT corpus confirm his northern connections: Gwalchmai talks of having drunk wine with Owain Gwynedd at Caernarfon near the land of Hiriell, CBT I 9.140 *Yn Aruonic caer ger Hiryell beu*; Owain is styled as *castell Hiriell* by Seisyll Bryffwrch (CBT II 22.45), and his praise resounds in Cynddelw's fine line, CBT IV 4.152 *G6nn oet h6nn oet Hiryell Gwynet!*, and again in CBT IV 1.33 *Hiryell hiryein*. Owain's son, Dafydd, is described as the veteran of Bro Hiriell, CBT II 27.10 *Heneuyt Bro Hiryell*; and Llywelyn ab Iorwerth is the lord of Hiriell's land in CBT VI 20.50 *Yn Ystrat Meuryc anystywell—lu/ Y am ly6 Bro Hiryell*. In CBT VI 13.17 a Deheubarth prince, Rhys Ieuanc, is compared in valour to Hiriell, see CBT IV 193. 14c poets

8 Yn wir dymbi Romani kar

continue to refer to him — Iolo Goch's praise of Owain Glyndwr, GIG 9.17 *Hiriell, Cymru ddihaereb*; GGM I 3.17 *traul mil hil Hiriell*; GGM I 7.49 *Daeth am ddraig mil hil Hiriell*; GPB 8.24 *nid mal Hiriell* (satire); GLlG 3.63 *o fro Hiriell*; *YB* 18 (1992), 105.72 *ail i Hiriell*. In CA 569 *keingyell hiryell oe law* in an awdl praising Heilyn *hiryell* was regarded as simply the compound adj. *hir* + *gell* (presumably the origin of the personal name as well), describing a battle-stave; a sceptic might wonder whether, especially in the light of the repeated element *gell*, whether it was not a personal name here, i.e. that Heilyn was wielding a weapon like that of old Hiriell of yore. *Tu* 'region' used adverbially is more likely than *ty* 'house', and cf. CBT III 17.14 *Yn y tir tu Hafren*. Uwch Hafren is not used as the name of a distinct area unlike Uwch Conwy, Uwch Aeron, Uwch Aled, etc.

64 **bydhawt Kymry kynnull yn discowen** *Bydhawt*, cf. §7.109 *bythawt breu breyryon*; again in political prophecy contexts, LPBT 1.67 *bydhawt penn seiron*; LlDC 1.38 (Ymddiddan Myrddin a Thaliesin) *bithaud kyffredin vy darogan*; LlDC (Oianau) 17.75 *y p[arche]ll yssy wiv bitaud mev*; LlDC 17.123 *bitaud ev kinatil a edmyccaur*; R585.9 (Gwasgargerdd) *byda6t g6aeth budelw no chrowyn*; R1049.41 (Anrheg Urien) *Gweith Cors Uochno o diangho byda6t detwyd*; R1051.3 (Moch daw byd) *Dygoganaf tyfyrru erymes tra bytha6t*; R1051.24 (Llynges Fôn) *byda6t dir dyuot*. Of Judgment Day, CC 20.55 *Tir bydawt tywyd*; CC 28.7 *Dit Braud bitaud ediwar*; EWSP 451.24b *byda(u)t dolur pan burer*; of Heaven to come, CBT I 30.7 *Byda6t nef dichleis*; elsewhere, CC 26.4-7 *bitaud ked*, etc.

Kynnull understood as a noun here 'gathering, collection', with G, and *Kymry* as genitive. *Discowen*: G s.v. *disgywen* 'lively, wanton; stubborn, etc.'; GPC s.v. 'splendid, proud, bold, brave, fearless; clear, manifest'. Used of poets, battlefield, warrior(s), and wrath by Cynddelw (CBT III 11.77; 16.106 and 107; 24.17; IV 6.236), but not used by other CBT poets. Elsewhere rare in poetry: LPBT 8.6 *ar pennawr disgowen* (rhymed with *Hafren*, as here); R584.34-5 (Gwasgargerdd) *disgiwen bun g6rth b6yth g6as*.

65 **y kynnif Katwaladyr bythit llawen** *Y* understood as 'to' with the topos of going joyfully to battle, as in PT II.30 *galyscein* (recte) *y wytheint oed llawen* (recte); CA lines 57 *chwerthin ognaw* and 429 *ryvel chwerthin*; EWSP 430.11 (of Cynddylan) *mor wylat/ gantaw mal i gwrwf y gat*. *Bythit* is not attested elsewhere in early poetry, and G 69 classes it provisionally with 3sg. imperative of vb *bot*.

66 **banieri (ms peneri) cerdoryon clot a gweithen** The ms reading *peneri* is a problem, and an emendation to *penweri*, pl. of *penwar* 'headstall, halter, muzzle', etc. seems difficult to accommodate. Other possibilities might involve *penn* 'chief', *ener* 'lord', *erhy* 'brave, bold, heroic', *peri* 'to incite', *Ceri* (the Powys region south of the River Severn), or *banieri* 'cries'. The last of these is tentatively restored, comparing CBT V 25.4 *beirt uannyeri*, and the idea of loud acclamations from the poets, e.g. CBT II 28.26 *Bannllef beirt y'th uoli*, etc. The second part of the line is either simply 'fame and battle', or *clot* as an adj. with *a* + noun syntax (GMW 37) and unrealised lenition.

67 **dedeuhawr** See on line 50 above.

68 **a'e lu a'e longawr** *Llongawr* 'ships' rare, but cf. LPBT 8.18 *dyrehawr longawr ar glawr aches*, a partly prophetic poem which has several lexical features in common with the present text.

8 Yn wir dymbi Romani kar

69 **a'e taryf yscwytawr** *Taryf* (and its compounds) are very common in CBT battle descriptions, with over 30 instances, but there is no close parallel with *yscwydawr*, only CBT IV 6.86 *Taryf ar yscwyda6*. The pl. form *yscwytawr* is instanced 10 times in the CBT corpus, and was still being used by Bleddyn Fardd in the 1280s.

70 **newityaw gwaywawr** See GPC s.v. *newidiaf: newid* for examples in a fighting context where it means 'to clash, exchange weapons'.

72 **y uod ef gwnelawr** *Bod* 'wish', used with vb *gwneuthur* in Echrys Ynys line 14 *gwnelit y vod*; with vb *digoni* LPBT 16.41.

74 **fflemychit ygno** *Ygno* presumably from *yng* (ModW *ing*) + *gno*, 'a renowned one in battle' (cf. CBT V 23.115 *fwyrgno*; I 3.3 *urno*. Unlikely to be a mistake for *ygo, yngo* 'there, nearby', unattested before the 14c (GPC). *Ygno* is understood tentatively in LPBT 9.62 as an otherwise unattested personal name (comparing *Gueithno, Mydno, Uchno, Elno, Clydno, Cibno*, etc.). Here, 'a famous one in battle' is preferred.

76 **yr meint y do** Understanding *y* + *y do*, with infixed dative 3sg. pron. The rare *do*, 3sg. pres. of vb *dyuot*, is found also in §3.9, and in CBT II 21.19 *Ple do dial dywal dwys* (ms *pla ple do*; for a different emendation to *plo do*, see G 413).

77 **Nyt yscawn iolet** With form *yscawn*, cf. CBT II 14.42 *Lluch y dan ysg6yt ysga6n lydan* contra CA line 5 *ysgwyt ysgauyn lledan*, and see further on §4.4 *gnawt yscwyt yscawn ar gefyn yscawt*. Sole attestation of *iolet* 'desire'; its relations, *amiolet* and *eiriolet*, are common.

79 **Dydyccawt eniwet (ms ynwet)** If *ynwet* is for *enwet*, conceivably 3sg. impv. of vb *enwi* 'name, declaim, proclaim'. But a simple emendation to *e(i)niwet* 'harm, loss' yields better sense; on resulting length, note six syllables in lines 82 and 86.

80 **tra Merin Reget** On the Welsh knowledge of North Britain, see Haycock, 'Early Poets Look North', in BGod 7-39. See poem introduction.

81 **perif perchen ket** *Peryf* 'lord', most often for God, hence suggesting that this could perhaps be a parenthetic call to God for Cadwaladr to rule in Elfed. CBT VI 1.19 has *peryf* for a secular lord however.

82 **gwledychawt yn Eluet** See poem introduction. The vb *gwledychu* is very common in poetry, used extensively in prophecy, §1.17; R577-83 (Cyfoesi) *passim*; LlDC 15.6 and 20 (Bedwenni); LlDC 17.145 (Oianau); of God (CC 11.10); Alexander the Great (LPBT 16.2); and in the CBT corpus (13 instances, including CBT IV 4.221 *Gwletychawt mola6d mil ueirtyon*).

83 **hael hydyr y dylif** *Dylif* 'arrangement', specifically of cycles, e.g. LPBT 13.7 *dylif deweint a dyd* 'the patterning of night and day', or of patterns such as in weaving, see LPBT 3.12n. Here understood figuratively for 'plan' or 'strategy', comparing the denominative vb in CBT VI 14.9 *Pei achwir 6olawt y dyli6et fossawt*. The meaning, 'temperament, habit' is not impossible, but not attested, according to GPC s.v. *dylif¹*, until the 14c.

Hydyr y, cf. LlDC 18.147 *hydir y wir in y bro*; and eight instances in CBT corpus (3sg. and pl.); *hydyr* alone is very frequent.

85 **Wrth awyr yolif (ms awyryohif)** If the emendation *yohif* to *yolif* is correct (note that *iolaf* is the usual 1sg. form), the idea would seem to be that of 'praising to the skies', declaiming Cadwaladr's praise for all to hear. One might expect *hyt awyr*

8 Yn wir dymbi Romani kar

perhaps; or is there a comparison to suggest that the hero is endowed with the movement or the boundless nature of the *awyr*?

86 **gweith heinif** The same phrase, rhyming with 1sg. *golchif*, is found in LlDC 35.10 (Trystan fragments) *Gweith heinyw golchiw ar wi nvywron.*

9 Ymarwar Llud bychan

This poem abstracts its title, 'The Short Poem about Lludd's Discussion', from line 11 *kyn ymarwar Llud a Llefelis*, and the title may have been contrasting this short piece with a longer item, possibly *Gwawt Lud y mawr*, poem §7 in this collection, although that poem, disappointingly, has no mention of Lludd as such. In our poem, the brothers Lludd and Llefelys are paired, as in the tale *Cyfranc Lludd a Llefelys*,[1] and Brynley F. Roberts suggests that they were known as bringing deliverance from one or more *gormesoedd* or oppressions. In that tale, there were three *gormesoedd*: (1) the Coraniaid, who could hear everything going on; (2) a scream causing the land and animals and women to be barren (perhaps remembered in §7.65 *heb eppa, heb henuonha*); (3) food becoming scarce — only the food of the first night could be eaten (compare the shortage of provisions in §10.9-10). In Triad 36, the Coraniaid people, who came to Britain in the time of Caswallon son of Beli (and therefore during the time of Caswallon's brothers, Lludd and Llefelys), are said to have come from Arabia (*or Auia pan hanoedynt*). The second and third *gormes* were the Irish-Picts (the *Gwydyl Fychti*, also mentioned in §5.12) and the Saxons under Hengist and Horsa.

    The main thrust of the poem accords broadly with these concerns. A *gormes*, here called a 'myriad host of cruel violence', will conquer or threaten Britain: they are called 'the men of the land of Asia' and the unidentified 'land of Gafis'. These are a race of malign intent whose land is not familiar or known. Their weapons are strange (*gowyreis*), and they wear trailing mantles (*amlaes eu peisseu*). They are sea-raiders (*herwyr* (em.) *maris*), a people unlike any other. Nothing of this description brings to mind the Vikings; however it is worth noting T. Gwynn Jones's suggestion (reported in EVW 127) that they were the Danes, on the grounds that 'the Irish and Welsh, as Christians, seem to have regarded the pagan Danes as Saracens'.[2] A similar process sees the extension of the term *Idewon* 'Jews', so that it can be used indiscriminately for foreigners or enemies.[3] Returning to our poem, we note that the odd terms *Europin*, *Arafin* and *Arafanis* are employed, as well as possibly Latin *famen* 'language' (if calquing W. *ieith*, both 'language' and 'race') and *maris* 'of the sea'. Christ is cited as a true deliverer, one who antedated the *ymarwar Llud a Llefelys*, the 'discussion' or 'conversation' between Lludd and Llefelys. The ruler (*perchen*)

---

[1] CLlaLl. On its date, cf. on line 11 below. The priority between the tale, our poem and Geoffrey of Monmouth is still unclear.

[2] Welsh uses of *Sarasin* and related forms are discussed LPBT 310. On vague English uses of 'Saracens' to refer to pagan invaders of Britain, see Matthieu Boyd, 'Celts Seen as Muslims and Muslims Seen by Celts in Medieval Literature', in *Contextualizing the Muslim Other in Medieval Christian Discourse*, edited by Jerold C. Frakes (New York, 2011), 21-38, at p. 22.

[3] See LPBT 14, 310 and 346 on *Idewon*; cf. Alexander Falileyev, 'Why Jews? Why *Caer Seon*? Towards interpretations of *Ymddiddan Taliesin ac Ugnach*', *CMCS* 64 (2012), 85-118.

of Albion, *y wen Ynys*, shall be shaken or roused before a ruler (or empire) of Rome (*pennaeth o Rufein*).

Margaret Enid Griffths, EWV 125-8, dated the poem to the eleventh century, thinking that the foreigners referred to are probably the Saracens themselves, and that the First Crusade (1096-9) is in the background. Nevertheless, she finds it 'strange . . . that these people should be expected to come to Britain'. However, it is quite possible that the first of the imagined *gormesoedd* of the past should be exoticised in this manner. Yet little here apart from the Arabian reference matches the Coraniaid as experienced in the tale and in the triad. The final part of the poem seems to draw on apocalypse or Harrowing of Hell motifs (the swamp and lanterns), and there is a certain mention of Christ in line 10. There are odd linguistic forms not found elsewhere, such as *Brythonic*; and it is perhaps signicant that the locution *y Wen Ynys* 'Albion' is not found outside the Welsh translations of Geoffrey of Monmouth's *Historia Regum Britanniae*.

The poem is incomplete — the last line has no rhyme partner, and the reference to the men or territory of Wessex (*Iwis*) seems out on a limb from the rest of the piece, unless it is to recall with scorn those tenth-century Welsh kings who curried favour at Æthelstan's court, and who were being wooed in Armes Prydain to switch their allegiance.[4] They perhaps are being imagined as consigned to the Hellish swamp of line 16. The metre here is classical Cyhydedd Naw Ban, very much as in Armes Prydain, with regular 5+4 patterning and much internal rhyme.

---

[4] See introduction to poem §4.

9 Ymarwar Llud bychan
Book of Taliesin 78.18-79.8

En enw Duw Trindawt, kardawt kyfrwys,
In the name of God the Trinity, of wise charity,
llwyth lliaws, anuaws eu henwerys,
a myriad host of cruel violence,
dygorescynnan Prydein, prif van ynys:
shall conquer Britain, the pre-eminent island:
gwyr gwlat yr Ascia a gwlat Gafis,
the men of the land of Asia and the land of Cafis/Gafis,
5   **pobyl pwyllat enwir eu tir ny wys.**
a people of evil intent whose land is not known.
Famen gowyreis herwyr[1] maris
A race with inclined lances, sea-raiders,
amlaes eu peisseu, pwy eu heuelis,
their tunics trailing, what others are like them,
a phwyllat difuner,[2] ober efnis?
with a vain intent, a hostile action?
Europin, Arafin, Arafanis.
Europeans, Arabians, Saracens,
10   **Crist yawn[3] difryt diryd dilis**
Christ (was) a true salvation to the bound and reviled
kyn ymarwar Llud a Llefelis.
before the conversation of Lludd and Llefelys.
Dysgogettawr perchen y Wen Ynys
The ruler/owner of Albion shall be stirred/moved
rac pennaeth o Rufein, kein y echrys.
in the face of a lord from Rome, fair (to behold) the terror he provokes.
Nyt rys, nyt kyfrwys ri rwyf y areith
It is not . . . , not a skilful king of great speech
15   **a rywelei a ryweleis o aghyfyeith**
who'd see what I saw of the foreigners.
Dullator petrygwern llugyrn ymdeith,
There will be arranged a veritable swamp, a path (needing) lanterns,

---

[1] ms *herwyd*
[2] ms *dyvyner*
[3] ms *cristyawn*

9 Ymarwar Llud bychan

    rac ryuonic kynran   baran godeith.
in the face of a stout warrior with the roar of a great conflagration.
    Ry talaf Mab grat,   rwyf y areith.
May I merit the dear Son, of ready utterance.
    Kymry yn danhyal,   ryfel ar geith,
The Cymry gnashing their teeth (and) war on bondmen,
20   **pryderaf, pwyllaf   pwy y hymdeith,**
I worry, I wonder what their course will be,
    Brythonic yn Iwis   dydyrchefis.
the Brython-like ones who triumphed in Wessex.

1   **En enw Duw Trindawt**   Cf. poem openings invoking God, CC 22.1 *In enu Dom'ni meu y voli maur y uolaud*; PT XI.1 *En enw gwledic Nef goludawc*; PT XII.1 *En enw gwledic Nef gorchordyon. Kyfrwys* of God, CC 33.8 *pwy namyn kyfrwys a'e kyfrwyma*.

2   **llwyth lliaws anuaws eu henwerys**   Cf. AP lines 127-8 *Dygorfu Kymry y peri kat/ a llwyth lliaws gwlat a gynnullant*.

3   **dygorescynnan**   The only attestation of this compound of *goresgyn* 'overcome, overrun, conquer'. See General Introduction, 16, on *dy-* preverbs.

3   **prif van ynys**   GPC s.v. *bân* suggests that this is an instance of *ban*[1] 'exalted, renowned', etc. *Y Wen Ynys* is used for Geoffrey's Albion in line 12 below, as in the Brut y Brenhinedd translations of the *Historia Regum Britanniae*, e.g. BD 19 (I 16), also *yr Enys Wenn*, and *Ynys vel Veli* in §5.9.

4   **gwlat Ascia**   As well as the regular L. *Asia* (e.g. LPBT 25.50) are found the forms *Asicia* (CC 24.31 (BT) *Asicia, Affrica, Europa*), and *Agascia* (LPBT 16.19 *a chiwdawt Babilon ac Agascia mawr*), the latter perhaps to be emended to *Ascia*.

4   **gwlat Gafis**   G s.n. *Cafis* (*-ys*, or *Gafis*, *-ys*). Solinus locates near the Indus *urbem . . . Caphisam, quam Cyrus diruit* (54.2); this is called *Capisa* in Pliny, and *Cassica civitas* on the Hereford Map (Scott D. Westrem, *The Hereford Map* (Turnhout, 2001), 53, translates *Capisa*). It is north of present day Kabul. The Welsh translation of *Imago Mundi* (DB 97, White Book text) has *caer Gabes* in the extreme west of Africa but probably not modern Gabes which was *Tacape* (in Tabula Peutingeriana, etc.). Cadiz (L. *Gades*), under Moorish rule from 711 to 1262, may well be relevant, or the first of the two unidentified islands mentioned in Triad 35 (TYP[3] 85 *Gals* (?Galicia, Galatia) *ac Auena*, near *Mor Groec* 'the Greek sea').

5   **eu tir ny wys**   Commonly used pres. impers. of vb *gwybot*.

6   **Famen gowyreis**   G regards this as L. *famen*, pl. *famina* 'utterance, speech, word', a post-classical coinage, first recorded in the metrical Gospels of Juvencus, and well-known to us from the title *Hisperica Famina*. Is it here calquing W. *ieith* which can mean 'language', but also 'people, nation'? *Gowyreis* is understood with G and GPC as a hapax instance of a compound < *gowyr* 'bent, inclined' + *eis* 'lances', translated by Day, Arfau 497, as 'couched lances'. This mode of fighting with horizontal lance held beneath the arm is

9 Ymarwar Llud bychan

described very often in the later prose tales, the romances especially, but the evidence from the pre-1283 poetry texts is less conclusive, as Day discusses. Since we are dealing here with a foreign fighting force, it is not surprising that the poet should focus on different weaponry and dress.

6   **herwyr (ms herwyd) maris** *Herwyd* 'by means of' is not impossible, but *herwyr* yields better sense with L. *maris* 'of the sea', for sea-raiders or marauders. The fact that the two words *herwyd* and *herwyr* are sometimes collocated (as in CBT I 8.10, CBT II 1.149 and 28.26-7) may have led to the mistake.

7   **amlaes eu peisseu** The long tunics or coats noted as a distinguishing feature may be the extremely long flowing surcoats worn over armour which became common from the 12c. *Peis* < L. *pexa* was originally a garment of wool, but of marten pelts in the case of the boy Dinogad's celebrated garment, CA line 1101.

7   **pwy eu heuelis** The orthography *-is* (for *-ys*) is perhaps influenced by the rhyme for *maris* in line 6, but note again LPBT 15.14-15 *wrth pop heuelis/ wrth heuelis Nwython*. Not a common word (< *hafal* 'same as'), but cf. Moliant Cadwallon line 7 *heuelys y llong nar llu estrawn* (em.); CBT IV 6.47 *Llary Llacheu heuelys*. In *Cyfranc Lludd a Llefelys*, it is stressed that the like of the three oppressions (*teir gormes*) had not been seen: CLlaLl line 31 *ar ny welsei neb o'r ynyssed gynt eu kyfryw*.

8   **a phwyllat difuner (ms dyvyner)** The single *-n-* would tend to rule out a form of vb *dyfyn* 'to summon'. G suggests emending to *dy funer* 'to/for a lord', but preferable perhaps is GPC *difuner* 'without a lord, unprotected; free from payments or dues, privileged; ?futile', occasionally attested in early poetry: R580.20 (Cyfoesi) *Kyuarchaf ym diuuner ura6t*; CBT II 18.52-3 *Cof Ewein y'm callonn yd uyt,/ Di6uner ucher ac echwyt*; and see n. in CBT II 326 where the meaning 'lordless' is favoured (contra G), and comparison made with OE depictions of such figures, as in *The Wanderer*. 'Fruitless, vain' seems more likely in CBT IV 17.9 *Ouer, difuner, llyther llea6r*. Here apparently for foreign free-booters acting on their own impulses without the control of a lord.

8   **ober efnis** There is some uncertainty whether this is a native word, *g(w)ober* or else a borrowing from L. *opera*, with some instances having developed an inorganic *g(w)-*, e.g. CBT I 2.40 *cadr wober yv*; VI 10.40 *an cam wober*. The meaning 'work, deed' suits well, as in EWSP 451.24a *Berwit brat anuat ober*; CBT III 26.3 *gwythla6n y ober*; IV 4.290 *O dorri o derrwyn ober*; IV 8.17 *Yg Kemeis, yn treis, yn tra6s ober*; VI 10.16 *Dywedud traha trwe gam ober*. Note also *gorober* 'act, feat, exploit', CBT I 15.10 and 21.34; VI 5.37 and 18.126; and IV 4.282 *anober*. *Efnis*, atypical orthography again for *efnys* 'hostile, wrathful', especially common in CBT corpus.

9   **Europin Arafin Arafanis** The most common triad of continents is *Asia*, *Affrica* and *Europa*, as in LPBT 25.50-3; CC 24.31; and in the Welsh numerological triads, on which see Owen, TrArbennig 441-3. But the *Europin* form is not otherwise attested in MW; neither is *Arafin*, which can be assumed (with G) to be a form of Arabia, elsewhere rendered *Afia*, most often with preceding *eur* (CBT VI 3.28 *rudeur Afya*; V 8.16 *Eur Auya*; and examples in GPC² s.v. *aur*, comparing also *aur Opia* from Ethiopia). The Pen. 16 Triad 36 on the Three Oppressions notes the first as the people of the *Corryanyeit* (who have a starring part in CLlaLl) who came from Arabia: *a doethant eman yn oes Caswalla6n mab Beli, ac nyt aeth 6r un onadunt dracheuyn. Ac or Auia pan hanoedynt* (TYP³ 90).

9 Ymarwar Llud bychan

See IGE² 394 on *Yr Afia*; GGrG 5.27 is notable with *aur Arafia*. The *-in* endings are unlikely to be diminutive, but could they be the W. adjectival suffix (as in *derwin, lledrin, kyssefin, gwerthefin*, etc.), or forms attempting to give the effect of L. pl. *-ini*? The compound *arafin* 'fine weather' < *araf* + *hin*, attested from the 16c onwards, seems most unlikely. The third form, *Arafanis*, is equally baffling, perhaps coined purely for the rhyme. Is there any possible connection with the reviled lineage LPBT 9.77 *o blant Saraphin* (also associated with evil sea-voyagers)? — but see n. on that example where it is suggested that *Sarasin* 'Saracen' (GPC s.n. < ME *Sarasin(e)*) was perhaps written *Sarafin* in an exemplar and misinterpreted. HKB ch. 115 says that 'The island will be called by Brutus's name and the foreign term will disappear. From Conanus will come forth a warlike boar, who will sharpen his tusks on the forests of France. He will break all the tallest trees, but give protection to the smaller. The Arabs and Africans (*Arabes et Affricani*) will tremble before him: for his charge will carry him all the way to further Spain'.

10 **Crist yawn diffryt** On the basis of the ms reading *cristyawn*, G s.n. *cristawn* treats this example as one word, 'Christian, believer': and if so, 'a true salvation to the Christian'. But G s.v. *diffryt* favours separation into two words, as implemented here, which yields rather better sense. Geoffrey of Monmouth, HKB ch. 64, recounts the reign of Kimbelinus (Cynfelyn) who had been brought up by Augustus Caesar and knighted by him. He was 'so fond of the Romans that he freely paid them the tribute which he could have withheld'. During his reign was born Jesus Christ 'whose precious blood was redeemed the human race, bound beforehand in the chains of idolatry'. This event here is put before the *ymarwar* of Lludd and Llefelys.

11 **ymarwar Llud a Llefelys** The poem's title is partly abstracted from this line, with its uncommon vb and noun *ymarwar* 'to talk, converse, discuss; conversation, discussion' (< *arwar*, see below). The 13c poet, Llywelyn Fardd II (CLlaLl xx has the wrong date, confusing him with the 12c Llywelyn Fardd I), evidently knew of the episode or story by the same name: CBT VI 7.3-4 *Handwyf hua6dyl was a wys yn llys/ Ual Ymarwar Llut a Lleuelys* 'I am an eloquent lad known at court/ as in the conversation of Lludd and Llefelys'. He appears to be comparing his eloquence in praising king Llywelyn ab Iorwerth of Gwynedd with the clarity of the communication between Lludd and his brother Llefelys, conducted through a long horn of brass rinsed out with wine to sluice out an interfering demon. This comparison with the speaking trumpet may be a variation on the idea of the poet likening himself, and the effect of his declamation, to a horn. Prydydd y Moch, for example, boasts that he is like Oliphant, the famous horn of Roland, CBT V 23.203 *Wyf tebic Eliffant*. But Llywelyn Fardd may have had in mind the secret nature of the horn communication between the brothers, and that only certain people are privy to his eloquence in his patron's court. Cynddelw uses the word *ymarwar* to describe the distressed communication between the hosts of Powys following the death of Rhirid Flaidd and his brother Arthen, CBT III 24.34 *Neut amrygyt kyrt kyd ymarwar*. The simplex *arwar* 'delight, pleasure, joy, zest' (and denominative vb) is very common (15 instances in CBT corpus, a third of them by Prydydd y Moch).

12 **Dysgogettawr perchen y Wen Ynys** *Dysgogettawr* is an otherwise unattested instance of a compound of the vb *ysgogi*, GPC 'to move (away), budge, stir,

shake, tremble . . . agitate, excite, urge, motivate, inspire, stimulate; change', seemingly with impers. *-etor* (cf. §7.55n) influenced by fut. *-hawr* (GMW 121, though cf. LPBT 18.54n). Cf. CC 21.132 *dygettaur*. See General Introduction, 16 on compounds in *dy-* as a signature feature of prophetic discourse.

It is unclear who the *perchen* 'owner, ruler' is. *Perchen* is used of God and Christ, e.g. Edmyg Dinbych line 2 *perchen Nef a llawr*; CC 11.43 *perchen lleg egylyon*; 14.23 *Vy maurhidic nen, vy perchen, vy parch*; LPBT 18.45 *py awr ymeindyd y ganet Perchen*, etc. With *pen*, CC 13.3 *Duw penn perchen pob kiwdawt*; Tymhorau line 22 *edmig perchen pen sywedydd*; CBT IV 17.1 and 16 *Denggrat Benn Berchen, barch Brioda6r . . . Dynyaton Berchen, Benn bob eua6r*, etc. Of a secular ruler probably in PT VII.31 *y vd Prydein pen perchen broestlawn*; certainly so in Echrys Ynys line 20 *priodawr perchen*; §8.81-2 *perif perchen ket/ gwledychawt yn Eluet*; LlDC 16.3 *perchen Machrev*, etc. and common in CBT corpus where *perchen/pen* are frequently collocated.

Y Wen Ynys, 'fair' or 'blessed' island, a phrase not attested elsewhere in early poetry, but see on line 3 *prif van ynys*. The phrase is, however, used to translate *Albion* in some of the 14c manuscripts of the Welsh renderings of Geoffrey of Monmouth's *Historia Regum Britanniae* (HKB ch. 21 *Erat tunc nomen insulae Albion*, described as a well-situated, pleasant land): Pen. 21, 6ʳ *Ac yn yr amser hwnnw y gelwit yr ynys honn Albion. Sef oed hynny y Wen Ynys . . . . tec . . . oed yr ynys honn*, etc.; BD 19 *A 'r amser hvnnv y gelwit hi y Wenn Ynys*; Mostyn 117 (NLW 3036, in the same hand as Book of Taliesin), p. 1 *yr hon a elwit gynt y wen ynys*; RB II p. 40 *y 6en ynys* (pace GPC s.v. *ynys* p. 3819). The positioning of *gwen* before the noun may aim to suggest an old compound name, or reflect the initial position of the 'white' element in Albion: see BD 209. Note that some earlier versions in 13c manuscripts have the more prosaic order: e.g. Pen. 44, p. 16 *er enys wen*; NLW 5266, p. 1 *er hon a el6yt er Enys Wen*.

13 **kein y echrys** 'Fair/welcome his terror, horror', presumably of the effect on the foe cf. CBT IV 6.63 *Lloegyr echrys* 'one inflicting terror on the English'; CBT III 24.116 *echrys Ochren* 'having the terror of Ochren', etc. Most naturally understood as describing the *pennaeth o Rufein*, although the *perchen* of the previous line is also possible.

14 **Nyt rys, nyt kyfrwys ri rwyf y areith** *Rys* may be for GPC *rhes¹*, to be connected with vb *redec* 'to run', etc., see GPC s.v., or, more likely, with *rysed*, *ryswr*, *rysfa*, etc. perhaps with a meaning like 'splendid, bold; presumptuous, overweening'. This is uncertain, as is the etymology of the personal name *Rhys*, which could also be considered here. There is a Rhys Aerlludd mentioned in Oianau line 98, and Rhys Undant in LlDC 1.12 (Ymddiddan Myrddin a Thaliesin), as well as numerous historical figures, such as Rhys ap Tewdwr, Rhys ap Gruffudd, Rhys Gryg, etc. Some mentions of the name in CBT corpus are (naturally) collocated with *rwyf* 'pomp, pride, arrogance' (e.g. CBT II 24.11 *Rys rwyf anaw*; CBT VII 21.9 *O Rys, rwyf vuelyar*; CBT VII 3.16-17, VII 14.6-7, etc.). Or is this a mistake for *rwyd* 'easy, fluent' or *rwy* 'excessive . . . extreme', etc. It is difficult to know whether this figure is being praised or condemned.

15 **a rywelei a ryweleis o aghyfieith** It is difficult to know whether we have interrogative *a* at the beginning of the line ('did he/could he see what I saw of the foreigners?'), or rel. pron. (with unexpressed object antecedent, 'that which he saw, I have seen . . .'). All very uncertain, especially since the first part of the line

9 Ymarwar Llud bychan

is abnormally long. The *aghyfieith* are presumably the various foreigners already alluded to in lines 2, 4-9.

16 **Dullator pedrygwern llugyrn ymdeith** *Pedrygwern* is not listed by GPC (or G s.v. *gwern*) but presumably for *pedrywern* 'perfect or four-square alder staves' (or 'square-headed javelins', or even possibly 'square alder shield', Day, Arfau 450). If the former, i.e. staves, being arranged or drawn up (the vb *dullyaw*), this might bring to mind Geoffrey of Monmouth's account of Cassivellaunus's preparations before Julius Caesar's second attack on Britain: HKB ch. 59-60 'in the bed of the Thames, where Caesar would sail to Trinovantum, he planted beneath the waterline stakes of iron and lead, as thick as a man's thigh, to hole Caesar's ships from below'. This led to a great disaster, with mass casualties. This dramatic event was evidently well-known: it is recounted by Bede, HE I.ii, as well as by HB ch. 19-20: Julius Caesar's second attempt was foiled by Dolabella, proconsul to Belinus son of Minocan who 'put iron stakes and "battle seed", that is, caltrops, in the river ford'. But if, as Day suggests (Arfau 387), *pedrygwern* denotes shields, there may be a reference in our poem to a drawing up a four-square defensive arrangement, or simply to the serried ranks of warriors with their shields proceeding with lighted brands.

However, *gwern* is used most frequently in poetry to mean a swamp, often a key feature of hell in the Welsh medieval tradition. It was conventional to rhyme *gwern* and *Uffern*, in turn collocated with *llugyrn/-ern* (e.g. LPBT 18.20). If so, perhaps 'complete, utter swamp', one so dark as to have to be negotiated by lantern-light (*llugyrn ymdeith*, lit. 'a lantern going, retreating'), a slough of despond for the enemy. This second interpretation, though uncertain, perhaps accommodates *llugyrn* (possibly to be emended to *llugern* for full internal rhyme) more easily. Full internal rhyme if *llugyrn* were emended to *llugern*: for details on the forms *llugorn*, *llugyrn*, *llugern*, and their relationship to L. *lucerna*, see LPBT 5.9n and 18.20. CBT VI poem 20 (englynion in praise of the martial exploits of Llywelyn ab Iorwerth and his warband, possibly by Prydydd y Moch, CBT VI 299) collocates *dywalwern*, *drywern*, *rysswr*, *Rosed Diabret* in lines 64-5.

17 **rac ryuonic kynran** *Ryuonic* is not listed by GPC. If from *bon* 'bottom, base, root, stump, trunk, stock, stem' rather than 'rump, tail', then perhaps a meaning like 'stocky, stout' would be possible, and this is understood here, albeit tentatively. There is no obvious candidate *monic/mynic* (as opposed to *mynawc* 'noble'), nor *gwonic/gwynic*. A termination *-ic* attached to *ryfawr* is not impossible; other suggestions might include *ryodic* 'fine, noble', and *rywodic* 'eager' as in the hapax CBT VI 20.21 *rywodic lluoed* (if not for *ryodic*, see CBT 313).

However, line 13 *pennaeth o Rufein* might suggest a mistake for an adj. formed from the personal name *Rufawn* < L. *Romanus* 'Roman', i.e. *Ruuonic, in ModW orthography, *Rhufonig*. The name Rhufawn was certainly one to conjure with: it is instanced as the name of one of Cunedda's sons, the eponym of Rhufoniog, EWGT 13; and there is a Rhufawn Hir and a Rhufawn in the Gododdin (CA lines 378 and 1002), as well as a Rhufawn in Englynion y Beddau, LlDC 18.129 and 132. Rhufawn Bybr's burial-place (in Cornwy, Talybolion, Anglesey, GGDT 8.30) is mentioned by Hywel ab Owain Gwynedd, CBT II 6.2 *Gwytua Ruuaόn Bebyr, ben teyrnet*. Triad 3 records him, *Ruuawn Beuyr* son of Dewrarth Wledig,

9 Ymarwar Llud bychan

as the third of the *Tri Gwyndeyrn* of the Island of Britain together with Owain son of Urien and Rhun son of Maelgwn; he appears in CO line 183 as son of Dorath, and in *Breuddwyd Ronabwy* as son of Deorthach Wledic; and continues, as a touchstone of valour perhaps, in 14c Anglesey, GGM I 4.23: see TYP[3] 8, 489-90. Other personal names spawn adjectives, including Meurig (EWSP 414.1 and 2 *Meurygawc marchawg*), and Elffin (LPBT 12.22 *Elffinawc varchawc, medhwyrdy Ogled*); note also the hapax *Brythonic* in line 21. This interpretation would necessitate emending to *ruuonic*: the scribe may have had his eye on *ry talaf* in line 18. If so, 'in the face of a warrior like Romanus/Rhufawn'. Very uncertain, as is the identity of the *kynran* — if the *petrygwern* of line 16 is an infernal swamp, then Christ as Harrower of Hell is not impossible, especially in view of line 18.

17 **baran godeith** *Godeith* 'fire, conflagration', cf. EWSP 429.4a *Kynddylan callon godeith wannwyn*; EWSP 460.19c *ruthur godeith ar diffeith vynyd*; and 12 instances in CBT corpus, in battle contexts. *Baran* 'noise, roar' is extremely common: with *tan*, §2.19 *Rac baran Kynan tan tardawt*; CA line 832 *baran tan*; compound *gofaran* rhyming with *kynran*, CA lines 33-4.

18 **Ry talaf Mab grat rwyf y areith** GPC treats the hapax *grat* as an irregular borrowing from L. *gratus* 'beloved, dear'. A Latinate word, along with the vb *talu* 'to merit, deserve, to be worth', suggests that the *mab* in question here is Jesus. But He is referred to extensively by the poets as *mab rat* 'Son of Grace/ blessing', e.g. CBT I 24.27 *Argleitryat, Uab rat, ryhyt—o garchar*; CBT IV 17.108 *Y'r Mab rad, y'r Tad tec hynafyaeth*; CBT VI 9.15 *Bwyf gwastad gan Uab Rad reithgar*; CBT VI 24.37 *Pan dyfu y Mab Rat, oed reit 6rthaw*, and 43 *Vcheldat Vab Rat, rac r6yda6—y ha6l*; CBT VI 30.17 *Ni ddotto fy Rheen, Fab Rhad,—ei bechawd/ Yn erbyn fy mrawd, ddefawd ddifrad*; CBT VII 40.64 *Yd archaf y'm Tat, Yspryt a Mab Rat*; CBT VII 48.36 *Haeluab rad, y Dad a'e duc ataw*, etc. These examples argue strongly in favour of restoring *mab rat* in our example (despite G's doubts about its relevance s.v. *grat*), unless there is a sophisticated word play in operation here whereby a secular *mab* (the redeeming hero) is being given an adj. *grat* 'beloved' thus suggesting his proximity of function to Christ but yet without quite taking in vain the well-known phrase, *mab rat*.

19 **Kymry yn danhyal ryfel ar geith** Rare *danhyal* 'biting, gnashing of teeth', only attested otherwise (in an infernal context) in 14c GC 7.36-7 *Trist gosb, gost ffwrndost, gwst ufferndan./ Trinheion dynion (danial ogan)*. This suggests the poet is thinking of a cataclysm to come, when the world is turned on its head and war is waged on bondmen or captives (*keith*). Or else the *keith* of Hell are meant.

20 **pryderaf pwyllaf pwy y hymdeith** The two vbs *pryderu* and *pwyllaw* signal meditation on serious matters, and they are used together elsewhere in a religious poem addressing the problem of what sustains the world: LPBT 26.3-4 *Lliaws a bwyllaf/ ac a bryderaf*. The collocation recalls the famous father and son whose names are paired in LPBT 18.4 *Trwy ebostol Pwyll a Phryderi*. It may be that *pwyll a phryder* was perhaps a familiar pair of alliterating synonyms (like *ser a sygneu*) echoed in the poetry examples, and in the names of the Mabinogi characters. For vbs with direct object, CBT I 5.3 *Pryder pryderaf yn uawr*; V 1.55 *Pwyllaf a ganaf, a gen6ch,—ueirtyon*, etc. For *pryder* with *Prydein*, CBT II

9 Ymarwar Llud bychan

22.21; CBT III 14.27; 16.193; 21.67 (*Pryderi*); III 26.109-10; CBT IV 13.30; CBT V 1.81; CBT V 11.30, etc.

21 **Brythonic yn Iwis dydyrchefis** *Brythonic* is a hapax adj. form < *Brython* 'Briton' (cf. perhaps *ryuonic* recte *ruuonic* in line 17 above) but does it simply mean 'Briton(s)', or does it have some other force? A very tentative suggestion is made in the introduction that it may refer to tenth-century Welsh princes in attendance at Æthelstan's court. The *Iwis* 'Gewisse, Wessex men', AP 49-50, *B* 4 (1927-9), 45, are still being referred to in an elegy for Madog ap Maredudd (d. 1160). He is said to have conducted a bold raid *drac Iwys* 'beyond the Wessex men' (CBT I 7.122) as well as 'beyond Lincoln' (line 120 *tra Llynnwys*), where it is known that Madog was fighting in 1141, see CBT I 170. In both this example and the present, a territory yields better sense than the name of the people — the coterminous Welsh practice (*Kymry* = Wales, Welshmen) was perhaps applied to other peoples (cf. E. *Wessex* < *West Saxons*). The rare vb *dydyrchafu* 'rise, rise up, triumph' is attested otherwise only in §8.24 *dydyrchafwy dreic o parth deheu*. The final line is unrhymed, suggesting an incomplete text.

10 Darogan Kadwal[adyr]

The title marks this poem out as the only one in the Four Ancient Books (and in the Hendregadredd manuscript) to be called *darogan*. The poem is sadly incomplete, standing on the last surviving folio of the manuscript. A catch-word *ac am lan* is found at the foot of the page, facilitating a link to another quire, now missing. It presumably refers to a battle on a river, a commonplace in prophecy (cf. Conwy (§2.8), Gwy, Camarch, Peryddon, Tywi, Teifi, Eleri, etc.). The poem begins with a sketch of a death-dealing 'swift, noisy horseman' who appears to be making guerilla strikes from the mountains of Eryri, a refuge mentioned in other poems (see note on line 4). Then Cadwaladr is named: he may be the horseman just mentioned, but more likely he is billed as a superior leader who is able to make his headquarters on the lowland plains of Britain, not, it is implied, in some mountain fastness. That day will bring joy to the poet, and surely to his audience. But first there will be a period of privation, a common enough progression in prophecy, with the grasping Saxons demanding the best shares of the food, a suggestion of incest perhaps in line 14, corpses being devoured by ravens, and wounded men felled by the sword, presumably by the invaders. The metre is somewhat confused, using a tripartite line in the main, with a change to Cyhydedd Naw Ban in line 15.

10 Darogan Kadwal(adyr)
Book of Taliesin 80.17-27

Marchawc mwth misterin
A swift, noisy horseman
ar deu wyneb brwytrin ◇,[1]
on the two flanks of the fighting,
rodawc braw, llaw y treghi,
a dispenser of terror, dealing death to the weak,
ac yn Eryri ymolöi.
and taking cover in Eryri.

5 **Pan del Katwaladyr gogwna**
When Cadwaladr shall come he'll cause
ydoleu Prydein pen ma.
(his) headquarters (to be situated) in the meadows of Britain.
.... wc oes moes ny ma,

a minheu bydif ym ar*h*a.[2]
and I for my part shall be in my element.
Ys deubi Seis yna y erchi bwytta
The Saxon shall come then to demand the eating of
10 **dogyn gwyr o rys*w*yr**[3] **rosseda.**
the men's share by attackers of intemperate behaviour.
Jeuhawt gwreic gan y gwas,
The wife shall be yoked by her servant,
hen gas ny ma.
an old enmity/enemy ....
dogyn gwyr o ryfyr.
the men's share of ....
A weleisti vyg kar a'm brawt?
Did you see my relation with my brother?
15 **Gweleis-i gelein vein a brein ar gnawt,**
I saw a slim corpse, and ravens on flesh,
ac arall ar darwein gwall grein cledyfawt,
and another bleeding from a wrongful felling by sword-stroke,
ac am lan .....
and on the bank of ...

---

[1] ms *berwyn*
[2] ms *arua*
[3] ms *ryfyr*

10 Darogan Kadwal[adyr]

1   **Marchawc mwth misterin**   Cf. with *mwth* 'swift', PT VII.9 *gochawn marchawc mwth molut Gwyron*; PT VIII.32 *Vn yw maon meirch mwth miledawr*; CA line 3 *meirch mwth myngvras*; CBT V 1.126-8 *Meirch breischir uch brasgeirch haluc,/ M6th, myggann, hirllam, haerlluc: na bwynt gynt/ No rywynt uch Ryd Nuc*. Prydydd y Moch uses *mwth* in two further instances, CBT V 11.15 and V 23.63, and one instance of pl. in CBT V 1.150 *Mythyon ueirch, fwyr tyweirch forta6l*, but none of the other court poets uses the word. Other alliterative lines with *marchawc* include EWSP 414.1 and 2 *Meurygawg marchawg meuen* and *Meurygawg marchawg maes*; CA line 812 *ar les Minidauc marchauc maon*; CBT I 2.19 *Metcvin kywran, marchauc mitlan, mann meidrolaeth*; etc.

    Misterin represents *mysterin*, found also as trisyllable in CBT VII 42.27 *G6eleis wyt yn trin a meirch mysterin* (pace CBT VII 487). This appears to be an adj. derived from the noun *mwstr/mwstwr* 'muster, gathering, noise clamour; commotion', etc. attested from 15c onwards (possibly from OF *moustr* 'a mustering of soldiers', perhaps through ME according to GPC). See also GPC s.v. *mwstrin, mwstring*, like the vb *mwstr(i)o*, of late attestation.

2   **ar deu wyneb brwytrin** ◇ **(ms berwyn)**   The length of the line and the need for a rhyme in *-in* suggest that G may be right to regard *berwyn* as a gloss (viewed by G as an adj. 'wrathful, angry', rather than a personal or place-name). *Brwydrin* is a synonym of *brwydyr* 'battle' (*brwydyr* + *-in*, GPC) as in CA line 609; EWSP 459; LPBT 5.190; CBT I 3.33 *Ergyrwaew brwydrin*; CBT VI 25.11 *taer ym mrwydrin*; CBT VII 46.13 *Aruaeth ehelaeth, hwyl gyrchyat—brwydrin*; or else an adj. 'pugnacious', possibly used nominally. *Deu wyneb*, cf. CBT IV 4.15 *Mur moreb deu wyneb Dyfnant*. Here, 'on the two sides or wings of the battle'.

3   **rodawc braw llaw y treghi**   Since the scribe of the manuscript is yod-shy, and since *-d-* is ambiguous, *rodawc* could represent either ModW *rhoddiog* 'generous, bountiful, munificent, full of gifts; ?thrown (of spear): giver, benefactor, donor', or else the common *rodawc* 'a round shield'. *Llaw* taken as adj. 'base, mean, small, sad' used nominally, with pre-verbal-noun *y* (~ *yn*), although *llawyr treghi* would be more natural in poetry.

4   **ac yn Eryri ymolöi**   There are at least 13 references to *Eryri*, the Snowdon mountain range in Gwynedd which provided a valuable refuge: see further §2.16n. The vb *ymolöi* 'to hide oneself, take refuge, withdraw to' is not otherwise attested in the medieval period, in contrast with the simplex vb *golo/golöi*.

5   **Pan del Katwaladyr gogwna**   On Cadwaladr, see General Introduction, 11. Forms like *pan dyfo*, etc. are naturally a common feature of prophetic discourse, but *pan del* is not so frequent: cf. R584.8 (Gwasgargerdd) *Pan del g6r g6rthryn y ar olwyn du*; LPBT 13.3 *Pan del y rihyd* (of God's majesty). Elsewhere, PT IX.3 *pan del vygwaessaf*; CBT I 6.22 *Hyd pan del Kynan (kein aduwyndaw6d)/ A Chadwaladyr ma6r, mur pob kiwda6d*, in a praise poem to Madog ap Maredudd by Gwalchmai ap Meilyr who maintains, in a conscious allusion to the prophecy style, that Madog has no peer, nor will have until such time as Cynan and Cadwaladr return to defend their people; St David, rather than a secular hero, is the deliverer for the poet, Gwynfardd Brycheiniog, CBT II 26.176-7 *Pan del ryuel a rwysc Fichti/ Ros eluyt, pob keluyt geil6 Dewi*, together with God elsewhere in the same poem, CBT II 26.59-60 *Ban del gofyn arnam-ny rybyt6n ofna6c/ Rac gormes kedyrn Cad Dybruna6c*. Other CBT instances tend to refer to

10 Darogan Kadwal[adyr]

the impending Judgment, e.g. CBT I 28.7 *Pan del rac Yessu trillu tralla6d*; CBT VII 33.81 *Pan del y trillu*; CBT III 3.77 *Pan del Bra6t rac bronn uchelseint*.

Gogwna: forms of the compound vb *gogwneuthur* 'make, cause' are otherwise restricted to CA line 1045 *gogwneif* and possibly line 1046 *gwygynei* (which CA 315 emends to *gogwn e*).

6   **ydoleu Prydein** *Dolyd* rather than *doleu* is the pl. form favoured in the CBT corpus, but *doleu* in Marwnad Cynddylan line 38 *Doleu Taw* (EWSP 176); LPBT 18.38 *Doleu Defwy*; 5.230 *Doleu Edrywy*; and 8.7 *Doleu Hafren*; and LPBT 4.68 *doleu dynwedyd* which appears not to be a geographical usage.

6   **pen ma** One would expect *pennaf ma* or *penn maeu*, so this looks like an old formation like *pencawr* (see Kenneth Jackson, 'Rhai sylwadau ar "Kulhwch ac Olwen"', *YB* 12 (1982), 12-23, at pp. 12-15) from **pennon magon* (gen. pl., replacing **mageson*). If so, 'chief of places', headquarters.

7   **. . . wc oes moes ny ma** The worn leaf which had evidently been the outer one for some time is particularly rubbed at the beginning of this line where there is room for four or five letters. Gwenogvryn Evans suggested *ae amlwc*. H-cd suggests 'ni'm oes ni'm â' perhaps because *ma* would not be expected again as a rhyme (unless *penma* in line 6 was regarded as a close compound perhaps). *Moes* with *oes* is a common collocation. The surrounding lines have a pentasyllabic first section.

8   **ym arha (ms arua)** *Ara/arha*, adj. 'joyful, pleasant delightful' (GPC²), as in LPBT 4.92 *buched ara* and Echrys Ynys line 19 *aros ara*; an abstract noun would suit here. As a vb, 'to delight, please', CBT II 18.20 *Ni'm arha aros agkyuyeith*. Without emendation, **arua < arf + ma* 'battle-position' (unattested).

9   **Ys deubi Seis yna y erchi bwytta** Perhaps omit *yna* for the length. *Deubi*, cf. LPBT 1.97 *a geissont gyfarws nys deubi*; LPBT 4.6 *nys deubi*; CC 20.159; the form is not attested in the CBT corpus. *Bwytta* is rare in poetry (as opposed to drinking!), but see CC 33.70 relating Luke 24 and Mark 16.

10 **dogyn gwyr o ryswyr (ms ryfyr) rosseda** The same four words at the start of the line are found below in line 13. GPC only notes *ry* + *byr* 'short'. But if *rysyr* (*f* and *ſ* confusion), perhaps a mistake for *ryswr* 'hero, fighter, attacker', etc. or, better for internal rhyme, for *ryswyr* (pl.). If so, cf. possibly CBT VI 20.65-8 *Tremynwys rysswr Rossed — Diabret/ Am deibryt Gwyned,/ Lloegyr gychwyn a'e mynn, a'e med,/ Llywelyn, llyw teyrned*. Another possibility could be *rysgyr* 'attack, rush, force', or (foregoing the alliteration) *rywyr* 'great men, heroes' (with the *w* written as *u* and wrongly modernised perhaps): cf. CBT V 10.11 *Hyt yt a clod rod rywyr*.

For the problematic *Rossed/rossed*, see note on §8.13. Here the vb noun *rysseda* (see GPC s.v. *rhyseddaf: rhyssedda, rhyseddu*) seems likely, and the variation in the first vowel is paralleled by the Red Book's *G6ell duhud no rosedha* (Diarhebion 17), a proverb seemingly reflected in R1056.18-19 (Gosymdaith line 78) *g6ell rihyd no ryssedha*. Further comparisons include *Broceniauc* and *Coheic* (for *Brycheiniog* and the personal name *Cyheig*), cited by J. Baudiš, *Grammar of Early Welsh* (Oxford, 1924), 23 and 24; and the treatment of *Rhydderch* as *Rodarchus* in VM, noted by LHEB 658 and 662. Richard Glyn Roberts suggests (personal communication) reading *dyhud* instead of *duhud* in the first example, understanding 'better is contentment than behaving prodigally', while Nicolas Jacobs understands Gosymdaith's *rihyd* as 'eternal glory'. *Rihyd* and *rossed* are

10 Darogan Kadwal[adyr]

      collocated in §8.45. The translation of our line is rather uncertain and takes the prep. *o* 'by' as introducing the agent of the vb noun *bwytta* in line 9.

11   **Jeuhawt gwreic gan y gwas** See General Introduction 11-12 on the 'world upside-down' theme in prophecy. This precise inversion is not paralleled in the early material.

12   **hen gas ny ma** 'old enemy/enmity'. *Ny ma* perhaps as in line 7 — *ny'm a* 'does not go to me'?

14   **A weleisti vyg kar** Ambiguous: *kar* 'relation' or 'friend', with *a* 'and' or 'with', possibly referring to, one of the signs of social inversion, see General Introduction, 12.

15   **Gweleis-i gelein vein a brein ar gnawt** *Brein/celein* is a commonplace throughout early poetry.

16   **ac arall ar darwein gwall grein cledyfawt** *Darwein/darwed*, see PT 59-60 for *ar darwed* meaning 'steeping, soaking'. *Gwall* and *crein* are understood here as adjs. describing the sword-stroke.

Index of forms discussed in the textual notes

References are to poem and line numbers; italics indicate emended forms, or comparanda. Forms are arranged according to the Welsh alphabet.

A
a'm bi 7.103
achadw 5.8
aches 2.12, 4.6
achestudyn 4.6
achwynogyon 3.41
achystudyn 4.6
adaned 3.27
atarrwy 1.2
adein 1.30
atvyd 2.7
atcorsan 4.1
atgoryn 4.1
Adonäi 7.24
adwyth 2.5
Adaf 1.41, 7.83
Addaon 4.8
adoer 2.9
aer 5.2
aerlin 3.22
aerlyw 3.22
Aeron 6.10
aethan 4.1
Aethwy 7.62
afar 3.38
afwyn 4.10
Affrica 9.9
agarat 8.42
agennis 6.13
agor 7.87
angar 7.23
angerdawl 7.76
agyfieithon 6.23
aghygres 7.103
Alclut 3.19, 6.15
Alt Clut 6.15
altirat 8.46
allfro 3.5
alltuted 8.32
am (< mab) 5.7
am 3.42, 6.12
am nodwy 1.7
amtir 1.33
amgant 3.11
amgor 7.56
amgyffreu 5.4
aMhanogan 5.7
amhryd 3.42
amiolet 8.77
amnodwy 1.7

amrwt 3.42
amrydar 3.42, 6.27
amwehyn 7.94
amwc 1.48
amygir 6.26
anan 1.36
anant 7.17
Anarawt 2.26
anaw 1.36
anchwant 7.10
anuonawc 2.1
anhawd 5.25
anhawr 5.25
anhed 4.4, 7.44
anoleithat 3.30
antared 7.23
anyan 1.36
ar 'against?' 8.49
ar 1.23, 6.1, a'r? 7.25
ar vrys 6.12
ar lleg 5.3
ar ofrys 6.12
ara 10.8
arab 8.2
Arafanis; *Arafia*; Arafin 9.9
arall 8.2
aralluro 1.45; arallvro 3.5
aranwynyon (ms) 6.21
arawt 7.91
arbet 2.29
arch 8.8
artir 7.53
Ard Nefon 6.18
ardyrched 8.9
areith 7.48
arua 10.8
arvedyd 7.72
argrat 8.42
arha 10.8
arlleg 5.3
arllwybyr 8.8
arofvn 3.10
arth 8.8, 8.18, 8.44
arwar 9.11
arwyd 6.2
arwyneb 8.10
Arx Alt Clut 3.19
arymes 2.12
Ascia 9.4
Asia 9.9

Asicia 9.4
-ator 7.55
awyryohif 8.85

B
balaon 4.8
balch 1.8; balcheeu 8.17
ban 3.48, 7.38, 9.3
banieri 8.66
bann 3.20
baran 2.19, 9.17
baranres 8.21
bargotyon 4.11
barnodeu; barnodyd 7.103
bat 2.14
bedman 8.40
bedyd 3.3
bedeu 8.21
bedrawt, betrawt 2.14
behet 8.40
beidadon 6.19
beidyeit 6.19
beleu 4.8, 7.38
Beli 2.3, 4.5
bereu 8.53
berthwyr 8.62
berw 4.8
berwhawt 7.52
berwhodawr 7.53
berwyn 10.2
beuder 3.52
bi 1.24, 7.49
bidan 4.1
bihit 8.40
billt (ms) 3.44
biw 3.8
Blathaon 4.8
bolch 3.50
bollt 3.44
bot y 8.29
branes 7.85
breeych 8.17
brehyr(y)eit 7.109
brein 8.7
brenin na vrenhin 3.44
breyryon 7.109
Brithanhäi 7.20
brithi 7.18, 7.20
brithni 7.18
brithöi 7.18

Index of forms discussed

brithret 7.93
briwhawt 2.21
bron 7.70
bronrein 1.28
brooed 8.10
brud/brut 2.28
brudyaw 2.28
Brun(e); *Brunanburh* 2.28
brwytrin 10.2
brwyn 2.21
Broceniauc 10.10
brychwyn 6.22, 8.52
Brython 4.29, 6.1, 7.102, 8.35
Brythonic 9.21
budyd 7.30, 7.33
budyn 8.56
Buch Vreith 7.49
bwlch 3.50
bwytta 10.9
byt 7.66
bydawnt 8.61
bydhawt 8.64
byhyt 8.40
bythawt 7.109
bythit 8.65

C
Cabes 9.4
kat 2.13, 2.28, 3.17
Kader Rhian 1.49
kadeithi 5.13
katuaon 3.42
Cadrawd Calchfynydd 3.1
Katwaladyr 2.19-20, 8.9, 8.49, 10.5
Catwallawn 6.17
kadwr 2.31
Käen 7.116
Cair Brithon 3.19
Caer Gabes 9.4
Caer Lleon 6.20
Caer Llion 6.20
Kaer Rian 1.49
Kaer Rywc; *Kaerrihoc* 1.49
Cafis 9.4
calch 3.32
Calchuynyd 3.1
Camlan 2.28
kamualhäu 1.44
canhator 7.55
cannwy 1.2
car 1.45
kared 7.23, 7.77
Karedigiaun 6.9
caslur 7.82
caslyn 7.82
Casnar 7.82

Casnur 5.6, *casnur* 7.82
Caswallawn 4.6
kattybrudawt; *kattybrunawc* 2.28
Cath Vreith 6.23
kathyl 7.1, 7.55
kaw, Kaw 5.3
Cawrnur 5.6
ked 4.6
kefyn, ar gefyn 2.4
ceidw 5.8
ceinmic 8.46
keinyadon 6.19
keir 1.45
ceironyd, *Ceirion(n)ydd* 7.34
keissut; *keissynt* 8.20
keithiawn; *keithyawr* 8.15
kelein 3.14
kelenic 8.47
Celi 5.27
cenuein 3.55
kenuyd 7.35
kennadeu; *kennat* 2.1
cennis 6.13
kerd 1.34, 7.34
kertassan; *kerdyn* 4.1
Keredigyawn 6.9
Kessarogyon 8.41
keudawt 2.2
ceugant 7.14
Clas Merdin 5.9
clawr 8.17
cled 8.48
cledyfal 8.6
cledyfar 8.6
clotleu 8.23
clotryd 3.2
Clud, Cludwys 3.15
Clydogau 8.11
coch 2.28
kogeu 7.68
cogni 7.22
Coheic 10.10
kollawt 4.12
colledigyon 7.105
colof(yn) §7 title
condigni 7.22
Conwy 2.8
crai 5.5
crei 2.7
crein 10.16
creith 2.8
credan 4.1
credeu 8.22
crëu 3.51
Creudyn 7.77
creulet 3.55
cri 5.5

Cristyawn 9.10
croywed 7.69
cud, cwd (*Gwr o Gud*) 4.24
cuinhaunt 8.61
cwffwn 7.113
cwydaf 7.114; cwydynt 8.22; kwydynt-wy 3.61
cwyn 2.20
kychwedyl 2.1, 3.1
cyfagar 8.3
kyfamrud 4.25
cyfarch 7.63
cyfarfot 3.29
cyfedach, cyfedwch 5.1
cyflawddon 6.5
kyfleudon 6.5
kyflewynt 8.48
cyflogawt 2.7
kyfranant 6.9
kyfret 7.79
kyfryssed 6.3
cyfwyre 3.36
Cimuireg, *Comereg* 3.36
cyfylchi 3.58
kyffestrawn 3.57
kyffin 7.113
cyffreu 5.4
cyffwrn 7.113
kygein 1.34, 1.37
kyghan 7.28
cyghyr 7.39
kyhoed 7.28
cyllellawr 7.73
kyllestric 7.116
Cyminawd 8.25
kymon 6.8
kymrwy 1.14
Kymry 2.18
kymyscyn 3.26
kyn no 7.97
Kynan 1.16, 2.19
kynechreu 8.12
kynnif 8.23, 8.49
kynnull 8.64
kynut 7.64
cyrchu 8.6
kysson 6.7
cystlyned 4.13
cystudyn 4.6
kywrisset 6.3

Ch
chwannawc 4.15
whechet 5.17
chwedleu 3.1
chwedyl 2.1

Index of forms discussed

D
da 3.3
datwyrein 7.101
Daethwy 7.62
dangossan 4.1
dande 3.35
danhyal 9.19
daresteinat 3.56
darfu 7.26
daruuan 4.1
darlleawr 7.99
darmerthed 8.46
darofum 7.26
Daronwy 1.6, §1 title
darparan 4.1
darwed 10.16
darwein 10.16
darysceinat 3.56
deu 5.1
dedueu, deduon 6.6
Deheu 3.39
Deheubarth 3.2
deruyd 4.8, 7.32
deiliadon, deiliaid 6.19
deilwat, delwat 8.42
derlin 3.22
derlyw 3.22
derllys 8.18
derw 3.22
deubi 10.9
deuliw 5.1
deulwch 5.1
deulwyr 5.1
deune 5.1
deuryw 5.1
deuthan 4.1
Diabret 8.13
diachor 2.11
dialeu 7.95
diarchar 8.8
dibyn 8.19
didwynas 6.25
Difiau 8.25
diuryssint 4.1
difuner 9.8
diffeith 7.67
differth 1.1
diffreidyat 8.35
diffyrth 1.1
digawn 2.2
digorbit 4.1
dillyn 2.11
Din Alclud 3.19, 6.15
Din Guennham 6.12
Dindaethwy 7.62
Dineidwc 1.50
Dineidyn 1.50
direit 7.67

disgogan 4.1
discowen 8.64
disgrein 3.59
discreinawr 3.59
discyn 3.29
disgywen 8.64
diwarnawt 7.98
diwedyd 2.13
diwystyl 6.28
do 3.9, 8.76
dodynt 2.1
dodyw 3.1
doethan 4.1
Dolaethwy 7.62
doleu 10.6
dolhwyckyt 7.61
dolwys 7.61
dolyd 10.6
draganawl 7.60
dragon 3.43
dragonawl 7.60
dreic 5.4, 8.35
dremynt 1.51
drych 3.21
dryw, drywon 8.37
dullyat 3.55
durawt 2.25
dwyrein 7.99
dy 'from' 8.11, 8.57
dy dra 8.57
dybrunawc 2.28
dybryt 2.28
dybu 3.47
dybyd 3.47
dybydant 6.5, 7.3
dychyfrwy 1.52
dychysgogan 4.1
dyderbi 8.50
dyderuyd 4.8
dedeuant 1.18, 7.57
dydeuhawr 8.50, 8.67
dydranoneu 8.11
dydyrchafwy 8.24
dydyrchefis 9.21
dyf Ieu 8.25
Dyfet 3.8
Dyfrdonwy 1.15
dyfynhyn 2.25
dyg6rthryn 4.1
dygan 4.1
dygawn 2.2
dygedawr 7.80
dygnawt 2.17
dygobryssyn 4.1
dygodolyn 4.1
dygofi 5.15
dygogan 4.1
dygoglawd 4.1

dygollouit 4.1
dygorelwi 2.34, 4.1
dygorescynnan 4.1, 9.3
dygorfu 4.1
dygottorynt 4.1
dygwgei 4.1
dygyrchet 3.8
dyhed 8.42
dylanuan 4.1
dylif 8.83
dylochassan 4.1
dymbi 5.11, 5.28, 7.23, 7.40, 8.1; dimbi 5.28, 5.11
dymdygyrch 8.17
dymgöi 5.15
dyn(n) 6.15
Dyn Daryfon 6.15
Dyn Maerut 6.15
Dyn Riedon 6.16
Dynclut 6.15
dyouot 5.15
dyrchafu 4.5, 6.1
dyrchafyssyn 4.1, 4.5
dyrnawt 2.10
dysgogan 4.1, 7.32, 8.12
dysgogettawr 9.12
dyvyner 9.8
dywaled 3.3
dywalhau 1.44

E
ebryn 7.89
echen 7.82, 8.59
echlur 7.82
echrys 9.13
echwyd 3.15
edryssed 8.27
edyrn 2.10
efnis, *efnys* 9.8
efret 2.35
efrefwys 3.16
eglwc 1.46
ehaer 5.2
ehalaeth 4.3, ehelaeth 1.22
ehofyn 5.2
eidolyd 7.10
Eigyl 8.32
eillon 1.25
einiwet 8.79
eirig 8.46
eiriolet 8.77
eirwyn 3.21
eiry 3.21
eis 9.6
eissilled, *eissyllyd* 8.33
eithyt 7.62
eleirch 8.17
Elffinawc 9.17

Index of forms discussed

Elöi 5.26
Eluet 8.82
elyrch 8.17
emellin, emellun 8.51
eniwet, enwet 2.35, 8.79
eppa 7.64
erchwyrn 2.10
Erechwyd 3.15, 3.62
ergenhyd 7.35
erglywaw 7.91
ergrynaf, *ergrynaw* 7.116
erhy 2.18, 8.29
erwyn 3.21
ery 8.29
eryf, eryuet 3.62
Eryri 2.16, 5.24, 7.44, 10.4
eryron 8.7
escar 3.11, 8.4
esclwch 3.34
escorant 7.9, escori 5.22
-*etor* 7.55
etwaeth 1.18
eurgyrn 5.5
eurobell 3.55
euroi 7.21
Europa; Europin 9.9
eurröi 7.21
eurynni 7.42

F
Vel Ynys, Y 5.9

Ff
famen 9.6
ffaw 8.35
Ffichti 5.12
fflet 7.110
fflemychawt 8.63
ffraeth 1.24
ffreu 5.4
ffrwytheu 1.14
fwyrgno 8.74

G
Gabes 9.4
gadent 6.27
Gafis 9.4
galwhawr 8.54
geu 6.6
geir 6.8
genem 3.55
genhyd 7.35
genhyn 4.2
geunis 6.13
girat 3.52
glaswawt 2.34
glesni 2.34
glew 3.3

Glyn Aeron 6.10
gnawt 2.3, 2.29
gobell 3.55
gober 9.8
gotwyllyd 7.70
godeith 9.17
gofri 7.41
gofrwy 1.2
gofunet 8.12
gofur 7.66
gogan(u) 4.1
gogant 7.1
Gogled 7.81
goglyt 7.114
gogwn 8.43
gogwna, *gogwneif* 10.5
gogyfarch 3.17
gogyfeirch 3.41
goiaen 8.60
goleu 3.40
goleith 3.11
golwch 8.7
golwc 1.51
golludyon 6.13
gollychant 8.7
gonofant 7.12
goreu 3.40
gorchordyon 6.3
gordyfynt 8.39
gorerefein 3.62
gorescyn 4.16
goruyn; *goruynt* 6.6
gorfynt 8.39
gorgolchei 3.53
gorgolchel 3.53
goryein 1.31
gorllechant 8.39
gorlluddiaf 6.13
gorllwyd 6.13
gorllwython 6.13
gorman 7.27; gormant 7.11
Goronwy 1.10
gorynt 6.6
Gossulwyt 3.20
gowyllt 3.44
gowyr 9.6
gowyreis 9.6
grannwynn; granwen 3.25; granwynyon, garanwynyon 6.21, 8.52
grat 9.18
grayan 3.14
grefiat 5.2
greidawl 3.25
grëu 3.51
gro 3.14
gryn 3.24, 8.54
gwaet gwyr 7.12

gwaetlin 8.4
gwaedvenni 5.22
gwalhäu 1.44
gwan 1.39
gwanflet 7.110
gwanfret 7.110
gwarthfar; *gwarthfor* 7.57
gwarthmor 7.57
gwas 8.25
gwawt 1.34, §7 title
gwayawawr, *gwaywawr* 3.22
gwed 8.28
gweddawt 2.18
gwedw 1.29
gweglyt 7.114
gwehenyawdyr 3.30
gwehenyt 3.30
gwehyn 4.11
gwelych 6.10
Gwenhwys 3.56
gwenwyn 7.81
gwenwynuyd 7.81
gwerescyn 4.16
gwerin 7.115
gwern 3.42, 9.16
gweryt 5.20, 7.25
gwc 1.48
gwirawt 2.3
gwisc 1.41
gwledychawt 8.82
gwledychwy 1.17
gwnahawnt 8.61
gwnahawt 2.8
gwned 7.41
gwober 9.8
gwollycha 8.7
Gwr o Gud, Gwr o Gwd 4.24
gwrd 1.22
gwrgun 3.45
gwrit 8.8
gwrthenedic, gwrthuenedic (sic) 8.58
gwrthyat 3.50
gwryawc 1.30
gwryt 8.8
gwrys 8.8
Gwydno 3.13
gwydueirch 7.80
gwyduet 1.42
gwyduilet 1.42
Gwydyl Ffichti 5.12
gwygynei 10.5
Gwyllyonwy 1.15
gwyllt 3.44
gwynyeith 2.8
gwynofi 7.12
gwyrein 7.85

Index of forms discussed

gwyrin 7.85
Gyfylchi, Y 3.58
gynhon 4.26
Gynt, gynt 2.17, 4.26, 5.22

H
haelder 4.12
haelon 3.40; *haelyon* 4.9
haer 5.2
Hafren 8.57, 8.63
heu 5.18
heuelis 9.7
henuonha 7.65
henyn 7.83
hermyn 7.81
herwyd 9.6
herwyr 9.6
hëyrn 2.10
hinon 7.108
Hirell, *Hiriell* 8.63
hoelyon 4.9
hoywwed 7.69
hwedyd 7.72
hydyr 8.83
hywedyd 7.72
hywred 8.26

I
Iago 4.7
Iceni 3.19
Idno 3.8
Idwal 2.26, 4.7, 6.21
iddun 7.75
yogyfeirch 3.41
yohif 8.85
iolet 8.77
yolif 8.85
iolin 3.56
-itor 7.55
Iwis 9.21

L
leu 3.3
linx 5.21

Ll
llachar 3.22, 8.9
llat 5.4
lladassan 4.1
llafaro 3.7
llafasaf 3.9
llam 1.46
Llanrian 1.49
llanw 1.2
llara, *llary* 3.5
llathyr 8.23
llaw 10.3
llawd; *Llawdden* 6.5

Lleenni 7.43
lleeu 5.4
llef 2.31
Llefelys 9.11
llefessit 3.9
lleg 5.3
lleiseu 5.4
Lleminawc 4.14
llenyn 3.22
llestreu, *llestri* 5.4
lletcynt 2.2
Lleu 3.3
lleueu 5.4
lleutired 3.39, 8.47
lleuueryn 3.22
llew 8.18
lliaws 7.93, 8.59
llin 2.26
llithrant 8.33
llongawr 8.68
llogoed 7.54
Llonion, Llonyon 6.12
lluch 8.9
Llud 4.6, 9.11
lludedic 4.9
llugern, *llugorn*, llugyrn 9.16
lluman 3.22
lluoed 4.28
llurygogyon 8.36
lluwch 5.1
llüyd 4.28
llwch 5.1
llwdyn 1.40
llwybyr 8.28
llwybryn 4.1
llwytged 5.22
llwyded 5.22
llydan lyn 8.55
Llyminawc 4.14
llyn 5.1, 7.80
llyry 8.14

M
ma 10.6
mab dyn 8.2
Mab grat 9.18
mab mam 8.2
Mabon 3.17, 3.25, 3.44
maer 2.6
mäes 7.90
Maes Gwyddnau 1.49
Mays Maichghen 1.49
Manogan 5.7
marchogaeth 1.27
maris 9.6
marwhawt 2.6
Mathonwy 1.12

maw 8.3
med 8.28
medant 7.7
medeu 8.21
medhawnt 8.62
megedorth 1.48
mehyn 4.4, 7.92
Mei 2.7
meib 4.5
meillon 6.26
mein 5.3
meint 2.2
meindyd 3.61, 7.52
meinwen 3.14
meiwyr 7.74
Mellun 8.51
Menei 2.7
menhyt 7.59
Mercher, Merchyr 7.7
merin 7.111, Merin Reget 8.80
meryd 7.86
meuoed 8.52
Meurygawc 9.17
mi nyt 3.28
mil 7.112
milet 7.86
mirein 5.3
misterin 10.1
modrydaf 5.6
moel 3.33
Moni 7.43
mwstr, mwstwr 10.1
mwth 10.1
mwyedic 5.3
mygedorth 1.48
mynawc 5.7, 7.92
Mynogan 5.7
mynnyt 7.59
mysterin 10.1

N
nachwyaf 7.114
nawt 2.29
nebawt 7.91
ned 3.46
Nefon 6.18
nefwy, Nefwy 1.1, 1.8, 6.18
neut 1.6
newityaw 8.70
niant 7.17
nodwy 1.7, 6.14
nonneu 8.11
Nordmandi, Nordmannyeit 5.16
Nordmein, Nordmyn 5.16
Nordmynmandi 5.16
Normadi, Nortmin 5.16

Index of forms discussed

nothwy 6.14
Nowy 6.18
nu 1.45, 5.6, 7.19
nuchawnt 8.55, 8.61
nuchien 3.48
Nuedi 7.19
nugiaw 8.55
Nuoes 7.19
nur 5.6
nwy 1.14
nwyfiant 7.17
ny ma 10.7, 10.12
nychein 3.48
nyth 3.41

O

o 6.2
o'e 4.18-19
o'r pan 6.26
ober 9.8
ochwynogyon 3.41
odit 1.11, 3.7
oduch 5.4, 6.1
oheni 5.19
ohonaw 2.27
olwyn 4.9
or 3.42
Orsedd, Yr 8.13
-*otor* 7.55
Owein 3.18, 3.62
owillt (ms) 3.44

P

pabl 3.5
pair 8.62
pan 1.13, 8.43
pan y 5.27
par 8.2
peblet 3.5
pebyllyawnt 8.38, 8.61
pechadur 5.13
pedeirieith 1.20, 7.47
pedrydan(t) 2.33, 3.35
pedrygwern; *pedrywern* 9.16
peiron 8.62
peisseu 9.7
peithiawc 7.4
pelre 6.22
pellt 3.44
pellenawc 4.28
Pen Blathaon 4.8
Pen Cristin 7.87
pen ma 10.6
pencawr 10.6
peneri 8.66
Pengyfylchi 3.58
penllüyd 8.36
pennaeth 5.11

pennaeth weisson 4.13
Penryn Blathaon 4.8
perchen 8.36, 9.12
perchyd 8.36
perffeith 7.46
perif 8.81
perit 3.43, 8.43
Peryddon 6.15
peryf 8.81
Peryfon 6.15
pilleu 8.18
pleit 5.1
plo 4.7
plwyff 6.1
pop tri 2.15
pobyl 3.5
Porth Wydno 3.13
Porth Wygyr 6.24
Porthaethwy 7.62
porthyn 4.1
Powys 6.5
preid 3.56
pren 1.5
presswyl 7.95
priawt 2.13
prit 8.16
prudhau 2.28
pryderaf 9.20
pryt 8.16
Prydyn 4.7
puchysswn, *pucsaun* 7.75
pwmpäi 7.25
pwy 1.45
pwyllaf 9.20
pybyl 3.5
pylleu 8.18
pymhet 1.40

R

Rodarchus 10.10
Rodawys 3.21
Romani 8.1

Rh

rageu 8.20
reei 3.51
Reget 8.80
rëi 3.46
rein 1.28, 3.34
reiniaton 6.19
Rën 1.53
Reon 1.49
rhes 9.14
ret 2.35
rewinyaw 4.17
Rian 1.49
rieu 3.40
riuant 7.17

rihyd 8.13
rodawc 10.3; *rhoddiog* 10.3
Rossed, rossed 8.13, 8.45, 10.10
rosseda 10.10
Rufein 1.33, 7.102
Rufawn 9.17
Run 1.48, 3.46
rwy 1.14
rwyf 2.3, 3.43
rwython 6.14
ry'th 5.6
ryamwc 1.53
ryanet 5.2
rybud 8.20
rychwant 7.8
ryt 3.42
Ryt Alclut 3.19
Ryt ar Taradyr 6.24
rydadlas 8.25
rydyrchafwy 6.1
ryerchit 5.2
ryfed 5.17, 8.45
ryfedawt 2.23
ryferthwy 1.26
ryuonic 9.17
ryfyr 10.10
ryffreu 5.4, 8.15
rygeidw 5.8
rygreat 5.2
rygyrchynt 8.6
rygystlyned 4.13
ryn 6.10
rynawt, *rynnawd* 1.52
rynnu; rynyaw 1.38
ryodic 9.17
ryodres 7.8
rys, Rys 9.14
rysed 9.14
rysgyr 10.10
ryssed 8.13
rysseda 10.10
ryswyr 10.10
rythrychynt 8.6
Rywc 1.49
rywodic 9.17
rywyr 10.10
ryyscrifyat 5.2

S

sadiaw 7.54
Saeson 2.17
saeth 8.53
Seis 2.17
Saraphin; *Sarasin* 9.9
Seithenhin, Seithennin 1.49, 7.86
seithin 7.86

Index of forms discussed

sychet; sychediedi 7.21
syllu 1.42
symudant 7.48
syw, sywedyd, sywedydyon 7.104

T
taenawt 3.38
taflwy 1.2
taleu 8.22
tam 8.17
tandawt 2.22
tannwy 1.2
Tarad(y)r 6.24
Taranhon, *Tarannon* 8.11, 8.38
tardawt 2.19
tardei 3.32
tarth 3.12
taryf 8.69
tebet 8.40, 8.52
techin 4.1
tëi 2.22
Teiui 6.11
teithi 5.8
Teithy Hen 1.49
teithiawc 5.10, 8.34
tertyn 4.1
teruyn 7.100, 8.19
tewis 6.13
tir Gwydno 3.13
tiryon 7.100
tith 7.71
tonneu 8.11
toruenhawl 7.71
tormennawc, tormynnawc 7.71
torroed 7.37
torrynt 8.22
torwynnaf 7.71
tra 7.105
trablud 3.50
trachwres 3.6
traeth 3.40
tragwynawl 7.60
trangwy 1.2
traghawt, traghwy 8.30
Trahannon 8.38
tramerin 7.111
tramwy 1.2
tratrachwres 3.6
trefdyn 7.76
treis, treissyn 4.1
treithin 4.1
Tren 8.38
triganed 8.5
troch 2.11
trwy 7.69

trwydet 3.13
trychu 8.6
trydar 8.5, 8.30
trydw 7.84
tryganedd 8.5
trygar 8.5
trymluawc 2.11
tu 3.23, 8.63
tuded 8.31
tudyn 4.6
Tuman 3.22
tuth; tuthiolyd 7.71
twym 3.12
ty 2.22
tyfhawt 2.27
tyghettor 7.68
tyno 7.90
tyrch 8.22
tyruawt 8.27
Tywi 6.11

U
vch 7.88
udu 3.20, 7.75
udud 7.75
udun, *vdun* 3.20, 7.75
udunt 7.75
udyn 3.20
vn eir 6.8
urdedic 8.58
vrthenedic 8.58
vrdin, *urdyn* 7.96
urno 8.74

W
Wen Ynys, y 9.12
whechet (ms) 5.17
Winued, *Winwæd* 8.43
wy nyt 3.28
wylhawt 7.36
wyneb 4.21
wysg 1.41

Y
y mawr, Gwawt Lud §7 title
ycheirie 8.46
yd yr 3.54
ydu 7.75
ygno, *Ygno* 8.74
Ygwen 3.19
ymarwar 9.11
ymchoeles 3.15
ymdeithic 4.10
ymellun 8.51
ymgelann 4.1
ymgygein 1.37
ymolöi 10.4
ymträu 1.41

ynyal 7.89, 8.10
ynwet 8.79
Ynys vel Veli 5.9
Enys Wen 9.12
yrat 3.52
Yrechwyd 3.62
yrof 3.10
yssadawr 7.54
ysbenyt 4.7
yspydawt 2.5
yscafael 3.33
yscafyn 2.4
ysgai 5.5
yscarant 3.11, 7.6
yscawnt 2.4
yscawn 2.4, 8.77
yscein 1.35
ysceinat 3.56
ysci 5.5-6
ysgïen 5.5
yssit 1.9
ysglyfiaf 3.34
ysgodogyon 2.4
ysgor 5.22, 7.9
ysgrifiad, ysgrifyaw, ysgriuen 5.2
yscwytawr 8.69
ystaenawt 3.38
ystic 4.21
ystrat 3.4

Conspectus of the Book of Taliesin

The prophetic poems are indicated in bold type and the ten poems edited in this volume are numbered. The Book of Taliesin, incomplete at beginning and end, and with further missing quire(s), may have contained in front of the extant first quire some or all of the whole block of prophetic material in the Red Book of Hergest:

i	Anrec Vryen	R 1049.7-1050.6
ii	Mal rot yn troi	R 1050.7-23
iii	Moch da6 byt	R 1050.25-1051.3
iv	Llynghes Von	R 1051.5-29
v	Crist Iessu	R 1051.31-1053.15
vi	Mor y6 g6ael g6elet	R 1053.17-42

	Prif Gyuarch Geluyd (acephalous BT text = R1054)	**BT 3.1-12, LPBT 1**
	Ren Nef ry'm awyr dy wedi	BT 3.12-24, CC 17
	Archaf wedi y'r Trindawt	BT 3.25-4.12, CC 19
	Marwnat y Vil Veib	BT 4.13-6.16, 7.2-12, CC 24
	Latin 'sequence' *Qui venerunt angeli*	BT 6.17-7.1, CC pp. 256-7
	Buarth Beird	BT 7.12-8.20, LPBT 2
	Aduwyneu Taliessin	BT 8.21-10.3, LPBT 3
	Yrymes Detbrawt (Armes Dyd Brawt)	BT 10.4-13.1, CC 20
	Arymes Prydein Vawr	**BT 13.1-18.25, AP**
	Angar Kyfu*n*dawt	BT 19.1-23.8, LPBT 4
	Kat Godeu	BT 23.9-27.12, LPBT 5
	Mabgyfreu Taliessin	BT 27.13-28.21, LPBT 6
1	**Daronwy**	**BT 28.22-29.20**
	En enw gwledic Nef goludawc (Gwallawg 1)	BT 29.21-30.23, PT XI
2	**Glaswawt Taliessin**	**BT 30.24-31.20**
	Mydwyf Merweryd	BT 31.21-32.25, LPBT 7
	Golychaf-i Gulwyd	**BT 33.1-34.14, LPBT 8**
	Kadeir Teyrnon	BT 34.15-35.21, LPBT 9
	Kadeir Kerrituen	BT 35.22-36.22, LPBT 10
	Kanu y Gwynt	BT 36.23-38.10, LPBT 11
3	**Kychwedyl a'm dodyw o Galchuynyd**	**BT 38.11-40.3**
	Kanu y Med	BT 40.3-20, LPBT 12
	Kanu y Cwrwf	BT 40.20-41.15, LPBT 13
	Teithi Etmygant	BT 41.16-42.15, LPBT 14
	Edmyc Dinbych	BT 42.16-44.16, BWP 155-72
	Plaeu yr Eifft	BT 44.16-45.9, CC 9
	Trawsganu Kynan Garwyn	BT 45.9-46.4, PT I
	Llath Moessen *recte* Gwyeil Jesse	BT 46.5-47.18, CC 11
	'Canu y Meirch'	BT 47.19-48.27, LPBT 15
	Ygofeisswys byt (Alexander 1)	BT 51.1-52.5, LPBT 16

Conspectus of the Book of Taliesin

	Ar clawr eluyd (Llvruc Alexandyr)	BT 52.6-17, CC 3
	Anryuedodeu Allyxander (Alexander 2)	BT 52.18-53.2, LPBT 17
	Ad Duw meidat (Llath Voyssen)	BT 53.3-54.15, CC 10
	Preideu Annwfyn	BT 54.16-56.13, LPBT 18
	Arwyre gwyr Katraeth gan dyd	BT 56.14-57.13, PT II
	Uryen Yrechwyd	BT 57.14-58.12, PT III
	Eg gorffowys	BT 58.13-59.6, PT IV
	Ar vn blyned	BT 59.7-60.7, PT V
	Gweith Argoet Llwyfein. Kanu Vryen	BT 60.7-26, PT VI
	Ardwyre Reget ryssed rieu	BT 61.1-62.16, PT VII
	Yspeil Taliessin. Kanu Vryen	BT 62.16-63.24, PT VIII
	En enw gwledic Nef gorchordyon (Gwallawg 2)	BT 63.25-65.5, PT XII
	Dadolwch Vryen	BT 65.5-24, PT IX
	Marwnat Er*cwl*	BT 65.24-66.8, LPBT 19
	Madawc Drud	BT 66.9-11, LPBT 20
	Erof Greulawn	BT 66.11-17, CC 15
	Marwnat Corroi m. Dayry	BT 66.18-67.8, LPBT 21
	Marwnat Dylan eil Ton	BT 67.8-17, LPBT 22
	Marwnat Owein	BT 67.18-68.4, PT X
	Echrys Ynys	BT 68.5-69.8, BWP 172-80
	Mydwyf Taliessin ('Cuneda')	BT 69.9-70.16, LPBT 23
4	**Dygogan awen**	**BT 70.16-71.6**
	Marwnat Vthyr Pen	BT 71.6-72.8, LPBT 24
5	**Kein gyfedwch**	**BT 72.9-22**
6	**Rydyrchafwy Duw ar plwyff Brython**	**BT 72.23-73.19**
	Trindawt tragywyd	BT 73.20-74.11, CC 8
7	**Gwawt Lud y mawr**	**BT 74.12-76.14**
8	**Yn wir dymbi Romani kar**	**BT 76.15-78.18**
9	**Ymarwar Llud bychan**	**BT 78.18-79.8**
	Kanu y Byt Mawr	BT 79.8-80.6, LPBT 25
	Kanu y Byt Bychan	BT 80.6-16, LPBT 26
10	**Darogan Katwal[adyr]**	**BT 80.17-26**

Cysodwyd ac argraffwyd yng Nghymru

2013